European Cinema and Continental Philosophy

THINKING CINEMA

Series Editors:
David Martin-Jones, University of Glasgow, UK
Sarah Cooper, King's College, University of London, UK

Volume 8

Titles in the Series:

Afterlives: Allegories of Film and Mortality in Early Weimar Germany by Steve Choe

Deleuze, Japanese Cinema, and the Atom Bomb by David Deamer

Ex-centric Cinema by Janet Harbord

The Body and the Screen by Kate Ince

The Grace of Destruction by Elena del Rio

Non-Cinema: Global Digital Filmmaking and the Multitude by William Brown

Sensuous Cinema: The Body in Contemporary Maghrebi Film by Kaya Davies Hayon

European Cinema and Continental Philosophy

Film as Thought Experiment

Thomas Elsaesser

BLOOMSBURY ACADEMIC
NEW YORK • LONDON • OXFORD • NEW DELHI • SYDNEY

BLOOMSBURY ACADEMIC
Bloomsbury Publishing Inc
1385 Broadway, New York, NY 10018, USA
50 Bedford Squre, London, WC1B 3DP, UK

BLOOMSBURY, BLOOMSBURY ACADEMIC and the Diana logo are trademarks of Bloomsbury Publishing Plc

First published in the United States of America 2019

Cover design by Eleanor Rose
Cover image: Film, *Melancholia*, 2011, © Zentropa/The Kobal Collection

A catalog record for this book is available from the Library of Congress

ISBN: HB: 978-1-4411-2949-9
PB: 978-1-4411-8221-0
ePDF: 978-1-4411-1065-7
eBook: 978-1-4411-6261-8

Series: Thinking Cinema

Typeset by RefineCatch Limited, Bungay, Suffolk
Printed and bound in the United States of America

To find out more about our authors and books visit www.bloomsbury.com and sign up for our newsletters.

CONTENTS

ACKNOWLEDGEMENTS

This book was longer in the making than I would have liked, and so my first and foremost thanks go to the 'Thinking Cinema' series editors, Sarah Cooper and David Martin-Jones for their patience and persistence. It still feels like I let it go before its time – a feeling tempered by the thought that there is never a good moment to try and say something definitive, least of all about 'Europe' or about 'cinema'.

Several intellectual itches prompted me to take up these challenging topics once more. One was an urge to further develop ideas first put forward in the chapter on 'double occupancy and mutual interference' from my previous book on *European Cinema*, and to do so by 'enlarging the context'. Another had to do with a growing interest in film philosophy: our book on *Film Theory: An Introduction through the Senses* led me to think that some issues which had preoccupied film studies could do with a fresh approach and that film theory, too, might benefit from enlarging the context.

I also had the growing intuition that there was indeed another way of bringing *European cinema face to face with Hollywood*, given that cinema in the digital age requires a different 'ontology'. The tendency among European directors towards 'film as thought experiment' corresponded in some yet to be fully specified ways to what I had earlier tried to identify as 'mind-game films' in American cinema since the 1990s, well aware that these mind-game films had European predecessors in the works of Fritz Lang, Luis Bunuel, Alain Resnais, for instance.

But it required specific occasions to make me take these thoughts to a point where I wanted to write about them. Sincere thanks go to my hosts at various conferences and to panel chairs: my good friends in Tel Aviv: Nurith Getz, Michal Friedman, Boaz Hagin, Raz Yosef, Sandra Meiri and Anat Zanger, who invited me to a conference on 'Ethics and the Cinematic', where I first presented on Fatih Akin and the Ethical Turn in 2008; Henry Bacon, of the University of Helsinki, where I was able to talk to a very knowledgeable audience about Aki Kaurismäki's *The Man without A Past* in 2009; Anja Streiter and Hermann Kappelhoff whose conference at the Free University Berlin on 'Singulär Plural Sein' gave me the opportunity to reflect on Claire Denis' *Beau Travail*, also in 2009. Hent de Vries invited me to Johns Hopkins University in 2012, where I first presented on Lars von Trier's *Melancholia*. My thanks also go to Josef Früchtl, Natalie Scholz and Rachel Esner for watching Christian Petzold's *Barbara* with me at the Cinecenter on a cold winter's night in Amsterdam: our conversation afterwards was the impetus for me to want to find out why I liked the film so much. Cathy Portuges of the University of Massachussetts asked me to present *Barbara* at her annual Massachusetts Multicultural Film Festival in March 2013, and at Mainz University Oksana Bulgakowa was my host in December 2015 for another lecture on *Barbara*. My one regret: that I was not able to tell Harun Farocki how much I loved this film, on which he is credited as co-writer.

In 2010 I resolved that these isolated talks on films and directors I admired should become part of a book, since common themes, similar constellations and an overarching idea about a 'cinema of abjection' had taken hold of me. A conference at King's College London on *The Europeanness of European Cinema* in June 2010 had given me the opportunity to sketch the outlines of such a book, and the chapter 'European cinema into the 21st Century: Enlarging the Context' is an expanded version of the talk given at King's.

The opportunity to think more coherently about the relation of film and philosophy came during my time as Fellow at the Internationale Kolleg für Kulturtechnikforschung und Medienphilosophie (IKKM Weimar) in 2012, where I had the good fortune not only of having Lorenz Engell and Bernhard Siegert as my amazingly inspiring hosts, but was able to share my work and benefit from regular conversations with Christiane Voss, Francesco Casetti, David Rodowick, Michel Chion, Tom Levin, Siegrid Weigel, Rick Altman and Jimena Canales. A version of the chapter 'Film as Thought' was presented there in December 2012 under the title 'Film and Philosophy After Deleuze'. My thanks also to Philippe Gauthier who was kind enough to invite me onto his 2014 SCMS panel, where I talked about philosophy and film as either a friendly or a hostile takeover bid, which gave rise to a lively discussion with William Brown, echoing my topic.

At Yale in 2011, and later Brown University in 2012, I was fortunate enough to have a captive yet critical audience of graduate students with whom to explore further the concept of the abject as I detected it also in films of Michael Haneke, Mike Leigh, the Dardenne Brothers, Chantal Akerman, Agnes Varda, Bela Tarr, Pedro Costa, but in many Asian films, too, notably from Japan, South Korea, Taiwan and Thailand. Thanks to Edwin Carels, I was invited in 2017 by the director of the International Film Festival Rotterdam, Bero Beyer, to give a talk on 'A Cinema of Abjection', using some of the festival's films of that year as my examples. There, Kevin B. Lee, of whom I had long been a fan, thrilled me with his probing questions. Other productive presentations of 'A Cinema of Abjection' in 2017 were at the Arsenal, Berlin (my thanks to Michael Wedel and Hermann Kappelhoff of *Cinepoetics*), the University of Regensburg (with thanks to Christian Wagner and Markus Stiglegger), at New York University (my thanks to Marina Hassapopoulou) and at King's College London (organized on behalf of the graduate students by Hannah Pavek).

The chapter on 'Film as Thought Experiment' was first presented at the University of Pennsylvania in February 2016 – my thanks to Tim Corrigan, a loyal friend for decades – and subsequently at Stanford University in March 2016, on the kind and generous invitation of Scott Bukatman. My former Yale students Seung-hoon Jeong and Jeremi Szaniawski asked me to contribute a chapter to their book on Global Authorship, which allowed me to gather my thoughts on the dynamics of autonomy and (in)dependence, of creativity and constraint typical of festival films also in relation to my theme of 'abjection'. My thanks to them for agreeing to let this essay serve a double function.

Throughout the years the chapters benefitted enormously from the on-going conversations with my many friends and trusted colleagues in New York, London, Berlin, Frankfurt, Paris and Amsterdam: among them Alex Alberro, Nora Alter, Dudley Andrew, Nico Baumbach, Claire Bishop, Barton Byg, Zoe Beloff, Noam Elcott, Angela Dalle Vacche, Jane Gaines, Lev Manovich, Charlie Musser, Dominic Pettman, Dana Polan, Amie Siegel, Shelly Silver, and Kenneth White; Laura Mulvey, Geoffrey Nowell-Smith, Murray Smith and Ginette Vincendeau; Noll Brinckmann, Gertrud Koch, Raya Morag, Hito Steyerl and Robert Burgoyne; Malte Hagener, Vinzenz Hediger and Danny Fairfax; Raymond Bellour, Christa Blümlinger, Michèle Lagny and Antonio Somaini; Patricia Pisters and Josef Früchtl, with whom I started the first Amsterdam School of Cultural Analysis Film-Philosophy Graduate Seminars in 2006. From our 'Cinema Europe' group, Melis Behlil, Tarja Laine, and Ria Thanouli continue to be valued interlocutors. And thanks also to my friend-at-large, Dina Iordanova, who shares my concern over the future of Europe and its 'abjects'.

The greatest debt of gratitude for keeping me at it, and for fully engaging not only with my thinking but also with my prose is owed to Warren Buckland. His intellect, logic and erudition were particularly valuable in the discussion of the philosophical turn in film studies, where his broad knowledge of both continental and cognitivist-analytical philosophy proved a special asset. Floris Paalman also read substantial parts of the manuscript, and offered a particularly helpful summary of the chapter dealing with Europe as political thought experiment. With Seung-hoon Jeong I have shared over many years my thoughts on the various uses and abuses of the concept of abjection, and he was one of my closest and most painstaking readers of the chapter in question. Drehli Robnik's familiarity with and lucid exposition of the film-philosophy of Jacques Rancière have also been most welcome and appreciated. While presenting from the manuscript at Gdansk University in the winter of 2017, Mirek Przylipiak and Agnieszka Piotrowska also offered generous comments.

My thanks, finally, to the publishers and editors for granting permission to use previously published material, details of which are below. Besides the editors already mentioned, I want to acknowledge the excellent editorial work of Mary Harrod, Mariana Liz and Alissa Timoshkina, as well as of Bonnie Honig and Lori Marso. When it comes to editorial work, however, I must return to Sarah Cooper and David Martin-Jones: they read all the chapters with great care and sensitivity, making helpful suggestions throughout and generally being most constructive. They also provided me with two outstanding assistants: Laurence King and Chelsea Birks, who checked the footnotes, completed the bibliography and established a filmography, with Laurence also providing the index. They have my warm and heartfelt thanks.

At Bloomsbury, my manuscript was expertly steered through the production process by many hands, with special thanks to Katie Gallof and Erin Duffy.

The book is dedicated to Silvia, with love, and for support that only she knows how to give.

Chapters that have been previously published are:

Chapter 1: Thomas Elsaesser, 'European Cinema into the 21st Century: Enlarging the Context?', in Mary Harrod, Marina Liz and Alissa Timoshkina (eds), *The Europeanness of European Cinema: Identity, Meaning, Globalization* (London: I.B. Tauris, 2014), 17–32.

Chapter 7: (in German) Thomas Elsaesser, 'Postheroische Erzählungen: Jean Luc Nancy, Claire Denis und *Beau Travail*', in Hermann Kappelhoff, Anja Streiter (eds.), *Die Frage der Gemeinschaft: Das westeuropäische Kino nach 1945* (Berlin: Vorwerk 8, 2012), 67–94.

Chapter 8: Thomas Elsaesser, 'Hitting Bottom: Aki Kaurismäki and the Abject Subject', *Journal of Scandinavian Cinema*, vol 1, no 1 (2011), 105–122.

Chapter 9: Thomas Elsaesser, 'Politics, Multiculturalism and the Ethical Turn: The Cinema of Fatih Akin', in Boaz Hagen, Sandra Meiri, Raz Yosef, Anat Zanger (eds.), *Just Images: Ethics and the Cinematic* (Newcastle: Cambridge Scholars, 2011), 1–19.

Chapter 10: Thomas Elsaesser, 'Black Suns and a Bright Planet: Melancholia as Thought Experiment,' in Bonnie Honig and Lori J. Marso (eds.) *Politics, Theory, and Film: Critical Encounters with Lars von Trier* (New York: Oxford University Press, 2016), 305–335.

Chapter 11: Thomas Elsaesser, 'A Thought Experiment: Christian Petzold's *Barbara*' in Christy Wampole (ed.), Special issue 'Narration and Reflection', *Compar(a)ison* I/II, 2010 [2015], 187–206.

Chapter 12: Thomas Elsaesser, 'The Global Author: Control, Creative Constraints and Performative Self Contradiction' in Seung-hoon Jeong and Jeremi Szaniawski (eds.), *The Global Auteur: Politics and Authorship in the 21st Century* (London: Bloomsbury 2016), 21–42.

1

European Cinema into the Twenty-first Century

Enlarging the Context?

In this troubled world, Western Europe has, in fact, become a fragile island of prosperity, peace, democracy, culture, science, welfare and civil rights. However, erecting walls against the rest of the world may undermine the very fundamentals of European culture and democratic civilization . . . But the overcrowded and aged Western Europe of the late twentieth century does not seem as open to the world as was the young, mostly empty America of the beginning of the century.[1]

As Europe is becoming more like the United States a hundred years ago – a continent of immigrants seeking a better life – one of the most familiar ways of asserting its cultural identity, namely defining itself in opposition to America, is becoming increasingly obsolete.[2] The same may hold for European cinema, which has often been cast as the 'good' object, by comparison with Hollywood. Critics tended to line up directors and national cinemas along

---

[1] Manuel Castells, 'European Cities, the Information Society and the Global Economy', *New Left Review* 1, no. 204 (March–April 1994): 22–3.

[2] Overviews of the debates can be found in Alexander Stephan (ed.), *The Americanization of Europe: Culture, Diplomacy, and Anti-Americanism after 1945* (New York: Berghahn Books, 2007); Philipp Gassert, 'The Spectre of Americanization: Western Europe in the American Century', in Dan Stone (ed.), *The Oxford Handbook of Postwar European History* (Oxford: Oxford University Press, 2012); and Volker R. Berghahn, 'The debate on "Americanization" among economic and cultural historians', *Cold War History* 10, no. 1 (February 2010): 107–30.

opposing values: 'art versus commerce', 'auteur versus star', 'critical prestige versus box office', 'realism versus dream factory', or – after Gilles Deleuze – 'the movement image versus the time image'. These and many similar constructions of identity through binary difference helped disguise the fact that the major changes – geopolitical, demographic and technological – which have affected how films are being produced, distributed, viewed and used in the new century, have left especially the national cinemas of Europe in a crisis. This crisis of identity was the major topic of my previous effort to define *European cinema*, whose title, *Face to Face with Hollywood*, reflected that Europe, and more specifically its cinema, has, in the later part of the twentieth century, supported its sense of self-importance by positioning itself 'face-to-face' with the Other.[3] Take away this prosthetic self-construction, what kind of identity is there for European art cinema and its auteurs? Do directors still feel allegiance to their nation and to authorial self-expression or do they pay attention to the diffuse audiences (and juries) at film festivals, hoping to ensure press coverage, exposure on television, screenings at the few remaining art houses and sales in the dwindling DVD market?

Traditionally strong filmmaking nations like France, Italy and Germany may still boast world-class festivals at Cannes, Venice and Berlin, but the films showcased and winning prizes often come from outside Europe. Looked at 'from outside' (including from the United States), films made in Europe now share the generic label 'world cinema', where they compete with productions from Turkey and Thailand, Iran and Mexico. This apparent 'demotion' of European cinema to 'world cinema' status might be regretted or lamented, but it is hard to overlook. It stands in sharp contrast to the rise of Asian cinema, notably that of South Korea, Thailand, The Philippines, Taiwan and increasingly also mainland China. Many of these countries have ambitions to compete as commercial rivals to Hollywood, while successfully performing as artistic rivals to Europe. European Cinema joins the prefix 'Euro' as not only connoting a beacon of hope shining from the island of prosperity and the rule of law, but often enough also the link to cheapness and crisis, not wealth or welfare: Euro-trash, Euro-pudding, Euro-shopper, Euro-crisis. Provided one can acknowledge the realities of these changing ideas of 'Europe' such trans-valuations also represent an opportunity: first, to let the label Europe find its own fluctuating 'value' on the stock-exchange of cultural capital, and second, to rethink what Europe means to the world not just in matters of cinema. Less may be more: a diminished standing and lower expectations could clear the path for European cinema to ready itself for renewal.

The present book sets itself this task: to look at European cinema through a new lens, that of philosophy and political thought. It starts from three

---

[3] For a more detailed assessment of these issues, see Thomas Elsaesser, *European Cinema: Face to Face with Hollywood* (Amsterdam: Amsterdam University Press, 2005).

interrelated premises: first, that contemporary (European) philosophy has something to say about cinema (as argued in Chapter 2 'Film as Thought: The "Film and Philosophy" Debate'); second, that the demotion of European art and auteur cinema is an opportunity for such a cinema (including for its directors as auteurs) to attain a paradoxical kind of autonomy (as proposed in Chapter 12 'Control, Creative Constraints and Self-Contradiction: The Global Auteur'); and third, that this requires a notion of cinema as having the status and function of a 'thought experiment'. Argued in greater detail in Chapter 3, 'Film as Thought Experiment', such thought experiments – common in philosophy and in physics – can be didactic parables or imaginary scenarios that address hypothetical 'what if?' situations. They can posit something as conceivable, and thus as possible, even if not realizable in practice, or they can address a crisis situation by 'thinking the unthinkable'. Such a crisis situation is a given in the Europe of the twenty-first century, both artistically and politically, indicative that the thought experiment may have emerged as the appropriate response: a proposition I also argue in Chapter 4, '"Europe": A Thought Experiment'.

The idea of the thought experiment tries to respond to several problems. With respect to cinema, it names films that neither compete with Hollywood (in the classic self–other construction), nor oppose themselves to Hollywood (in the classic anti-stance of art and avant-garde cinema). They also skirt another danger, which is to slip into a kind of self-exoticism or auto-ethnography: representing yourself to the Other, as you imagine the Other imagines you, which is the perennial temptation of festival films and of the 'new (national) waves' that festivals periodically presented to the world. Instead, cinema as thought experiment identifies films that can be referenced to the core philosophical principles and political values of European democracy, testing the appeal or traction that ideals such as liberty, fraternity and equality still have in today's Europe. Films can do this overtly, with narratives of migration and multicultural communities, showing the disintegration of families, mechanisms of exclusion and discrimination, but they can also do so more implicitly when the individual's relation to power and the state is at issue, or when crafting parables that confront characters with difficult or impossible ethical choices. Secondly, given the disappointments and frustrations that the European Union elicits among its members collectively and individually, it may be time to declare this very idea of a united Europe a political experiment badly in need of renewing itself as a *philosophical* thought experiment. As Roberto Esposito has pointed out, the notion of Europe as above all a philosophical idea has a long tradition:

> [There is] something that pertains to the philosophical character of the very constitution of Europe. Not possessing definite geographical boundaries, at least in the East – its distinction from Asia is problematic, considering that two large countries, Russia and Turkey, stretch between

> the two continents – Europe, from the beginning, has defined itself from the perspective of the constitutive specificity of its philosophical principles: the freedom of the Greek cities as opposed to the Asian despotic regimes. Although these principles were often contradicted and reversed into their opposite, the idea of Europe is inseparable from them.[4]

Just as frequently, however, this very priority given to Greek politics and philosophy, together with Judeo-Christian religion and ethics in any definition of Europe has been criticized as Eurocentric, suppressing the debts to other civilizations, setting up a successive series of distorting mirrors, as well as acting as an elitist and exclusionary narrative even with respect to Europe's own indigenous populations and their cultures.[5] These historical issues – too broad to be considered here – form the outer horizon, as they inform the debates on Europe's diminished role in a globalized world. Where and how to de-centre and re-centre Europe thus remain relevant to the topic in hand, namely European cinema's own reduced role in world cinema.

One of the qualities of European cinema at least since the end of the Second World War has been its reflexivity, its inward turn, as well as its unique form of ruminating, speculative self-scrutiny. The films of Roberto Rossellini, Ingmar Bergman, Michelangelo Antonioni, Alain Resnais, Jean-Luc Godard, Agnès Varda, Chris Marker, Andrzej Wajda and Alexander Kluge have always been 'philosophical' in this respect, thanks to intense self-interrogation, political critique and a probing of limits (of what it means to be European). As this generation has passed on or is handing over, a less personal and existential kind of philosophy has come to the fore also in filmmaking: embracing a political philosophy that once more examines the kinds of intimate or extended community that liberal democracy provides for its citizens, once outside their comfort zone and confronted with the Other, as neighbour, stranger, antagonist or object of desire. These questions are deeply interwoven with how we think about cinema as a practice

---

[4] Roberto Esposito, 'An Interview with Roberto Esposito', interviewed by Diego Ferrante and Marco Piasentier, *The Philosophical Salon*, http://thephilosophicalsalon.com/from-outside-a-philosophy-for-europe-an-interview-with-roberto-esposito-part-one/ (accessed 27 December 2016).

[5] Among the many studies challenging Eurocentrism, Josep Fontana's *The Distorted Past: A Reinterpretation of Europe* (Cambridge, MA: Blackwell, 1995) sounds the familiar polemical note: 'Europe's history has been . . . a process of self-representation that has employed any number of such [distorting] mirrors . . . the barbarian, the Christian, the feudal, the devil, the rural, the courtly, the savage, "progress," and, finally, the mob. Each has thrown back different visions that, throughout all their many transformations, have served consistently to assure Western Civilization that it is superior to all other civilizations and deserves to dominate the planet.' Anthony Pagden, reviewing Fontana's book in *American Historical Review* 102, no. 5 (1 December 1997): 1469.

commensurate with the digital age, with social networks and the ubiquity of the moving image not only in film and television, but also in art spaces, in design and in advertising. Another way is to think of cinema as a space that confronts us with our 'being in the world', welcoming cinema as an ever surprising or startling *encounter*, one that touches us in our ethics and politics, that challenges not just specific ideas or beliefs, but entire value systems, maybe even proposing quite radical insights into how life can be lived and imagined – as individuals, as social beings, as part of humanity. Film as thought experiment wants to suggest a philosophical framework for such an idea of cinema as a political ethics.

This philosophical framework starts with the idea of no longer thinking of the screen as either a 'window-on-the-world' or a 'mirror-to-the-self', the two abiding aesthetics and enabling epistemologies – apparently diametrically opposed – that have characterized our critical approaches to modern European cinema. Since the end of the Second World War and the revival of European art cinema, the paradigm of the 'window' has stood for an art of transparency and realism, exemplified by neo-realism and theorized by André Bazin and Siegfried Kracauer, while 'mirror' came to signify the European auteurs' modernist turn to self-reference, reflexivity and distanciation, exemplified by the 'play' metaphors in Resnais and Jacques Rivette's films, Federico Fellini's doubling of the director via an alter ego in the narrative, Bergman's portraits of the artist as magician and manipulator, and in Godard's films about filmmaking, and of treating words as images and images as signs. Cinema as mirror was theorized in *apparatus theory* (Jean-Louis Baudry), combining Freud and Plato, and based on concepts like *mise en abîme* (Christian Metz) or *suture* (Jean-Pierre Oudart and Stephen Heath), while mostly relying on Jacques Lacan's concept of the *mirror-phase*, according to Lacan the key in the development of human identity and subjectivity.[6]

What would be an alternative ground from which to reassess and reposition both of these cinematic epistemologies? The extraordinary success of the philosophy of Gilles Deleuze among film theorists is in part due to his bold move of dispensing with the entire conceptual arsenal associated with the optical vocabulary of eye, gaze and look, as well as discarding transparency, reflection and representation (along with identity and difference), making them suddenly seem expendable to an understanding of cinema. By claiming for the moving image a new kind of materiality, an existence in time beyond the ephemeral and the moment, as well as investing it with energy, with agency and intensities – in short, with something akin to a life-form of its own – Deleuze began defining for a whole generation a new rapport with cinema, whether contemporary, modern or classical. By

---

[6] For useful summaries of these concepts, see Edward Branigan and Warren Buckland (eds), *The Routledge Encyclopedia of Film Theory* (New York: Routledge, 2014).

resolutely affirming the co-extensiveness of cinema and the spectatorial body, rather than their critical distance from each other – previously theorized as mis-cognition, disavowal, fetishism – and instead connecting cinema more directly to our senses, to affective flows in either direction, he 'freed up' other perceptual faculties than the eye, and at the same time, dignified films with a capacity for being a world, rather than reflecting one, and for film spectators as 'being-in-the world' rather than merely having imaginary access to the world. What was so attractive about Deleuze's film philosophy, then, was not only that he talked about all the things that contemporary audiences (and indeed, filmmakers) seem to be interested in – affect, time, embodiment, the virtual and the actual – but he did so in a way that jolted one's thinking quite generally, conveying a bracing conviction that there was light at the end of the modernist/postmodernist tunnel. And sure enough, Deleuzian approaches to films, not only those made in Europe, have begun to bridge the gap between traditional auteur studies, essentializing studies in 'national cinema' and the worlds of cinema that exist or have emerged elsewhere than Europe and are animated by political topics and ethical or spiritual concerns.[7] Deleuze also provided 'toolboxes' by which to discuss films made in Europe, but otherwise difficult to classify. Such approaches often testify to a renewed 'love' of (contemplative, 'slow') cinema, distinct from classical cinephilia and yet subtly continuing to celebrate cinema's life-sustaining and life-affirming powers, even where the criteria of value differ from 1950s cinephilia, which tended to construct the loved object either in the mirror image of high art, or as precious precisely in relation to the ever present anxiety of loss and ephemeral transience.[8]

A comparative study of the different metaphors and paradigms as they pertain to the cinema was the subject of another book, from the perspective of the changes that the digital turn had brought to the cinema, especially as they related to the body and the senses.[9] The present study pursues another way of understanding the current conjuncture, in which European cinema finds itself either as an entity without identity or with too many identities. It follows on from earlier attempts to describe the hybrid and hyphenated identities of European cinema and to come to grips with the dilemmas endemic to European cinema, for which I coined the concept of 'double occupancy'. It was a phrase I took from hotel-speak, to make the connection to 'hospitality', that is, of how to accommodate the stranger, the intruder,

[7] Directors that come to mind are Apitchatpong Weerasethakul, Rithy Panh, Lav Diaz, Carlos Reygades, Phan Dang Di and Jia Zhangke.

[8] For recent studies of cinephilia, see Malte Hagener and Marijke de Valck (eds), *Cinephilia: Movies Love and Memory* (Amsterdam: Amsterdam University Press, 2005).

[9] Thomas Elsaesser and Malte Hagener, *Film Theory: An Introduction through the Senses*, 2nd edn (London and New York: Routledge, 2015).

the guest – both from without, and already inside.[10] I even tried to up the ante, by referring to the auto-ethnographic impulse of festival films, showing the respective others the face they want to see, as the 'mutual interference in the internal affairs of the other', a phrase used in political discussions in Brussels about post-national concepts of sovereignty, and to which I gave a positive, empowering and at the same time suitably risk-taking and dangerous meaning. Less positively phrased, it recurs (in Chapter 12) as the challenge faced by auteur cinema on the festival circuit, where films often enough find themselves 'serving two masters'.

Can we understand this epithet 'European' not just at the crossroads of multiply intersecting national trajectories, serving not two (or more) masters, but serving also several (universalizing) ideals, recognized as 'European'? A first step, already taken in my previous book, is to look at contemporary cinema under the general conjuncture of globalization, capitalism and the ensuing crisis in (Western) democracy. But now going beyond the dynamics of self and other, invariably associated with the cinema when we remain within the vocabulary of window and mirror, I want to understand the epithet 'European' across the different dynamics of both antagonism and mutuality. It requires one to factor in the judgement of others (Europe's diminished influence), as well as Europe's self-image (still occupying the moral high ground), which when taken together, lead to my central thesis already alluded to: namely that the new marginality of Europe (not only) *when applied to the cinema* should be seized as an opportunity even more than seen as an occasion for nostalgia or regret.

At first glance, the negatives seem overwhelming: European cinema is artificially kept alive with government subsidies, Council of Europe directives and cheap television co-production deals. Bolstered by being co-opted for cultural tourism and city branding, it speaks on behalf of no constituency, and, for the most part, speaks to no public other than festival audiences, loyal cinephiles and to university students. Looking closer, these apparently fatal weaknesses can yet be turned to advantage: precisely because they exist at the margins, in a sphere of disinvestment and disinterest, European films have a special kind of freedom, which is also a power and a strength. Having 'lost' the (illusory) status of not only standing for 'art', but also for integrity and authorial independence (braving Hollywood's 'cultural imperialism'), films made in 'Europe' have little or nothing (else) to lose. Precisely because they exist in a disinterested universe, European films can so easily become Deleuzian, in the sense that *their inconsequentiality either in economic or ideological terms frees them from the burden of being*

[10] Thomas Elsaesser, 'Real Location, Fantasy Space, Performative Place: Double Occupancy and Mutual Interference in European Cinema', in Temenuga Trifonova (ed.), *European Film Theory* (New York and London: Routledge, 2009), 47–61.

'representative': it allows them to develop 'lines of flight', a different kind of affective presence, and above all, a new kind of autonomy. This is the key 'political' thesis of the chapters that follow.

Consider the following: unlike Hollywood films, European cinema does not have to prove that it is 'post-9/11' or 'post-racial', that it has global audience appeal or that its films play equally well as a gripping adventure story and as a video game, that they hold up to repeated viewing on a DVD, or that they are still in the public's memory when it is time to sell the television rights to cable and the syndicated networks. Not having to 'reflect' or promote a specific ideology, and therefore not being answerable to the kinds of critique that Hollywood films are routinely subject to (nor to the allegorical and symptomatic readings common in cultural studies) does give a filmmaker a special kind of privilege and freedom. European cinema can, as a consequence, more easily transcend or ignore the geometry of window and mirror. It is these fixed spatial coordinates – such would be the argument – that make such ideological readings possible in the first place, because of the mimetic-representational correspondences they imply about the relation of cinematic realism (however stylized) to physical reality (however ideological). Not to be beholden to window and mirror thus opens up possibilities beyond the Euclidian space–time continuum, its linearity of temporal succession and its geometry of representation, as inherited from Renaissance perspective.

In contrast to European cinema's relative irrelevance, Hollywood not only continues to work on the US's national traumas as well as past and present political histories.[11] It also actively seeks out answers to the challenges of new technologies, and therefore still qualifies as the industrial avant-garde of cinema and visual media in general. It strains to remain a powerful force in innovation, across the different media platforms and formats, even if it means entering into unholy alliances with, for instance, the military-entertainment complex (when it comes to computer games, but also in the many films that have the US military as their subject or setting). As a consequence, Hollywood's genres take account of the widespread non-entertainment uses of simulators, of acting at a distance, of animation and 3-D rendering, making pleasurable and investing with libido the general militarization of civil society and the security state. In all these areas, European cinema trades on a narrower, now almost entirely antiquarian definition of avant-garde, and does not seem to have a particular ambition other than to preserve and perpetuate itself. As governments benefit from promoting one of the most cost-effective forms of

[11] The traumas: *Syriana*, *Argo*, *Zero Dark Thirty*, *American Sniper*, *Good Kill*; *Margin Call*, *The Big Short*, *The Wolf of Wall Street*. The histories, past and present: *Lincoln*, *12 Years a Slave*, *Bridge of Spies*, *Citizen Four*, *Snowdon*.

cultural subsidy, so do the filmmakers: the two (European governments and the filmmaking communities) continue to exist in a beneficial relation of 'antagonistic mutuality', more harmless perhaps than the overt cooperation of Hollywood and the military, but no less in need of examination and analysis (see below).

Therefore, in order to come to another approach to European cinema, I am dispensing with the usual taxonomies, not only by not focusing on individual national cinemas, but also leaving aside the interpretative schemata of a) classical film theory (ideological critique) and b) cultural studies (the politics of representation and identity), while also excusing myself for not (altogether) adopting the Deleuzian toolbox of the 'time image', 'crystal', 'minor literature' and the disruption of the sensory-motor schema, which have become the customary consequences of rejecting both a) and b). Instead, I begin by invoking three readily available narratives that try to explain the collapse of relevance within the geopolitical context of Europe's new marginality.

First, the narrative of globalization and the end of the Cold War: Europe from 1945 until 1990 had a unique strategic value for the US as its buffer zone and front-line of defense against the Soviet Union; since the 1990s Europe has lost much of its political significance for the US, which has turned to China, Asia and the Middle East. Globalization has decisively shifted the epicentres of power, and the bi-polar face-to-face of Europe either vis-à-vis the US or in confrontation with the USSR has given way to a much more complicated (but also traditional) geopolitical calculus. One witnesses here the downsides to the upsides of the European Union: in a few brief decades, it has established a partnership between nations that used to be arch-enemies, notably France and Germany, Britain and France, Germany and Britain, and it has healed or at least recalibrated the East–West divisions brought about by the Cold War. It has brought prosperity to Europe's impoverished periphery, notably to countries like Spain, Portugal, Greece and Ireland – even though only after the Euro-crisis of 2008 have the citizens of these countries realized the price to be paid for this sudden wealth, by way of unsustainable debt and draconian austerity measures, followed by a sharper North–South divide and resurgent 'Fortress Europe' populism.

Second, heroic and post-heroic narratives: Europe, based as it has been on its nation-states, with their firm borders, distinct peoples, languages and territories, has gradually lost these markers of 'identity through differentiation'. Within the European Union there are hardly any borders: Europe has absorbed millions of 'foreign' nationals (be they from within or from outside the EU), it has become multinational, multi-religious and multi-ethnic, there has been an unprecedented mobility of goods, labour, people and property – making room for theories of immunization and auto-immunity as a political philosophy when recasting inside–outside relations.[12] The self–other dynamic no longer applies as the 'Gestalt' model regulating self-perception, except as populist *ressentiment*, mostly on the (extreme) right of the political spectrum, where its virulence is like the phantom pain of loss (of sovereignty).[13] In short, Europe no longer has a *heroic narrative* of self-identity and self-creation. The French and American Revolutions, Rousseau and Hobbes' social contract leading to democracy, the critical hermeneutics of the Enlightenment, which established empirical knowledge, technological improvement of life and the prospect of unlimited progress: all represented European narratives of heroic-collective self-creation and self-realization.

Now that we know how much this heroic narrative was also based on imperialism, slavery and colonialism, on exploitation and exclusion, not everyone is quite so proud of it, while others are in collective denial, trying to revive national exceptionalism. Central and Eastern Europe – partly as a consequence of freedom from Soviet totalitarianism – have seen a resurgence of such post-nationalism, but it is one born out of fear and resentment, clinging to the remnants of the heroic narrative in distinctly unheroic times of corruption and cronyism. This post-national condition has led neither to a credible post-heroic narrative (as suggested in Chapter 4, on '"Europe": A Thought Experiment', and Chapter 6 on 'Post-Heroic Narratives and the Community to Come') nor to a whole-hearted embrace of globalization, other than in the form of tourism, leisure and consumption. Instead, (cultural and political) Europe has turned obsessively inward, towards the past, towards commemoration and collective nostalgia, while economic Europe is buoyed by Germany's manufacturing exports, France's military and aviation technology and Britain's financial services.

The third narrative maintains that Europe has undermined itself philosophically (since Nietzsche) through secularization, scepticism, nihilism,

---

[12] On this topic, see Hannah Richter, 'Beyond the "Other" as Constitutive Outside: The Politics of Immunity in Roberto Esposito and Niklas Luhmann', *European Journal of Political Theory* (July 2016), which uses the concept of immunization to break down the self–other divide, arguing that (according to Esposito) a community can sustain its relations through introversive immunization against an undefined outside, and (according to Luhmann's immunity theory) that politics relies on immunization through contradictions to reproduce its functional role as a decision-making institution, but is exposed to potential rupture through the political openness immunity introduces. http://ept.sagepub.com/content/early/2016/07/14/1474885116658391.abstract (accessed 18 December 2016).

[13] Apart from such established parties of the right as France's Front National and Italy's Liga Nord, there have sprung up since the 2000s a plethora of right-wing parties in Britain, Denmark, the Netherlands, Italy, Spain and Greece. Most are anti-immigrant and anti-Islam, notably the German Pegida. See Kate Connolly, 'Pegida: what does the German far-right movement actually stand for?', *Guardian*, 6 January 2015, https://www.theguardian.com/world/shortcuts/2015/jan/06/pegida-what-does-german-far-right-movement-actually-stand-for (accessed 18 December 2016).

critical theory, epistemic relativism and deconstruction.[14] It has systematically cast doubt on its own moral, epistemological and ontological foundations, most notably by challenging from within the universality of values of Enlightenment humanism, and in the process has embraced a form of social constructivism and relativist multiculturalism that ends up distrusting the legitimacy of its political institutions, undermining civic pride, citizenship and solidarity, breeding instead both cynicism and apathy.

This third narrative of decline would, then, be about the supposedly corrosive effect of post-metaphysical philosophy and deconstruction, the dominant intellectual trends from the 1950s to the 1990s, taking in existentialism, structuralism, anti-humanism and deconstruction. Rejection or overcoming this anti-foundationalism and anti-universalism is what unites an otherwise very disparate group of philosophers currently also drawn on in film studies, most of whom figure in the chapters that follow: Deleuze, Jacques Rancière, Jean-Luc Nancy, Alain Badiou, Emmanuel Levinas (as well as Michel Foucault).[15]

In their respective ways, each is making strong claims for how one might revitalize European universalism after deconstruction, of how to renew the social contract, after socialism, and how to build on the dissenting energies of religion – notably the Christian heritage – after secularism: all in order to give new meaning both to the term 'Europe' and to that of 'community'. The aim is to rescue some of the energies that went into the great utopian or 'progressive' social projects which dominated European political and social thinking over the past 200 years, and which failed so catastrophically in both its fascist-millennial and socialist-egalitarian variants. To these French names I add Giorgio Agamben, whose notions of bio-politics (after Foucault) and the concept of 'bare life' (after Hannah Arendt) have had considerable impact, and whose work will be discussed in greater detail in several chapters. The philosopher who makes regular appearances by way of commentary and asides is Slavoj Žižek, not least because his range of references so readily includes the cinema. Also worth mentioning is the German philosopher Peter Sloterdijk, who has written extensively about 'Europe'. For instance, in a

[14] See Roberto Esposito, *From Outside: A Philosophy for Europe* (London: Polity Press, 2017), and an extended interview with Esposito, http://thephilosophicalsalon.com/from-outside-a-philosophy-for-europe-an-interview-with-roberto-esposito-part-one/ (accessed 18 December 2016).

[15] Each of the philosophers named could be said to rethink the 'foundations' of European 'identity': Gilles Deleuze and 'multiplicities' (repetition and difference, rather than identity, negativity and difference); Jacques Rancière and 'radical equality' (how to renew the social contract); Alain Badiou and 'the event' (revitalize European universalism); and Jean-Luc Nancy and 'being singular plural' (how to redefine community and togetherness). Some – notably Badiou, Žižek, Agamben – also ask themselves how to build a new politics on the dissenting energies of the Christian religion. Exploring the cinematic implications of such a new politics is part of another project.

book called *Zorn und Zeit* ('Anger and Time') he argued for a return to the virtues of anger and pride (as opposed to resentment), which he traces back to Homer's *Iliad* (the anger of Achilles with which the epic begins) and the concept of *Thymos* (courage, spiritedness, the struggle for recognition) – what I have called the 'heroic narrative' of self-fashioning.

The contrast to Homer's *Thymos* is Plato's *Eros*, which has degenerated, according to Sloterdijk, in contemporary consumer culture, into a cult of desire and lack, guilt and shame, instant gratification and deferred action. So far so banal, you might say, but Sloterdijk goes on to argue that these great social achievements and political projects of Europe have been made possible by what he calls the collection, conservation and channelling of *Thymos*, that is, righteous anger and pride, institutionally administered by Christianity, Capitalism *and* Communism, of which the socialist revolution was the last beneficiary, but where, after the heroic phase of the workers' movements and the collapse of socialism, all that is left is resentment. Now that each of the three Cs has lost credibility and status, the frustrated collective *Thymos* is being dissipated and defused, Eros-fashion, by different forms of therapy, ranging from psychoanalysis to granting everyone victim-status, from ostentatious displays of empathy in television talk-shows to the spectacle of pure aggression in reality television.[16]

Even if such generalizations border on polemics and caricature, the argument would be that these different philosophical takes on Europe's malaise nonetheless provide something of a cognitive map also for positioning European cinema in and for the twenty-first century. The subtitle of this chapter, 'Enlarging the Context', is meant to invoke a famous saying by Jean Monnet, one of the intellectual and political founders of the European Union: 'If you have a problem that you cannot solve, enlarge the context.'[17] In my case, the 'problem' would be European cinema's loss of status and apparent marginality, while 'enlarging the context' would be my suggestion to see it as an act of liberation and experiment, rather than denying it or arguing it away. But enlarging the context can also mean placing 'marginality' within a broader political and philosophical context: the crisis of European governance and sovereignty, the weakness of the humanities in the universities, and the collapse of the left both politically and intellectually in

[16] What a return to Thymos might look like has been demonstrated by the rise of AfD (Alternative für Deutschland), a German political party on the extreme right. Its chief thinker, Marc Jongen, is the long-time assistant of Peter Sloterdijk who was obliged to distance himself from the AfD and its programme. For a summary of the debate, see https://www.heise.de/tp/features/Der-Parteiphilosoph-der-AfD-von-dem-Anhaenger-den-grossen-Wurf-erwarten-3378874.html (accessed 18 December 2016).

[17] The phrase is attributed to Jean Monnet, as, for instance, cited in the title of the opening speech at the Unrepresented Nations and Peoples Organization conference, The Hague, 29 September 2006 http://www.unpo.org/content/view/5526/81/ (accessed 18 December 2016).

Europe. This broader context in turn coincides with what could be called the three traumas of Europe: these partly overlap with the narratives earlier invoked, by which Europe's decline is seen from the 'outside', except that this time, they are focused on the anxieties experienced 'from within'.

First, we have the trauma of Europe's bio- and body-politics, that is, the adverse demographics of ageing and lack of reproduction, the obsession with wellness and health care, but also the new cult of children, the precariousness of childhood, with the attendant anxieties of 'abuse'; the apprehensive but ambivalent concern about the environment, about genetically manipulated foods, and the palliative, self-therapizing effects of being a 'green consumer', the debates over euthanasia and over who has the right over one's body: the individual (woman) or the state.

Second, we have the 'trauma' of the Holocaust, and its paradoxically foundational role for Europe as the (re-)civilizing project for a new moral compass. A major shift has taken place in our understanding of the twentieth century and, in particular, the Second World War, whose remembered reference point since the 1970s has become the Holocaust. As this memory of the Holocaust is being Europeanized, its political function and afterlife have changed. Once a monstrous crime committed by the Germans as a people and a nation, it has become a moral catastrophe and humanitarian disaster in which all Europe has a share of blame and guilt, so that its annual remembrance and public memorialization is now the rallying point for a specifically 'European' moral and cultural unity.

Third, we have the trauma of the confrontation and accommodation with Islam. More than a thousand years of contact, of hostilities, conquest and alliances, around Turkey and the Ottoman Empire (for Germany, Austria and the Balkans), with Arabs and Mediterranean Islam (for Spain and France) and with Islam in the former colonies (for Britain, France and the Netherlands) are now being revived and relived under different signs: of immigration rather than military conquest; of coexistence rather than crusade; of human trafficking, drugs and the prostitution of women, rather than spices, silk and trade; of homegrown Diaspora radicalism rather than exotic, tourist 'Orientalism'.

All three contemporary traumas, I believe, can be related to tendencies in European cinema. Bio-politics and the body are very present in French cinema, notably by its women directors: Catherine Breillat, Claire Denis, Coline Serreau, for instance; children, or the death of children, is almost the defining theme of Italian cinema, from *Cinema Paradiso* (1988), *La Vita e bella* (1997) and *The Son's Room* (2001), to *Lorenzo's Oil* and the 2010 Cannes entry, *La Nostra Vita*. Sexuality and old age have been a theme in Italian (Paolo Sorrentino's *Youth*, 2015) German (Andreas Dresen's *Cloud Nine*, 2008) and Romanian films (Cristi Puiu's *Death of Mr. Lăzărescu*, 2005). This body politics on screen is matched by a near-universal turn in film analysis to embodied forms of spectatorship, of a 'cinema of touch', of 'intimacy', of '(physical) extremity', 'of skins and screens' and 'haptic modes of vision'.

The role of the cinema in helping create the iconography and cultural memory of the Holocaust in and for Europe can hardly be overestimated – by now, there have even been several 'waves' within this genre alone: the 'mode retro' in France, from *Lacombe Lucien* (1974) and *Au Revoir les Enfants* (1987) to *Le Dernier Métro* (1980) and *M. Klein* (1976), followed by the German 'Hitler-wave' of films by Hans-Jürgen Syberberg, Rainer Werner Fassbinder, Edgar Reitz, Margarethe von Trotta, Helma Sander-Brahms, followed by the anti-retro films such as Claude Lanzmann's *Shoah* (1985) or Harun Farocki's *Images of the World* (1989), itself succeeded by films featuring Jewish protagonists of the subsequent generation (*Rosenstrasse*, 2003, *Aimée & Jaguar*, 1999, and *Abraham's Gold*, 1990), and finally films showing the perpetrators as victims, such as *Downfall* (2004) or *The Reader* (2008), and the victim as perpetrator (*Son of Saul*, 2015).

The challenge of Islam and migration, of multiculturalism more generally and especially the gap across the generations, has in each country of Western Europe produced its own genre or sub-genre of films that either renews traditions of neo-realism with closely observed faces and everyday fates, in the semi-documentary idiom of Michael Winterbottom's *In this World* (2002), Pawel Pawlikowski's *Last Resort* (2000) and Lukas Moodysson's *Lilya 4 Ever* (2002), or in the generational conflict and star-crossed lovers films like Fatih Akin's *Soul Kitchen* (2009) and Abdellatif Kechiche's *La Graine et le mulet* (2007). Some have found a new fusion between youth cultures, drug cultures and music, as in the films that followed the classic of the genre, Mathieu Kassovitz's noir-blanc-beur film *La Haine* (1995), such as *Trainspotting* (1996), *24 Hour Party People* (2002) and *Enter the Void* (2009). Several of Fatih Akin's films can stand as examples, although as I argue in Chapter 9 on Akin ('Experimenting with Death in Life'), the multicultural setting may also serve as the conveniently topical framework for raising ethical issues of a more existential kind.

Most remarked upon, in this context, has been the emergence of so many hyphenated filmmakers in Europe – Turkish-German, Asian-British, Maghreb-French, Albanian-Italian – as if the cinema, for these mostly second-generation immigrants, had proved the ideal mode of expression in which to be affirmative about living conditions and personal circumstances that, from a strictly sociological point of view, would have made them marginal and outcasts.[18] Here, festival cinema, across the more level playing

[18] See, among others, Elizabeth Ezra and Terry Rowden (eds), *Transnational Cinema: The Film Reader* (London and New York: Routledge, 2006); Cary Rajinder Sawhney, *Asian-British Cinema – From the Margin to the Mainstream* (Screenonline); Carrie Tarr, *Reframing Difference: Beur and Banlieue Filmmaking in France* (Manchester: Manchester University Press, 2005); Will Higbee, *Post-beur Cinema: North African Emigre and Maghrebi-French Cinema* (Edinburgh: Edinburgh University Press, 2013); Sabine Hake and Barbara Mennel, *Turkish German Cinema in the New Millennium: Sites, Sounds, and Screens* (Oxford: Berghahn Books, 2012).

field of 'world cinema', allows the hyphenated Europeans to deftly affirm multiple allegiances and credibly embody different kinds of authenticity, once the Europe–Hollywood asymmetries no longer determine the respective self-image, of either wanting to 'become American' or defining oneself against Hollywood.

I suggest that in each case, Europe's 'traumas', insofar as they serve as a resource for European cinema, should indeed be seen as the basis for a liberating move, rather than a handicap. Here, too, the new marginality of European cinema reveals itself as its potential strength. While I shall not argue this in detail for each of the three traumas, and am concentrating instead on another triad – liberty, equality, fraternity – I can briefly illustrate the general point. For instance, one understanding of *freedom* – not in the French sense, which asserts that everything is permitted, so long as it does not harm another, nor the freedom that artists usually claim for themselves, when insisting that their work is responsible to no one other than their desire for self-expression – is not as 'freedom from', nor 'freedom, in order to', but another (Kantian) model, which is also that of Kafka, or Herman Melville's Bartleby: 'the freedom to choose not to'. It gives rise to my key philosophical-ethical-political concept which runs throughout the book, namely 'abjection'. Abjection, in the expanded definition that I shall give it, connects both with the idea of Europe in political crisis and with (its) cinema as thought experiment. Certain films qualify as thought experiments, insofar as they can best be understood as testing Europe's political values through states or moments of abjection: abjection becoming the degree zero of what it is to be human today. This differs from the meaning of abjection as primarily a psychoanalytic concept of relevance to gender and femininity, by adding to it a political as well as an ethical dimension. Abjection in this sense is neither to be confused with victimhood, nor shall I interpret it as 'resistance' and 'critique'. Instead, it figures as the freedom to assert – and to inhabit – a position of extreme marginality and exclusion, imposed by the Other. As a consequence, the ethics of abjection derives from the fact that the abject has nothing more to lose, but also has no claims to make, thus commanding a particular kind of freedom that probes the limits of both freedom and the law.

However, Julia Kristeva, to whom we owe the concept of abjection as pertinent to discussions of subjectivity, identity, personhood and gender, has also associated it with creativity, a connection I shall explore in relation to the figure of the film auteur, arguing that abjection can also mean the freedom to impose on oneself certain (creative) constraints or limits. This is a stance for which I might have chosen a number of prominent European directors, such as Krzysztof Kieslowski, Claire Denis or Tom Tykwer, but where Lars von Trier and Michael Haneke will serve as my primary examples in Chapter 12, 'Control, Creative Constraints and Self-Contradiction: The Global Auteur'.

I want to claim that the general condition of *marginality and irrelevance* of European cinema precisely raises the possibility of freedom, in the sense of requiring a filmmaker to think of the kinds of self-imposed limits which can make this freedom from either box office or social accountability aesthetically and ethically meaningful. Jon Elster, a social philosopher, has spoken of creative constraints as a key to innovative thinking not just in the arts but also in business and management, and he has argued that creative people 'self-bind' themselves to arbitrary sets of constraints whenever there is not sufficient constraint present in their environment or if the problem at hand is not yet defined clearly enough. One of the examples Elster provides for an arbitrary creative constraint happens to be the 'film director [who] decides to shoot in black and white so as not to be tempted by the facile charms of color photography'[19] – a reference that would seem to fit perfectly the case of Michael Haneke's *The White Ribbon* (2009), had it not been written some ten years before the film was made. The other case I shall discuss is that of Dogme 95, the Danish manifesto for a new cinema, instigated by Lars von Trier and Thomas Vinterberg, but whose implications are most systematically explored in the form of thought experiments in von Trier's films.

The chapters on Aki Kaurismäki's *The Man without A Past* (2002) and Christian Petzold's *Barbara* (2012) can be seen as further instantiations of the politics of abjection. The former tests the proposition 'What if a man loses his identity along with his memory?': a human tragedy and a personal disaster, but also the chance to use his abject state and mental blank as the *tabula rasa* to not only reinvent himself, but to (re)discover an entirely different world of humanity, and a new form of sociability and solidarity. Petzold's *Barbara*, in my reading, is also a thought experiment of abjection: this time the proposition is 'What if an entire state and nation becomes abject?', also requiring people to 'reinvent themselves' under extremely adverse conditions that entail difficult ethical dilemmas.

To conclude, in the chapters that follow I shall be combining reflections on European political and philosophical thought in the age of the post-nation-state with thinking European 'cinema' beyond the self–other divide of the old Europe–Hollywood divide, as well as beyond the tendency of self-exoticism in 'world cinema'; that is to say, beyond cinema as window and cinema as mirror. What mutuality and antagonism are for the deadlocks of national interest and trans-national sovereignty on the ever more rocky road to a united Europe and a new universalism of human rights and responsibilities, I claim, creative constraints and performative self-contradiction are for an auteur cinema on the way to reimagining 'autonomy' in the face of

---

[19] Jon Elster, *Ulysses Unbound: Studies in Rationality, Precommitment, and Constraints* (Cambridge: Cambridge University Press, 2000), 2.

cinema's 'ubiquity' in the digital age. To put it in more polemical terms: just as the European Union is both promoted and demoted by the rest of the world, held up as a commendable example of some of the most progressive thinking in matters of sovereignty, statehood, solidarity and human rights, while being also reviled for its bureaucratic muddles, waste, petty chicanery, arcane regulations and endless deferrals, so European cinema is both praised for having given the world the film auteur with the status of sovereign artist, enjoying seemingly unlimited freedom, while also dismissed as otherworldly, inward-looking and irrelevant.

Against this binary stalemate, I shall argue that the discrepancy between the way European cinema is seen from without – as part of the exotic-ethnographic mix going by the name of world cinema – and how it sees itself from within – as the stronghold of cinema as autonomous art – might be overcome by making its marginality, seeming irrelevance and unaccountability the starting-point for a new way of recasting the 'political' legacy of Europe across different kinds of foundationalism, universalism and voluntary constraints on freedom. In other words, my claim is that European cinema is working on something after all: reworking a legacy – the universalist values and political ideals of the Enlightenment, albeit in a different key. It reworks them for the twenty-first century, but does so from a position of 'tactical weakness': equality as abjection, fraternity as antagonistic mutuality, and freedom as the freedom to choose one's own limits and contradictions. It may not seem much, but as a project it reaffirms the Europeanness of European cinema as part of what it is not (yet), rather than against what it can no longer be.

2

Film as Thought

The 'Film and Philosophy' Debate

From being erstwhile foes and then indifferent strangers, philosophy and film have recently joined hands, unlikely partners providing solace to one another in a sometimes felicitous, sometimes fractious, marriage of convenience.

ROBERT SINNERBRINK

Introduction

Few living philosophers have been featured in films: Jean Luc Godard's *Vivre sa Vie* (1962) has Brice Parrain talk to Anna Karina in a café, and in *La Chinoise* (1968) Francis Jeanson gives Anne Wiazemsky a tutorial during a train ride; Marshall McLuhan intercepts a cinema queue in Woody Allen's *Annie Hall* (1977), and Jacques Derrida gives a memorable interview to Pascale Ogier in Ken McMullen's *Ghost Dance* (1983).[1]

---

[1] For the record, there are a few biopics of philosophers: Roberto Rossellini's television programmes on *Socrates* (1971), *Blaise Pascal* (1972) and *Descartes* (1974), Derek Jarman's *Wittgenstein* (1993) and Margarethe von Trotta's *Hannah Arendt* (2012); there is *The Ister* (2004), which features a number of philosophers commenting on Heidegger's commentary on Hölderlin's Danube poem, and not forgetting, of course, the many films with and about Slavoj Žižek: without counting the YouTube videos of his lectures and interviews, there are *Žižek!* (Astra Taylor, 2006), *Alien Marx & Co: Slavoj Žižek* (Susan Chales de Beaulieu, 2005), *The Pervert's Guide to the Cinema* (Sophie Fiennes, 2006) and *The Examined Life* (Astra Taylor, 2010), which also features, among others, Judith Butler, Martha Nussbaum, Michael Hardt and Avital Ronell.

But how alive is philosophy in 'film' as a medium and art form? The answer seems to be 'more and more', considering how the question has exercised some of the best minds in cinema studies and in philosophy for the past three decades. It has generated much on- and off-line debate; a terminology has evolved that distinguishes between *philosophy of film*, *film and philosophy*, *film philosophy* and *film-philosophy*, necessitating any number of books, readers and monographs published with these two words in their title, including a bold conflation of both into *Filmosophy*.[2]

As so often in the history of the young discipline that is film studies, the positions taken on the subject divide between a North American contingent and a continental one, the former inspired by analytical philosophy, cognitivism and more recently the neurosciences, the latter inheriting the cinephilia of Paris auteurism, but now buttressed variously and philosophically by Nietzschean anti-metaphysics, Henri Bergson's vitalism, Edmund Husserl's phenomenology, Martin Heidegger's *Weltbild* and Jacques Derrida's deconstruction, as well as returning to the anti-Cartesianism of Gottfried Wilhelm Leibniz and Baruch Spinoza, as championed by Gilles Deleuze. The divides are never that neat, of course: hardline film-cognitivists can come from Europe (Torben Grodal, Ed Tan), while American film scholars Alan Casebier and Vivian Sobchack have done much to revive an interest in Merleau-Ponty's phenomenology, and Patricia Pisters has tried to find common ground between Deleuze and the neurosciences. As in previous schools of thought about cinema, North American and British universities have been the conveyor belts and transmission wheels for French thinking, and *film: philosophy* is no exception: for instance, books on Gilles Deleuze in English outnumber those in French by about 5 to 1.

Indeed, it was the wide reception of Deleuze's cinema books, once they had been published in an English translation in the late 1980s (Deleuze 1986, 1989), that provided the major impetus for the whole field to emerge in its current form, also giving the North American faction (notably the combative Noël Carroll) a new opponent, having previously presented a united front under the heading of 'post-theory' rather than 'philosophy of film'. In France, on the other hand, the international success of Deleuze's *Cinema I* and *II* in turn prompted several established philosophers – all in their seventies – also to write books on cinema: among them Jacques Rancière, Jean-Luc Nancy and Alain Badiou. To complicate matters further,

---

[2] See Daniel Frampton, *Filmosophy* (London: Wallflower, 2006). Overviews from these different perspectives can be found in Cynthia A. Freeland and Thomas E. Wartenberg (eds), *Philosophy and Film* (London and New York: Routledge, 1995); Noël Carroll and Jinhee Choi (eds), *Philosophy of Film and Motion Pictures: An Anthology* (Malden, MA, and London: Blackwell, 2005); Daniel Shaw, *Film and Philosophy: Taking Movies Seriously* (London and New York: Wallflower, 2008). For online discussion, there is also the well-kept website *Film-Philosophy* (www.film-philosophy.com).

Deleuze's pre-eminence became such that in the wake of his impact another (living) American philosopher of film was rediscovered: Stanley Cavell, who – inspired and influenced by André Bazin – had published *The World Viewed: Reflections on the Ontology of Film* as early as 1971, at a time when Bazin, and his use of the terms 'realism' and 'ontology', had almost entirely negative connotations for the serious film theorist. These two maligned terms are now key references in the 'new philosophies of film'.

The present volume does not set out to make a major contribution to this burgeoning field, nor does it engage in the polemics that have arisen. It does not even attempt to mediate between the opposing factions, as some recent books on the subject have tried to do.[3] Nonetheless, it is informed by these debates, and – in this chapter – sets out to understand the symptomatic nature of the philosophical turn in film studies. Inevitably, it means recapitulating some of the narratives that have become *doxa*, in order to provide some justification for entering the fray at all, and this so late in the day. It is to stake a more modest claim, or rather to explore and test a more modest proposal: not necessarily that *films can think*, but rather that a certain class of films may be best understood as borrowing the rhetorical strategies of a *thought experiment*. Whether this makes them 'philosophy' is a question I leave open, not least because I am neither a trained philosopher, nor do I intend to become a film-philosopher. As a film historian – and historian of ideas – I am, however, passionately interested in the problems that I believe film philosophy wants to provide answers for, and the problem I am most concerned with here is the film form that has evolved among European filmmakers since roughly the mid-1990s, and why it seems to me symptomatic of larger issues.

In subsequent chapters, this book therefore focuses on individual European films and filmmakers, but within a different context: one that regards 'Europe' in the twenty-first century – a continent in decline and, some would argue, in disarray – as a philosophical problem, as well as a political one. My contention is that in response to this philosophical problem – how to manage, defend, jettison or redefine the values of the Enlightenment – European cinema, when considered under specific aspects of the thought experiment, has generated some fresh thinking: of the kind that, at least in the present political stalemate, cinema alone seems capable of doing. The thought experiment, that so many films from Europe are intent on staging, revolves around the question of how to test, and possibly reboot, the values that are generally identified with Europe's legacy, such as *liberty*, *equality*, *fraternity*, and they do so by putting

[3] See, for example, books that try to bridge the gap between cognitivism and continental approaches, such as Robert Sinnerbrink, *New Philosophies of Film: Thinking Images* (London and New York: Continuum, 2011), as well as Patricia Pisters' attempted synthesis of Deleuze, the neurosciences and cognitivism in *The Neuro-Image: A Deleuzian Film-Philosophy of Digital Screen Culture* (Stanford, CA: Stanford University Press, 2012).

into play a paradoxical form of negative agency that I associate with the concept of *abjection.*

Film and philosophy: a new alliance or old friends?

But first a brief sketch of the narrower horizon within film studies. What are the reasons for film and philosophy to join efforts? Is it the old combat (American pragmatism versus continental metaphysics) in a new guise? Or is it the digital turn and the 'death of cinema' arguments, leading to a rethinking of the 'ontology' of cinema? Both questions are exciting and challenging, for they offer an opportunity for new thinking also from outside the discipline itself, rather than yield to melancholy and the sense of loss. With the help of philosophy, as the traditional arbiter of foundational problems, might it be possible to write a new history of film theory? Or even begin to understand what has been the importance of the idea of cinema, not just in the twentieth century, but within modern representational thought, such as the last 500 years of image-making and image-circulation? Or perhaps cinema is not primarily about imaging at all, and needs to be seen separately from the various pictorial traditions and media – painting, dioramas, photography – with which it is usually associated? Maybe it affects us most directly as movement, as flow, energy or intensity, as the rhythmic articulation of time and duration? In each case the question of what connection cinema has with philosophy would pose itself differently.

But what is drawing philosophers to cinema, and why do they think it is worth their attention? One no doubt hasty and superficial answer would be that the modern sciences, whether the neurosciences or quantum physics, have reawakened anxieties about the status of reality and the visible world, keying into the seemingly timeless philosophical debates around scepticism, that is, the possibility that the material world we apprehend with our senses and bodies is merely a cleverly engineered illusion. From Plato's cave parable to Descartes' rigid divide between *res cogitans* (mind) and *res extensa* (matter), explorations of such idealism and its obverse, radical scepticism, have been philosophy's dominant preoccupations, whose rebuttals by Kant, Heidegger, Wittgenstein or Gilbert Ryle have not settled questions of the nature of consciousness, the existence of other minds, or the reliability of perception.

But why choose cinema as an object of study for such issues? And how does the present philosophical preoccupation differ from the tendency within film theory of having been 'philosophically literate' not only from the very beginning, but having accurately reflected the changing trends and strands in philosophy? Between 1916 and 1936, film theory's debt to philosophy runs from Hugo Münsterberg's cognitive psychology and Béla Balázs' phenomenology to

Rudolf Arnheim's Gestalt psychology and Walter Benjamin's messianic Marxism (not forgetting Henri Bergson's ambivalently anti-cinematic cinematic philosophy of movement). After 1945, philosophically grounded film theory oscillates from André Bazin's phenomenology to Metz' structural linguistics, and includes *Screen* theory's many philosophical debts: to Jacques Lacan's Hegel, via Louis Althusser's Marx and Michel Foucault's Nietzsche (Foucault also providing an indispensable source for the new film historiography and media archaeology[4]).

What, then, is the agenda that brings philosophy and film together *now*? First, some negative reasons. The most frequently voiced narrative is that 'the rise of the new philosophies of film, which have drawn heavily on analytic philosophy, aesthetics and cognitivist psychology, has coincided with the decline of 1970s screen theory'.[5] Coincidence, correlation, conjuncture, or cause and effect? The reasons for the decline of '*Screen* theory' are said to be due either to the challenge from a more 'powerful' cognitive-analytic paradigm,[6] or the general realization that it rested on three weak, if not altogether damaged/discredited conceptual pillars: Saussure's linguistics, Althusser's Marxism and Lacan's psychoanalysis. Robert Sinnerbrink also states more positive reasons: '[The new film philosophies are] distinguished by the effort to recast many of the problems of classical film theory – concerning the ontology of film, the question of film as art, questions of narrative, character, authorship and genre – within a philosophically renewed and theoretically transformed paradigm (supplanting the older paradigm of psychoanalytic-semiotic film theory).'[7] The implication seems to be that philosophy can assist in putting cinema as an object of study and film studies as a discipline on a more secure epistemological footing by aligning them more closely with the reigning scientific paradigms of the day. A countervailing film philosophy would stress the need to enlist philosophy for a more 'culturalist' agenda, as argued by David Rodowick, when he writes that we need 'a philosophy of the humanities critically and reflexively attentive in equal measure to its epistemological and ethical commitments'.[8]

Rodowick regards the cognitive and analytic attack on *Screen* theory as an attempt to dismiss the humanities more generally, and sees the

---

[4] Thomas Elsaesser, *Film History as Media Archaeology* (Amsterdam: Amsterdam University Press, 2016).

[5] Sinnerbrink, *New Philosophies of Film*, 3.

[6] 'Cognitivism, analytic philosophy and, more recently, neuroscience and evolutionary biology have begun to coalesce into a formidable research paradigm. The latter maintains that film studies, ideally, should draw on the best available science, be compatible with philosophical naturalism, and demonstrate cumulative, testable results. We might define these, respectively, as the *culturalist-historicist* versus the *cognitivist-naturalist* approaches to film' (Sinnerbrink, *New Philosophies of Film*, 4).

[7] Sinnerbrink, *New Philosophies of Film*, 4.

[8] David Rodowick, 'An Elegy for Theory', *October* 122 (Fall 2007): 91–109.

philosophical study of cinema as holding out against the dominance of the empirical or experimental sciences. Considering that much of the philosophy brought to bear on cinema during the 1970s tended to be anti- or post-humanist, this may seem a surprising turn, but if we are to ask afresh what is cinema, then it is important not to have determined in advance the sole epistemological ground from which to pose the question.

It is in this sense that the problems raised by *Screen* theory have not gone away, however much the answers may have proven unsatisfactory, inadequate or conceptually flawed. The list of problems is long. Beginning with Metz's 1964 essay 'Cinéma: langue ou langage?'; followed by the issues of filmic realism and illusionism; film and ideology;[9] theories of the subject articulated through the cinematic apparatus (*dispositif*); and the gendered subject effect of looking (the male gaze) coupled with the cinematic apparatus as a *bachelor machine*. While none of these issues have been definitely laid to rest, and have either been abandoned or replaced by more pressing ones arising from the move from analogue to digital images, one implication of *Screen* theory was that it installed a hermeneutic model that probed a film's 'unconscious', and thus if only by default raised the possibility that a film has a mind, or rather (if one takes a Deleuzian perspective): what is 'mind' in a film and what is 'matter'?

Yet it may be necessary to also revise some of our common assumptions about hermeneutics – notably re-examine what is usually termed the *hermeneutics of suspicion* (also known as 'critical readings') in light of today's more proactive and interactive spectators (who practise hermeneutics either as a way of showing off their hard-won expert knowledge, or who are seduced into hermeneutics by enigmatic scenes or ambiguous endings, puzzling character motivation or plot twists). What I will be arguing is that the hermeneutic approach most likely to build a viable procedural bridge between film and philosophy is one that considers a film's reality-status as well as its propositional character to be that of the *thought experiment*. Thus Chapter 3 will make the case for a hermeneutics modified to carry the limited claims and heuristic value of a thought experiment. Here the main philosophers challenging hermeneutics – after Hans Georg Gadamer and Paul Ricoeur forcefully arguing for hermeneutics – would be besides Deleuze, Slavoj Žižek and Friedrich Kittler. Of special value is the latter's insight that the mechanical and electronic media have recorded and transmitted more sensory data about the world than human perception can process at any given time and in any hitherto known form (including narrative). Hence the need to filter, select,

[9] Realism as an ideological illusion (which, as I shall argue below, is best understood as a negative epistemology) can also be traced back to much older debates, that is, Plato, since the philosophical core of these debates is Plato's priority of the concept (logos) over the image (distrust in the image).

abstract, subtract – which is what I see hermeneutics as doing, while the thought experiment suggests itself as the formal or rhetorical device, given its special position between the particular and the general, the concrete case and the general code that can reframe different interpretative moves.

The idea of film as a thought experiment has been argued by Thomas Wartenberg and several other scholars who have pointed to its merits but also drawn attention to its limits as a concept and analogy.[10] Sinnerbrink, who is also sympathetic to film as thought experiment, sees it as an honest compromise, paving the way for a 'greater interactive engagement between the rationalistic style of traditional *philosophy of film*, and the minor, interdisciplinary tradition of . . . *film- philosophy*'.[11] Less ecumenical than Sinnerbrink, who wants to reconcile or least find common ground between the analytical school and the continental one, I think of the thought experiment as answering to a more limited challenge – that of a new understanding of recent European cinema, given that I lean towards the European side of the 'continental divide', both for my political-philosophical agenda and for the films I cite as case studies. It does not mean that I subscribe to Deleuze's agenda about 'modern cinema' as characterized by the 'time image'. In this respect, I find myself more actively engaged with the critique of Deleuze by Rancière and Badiou, while at the same time recognizing their (and thus also my) substantial debt to Deleuze.

If one focuses on questioning both the epistemology of cinema (is it a form of thought? What kind of knowledge does it generate?) and its ontology (as in the formula 'Cinema: a form of art, or a form of life?'), then one's inspiration must invariably include Deleuze, who tends to encourage the recklessness of the latter formula. But even a foolish move is not necessarily a misstep, when one sets out to contribute to a form of thinking about our post-human condition that does not implicitly start from, and remains circumscribed by, the presumptions of the natural and the experimental sciences as providing the only kind of knowledge either pertinent or admissible for an understanding of the spectrum of the human and its symbolic forms, be they logic, mathematics, language or images.

More specifically, the problems of classical film theory that Sinnerbrink hopes film philosophy can recast, include 'the minds of film', 'the nature of movement', 'time: reversible or irreversible', 'sensation, affect and embodiment', 'other minds and other worlds', 'singularity' and finally 'agency', while 'narrative' is a category best broken down into different constituent parts, such as, on the one hand, causality, sequentiality, linearity and distributed

---

[10] See Thomas Wartenberg, *Thinking on Screen: Film as Philosophy* (London: Routledge, 2007).

[11] Sinnerbrink, *New Philosophies of Film*, 3. Sinnerbrink calls this 'an alternative approach that combines aesthetic receptivity to film with philosophically informed reflection' (ibid.).

agency, and on the other, storage, retrieval (memory), the organization and classification of data (database logic), as well as user orientation (perspective, point of view) and interpellation (deictics, mode of address).

A new ontology of film

Looking back, one could argue that, for the first fifty years of film theory ('Classical film theory', up to 1964), the overarching question was *Is film 'art'*? This debate lingers on in the 'philosophy of film' (Carroll, Bordwell, Sinnerbrink, Murray Smith), albeit in a somewhat different formulation and across a different paradigm, namely: 'What is aesthetics?' (and by extension, 'What is art in the twenty-first century?'). For the second fifty years of film theory, the main approach was epistemological, and centred around *Screen* theory, whose questions were listed above ('Is film a language?; filmic realism and illusionism; film and ideology; the subject effect of the cinematic apparatus'). Obviously, there were other issues as well, most notably auteurism (which initially belonged to the 'Is film art?' debate, but which in a final chapter I try to open up to 'film as thought experiment') as well as genre study (from literary theory and anthropology).

Unlike the philosophers of film mentioned above, Cavell, Deleuze and Nancy do not focus on aesthetics, but are very much more concerned with a new ontology that cinema has brought into the Western world, that is, a new taxonomy of what exists and what does not, what is alive and what is not, and have thus provided philosophy with an enigma and challenge, rather than using cinema merely for the illustration of reality or the representation of what exists. For the new century, therefore, one could argue that the overarching question is *Is film a reality that thinks?* See Fig. 1 for an overview of the relation between these theories (as well as cognitivism).

While it might thus appear that the turn to philosophy in film studies is a conjunctural move, as much dictated by changing intellectual trends and the vagaries of academic institutional life, I believe there is an inner necessity, which cannot be explained merely by the inner logic of the discipline, by academic politics, the swing of the pendulum in academic fashion and any other contingent, but rather by pertinent factors we might care to name. This inner necessity I connect with two priorities. First – as just indicated – there is the need to elaborate a new ontology of cinema, by subsuming its previous ontology (based as it was on the photographic image) under a more encompassing classificatory scheme that does not juxtapose analog to digital, but makes the *photographic ontology* of cinema merely a historically contingent if crucial modality of the *graphic mode* in its wider sense. The second priority has to do with post-war European cinema's legacy of humanism, scepticism, reflexivity and realism.

Name	Ontology 1: Film as Art (Classical Film Theory)	Epistemology (*Screen* Theory; 'Contemporary' Film Theory)	Cognitivism	Ontology 2 (post-epistemological ontology): Film as Thought
Key Theorists	André Bazin (ontological realism); Rudolf Arnheim (ontological formalism); plus the 'philosophers of film': Noel Carroll, David Bordwell, Robert Sinnerbrink, Murray Smith.	Christian Metz, Jean-Louis Baudry, Jean Luc Comolli, Stephen Heath, Colin MacCabe, Laura Mulvey.	Classical cognitive theories: Jerry Fodor (psychology); Noam Chomsky (linguistics); Bordwell (film theory). Naturalistic or ecological cognitivism: J.J Gibson (psychology); Joseph Anderson (film). Embodied mind: George Lakoff (philosophy); Clark and Chalmers (psychology); C. Plantinga and G. Smith (film theory).	Stanley Cavell, Gilles Deleuze and Jean Luc Nancy.
Questions/ Issues	Is film an art?	Is film a language?; the critique of filmic realism as illusionistic and ideological; the social coding of subjectivity via the cinematic apparatus.	Classical cognitive theories. Internalism: locates mental processes in the brain; naturalistic or ecological cognitivism, externalism: locates meaning, thought and the mind in the external data (the body, tools of reasoning, the environment); embodied mind: internal+external – how does the body and emotions govern filmic perception?	Concerned with a new ontology that the cinema has brought into the Western world. The overarching question is: *Is film a reality that thinks?*

FIGURE 1 Film and Philosophy: Art, Epistemology, Ontology.

Another historical reason for 'film and philosophy' is our culture's slow transitioning from a 500-year episteme: the central perspective as the dominant representational system, now superseded or supplemented by other visual interfaces. It alters how we picture and experience the world, assigning a different function also to our eyes as the primary organ of perception and observation. If our perceptual field is now pre-formatted by a century of cinematic reality, it is in the process of becoming 'augmented reality', the new default value of 'reality' *tout court*. Even the word 'medium' may one day become as obsolete as the word 'ether' became when electromagnetic waves were identified as what they were responsible for and capable of. Hence my belief that the 'philosophical turn' in film studies is most usefully understood as an attempt to include film in what is real, in what exists and in what is alive (which exceeds, or questions, the anthropocentric view, and thus may bring us also to the limits of traditional notions of 'the humanities' acknowledging the important place of one of cinema's most characteristic features, namely its 'automatism' – see section below). Evidently, I am alluding to a complex, multifaceted and conflicted process, requiring a brief explanation about the notion of 'ontology'.

What do I mean by ontology in this context? The simplest response is to say, instead of asking 'What do films mean'? or 'Is this film a truthful representation of x . . .?', it says 'These images exist, so what do they do, how do they affect me, what realities in their own right do they constitute, how do they organize, partition, classify the visible (and invisible) world, and how do they draw the line, if at all, between animate and inanimate, between human beings and things, the actual and the virtual?' From such an 'ontological' position, for instance, spectatorship, subjectivities, subject positions are of subordinate and secondary concern to a film philosopher such as Deleuze, who thinks cinema outside of the viewing subject (the primary context of cinema within cultural studies and gender, for instance). Instead, he asks, what 'are' images – what kind of agency do they have, how do they affect our bodies and senses, what energies do they release, what ideas do they put in circulation, what connections do they establish?

Ontology in a more philosophically concise way is the study of everything that exists, of 'being'. To give a classical definition such as one finds it in a dictionary: 'Ontology is the philosophical study of the nature of being, becoming, existence, or reality, as well as the basic categories of being and their relations. Traditionally listed as a part of the major branch of philosophy known as metaphysics, ontology deals with questions concerning what entities exist or can be said to exist, and how such entities can be grouped, related within a hierarchy, and subdivided according to similarities and differences.'[12] When Deleuze insists that in his *Cinema* books he is providing not a history of cinema but a 'natural history', he is alluding to a taxonomy and a classification system of all the moving images that do and can exist, thus turning his natural history towards ontology. On the other hand, the key distinctions for which his *Cinema* books are best known are not the categories and subcategories of images, but the break between the 'movement image' and the 'time image': a distinction that has been (mis-)understood as a historical periodization more than an ontological categorization, an ambiguity or even a muddle, to which Deleuze himself has contributed and for which he has been taken to task many times, notably by Rancière.[13]

Ontology, however, can also be understood in a more specific sense. For Fredric Jameson, in his book *A Singular Modernity: An Essay on the Ontology of the Present*, ontology almost means the same as the Marxist (or Adorno's) category of 'totality', and for Jameson the ontology of the present is that we are unable to think beyond the present (the untranscendable horizon of capitalism). From being an 'ideology' (which one can critique from a position 'outside') it has become an 'ontology' (there is no outside to this inside), which makes 'modernity' – and postmodernism, its fidgety inside-outside-inside offspring – our ontology.[14]

Secondly, because we no longer have 'history' (the Enlightenment idea of progress, the workings of the world spirit, the perfectibility of the human race, the dynamics/dialectics of class struggle, etc.) as our grounding, we

---

[12] See http://en.wikipedia.org/wiki/Ontology (accessed 23 October 2016).

[13] Jacques Rancière, 'From One Image to Another: Deleuze and the Ages of Cinema', in *Film Fables*, trans. Emiliano Battista (Oxford: Berg, 2006), 107–24.

[14] Fredric Jameson, *A Singular Modernity: Essay on the Ontology of the Present* (London: Verso, 2002).

cannot assume a *telos* or put our trust in 'time', and thus we are in an 'ontological' situation, in the sense of having to face the 'groundless ground of being'. Foucault's periodization scheme – his different epistemes in *The Order of Things*, or in *The Archaeology of Knowledge* – tried to address a similar problem: retaining some notion of history, and assuming that the boundaries of our knowledge at any given time (our ontology) are determined by a set of material, political, institutional and discursive constraints ('practices') which exceed the material-economic constraints previously presupposed by Marxism as the main determinants (besides the class struggle). Rancière, who also uses the word 'ontology', albeit negatively in relation to Deleuze, puts it like this:

> An ontology can be a supplementary tool for bringing such and such knot of 'politics and philosophy' or 'aesthetics and politics' to light. But an ontology remains a kind of poem and you still have to understand how it constructs poetically its own relation to what it is supposed to ground.[15]

In other words, from a post-Nietzsche, post-Heidegger position, only a 'poetics' can be the groundless ground of being. In this sense, Deleuze's philosophy of cinema would be such a poetics, because it proposes exactly that: to see cinema as an ontology, in the sense of instantiating the groundless ground of our being – and reconciling us to it (renewing our 'belief in the world').

At its most elementary, a new ontology for cinema in the twenty-first century would be a classification system that lets go of many of the categories we usually deploy in film studies (such as 'author', 'genre', 'realism', 'fiction', 'documentary', 'avant-garde', 'classical/post-classical Hollywood', 'post-cinema'). Secondly, it means letting go of 'representation' as the central category, such, for instance, as it is underpinning almost all the work in cultural studies, with respect to the representation of race, class, sexual orientation, ethnic or religious minorities. The new classification is not entirely arbitrary or self-chosen, but assesses cinema in the light of many of the traditional areas of philosophy, such as epistemology and the philosophy of knowledge (how do we know what we know), philosophy of mind (other minds, other worlds), aesthetics (the relation between truth and beauty, or between the beautiful and the sublime) and hermeneutics (man-made sign systems and symbolic action).

But then, we should turn this round, and also look at cinema with categories that are relevant to the audience as human beings, where films might still be seen as coded texts and symbolic actions, but where cinema is also an event and an experience *of* the world, and of us *in* the world – as Cavell might have put it – but also of other forces, forms and faculties

[15] Jacques Rancière, *Hatred of Democracy*, trans. Steve Corcoran (London: Verso, 2009), 300.

present.[16] What distinguishes cinema from the other arts is its inherent heterogeneity but also its egalitarianism (it brings very different entities into play, but can assign them equal significance or treat them with equal indifference): already Jean Epstein's theory of *photogénie* recognized this levelling (or elevating) quality that confers beauty on humans and objects, regardless.

Speaking of equality brings me to my second agenda point (taken up in some detail in Chapters 4 and 5): the fate of European cinema, as part of the state of Europe in the twenty-first century, its tradition of humanism and realism, its democratic aspirations – in short, the values it was able to project from the days of neo-realism to its decline in the 1980s, signalled by the fading of the last of the great new waves, that of the New German Cinema. Here, the philosophical import encompasses how globalization has changed our view of human rights and challenged ideas of the social contract, transnationalism and solidarity, but also how to assume the legacies of nihilism and existentialism, and the 'groundless ground' of deconstruction. For instance, there is the view that the auto-critique of the Enlightenment project, conducted so vigorously by European intellectuals during the second half of the twentieth century, has pulled at and dug out the roots of Europe's own value systems – with the result of accentuating the radical scepticism mentioned above, of the European philosophical tradition since Descartes and Kant, while unable to counter the empiricist challenge that has come from the experimental sciences and the advances in technology, in medicine and in the use of natural resources.[17] In Chapter 4 I propose to address European scepticism and groundlessness, the loss of a binding value system and the apparent interchangeability of everything with everything else, usually referred to as postmodernism, but where cinema – with its inherent egalitarianism – may have played its part as well.

These factors require a look at European cinema not only as Hollywood's 'other', but in the new context of 'world cinema', whose preoccupations are political, insofar as the old political questions are being presented as ethical dilemmas. One can enumerate a number of political issues – the local effects of globalization, the pressure on traditional modes of life and especially on the patriarchal family, the position and rights of women, migration and

[16] For a preliminary sketch of such an ontology, see Thomas Elsaesser and Malte Hagener, *Film Theory: An Introduction through the Senses*, 2nd edn (London and New York: Routledge, 2015), which has a chapter on 'Mind and Brain', while also suggesting some of the reasons for breaking with the idea of 'cinema as window on the world' (the 'realist' paradigm), and 'cinema as mirror of the self' (the 'modernist-reflexive' paradigm).

[17] The critique of the Enlightenment critics can range widely: from Richard Rorty's *Achieving Our Country: Leftist Thought in Twentieth-Century America* (Cambridge, MA: Harvard University Press, 1998) to Alan Sokal and Jean Bricmont, *Fashionable Nonsense: Postmodern Intellectuals' Abuse of Science* (New York: Picador, 1998).

labour – and ask how does world cinema respond to them? But one can also look at how one particular world cinema, in this case coming from the formerly national cinemas of Western Europe (including France, Italy, Germany, Poland, Belgium, Denmark, Finland) thinks the classic philosophical values and ideals, such as liberty, equality, fraternity, have fared or have faded. In this context, the new 'universals' are especially telling. Social justice, human rights, equality before the law, protection of the environment (across the vanishing nature–culture divide) are being amplified and redefined across the demand for *dignity* (see Michael Rosen, *Dignity*), *recognition* (Axel Honneth's *The Struggle for Recognition: The Moral Grammar of Social Conflicts*) and *respect* (Sloterdijk's 'Thymos' in *Rage and Time: A Psychopolitical Investigation*), to which one may add the 'conservative' demands and values, such as 'sanctity of life', 'spirituality' and 'self-worth' (as proposed by Georg Lakoff's *Metaphors we Live By* and by Jonathan Haidt's *The Righteous Mind*, and as applied to cinema by Carroll or Anne Bartsch).[18]

The wider horizon: what is cinema good for?

For me, the divisions, schools and factions around the 'philosophy of film' and 'film as philosophy' are embedded in the broader horizon I already alluded to, which is not adequately characterized by making the distinction between 'analytical' and 'culturalist', or North American and continental. Rather, the 'philosophy: film' turn must also respond to a deeper set of concerns and challenges: not only 'What is cinema?', but 'What is cinema good for?' This is probably not a question that would be understood in Hollywood ('It's good for making money and for becoming famous' would probably be the answer), but one that Europeans tend to worry about. Is cinema making a theological point, in that it promises us immortality, or is it an 'invention of the devil', holding us in thrall to images, that is, idolatry, leading to self-regard, egoism and hubris? Given how the distrust in images is deeply ingrained in all the 'religions of the book' (Judaism, Christianity and Islam), and how images also worried the Greeks, notably Plato, who famously opposed the deceptive 'image' (icon), belonging to the realm of mere appearance, to the abstract but veridical 'concept' or 'idea' (logos), the question is not one that a film philosophy can ignore, although I shall only mention it in passing.

Closer to home, and nearer to our time, there are various ways one might specify the question 'What is cinema good for?' in the sense of what it has contributed to culture and human civilization. Phrased even more anthropologically, how does cinema figure in humans' adaptation to their environment,

[18] Noël Carroll, 'Movies, the Moral Emotions, and Sympathy' and Anne Bartsch, 'Vivid Abstractions: On the Role of Emotion Metaphors in Film Viewers' Search for Deeper Insight and Meaning', both in *Midwest Studies in Philosophy* 34 (2010): 1–19 and 240–60.

what is cinema's ecology, so to speak? Several 'answers' have emerged, either implicitly or explicitly: (1) Bazin's notion that cinema is a way to defeat death, by preserving an imprint of life, like a cast or a mould, or the envelope of a mummy; (2) Edgar Morin's claim that it answers to 'man's age old desire for a double, a likeness,' a mirror in which mankind can reflect its deeds and vanities;[19] (3) cinema is a window on the world, a static vehicle that allows us to travel without leaving home, as it were; or (4) cinema as a disembodied eye that can go everywhere and knows no shame and no taboo, but also no social barriers or physical obstacles; (5) cinema has been for the twentieth century what the novel was for the nineteenth and oral tales and recorded myths for the past 5,000 years: the storytelling medium through which a human group or community, from family and tribe to nation and the globe, not only make sense of the world, but speak to each other and negotiate the aspirations as well as test the boundaries that make social life possible; (6) the photograph and moving image also have their share in making possible 'acting at a distance'.[20] It helps to calculate and control the environment, to measure and to modify: this would embrace all the non-entertainment uses of the cinematic apparatus in medicine, the sciences, in monitoring and surveillance, for the military and in space exploration for weather reports and news coverage on television. (7) Along the same lines, but now once more including fiction film, and extending it, to say, computer games, one could trace cinema's role in 'mastering' life through simulation and play, which also has a scientific variant (the scientific experiment that requires computer simulation).

In this way cinema can be inscribed in the evolutionary arc of 'homo ludens': man at play, considered as both an ontogenetic (individual) and a phylogenetic (species-related) dimension. Play is essential for the formation of a self, and organized play leads not only to sociability, but also to the spirit of adventure and experimentation; after all, the modality of 'what if' or 'make-believe' is obviously a cardinal property of cinema, even as – and perhaps because – it is also on the side of reality and document.

Cinema – humanism's last hope or the true face of technological determinism?

This anthropological perspective quickly comes up against cinema's inherent debt to technology, and whether its scope and development is technologically

[19] Edgar Morin, *The Cinema, or the Imaginary Man* (Minneapolis: University of Minnesota Press, 2015), 30–1.

[20] On acting at a distance, see Lev Manovich, 'To lie and to act: Potemkin's villages, cinema and telepresence. Notes around Checkpoint '95 project', *Ars Electronica* 1995 catalogue, Linz, Austria, http://manovich.net/index.php/projects/to-lie-and-to-act-potemkin-s-villages-cinema-and-telepresence (accessed 14 December 2016).

determined: is cinema 'an extension of man' in Marshall McLuhan's phrase, that is, a way of mastering and appropriating the world by prosthetically extending human physical faculties and the senses, or – especially when externalizing mental faculties – is there an inverse relation, where we 'outsource' our minds and feelings to such an extent that the machines take over, as pictured in so many technophobic fantasies and sci-fi scenarios (e.g. *War of the Worlds*)? According to media theorist Friedrich Kittler, the issue is less dramatic: technological determinism has undeservedly been getting a bad name; it is the natural condition of being human, because at every stage of evolution, it was the media of communication – language, writing, printing, mechanical recording, mathematical calculation and algorithmic computation – that defined what a given epoch considered 'human' and 'social'. Tools and machines are an integral part of the sociability of humans as a species: there never was a pristine humanity, in unmediated harmony with nature – technology is the medium within which we are human.[21]

If we are indeed determined by the technical media we use, and if our dependence on them makes them all but invisible, does it matter whether we are in charge of the technology we use, while being used in turn? Assuming there is a kind of co-evolution of humans and their technologies of communication and self-presentation, what exactly are the terms and modalities of this coexistence? Living with intelligent machines, depending on a networked super-brain, entering what is being called the post-human condition, after having inaugurated the *anthropocene*, that is, the era, arguably since the Industrial Revolution, where the impact of human behaviour, habitation and proliferation on the Earth has become so significant in its consequences for the atmosphere, the environment and the entire eco-system that it merits its own geological name?[22]

In this grand narrative, cinema has a minor, if measurable, role as a facilitating, translating and possibly 'transitional' instance, whether conceived in terms of turning the world of things, of objects and places into images, and therefore making them mobile, fluid, virtual and malleable (in size, scale and texture), as well as desirable and affectively charged, or whether we assign to cinema the function of cultural memory, the preservation of the past in the very terms, shapes, forms and movements of that past. One could also argue that cinema's role has been to help regulate

[21] A similar argument is developed within the cognitivist paradigm: in the 'extended mind' argument, cognition is not limited to the brain, but involves the body, and the body interacting with tools and, finally, interacting with the environment. Nonetheless, the cognitivists would generally maintain the concept of harmony between humanity and nature. For a classic statement of the extended mind argument, see Andy Clark and David J. Chalmers, 'The Extended Mind', *Analysis* 58 (1998): 7–19.

[22] See Simon L. Lewis and Mark A. Maslin, 'Defining the Anthropocene', *Nature* 519 (12 March 2015): 171–80.

and control human bodies and their perceptual input through different kinds of libidinal investment and affect, that is, what, with a nod to Foucault, one might call 'discipline through pleasure', and what Žižek called 'the injunction of the superego to Enjoy!', or as Miriam Hansen, with reference to Benjamin, phrased it: 'the mass production of the senses'.[23] Contrast this rather critical, negative assessment with the more typically American version that believes in simulation of all kinds, and prefers, whether in the nursery or in the military, a ludic way of preparing its citizen for the challenges of life, by simulating every conceivable situation in terms of a game environment, a test (drive) or a (sports) competition.

Within the same problematic of what cinema is/is good for in the twenty-first century, is the emergence of 'the cinematic': that particular way of apprehending the world, which – at the limit – acts as a symbolic form, one that is not identical with Erwin Panofsky's Renaissance perspective as 'symbolic form', but in active conflict with it. At once ubiquitous and invisible, 'the cinematic' encompasses ways of seeing, experiencing and acting upon the world that are not tied to either a specific *dispositif*, platform, medium, let alone to specific films (avant-garde or mainstream, art cinema or blockbuster). In *The Language of New Media* (2001), Lev Manovich has made himself one of the spokespersons of this view, suggesting that the cinematic (along with the book and the office desktop) was one of the interfaces initially adopted by computer manufacturers and software designers when they set about making the personal computer 'user-friendly' and familiar. With the ubiquity of mobile devices, on the other hand, interfaces more directly try to emulate the body and the senses, becoming 'intuitive' and tactile, most notably through surface contact: screens become touch-screens, that is, not screens in the traditional sense at all, and the phone an extension of the hand, not the ear.

The cinematic would then either be the ideology typical for a certain phase of capitalism (Jonathan Beller's 'Cinema, Capital of the 20th century', in analogy to Benjamin's 'Paris, Capital of the 19th Century' and Jameson's *Postmodernism or the Cultural Logic of Late Capitalism*) or have to do with what I call the 'here-me-now' deictic configuration of 'presence', which bridges the gap between cinema in its classical form and such contemporary devices as mobile phones and tablets, in the sense of preparing us for the perpetual 'now' of the Internet and of social media.

The film that thinks

These are some of the considerations and caveats that accompany 'film as philosophy' as it aims to overcome normative definitions, that is, what

[23] Miriam Bratu Hansen, 'The Mass Production of the Senses: Classical Cinema as Vernacular Modernism', *Modernism/Modernity* 6, no. 2 (April 1999): 59–77.

cinema 'is', in favour of ideas that support cinema's shape-shifting and permanent becoming.[24] What characterizes the 'continental' school in this respect is the assumption or assertion that film can be a mode of thought. This is strongest in Deleuze, and has been taken up in various ways by his advocates: Jacques Aumont, Raymond Bellour, Patricia Pisters and Daniel Frampton (the 'film-mind'), among many others. The question is then 'Is this a metaphor or can we understand it in some other way?' And if we accept that film is thought, then the secondary question is what is the nature of the mind that thinks in cinema: is it singular and embodied or is it trans-individual, is it the hive-mind of networked collectives? Or is it the unconscious of film in the sutured play of absence and presence, on-screen and off-screen space? Or do we first need to redefine mind, brain and consciousness (as the neurosciences and philosophers of mind are proposing) before we can even determine in what sense cinema can be said to 'think'? And finally, does cinema think across some kind of language or in non-linguistic 'concepts'?

If cinema, despite its brief history, can be shown to belong – logically and as both phenomenon and symptom – to Western modernity in the broadest sense, which began with the Renaissance, the Enlightenment and the Industrial Revolution, and ended somewhere in the mid-twentieth century (and from which cinema, as we know it, has inherited important features), then the historicity of our own moment in time or epoch also needs to be taken into consideration. Practically, this means that cinema cannot remain unaffected by the larger forces changing the world around us, something we are only too aware of when we think how much the change from photographic to post-photographic, that is, digital imaging, initially put the field in disarray, and led film studies into a crisis. Consider, as symptom of this crisis, the following statements by two of the most eminent scholars of the discipline: 'The live projection of a movie in the film theatre, in the dark, the predetermined time

---

[24] 'A title card in Jean-Luc Godard's 1966 film *Masculin-Féminin* quotes Maurice Merleau-Ponty, stating, 'le philosophe et le cinéaste ont en commun une certaine manière d'être, une certaine vue du monde qui est celle d'une generation'; 'the philosopher and the director have in common a certain way of being, a certain view of the world, which is that of a generation'. This quotation raises several questions: what is the place of philosophy vis-à-vis film? Does the filmmaker dictate the philosophy of a film? To what extent is philosophy made manifest in film? Does film exceed philosophy in expressing or exploring metaphysics, epistemology and other human concerns? These have been key questions in the study of the moving image throughout the discipline's history. In *The World Viewed: Reflections on the Ontology of Film* (1971), Stanley Cavell would propose a philosophy of film as a moving image of scepticism by reworking Cartesian methodological doubt. Recently, scholars have moved from the classical question 'What is cinema?', posed by Bazin and Cavell, to new questions: 'What was cinema and how will the medium shift in the new digital landscape? How will these digital images engage in and with philosophy? Perhaps the moving image is philosophy, regardless of apparatus specificity or authorial intent' (Call for Papers, Film and Philosophy, How Films Think, University of Florida, 5–7 November 2010).

of a more or less collective session, has become and remains the condition of a unique experience of perception and memory, defining its spectator, a condition that all other viewing situations more or less alter. And this alone is worth calling *cinema*' (Raymond Bellour).[25] And: 'Today it is a crucial point, which I think we can make a good criterion of what is cinema: any film presentation that leaves me free to interrupt or modulate this experience is not cinema' (Jacques Aumont).[26] These positions draw a firm line, but seem to forget that such definitions are themselves historically conditioned and contingent, given that the experience they posit as a norm not only cuts itself off from the present but also from the past: the first two decades of cinema's existence.[27] If the German sociologist Dirk Baecker is right, and 'it is the unknown future that is experienced in its present as crisis',[28] then, contrary to Bellour and Aumont, cinema, from the historical as well as philosophical perspective, is in crisis, because it *has* a future, and in its opportunism and adaptability it is no different from mankind itself.

In other words, some of the seemingly very local but nonetheless tectonic shifts in film studies – the changes in authors' cinema, the decline of the film avant-garde, the emergence of world- or transnational cinema, the concomitant shift away from Europe as a hub for so-called 'innovative' filmmaking, the regrouping of talent around Asia and the film festival circuit rather than national cinemas – all these changes may stand in some ultimately analysable correlation with the wider power-adjustments we understand by the term 'globalization', which for us Europeans means the ground is shifting beneath out feet, as Brian Massumi aptly summarizes:

> We're leaving the world we Europeans inhabited since the late 15th century: Eurocentrism, Enlightenment; Monocular Perspective, Projection

---

[25] 'La projection vécue d'un film en salle, dans le noir, le temps prescrit d'une séance plus ou moins collective, est devenue et reste la condition d'une expérience unique de perception et de mémoire, définissant son spectateur et que toute situation autre de vision altère plus ou moins. Et cela seul vaut d'être appelé "cinéma".' Raymond Bellour, *La Querelle des dispositifs: Cinéma – installations, expositions* (Paris: P.O.L., 2012),14.

[26] 'Un film est un morceau de temps mis en forme – comme la musique mais avec d'autres moyens. Ce que nous propose la séance de cinéma, c'est l'expérience de ce temps, sans moyen d'y échapper. C'est aujourd'hui un point crucial, car toutes les autres présentations de films nous laissent, au contraire, libres d'interrompre ou de moduler cette expérience.' Jacques Aumont, 'Que reste-t-il du cinéma?', *Trafic* 79 (September 2011): 95–107 (102).

[27] For the typical viewing experiences of cinema prior to the 1920s, see Charles Musser, *The Emergence of Cinema: The American Screen to 1907* (Berkeley: University of California Press, 1990), and Eileen Bowser, *History of the American Cinema: The Transformation of Cinema, 1907–1915* (Berkeley: University of California Press, 1990).

[28] '. . . die unbekannte Zukunft in ihrer Gegenwart als Krise'. Dirk Baecker, 'Zukunftsfähigkeit: 22 Thesen zur nächsten Gesellschaft', *The Catjects Project* (blog), 2 July 2013, https://catjects.wordpress.com/2013/07/02/zukunftsfahigkeit-22-thesen-zur-nachsten-gesellschaft/ (accessed 14 December 2017).

> and Vanishing Point, the Notion of a Future and a Past lined up on a linear trajectory; the Ground has moved from under us: perspective, upright, forward, back, up down; the Individual has become dividual: sensation, perception, the different senses, de-hierarchized, de-territorialized. The Unconscious is de-personalized, 'out there' in the form of contingency and coincidence. Affect is de-localized.[29]

If cinema cannot adapt, or indeed, if we cannot adapt our own perspectives on its history, then much of our knowledge might become obsolete, or at least find itself reframed and rephrased without us, or behind our backs, to the point where what is being rethought and refigured appears merely unthought and disfigured. Film and philosophy might assist us in avoiding that fate.

The mind-game film

An earlier attempt to respond to the film philosophy 'turn' was to take a closer look at a specific body of contemporary films, which I consider something like the new avant-garde: not in relation to some formalist or modernist agenda, but in relation to these anthropological or epistemic transformations alluded to above. These films I subsumed under the label 'The Mind-game Film', but it is a category that I described only partially, and analysed by way of a few provisionally formulated hypotheses. I have since argued that it is around such films that one can track some of the major concerns about time, space, individual agency, the single point of view, the linear projection of the arrow of time, the normativity of the goal-directed, purposive individual, and so on.[30] Mind-game films signal the breakdown of an episteme in Foucault's sense, notably that identified by Massumi, but they are sufficiently open-ended and ambiguous to embody the cinematic form most directly responding to the networked, distributed nature of contemporary agency, to which answer the flexible (but also precarious and volatile) subjectivities needed to function within neoliberal democracy and global capitalism. As mainstream cinema is adapting to such realignments of the body and the senses, with faster cutting rates and frequent changes of perspective and scale, mind-game films emerge as symptoms of this adaptation, but in the form of test-runs or prototypes, stretching or twisting the underlying parameters of temporal and causal relations, of character-consistency and the perceptual boundaries between reality and hallucination, optical illusion and data-based simulations.

---

[29] Brian Massumi, 'The Autonomy of Affect', *Cultural Critique* 31 (Autumn 1995): 83–109.

[30] Thomas Elsaesser, 'Contingency, Causality, Complexity: Distributed Agency in the Mind-game Film', *New Review of Film and Television Studies* 16, no. 1 (2018): 1–39.

As the name suggests, mind-game films may also be emulating the workings of the mind, sometimes depicting seemingly aberrant, abnormal behaviour, in a protagonist who nonetheless functions as the controlling consciousness, except that things seem to be out of control. In this fashion, the film as a whole seems like a mind, allowing what we perceive to oscillate between different levels of reality – presenting a purely imaginary world or a paranoid projection with the same degree of density of detail and specificity as we would expect from a photographically produced, bodily verifiable representation of observable reality. Mind-game films, I want to suggest, are a good case for justifying one of the central claims that some film philosophy scholars want to make, namely that films can not only represent but constitute a form of thought – at which point it also becomes possible to draw a comparison between mind-game films and films as thought experiments, each being the version of a distinct conception of cinema, but each responding to the crisis of cinema alluded to above.

Cinema thinks: can one specify some of the things this implies? For instance, it might require an entirely new language with which to speak about cinema, and this is indeed the case when one reads Deleuze, Jacques Rancière, Jean-Luc Nancy or Giorgio Agamben on cinema.[31] If we are indeed in the midst of an epistemic shift, of which cinema registers the seismic tremors, then there may indeed be good grounds for new categories and concepts, and this is very much what Deleuze sets out to provide in his *Cinema* books: a *film philosophy*, rather than a *philosophy of film*.

Secondly, to say that film is thought is to claim for cinema something like an active, interventionist role in some of the transformations just itemized, and thus to argue for a new kind of agency for aesthetics in politics: this would be Rancière's agenda, and why he puts cinema –strategically – at the forefront of his politics, the 'distribution of the sensible', and explains his militant stand for a radical equality, of which he regards cinema to be the (as yet unfulfilled) promise.[32]

Thirdly, to connect film with thought is to imply not just a different langue and new concepts, but – by way of a new taxonomy or classification system – to assert that *cinematic thought may be the name for a new ontology of*

---

[31] See Gilles Deleuze, *Cinema 1: The Movement Image*, trans. Hugh Tomlinson (Minneapolis: University of Minnesota Press, 1986), and *Cinema 2: The Time Image*, trans. Hugh Tomlinson (Minneapolis: University of Minnesota Press, 1989); Jacques Rancière, *Film Fables*, Jean-Luc Nancy, *L'Evidence du film: Abbas Kiarostami/The Evidence of Film*, edition bilingue français-anglais (Brussels: Yves Gevaert, 2001); Giorgio Agamben, 'Notes on Gesture', in *Means Without End: Notes on Politics*, trans. Vincenzo Binetti and Cesare Casarino (Minneapolis: University of Minnesota Press, 2000).

[32] The philosophical positions of Nancy, Rancière, Agamben and Alain Badiou with regard to specific questions of cinema, politics and ethics will also be argued in more detail in the subsequent chapters.

cinema: in the sense of an ordering system that can map for us a world whose basic categories have changed, under the impact of new forms of relationality, mutuality and interdependence, a new (a-)causality and interactivity. For these forces the mediated environments and augmented realities, generated through electronic sounds and images and supported by less visible but even more consequential algorithms and applications, can stand as both the outward manifestation and the inner logic. Cinema in its capacity to record and store, to replay and manipulate, to stage and to edit the perceptible world, may well be thought of as both forming and performing *life*.

What such a new ontology would acknowledge is that crucial distinctions in our Western world picture, such as the divides between object and subject, inner and outer, active and passive, real and virtual, appearance and reality, animate and inanimate, intelligent and stupid, truth and lie, have either vanished altogether or are undergoing transformations that leave us, apparently, without ground or anchor, without path or perspective. The first to argue for such an ontology beyond dichotomies was perhaps Maurice Merleau-Ponty, in his 'Cinema and the New Psychology' from 1947.[33]

A brief further reflection is in order, touching on the anthropological question, raised earlier: 'What is cinema good for?' In light of some of the answers given above, about 'disciplining' the body through pleasure, or 'mastering' life through play, the question arises: what changes are at stake with the claim that film is (a form of) thought? The claim can be construed as supporting, albeit implicitly, the notion that cinema is an intermediary stage or transitional link, between human beings thinking *individually*, but in fact having prospered as a species, because of storing, transmitting and sharing the fruits of this thinking *collectively*. Now that human beings are handing over much of this collective thinking to so-called 'smart' devices, or to a hybrid man-machine symbiosis (understood as 'artificial intelligence' rather than 'the hive mind'), what happens to innovation and new thinking, if all we do is recycle, repackage and repurpose the collective wisdom so far accumulated? In other words, arguing that 'film is thought' might commit one to a much wider set of presuppositions and assumptions than merely this counter-intuitive statement, made – so some claim – above all to give the general irrelevance of cinema an overextended compensatory shine. Rather, it positions cinema

[33] Merleau-Ponty, for instance, comments on the suspension of dichotomies in cinema: 'Si donc la philosophie et le cinéma sont d'accord . . . c'est parce que le philosophe et le cinéaste ont en commun une certaine manière de prendre position en face du monde . . . Encore une occasion de vérifier . . . que, selon le mot de Gœthe, "ce qui est au-dedans est aussi au-dehors".'; 'If therefore philosophy and cinema are in agreement . . . it is because the philosopher and the filmmaker have in common a certain way of taking a position vis-à-vis the world . . . Yet another opportunity to verify . . . that, according to Goethe's words, "what is inside is also outside".' Maurice Merleau-Ponty, 'Le cinéma et la nouvelle psychologie', *Les Temps Modernes* 26 (November 1947): 943.

as collective thought, perhaps best imagined as the Trojan horse in the battle of the algorithms to enter and penetrate the inner recesses of our subjectivity, and thus not just disciplining but actively modelling the senses and reformatting the mind. If this is so, then it is necessary to perhaps make a further point: the sort of intelligent machines, from which might emerge a collectively networked and interdependent intelligence, are not only much faster in transmission than previous technologies, but also much more widely accessible. It is a process that will both accelerate this sharing of intelligence that has made our species so successful in an evolutionary sense and make the enabling technologies less visible and thus more easy slip out of (individual or collective) consciousness and control. The possibility that it might eliminate hierarchies and level traditional power structures and, at least in principle, give a push to social equality and the wider distribution of goods, benefits and rights, would be the silver lining of this otherwise dark 'cloud'.

Insofar as today's globalizing network society is premised on interrelation, interdependence and 'real-time' interaction, it does so on the basis of mathematics and electronics, setting out to model and capture the human and the natural world in algorithms, through data mining, graphs and diagrams. As they do so, these technologies invariably shape the world in their own image, which is to say, by a logic quite different from ours. It is under this aspect – already touched on when I mentioned Friedrich Kittler – that one has to consider the digital image within the larger, philosophically informed framework, as well as within the political horizon that tries to align the humanities and the arts with the hard sciences: a (hostile) takeover in the making, or the moment for a radical rethink? Either way, it shows cinema poised between several seemingly unbridgeable gaps, where it is called upon to either mediate or play the double agent.

Automatism: after Deleuze

If film philosophy takes over from film theory, it is still confronted with the same question that preoccupied film theory. Not (only): is film art, and if so what sort of an art?[34] But also: are images on the side of perceptual reality and physical sensations, or on the side of language, code and sign? And do we have to choose? One version of the history of film theory sees it as a sequence of back-and-forth swings between the materiality, substantiality and physical presence of moving pictures ('realists'), and their immateriality, abstraction, graphism and diagrammatics ('formalists'). The move from

[34] Is cinema like painting and photography, or more like sculpture and dance, like architecture, or as a time-based art, is it more like music? Or a *Gesamtkunstwerk*, or none of the above, and is art *sui generis*?

theory to philosophy ups the ante, as it were, but it may also promise a new synthesis of these questions, perhaps even shows that the original questions were badly posed (a task that philosophers are traditionally proud of, that is, of showing that difficult questions do not require an answer, but disappear when one points out that the question is badly put, that it contains logical flaws). If it was badly posed, how can we pose it differently?

This is why Deleuze looms so large and why almost everyone contributing to film/philosophy comes 'after Deleuze'. One of the key claims Deleuze made was that moving images not only have agency and 'think', but do so in a philosophically valid sense.[35] Thanks to a series of analogies, mostly derived from Bergson, Deleuze can argue that cinema is philosophy because both perception and mentation/cognition are fundamentally cinematic.[36] But another key feature of Deleuze's intervention is the generally positive evaluation he gives to cinema's *automatism*, understood as the inherent capacity of the camera, whether photographic or cinematographic, to capture and register images by a mechanical process without the intervention of human intention or volition. From William Henry Fox Talbot's 1844 announcement of photography as 'the pencil of nature' to André Bazin's 1958 essay on 'The Ontology of the Photographic Image', the automatic registration of pictures has been the central fact discussed in any philosophical treatise on either photography or film. André Bazin's is the most canonical and celebrated formulation of cinematic automatism:

> The originality of photography in relation to painting lies then in its essential objectivity . . . For the first time, between the initial object and its representation nothing besides another object interposes itself. For the first time, an image of the exterior world is formed automatically without creative intervention by man, according to a rigorous determinism . . . *All the arts are based on the presence of man, in photography alone we enjoy his absence.* It acts on us as a natural phenomenon, like a flower or a snowflake, the beauty of which is inseparable from vegetable or earthly origins.[37]

---

[35] See Paola Maratti, *Gilles Deleuze, cinéma et philosophie* (Paris, Presses universitaires de France, 2003), and Patricia Pisters, *The Matrix of Visual Culture: Working with Deleuze in Film Theory* (Stanford, CA: Stanford University Press, 2003).

[36] 'If, as Bergson argues in *Creative Evolution*, both perception *and* intellect are cinematographic, we might even go so far as to say that each theory of cinema is a perceptual frame: only when placed together on the one, moving reel, do we get an approximation to the reality of film. *Cinema is philosophical because thinking is cinematic*', John Mullarkey, 'Film as Philosophy – A Mission Impossible?', in Temenuga Trifonova (ed.), *European Film Theory* (New York: Routledge, 2009), 74.

[37] First published in English as André Bazin, 'The Ontology of the Photographic Image', trans. Hugh Gray, *Film Quarterly* 13, no. 4 (Summer 1960): 4–9.

Besides Bazin and Deleuze, the list of those who noted photographic and cinematographic automatism and singled it out for special comment when discussing the cinema begins with Henri Bergson and Hugo Münsterberg, and includes Jean Epstein, Sergei Eisenstein, Rudolf Arnheim, Béla Balázs, Walter Benjamin, Siegfried Kracauer and Stanley Cavell, but also Jean-Luc Nancy, Alain Badiou, Jacques Rancière, as well as Roland Barthes, Susan Sontag, Roger Scruton, Kendall Walton, Noël Carroll and countless other philosophers of aesthetics.

The reason to return to the debate in the context of film/philosophy is that a more philosophical understanding of the cinema's automatism can trace another path not just from the analogue photograph to the digital image, but from cinema as an aesthetic phenomenon to cinema as ontology: something that has altered or at least affected our relation to – and being in – the world, and this in ways that one day might allow us to ask the question animating this chapter – 'Why cinema?' – a question that I consider 'philosophical' in a very primary, if not foundational, sense.

As already mentioned, for much of the first half of the twentieth century, the core of the debate was whether this photographic automatism disqualified cinema from being an art-form, unless human intentionality can be seen to intervene, through staging, framing, selection, but above all through montage and editing. One early dissenting voice was that of the French filmmaker Jean Epstein, who in his 1921 essay 'Bonjour Cinema' anticipates Bazin, when he writes:

> Cinema, by and large, doesn't do justice to the story . . . The drama we're watching is . . . unfolding on the curative slope to the crisis. The real tragedy . . . looms over all the faces; it is in the curtain and in the door-latch. Each drop of ink can make it blossom at the tip of the pen. It dissolves itself in the glass of water. At every moment, the entire room is saturated with the drama. The cigar burns on the lip of the ashtray like a threat. The dust-motes of betrayal. Poisonous arabesques stretch across the rug and the arm of the seat trembles. For now, suffering is in surfusion. Expectation. We can't see a thing yet, but the tragic crystal that will turn out to be at the center of the plot has fallen down somewhere. Its wave advances. Concentric circles. It keeps on expanding, from relay to relay. Is whether they get married in the end *really* all you want to know? . . . Cinema is true. The story is a lie.[38]

For Epstein, true cinema is the way the camera captures a door-latch or a burning cigarette in an ashtray, and he calls this automatism 'photogénie' –

[38] Jean Epstein, 'Bonjour Cinéma' [1921], in Richard Abel (ed.), *French Film Theory and Criticism: A History/Anthropology, 1907–1939*, vol. 1: 1907–1929 (Princeton, NJ: Princeton University Press, 1988), 242.

the capacity of the camera to imbue with grace and presence the most banal of objects or gestures. Exceeding language and making a mockery of meaning, *photogénie* is what the camera lens lays bare, directing the human eye to what it cannot discover directly, but what will fill the soul with suspense, emotion and wonderment. Epstein's passage (and a similar one by Virginia Woolf) launches a philosophy of disclosure and revelation that one also finds in Dziga Vertov's 'kino-eye' as well as in Walter Benjamin's 'optical unconscious', where the camera penetrates into aspects of reality that we register with our bodies and senses but that we may neither perceive nor process consciously. It reappears in Bazin and Cavell, becomes axiomatic as one side of an intertwined process in Rancière's idea of the cinema as a thwarted fable, and it receives its Heideggerian elaboration in Jean-Luc Nancy's notion of the evidence of film and its capacity for 'entbergen' (disclosure). As one on-line commentator puts it:

> Epstein's aesthetics is an automatist one, attributing the camera's disclosure of photogenic moments to its automated registration of a reality, too 'full' to be grasped by the human eye, let alone processed by our limited cognitive capabilities. But more important even than the camera's analytic properties to the conception of photogénie, was that the image contain – or be in – motion. Movement is the essence of cinema . . . captured best by the image of a smile slowly appearing on a face seen in close-up, [or even in] the anticipation of that smile.[39]

While on the one hand, such a view of *photogénie* stresses the inherent affectivity of the world when seized by the camera, it is the raw material that someone like Eisenstein wanted to shape into argument and discourse, through montage, rupture, attraction, and juxtaposition. Yet as much as Eisenstein might have wished to defeat and counter cinema's automatism, it is perhaps not without a certain irony that Roland Barthes was to develop his version of *photogénie* or automatism – namely his theory of the 'third' or 'obtuse' meaning, now around the 'stilled' image – precisely by taking as his examples several photograms from an Eisenstein film, *Ivan the Terrible*.

Another powerful artistic current that had been inspired by cinematic automatism were the Surrealists. They saw it not only as a way to get closer to reality through mechanical means and technical aids, but also an attempt to synchronize the workings of the human mind with the workings of the camera. It was, after all, Surrealism that promoted automatic writing as a way of stimulating the imagination, and of aligning the body, the eye and the

[39] Tom Paulus, 'A Lover's Discourse: Cinephilia, or, The Color of Cary Grant's Socks', *CINEA*, 25 October 2012, https://cinea.be/a-lovers-discourse-cinephilia-or-the-color-cary-grants-socks/ (accessed 14 December 2017).

hand, with the camera's capacity of capturing the flux and movement of sensation and of ever-changing impressions, but also by externalizing that which is not accessible to volition and conscious thought. André Breton made even bolder, political claims: 'An appeal to automatism in all its forms is our only chance of resolving, outside the economic plane, all the antinomies which, since they existed before our present social regime was formed, are not likely to disappear with it.'[40]

Trust and belief in the world

Writers not normally associated with Surrealism such as Ezra Pound, W. B. Yeats or Virginia Woolf were also after modes of impersonality, externalizing the soul, and some – like James Joyce – even practised versions of automatic writing. As David Trotter has shown, Joyce tried in the 'Wandering Rocks' section of *Ulysses* to enact in his prose and verbal punning a will-to-automatism that testified to 'a determination to view the world, for however brief an interval, as a machine would view it'.[41] Trotter's book is an attempt to write the cinema and pre-cinema of optical toys and stereoscopic views back into the canonical texts of high modernist literature. While ostensibly suppressing the existence of cinema, these writers' novels and poems are marked by an attempt to emulate cinema's effects even more than its techniques, and what Trotter finds is that in many cases it is the paradoxical combination of a heightened sense of presence with a melancholy awareness of absence that overcomes them, when commenting on the cinema's automatism. As Virginia Woolf famously put it: film reveals to us *life as it is when we have no part in it.*

Such is the ambiguous aspect of cinema's automatism that from the sensations it produces, writers and philosophers have asked themselves ethical questions, notably about what it means to be present to the world, while being absent to it. Perhaps no one has phrased it more sharply and pondered it more extensively than Stanley Cavell in his 1971 book, *The World Viewed: Reflections on the Ontology of Film.* Taking his subtitle and cue from Bazin, Cavell gives Bazin's ontology argument a different turn, when he asks himself what cinema's automatism means, not for the artist and for aesthetics, but for the viewer as citizen of a community and as member of the human race: 'The advent of photography expresses ... distance as the modern fate: to relate to the world by viewing it, [by] taking views of it, as [if] from behind the self.'[42] If the world is viewed without us

[40] Andre Breton, 'Limits Not Frontiers of Surrealism', in *What Is Surrealism – Selected Writings?* (New York: Pathfinder, 1978), 155.

[41] David Trotter, *Cinema and Modernism* (Oxford: Blackwell, 2007), 113–14.

[42] Stanley Cavell, *The World Viewed* (Cambridge, MA: Harvard University Press, 1971), 116–17.

having a part in it, does this merely breed the cynicism already expressed by Baudelaire, when in *Les Fleurs du Mal* he spoke of those who, faced with photographs of human misery and violence, 'swallow the world with a yawn', and give rise to the sad regrets of a Virginia Woolf, or is it possible to derive from this presence in absence a new kind of 'trust in the world'? For Cavell, this matter of trust is tied up with his main philosophical concern, which is scepticism: how can we know the world as it really is, how do we ever know what others think, how can we trust our spouses not to betray us, how do we know we're not in Plato's Cave? Dissatisfied with Descartes' answer of the cogito, with its infinite coils of self-awareness, recursiveness and self-doubt, Cavell welcomes the cinema as scepticism's antidote. Counter-intuitive as it may sound, cinema's automatism (precisely because independent of human intervention) guarantees a kind of externality and presence, hard to achieve by any other means. Cinema, furthermore, is a perfect expression of our modernity, in that it replicates our existential alienation, by bringing us close and keeping us distant all at the same time. As Cavell observes:

> In viewing films, the sense of invisibility is an expression of modern privacy or anonymity. It is as though the world's projection explains our forms of unknown-ness and our inability to know. The explanation is not so much that the world is passing us by, as that we are displaced from our natural habitation within it, placed at a distance from it. The screen . . . makes displacement appear as our natural condition.[43]

In other words, unlike Bazin's argument in support of film's ontological realism as a form of revelation and disclosure (which, let me be clear, involves a more complex and nuanced understanding of cinema than I have been presenting here, insofar as it is as much about imprint, inscription and trace as it is about visual or phenomenal perception, and thus also touches on memory, temporality and our mortality), Cavell takes solace from what is in effect a tragic view of life, as manifest in cinema's relation to the viewer. Cinema, by making us aware that the world can be so amazingly present to us, in all its singularity and manifest there-ness, while we are forever absent from it, can help us become reconciled with the world, because it anticipates our mortality and finitude.

Thus, automatism as the special and unique quality of cinema for Cavell is not to be equated with the mechanical, and on the contrary, belongs to a higher order of the human, which is why an ethical demand and mandate also flow from it. On the one hand, it frees our moral judgements and emotional capacities to the extent that it allows us to experience the world

---

[43] Cavell, *The World Viewed*, 39.

differently, dispassionately, in a disinterested, Kantian way, because we do not have to act or react, even though the world on the screen is so much more present, alive and 'there' than the world in which we *are* obliged to act, or are overwhelmed by our inability and impotence to act (when we should). Our exclusion from the cinematic world turns out to be a bonus because we can be in the world without having to be accountable: it both cleanses and extends our moral sense, as it were. On the other hand, this privilege also comes with a responsibility, the *bonus* might contain an *onus*, an obligation to engage in the world, to care for and take care of the world thus revealed to us in its naked beauty, unprotectedness and vulnerability.

Many if not all of these reflections belong to what one may now call 'after Deleuze is before Deleuze', in the sense that these reassessments of Epstein, Bazin and Cavell, in short, these rather more positive evaluations of cinematic automatism – because no longer tied to the question 'Is cinema art?', or to the primarily epistemological questions of realism, representation, miscognition and knowledge as power – are largely owed to the repercussions that followed in the wake of Deleuze's intervention.

Insofar as I am focusing attention on the status and function of automatism in Deleuze's thinking, the notion is complicated by the fact that automatism is a concept so pervasive in his – and Felix Guattari's – philosophy that it connects to almost everything else. It makes it difficult, for instance, to decide if the cinema is what gave rise to the notion of the 'spiritual automaton', or if cinema was merely a further exemplification of a much more general principle of connectivity, contingency and of different kinds of agency. The concept of the spiritual automaton originally came to Deleuze from Spinoza where it refers to the auto-movement of thought; it is what links one idea to another, independently from an object (or indeed a subject). Spinoza operates a reversal between the idea that thought is dependent on consciousness, and on the contrary, suggests that it is our consciousness that is dependent on the way thoughts are linked with other thoughts: not such an unreasonable idea, in light of what I earlier argued about artificial intelligence, the hive mind and the outsourcing of our innate faculties to automated systems driven by algorithms.

The fact, therefore, that Deleuze chose Spinoza (and Leibniz) over Descartes (and Newton) means that he opted for an alternative tradition in rationalism and materialism. Especially the way Spinoza in his *Ethics* describes bodies as potentialities for contact and connections resonated with Deleuze and might even establish an affinity with parts of Bruno Latour's thinking about the kind of de-centred, non-hierarchical and distributed agency which typifies Actor-Network-Theory.[44]

[44] See http://kvond.wordpress.com/2009/03/04/is-latour-an-under-expressed-spinozist/ and Jane Bennett's concept of 'Thing-Power', in *Vibrant Matter: A Political Ecology of Things* (Durham, NC: Duke University Press, 2010).

Generally, Deleuze's philosophical interest in cinema arose from his assumption that the automatism of the cinematographic image resembles mental operations: an analogy already elaborated in some detail by Hugo Münsterberg in 1916. Deleuze, on the other hand, takes the idea from Bergson, rephrasing the automatism argument in terms of Bergson's movement-image, by playing the earlier Bergson of *Matière et mémoire* off against the later Bergson of *L'Evolution créatrice*, where Bergson dismissed the cinema, indicting chronophotography as mere mechanical movement, whereas for Deleuze, cinema captures movement inherent in all matter, including the brain and thought. By insisting on the direct link between brain and screen, rather than connecting cinema and mind by way of analogical operations, as did Münsterberg, Deleuze seems to have distanced himself from both cognitivism and phenomenology, trying to avoid the 'rift between the order of consciousness and the order of the world. Instead, the image-movement of cinema is self-movement, automatic, soliciting the image of thought.'[45]

Confirmation is provided for Deleuze by all the spiritual automatons that people German Expressionist cinema. Its movie plots of somnambulists, golems, gamblers and hypnotists Deleuze reads as fictional-fantastic instantiations or anthropomorphic versions of cinema's automatism in all its positive ambiguity and uncanny effects. Hitchcock's denigration of actors as 'cattle' supports a similar reasoning, but it is Robert Bresson who most fully exemplifies for Deleuze the filmmaker, whose attrition of actors to the point of mental and physical exhaustion is designed to release a spiritual essence that transmitted itself to the spectator as 'thought'. In a 1960 television interview, Bresson did in fact state that he always induced a state of 'automatism' in his actors, and one of the minor players in *Pickpocket*, Pierre Leymarie, has gone on record of how he had to repeat the same action and dialogue over and over again, until the words and gestures became meaningless to him, emptying himself of all affect or conscious motor-coordination, until it felt like he was sleepwalking or under hypnosis. Bresson preferred professional models or lay players to trained actors, arguing in his *Notes on the Cinematographer* that 'nine-tenths of our movements obey habit and automatism. It is anti-nature to subordinate them to will and thought.'[46] With his minimalist, ascetic style the very opposite of Surrealist flamboyance, Bresson nonetheless considered automatism the most direct way of releasing – and thus recording – the mind's unconscious and the body's spirituality.

---

[45] Quoted in Francois Dosse, *Gilles Deleuze and Félix Guattari: Intersecting Lives* (New York: Columbia University Press, 2011), 419.

[46] Robert Bresson, *Notes on the Cinematograph* (New York: New York Review of Books, 2016), 17.

The *shift from vision and eye* to the *cinema as thought and mind* is perhaps the most momentous move in the transition from film theory to film philosophy. Changing the default value of what defines cinema and making of the *body a continuous perceptual surface* has a number of further consequences. First of all, it inaugurates a different *epistemology*: no longer does 'I see' equal 'I know'; it also challenges visualization and the image as an index of reliable truth or objective verification. Secondly, it acknowledges that in the neurosciences, the body is treated as perceiving, feeling, that is, processing sensory input through a variety of channels and organs: blood pressure, chemical changes, magnetic resonance and so on, that have now become measurable and quantifiable, which they are not if one were to rely solely on human sight or mental processing power alone.

While this redistribution of the faculties can be seen positively, as an undoing of hierarchies of the body and a liberation of the senses, such a different organization of perception can also have negative consequences. It ushers in surveillance and control, which replaces other, older power-knowledge regimes (analysed by Foucault, and extensively deployed in film studies) by proliferating the instances where the pleasure of the body and the delights of sight are used as additional mechanisms of control and surveillance (television, for instance, is, according to Deleuze, almost entirely an apparatus for additional social control,[47] and no doubt, he would have thought the same of the internet, had he lived to experience it). Conceivably, however, Deleuze might have had interesting things to say about the empowering as well as oppressive ubiquity of everything connected, and everybody online to everybody else, which the internet and especially social media have accustomed, if not addicted, us to. He would probably have seen the extraction of ever more data and useful information from our bodies and affects as a new phase in the linkage of thought and machines, and thus entirely in line with the cinema as a spiritual automaton.

Why is the assumption that cinema is matter and thought so important and not just a quirk by a uniquely original philosopher? Because it signals and affirms a new relation that human beings have with (mechanical, electronic) images, to which we can assign agency, and thus affects and effects, but also consequences and actions, or as one might say today, *images are data*. The background against which cinematic 'thought' then becomes important would be the digital realm, not in the sense of the loss of materiality of the index, however we define it, but as introducing a different status in our

---

[47] 'Cinema ought to stop "being cinematic", stop playacting, and set up specific relationships with video, with electronic and digital images, in order to develop a new form of resistance and combat the televisual function of surveillance and control. It's not a question of short-circuiting television – how could that be possible? – but of preventing television subverting or short-circuiting the extension of cinema into the new types of image.' Gilles Deleuze, *Negotiations 1970–1990* (New York: Columbia University Press, 1997), 76.

relation to images quite generally: not as objects to view or sights to contemplate, but as portals, passages, interfaces.

True, a vast number of images still serve to represent the world, and in all relevant respects behave like photographs, that is, they can be used for purposes of simulation, similitude and substitution, but often enough they are also (along with an increasing number of images generated by means other than optics) *graphic* ways of storing data, or even contain and convey instructions for action. This would be the basis for a new ontology of the image (if we still choose to call such displays of data 'images' and not diagrams), following on from, but also radicalizing, Bazin's notion that it is *human non-interference* in the production of photographic images that constitutes cinema's ontology, where the animated and the automated enter into a most felicitous union: a union amenable to both a spiritual, transcendental humanist reading (the beauty of the snowflake as part of God's creation) and a materialist post-human reading (the beauty of the snowflake as proof that life does not need us).

From the animated to the automated

How, then, does this relate to the Deleuzean claim that cinema is (a form of) thought? The short answer is: thanks to two moves. First, it presupposes the idea of radical immanence of thought, and second, assumes an equally radical exteriority of thought. Both come together in a materialism that encompasses everything that is animated and endowed with motion (whether measured in milliseconds or light-year eons, or not measurable at all), and its verso side: the universe's openness and constitutive incompleteness. Cinema would then be the sort of happy accident that allows us to formulate a philosophy, which keeps in flux and balance (as 'becomings') these two so apparently opposed views of the world – and us within it.

Deleuze's film philosophy has engendered many serious and critical responses by fellow philosophers, sometimes through a very direct engagement with his arguments, sometimes by implicitly drawing on his thought, as a way of developing their own positions. I will briefly discuss three of them: Badiou, Rancière and Nancy, once more focusing on how they view cinema's automatism, before venturing some concluding remarks that hopefully give an idea of where I would like to take this overall argument about cinema between the animated and the automated.

In his study *Deleuze: The Clamour of Being*, Alain Badiou introduces the concept of the 'automaton' in Deleuze early on, first as part of his general critique of Deleuze's notions of immanence, becoming and multiplicity. These, Badiou argues, are still dependent on an implied concept of singularity and totality (the All-One), and therefore, despite his best efforts to get rid of them, ground Deleuze's philosophy in transcendental and metaphysical assumptions. What Badiou claims is that the automaton depends on giving outside forces total power over what is still the subject. But first he has harsh words to say about Deleuzians:

> All those who believe that Deleuze's remarks may be seen to encourage autonomy or the anarchizing ideal of the sovereign individual populating the Earth with the productions of his/her desires are mistaken. They do not take literally enough the strictly 'machinic' conception that Deleuze has, not only of desire (the famous 'desiring-machines') but, even more so, of will or choice. For this conception strictly precludes any idea of ourselves as being, at any time, the source of what we think or do.[48]

Badiou here defends Deleuze against his admirers (and possibly his co-author Guattari) by saying that Deleuze's automatism has nothing to do with either 'desire' (it is purified, ascetic and aristocratic) or with 'spontaneity'[49] (it is impersonal and exterior):

> This figure of the automaton, which links up easily with that of the 'machinery' that produces sense, represents the veritable subjective ideal, precisely because it demolishes all subjective pretensions. The outside, as agency of active force, takes hold of a body, selects an individual, and submits it to the choice of choosing: 'it is precisely the automaton, purified in this way, that thought seizes from the outside, as the unthinkable in thought' . . . This 'purified automaton' is certainly much closer to the Deleuzian norm than were the bearded militants of '68, bearing the standard of their gross desire . . . We must, through the sustained renunciation of the obviousness of our needs and occupied positions, attain that empty place where, seized by impersonal powers, we are constrained to make thought exist through us.[50]

For Badiou, 'that empty place' is one which cinema may occupy, to the degree that it is an automaton. Finding convergence with Deleuze about the exteriority of both cinema and thought, Badiou emphasizes that this is a process of subtraction (of desire and need) and of voiding (of the subject's interiority), as opposed to cinema being celebrated as 'desiring machine': a

---

[48] Alain Badiou, *Deleuze – The Clamour of Being* (Minneapolis: University of Minnesota Press, 1999), 10.1.

[49] 'One of Deleuze's most constant themes is, moreover, that we only think when forced to think. Let this be a warning to those who would see in Deleuze an apologia for spontaneity: whatever is spontaneous is inferior to thought, which only begins when it is constrained to become animated by the forces of the outside.' Badiou, *Deleuze – The Clamour of Being*, 86.7.

[50] Badiou, *Deleuze – The Clamour of Being*, 11.2.

trope borrowed from Deleuze–Guattari's *Thousand Plateux*.[51] Rather, these processes necessitate a conceptual horizon, the 'impersonal powers'. We can only surmise what they are: contingency and indifference, but also beauty and philosophy ('we are constrained to make thought exist through us'). For all of these, cinema can be both vehicle and instance.

Jacques Rancière appears to have a very different disagreement with Deleuze, since he is above all troubled by the division between 'movement image' and 'time image', which he says cannot be grounded either historically or epistemologically. However, he does engage seriously with – and even expands on – the automatism of cinema. The true power of the machine cinema, for Rancière, is its indifference to hierarchies or taxonomies, making no fundamental distinction between the beautiful and the ugly, the valuable and the insignificant, the doorknob or the duchess (he cites Jean Epstein's 'Bonjour cinema'). Rancière is here at his closest to Deleuze, when he describes things and people before the camera as being 'in their state as waves and vibrations, before [they exist in] their qualification as objects, persons, or identifiable events by their descriptive or narrative properties'.[52] For the duality of mechanical recording on the one hand, and human intervention on the other (but also for Cavell's conundrum of cinema giving us simultaneously the presence of the world and our absence from it), Rancière proposes the concept of the thwarted fable.[53] Thus, in Rancière's version of automatism, the cinema is always already divided against itself. As a consequence, the history of cinema – and even more, the history of film theory – has been about how to deal with this thwartedness, that is to say, how to tame the contingent (raw sensory data) that automatism brings to light, into 'fables', that is, stories and narrative, while nonetheless not losing the 'force' (Badiou) and the 'life' (Deleuze) – which the contingent, the random and the fortuitous of this automatism bring to narrative, to character and, finally, to 'representation'.

Jean-Luc Nancy might not disagree with Rancière's reasons for considering cinema capable of reclaiming the world, provided that his radical equality can also be formulated differently. In a book ostensibly devoted to the films of Abbas Kiarostami, *L'Evidence du film*, Nancy – the most Heideggerian of the philosophers I am considering – also speaks about the non-human mechanical gaze and the human or expressive gaze of the camera. But he draws from this apparent dichotomy other conclusions than Deleuze or Rancière, mentioning neither a historical-political mission of cinema (as

---

[51] See, for instance, Ian Alan Paul, 'Desiring-Machines in American Cinema', *Senses of Cinema* 56 (2010), http://sensesofcinema.com/2010/feature-articles/desiring-machines-in-american-cinema-what-inception-tells-us-about-our-experience-of-reality-and-film/ (accessed 14 December 2017).

[52] Cited by Tom Conley, 'Cinema and its Discontents: Jacques Rancière and Film Theory', *SubStance* 34, no. 3 (2005): 96.

[53] Rancière, 'Prologue: Thwarted Fable', in *Film Fables* (Oxford: Berg, 2006), 1–20.

does Rancière) nor the historical breaks of the movement image and the time image (as does Deleuze). In fact, Nancy sharply differs from Deleuze in that he considers both classical cinema and modern cinema 'reactionary': classical cinema because it presumes that the world makes sense, and that cinema can show this sense in action, while modern cinema is reactionary because it is traumatized by the world no longer making sense: 'At the foundation of modern cinema are Deleuze's pure optical situations that occur when the link between man and the world has been broken. Modern cinema is therefore obsessed with the loss of the world of classic cinema and constantly tries to express this loss, either by deconstructing the forms of classicism or by formally emphasizing the loss.'[54] These are for Nancy two sides of the same false coin, because what cinema automatism reminds us of (to paraphrase and summarize a complex and subtle proposition) is that the world does not exist in order to make sense.[55]

By arguing that classical narrative organizes every element of a film toward a predetermined meaning, and modern cinema confronts a world that can no longer be understood, while representing this loss of meaning with the techniques of documentary and realism, Nancy is taking Bazin's neo-realist aesthetics and turning it on its head, while implicitly dismissing both Rancière's 'thwarted fable' and Deleuze's 'cinema as thought'. As Laurent Kretschmar puts it:

> Nancy's philosophical twist is that this loss of a meaningful world is actually a gain because a world without signification is the world itself. Not that the world is nonsense, but the 'sense of the world' is only conceivable once we have acknowledged that the world is not about meaning but is a mere locus for the meanings. And while we are becoming aware of that simple reality, the world opens itself. Overcoming what we saw as a loss literally gives us the world.[56]

Elsewhere Nancy compares the world with art:

> A world, or the world, what is it made for? In order to make world, that's all. No world is made for anything but itself . . . The world finds itself

[54] Laurent Kretzschmar, 'Is Cinema Renewing Itself?', *Film-Philosophy* 6 no. 15 (July 2002), http://www.film-philosophy.com/index.php/f-p/article/view/679 (accessed 14 December 2017).
[55] Nancy's thinking about 'sense' and 'world' traverses almost all his writings and can be found in Jean Luc Nancy, *The Sense of the World*, 2nd edn (Minneapolis: University of Minnesota Press, 2008), and Jean Luc Nancy, *A Finite Thinking* (Stanford, CA: Stanford University Press, 2003). See also Daniele Rugo, 'Nancy and the World Without Sense', in Daniele Rugo, *Philosophy and the Patience of Film in Cavell and Nancy* (Berlin and New York: Springer, 2016), 73–117, and 'Jean Luc Nancy: A Finite Thinking', https://seoulphilosophy.wordpress.com/2015/06/04/jean-luc-nancy-a-finite-thinking/ (accessed 14 December 2017).
[56] Laurent Kretzschmar, 'Is Cinema Renewing Itself?', *Film-Philosophy* 6, no. 15 (July 2002), http://www.film-philosophy.com/index.php/f-p/article/view/679 (accessed 14 December 2017).

> today in the position of art: it serves no design, it produces nothing, neither does it come from any other-world . . . [It is what it is, because it] knows that henceforth it cannot count on anything but itself – not on God nor on any historical eschatology.[57]

What we can infer is that whenever the cinema is able to disclose to us this existential fact – neither telos nor redemption – the world opens itself up. Letting go of meaning actually *gives* us the world, and cinema can thus be a means for freeing ourselves from the obsession with sense, not by representing the world, but by presenting it, in its there-ness, its self-evidence and self-sufficiency: the cinema as world and art, without human interference . . .

With such ideas Nancy is closer to Cavell than to Deleuze, in that he takes up the ethical challenge of cinema's automatism, when arguing that what makes cinema important is that it teaches us to live not just with impersonality, but with meaninglessness. This we should see as a gift – and in this respect Nancy joins both Cavell and Deleuze – in being able to envisage how cinema can restore trust and belief in a world, once we accept that it can cleanse 'the world viewed' of meaning and purpose, while giving us – and here one can cite Bazin once more – the self-sufficiency 'of a flower or a snowflake, the beauty of which is inseparable from its vegetable or earthly origins'.

Conclusion

Hopefully, these brief sketches of positions attributed to Deleuze, Badiou, Rancière and Nancy regarding the automatism of cinema in relation to thought, world and self allow me to return to my initial, philosophical question 'Why is there cinema, why does it exist?' and speculate where these arguments take one, if one is trying to identify agendas for European cinema in the twenty-first century, and to formulate a view as to this cinema's reality-status or 'ontology'. Common to the philosophers discussed would appear to be the position that cinema is a powerful agent not for instantiating subjectivity or artistic expressivity, but for getting rid of them, helping an ongoing and seemingly irreversible process of depersonalization of the sovereign subject and an exteriorization of all forms of interiority (soul, subjectivity, affect, desire).

For Deleuze, as we saw, cinema is the name for a state of being where matter is movement and movement is matter, and thus there is no fundamental difference between the animated and the automated. Nothing else needs to exist. Neither secured in a subject, nor constrained by human scale, size or

[57] Jean-Luc Nancy, 'Y a-t-il encore un monde?', interview with Claire Margat, *Art Press* 281 (2002): 55, translation as cited in Ginette Michaud, '*In media res*: Interceptions of the Work of Art and the Political in Jean-Luc Nancy', *Substance* 34, no. 1 (2005): 106.

proportion, cinema's automatic and autonomous movement ideally requires an entirely different set of coordinates, one where our brains and bodies are an integral part of the world, freeing us of interiority, healing the subject–object, mind–body splits, as well as the self-divisions and illusory self-presence of subjectivity by handing both self and thought over to the spiritual automaton.

Cavell seems to agree, when, in *The World Viewed*, one reads:

> So far as photography satisfied a wish, it satisfied . . . the human wish, intensifying since the Reformation, to escape subjectivity and metaphysical isolation. . . . Photography overcame subjectivity in a way undreamed of by painting, one which does not so much defeat the act of painting as escape it altogether: by automatism, by removing the human agent from the act of reproduction.[58]

Read today, the word reproduction has an extended semantic register, including mechanical, social and a bio-genetic reproduction: not all of them perhaps intended by Cavell, but there, for us, nonetheless.

Such a conclusion, however, would be too evolutionary and teleological for a philosopher like Badiou, who in paraphrasing Deleuze, is more categorical:

> For the automaton, who has *realized* this giving up of all interiority, there is only the outside . . . [But this] outside cannot be confused with anything so commonplace as a sort of external world. The automaton . . . is a simulacrum that is without any relation to other simulacra. It is, itself, the pure assumption of the outside. As Deleuze notes, concerning the canonical example of cinema – canonical because of what is evident in it: 'the material automatism of images' (*Cinema* 2, pp. 178–79): 'The automaton is cut off from the outside world, but there is a more profound outside which will animate it' (ibid., p. 179) . . . But what is the underlying principle of all animation? What populates the impersonal outside; what is it that composes forms therein? Let us call this 'element' of the outside 'force.' The name is appropriate for, inasmuch as it is translated only by a constrained animation, or by a setting into motion of the automaton-thought, the outside is only manifest as the imposition of a force.[59]

Cinema, as the emblem of all animation, thus also partakes in 'the forces of the outside' to which no external world corresponds (no realist aesthetics of transparency), but neither does a world of interiority and subjectivity (no mirror to the self). How, then, to imagine this force? Is it the untranscendable

[58] Cavell, *The World Viewed*, 21.

[59] Badiou, *Deleuze – The Clamour of Being*, 85.6.

horizon of capitalism, of which cinema is such an undeniable offspring? Is it the empty place that confirms the groundless ground of our being? Is it the eye-candy of illusionism that distracts us from our failure to comprehend either abstract numbers or quantum physics, that is, the forces that govern the universe? Badiou deliberately does not say, while nonetheless reminding us – and this would be another paradoxical sense in which cinema restores belief in the world – that these forces do exist. In their indifference and impersonality they might as well stand for 'the animated as the automated'.

Yet from another perspective, the philosophers' convergent if not unanimous verdict on cinema amounts to a proposition that makes cinema both historical and contemporary. Historical, in that during the roughly hundred years of its existence, it has done its job – thanks to its inherent automatism and the filmmakers' countermove: montage and editing. It has cured us of subjectivity, interiority, individuality and intentionality, one might add, at least as thoroughly as, for instance, the other narcissistic wounds inflicted by Darwinian evolution, Freudian psychoanalysis, Nietzschean nihilism and Marxism, all of which have also tried to wean us from believing we could either be fully present to ourselves, or in charge of our own fate. Having accomplished this, cinema could now become obsolete and outdated with dignity and pride, ready to be celebrated and commemorated, like any other human achievement that had done Hegel's 'cunning work of reason' (an older name for Badiou's 'forces of the outside') *behind our backs* – as Marx would add.

However, the cinema would also be contemporary, in that its digital reincarnation continues to ask: what world is it, to which its sounds and images can solicit us? A world we do not own or possess, a world that hosts us – in all our sensory capacities and moral faculties, but also in its indifference to us? In which case, does cinema exist – and continue to do so – not in order to enjoy *its obsolescence*, but rather to reconcile us humans to *our own obsolescence*? It's a troubling thought, but one worth thinking, nonetheless: in and with cinema, in and with film philosophy.

Both obsolescence and indifference, both 'reason' and 'forces of the outside', bring me back to European cinema, to the values of the Enlightenment and to the more fine-grained issues – political, aesthetic, ethical – that arise from these philosophical conundrums for individual filmmakers, and of course, for those writing about film as well. In the chapters that follow, I will address the question of cinema's exteriority with the proposal to treat contemporary cinema as providing 'thought experiments', while the tension (or potential equivalence) between *animated* and *automated* comes to the fore in a different guise: in its political and ethical dimension it underpins my choice of the central concept of abjection. The full 'post-human' implications of 'animated' and 'automated' will have to remain suspended, since 'abjection' is, after all, a humanist concept, derived from psychoanalysis, and since, from a European perspective, it is meant to maintain both the validity and urgency of the Enlightenment project.

3

Film as Thought Experiment

The previous chapters sketched the general background that led film studies to turn to philosophy. They also outlined some of the reasons that make new thinking about European cinema both possible and necessary, and signalled the need for a change in the default values if we are to reconstitute cinema – after the digital turn – as a theoretical object. My main (contentious) argument in the first chapter is that since the demise of national cinemas and the decline of auteur cinema, European cinema as a certain idea and practice has become less relevant, but that this apparent irrelevance may come with an unexpected bonus. It could yet turn out to be a strength, because it frees this cinema from ideological constraints and critical expectations, making the films potentially more experimental and engaged in 'serious games'. The second chapter added to this another layer, arguing that a substantial number of philosophers taking an interest in cinema identify its importance for philosophy in phenomena and properties that have little to do with either ideology or expressivity, and more with a voiding of interiority, a disclosure of the world that precedes or resists projection of intent and is inherently indifferent to meaning.

This is clearly a radical (abstract as well as counter-intuitive) move to tackle a topic as specific as national (or European) cinema. Yet it brings into view a different perspective: the freedom from ideological instrumentalization opens up the possibility of treating films as thought experiments – an idea already touched upon previously. As argued in the first chapter (and taken up in the concluding chapter on authorship), for a long time European cinema (existing primarily on the festival circuit where auteurs and national cinema are still the most common currency) was distinguished by the fact that directors and films served ideological ends that were deemed to be non-ideological: art and self-expression. Either speaking for the nation, or refreshing national stereotypes and tourist clichés for the benevolent gaze of the Other, auteurs were expected to uphold cinema as art. But being thrust into the role of critical conscience of their country, while also representing nothing but themselves, they were effectively obliged to serve two masters.[1] Liberated from both, European cinema can ideally face the bigger challenges: first, to embody the new epistemology and ontology of film (in part necessitated by the post-cinema condition of the digital image, and in part reflecting the same concerns as the critical intervention of continental philosophers: to complicate the reality-status of the moving image, now situated between art form and life form). The second challenge for this cinema is to be 'European' in a post-national sense, that is, to contribute to the continent's political experiment, which has rarely seemed more precarious. As a possible response to both these challenges I propose the term thought experiment, and the aim of this chapter is to introduce the concept more fully. 'Film as thought experiment' tries to ground the notion of 'film as thought' in a historical specificity and give it political urgency. In so doing it navigates a conceptual terrain between European cinema's (commercial, ideological) irrelevance and cinema's (inherent) indifference to traditional hierarchies and taxonomies, designating a (negative) space for a new ontology in the realm of the sensible, the visible and the thinkable.

The context I am here sketching differs in several ways from the debate that initially brought the notion of 'film as thought experiment' to critical attention. As mentioned in the previous chapter, the film philosophy debate pitted an analytically oriented 'philosophy of film' (which treats film and cinema as late additions to aesthetics and the philosophy of art) against film-philosophy, which wants to argue that certain films are not just pedagogically useful illustrations of classic problems in philosophy (free will versus determinism, the existence of other minds, radical scepticism about the knowability of the external world, the ethical limits of human law, the principle of utilitarianism), but are actual and even original contributions to philosophy, in a medium and a mode of thinking whose philosophical potential has largely gone unrecognized.[2] This latter position has been

[1] The argument about 'serving two masters' is taken up more fully and given an additional turn in the final chapter, 'Control, Constraints and Self-Contradiction'.

[2] There are by now a number of vivid and informative accounts of this debate, both in the form of articles and in book form. Often cited are Murray Smith and Thomas E. Wartenberg (eds), *Thinking Through Cinema: Film as Philosophy* (Hoboken, NJ: Wiley-Blackwell, 2006) and Thomas E. Wartenberg, *Thinking on Screen: Film as Philosophy* (London: Routledge, 2007). Early statements were by Stephen Mulhall, *On Film* (London: Routledge, 2001/2008) and Daniel Frampton, *Filmosophy* (London: Wallflower, 2006), followed by John Mullarkey, *Refractions of Reality: Philosophy and the Moving Image* (New York: Palgrave Macmillan, 2009). The debate is also well-presented in Paisley Livingston and Carl Plantinga (eds), *The Routledge Companion to Philosophy and Film* (London: Routledge, 2009), as well as Tom McClellan's essay 'Philosophy of Film and Film as Philosophy', *Cinema: Journal of Philosophy and the Moving Image* 2 (2011), http://cjpmi.ifl.pt/2-contents. In what follows, I rely extensively on Sinnerbrink, *New Philosophies of Film: Thinking Images* (London and New York: Continuum, 2011). Check also for what has already been referenced in full in previous chapters' footnotes.

dubbed (by its critics) the 'bold hypothesis',[3] mostly in order to ultimately reject it, conceding only that films, because they reach a wider audience, can usefully initiate debates that philosophers recognize as touching on their domain.[4] Calling it 'bold' was to argue implicitly for a more 'moderate' hypothesis, where films may possess some of the characteristics of philosophical argument, without fulfilling all the necessary conditions to count as philosophy.[5]

It was in the course of trying to find a compromise formula that, for instance, Thomas Wartenberg came up with the suggestion that films could have the status and function that thought experiments occupy in philosophy, where they are a recognized procedure and a valid tool of argumentation, albeit under certain, specifiable circumstances.[6] The advantage of the thought experiment was that it made room for two features that the opponents of the bold hypothesis deemed sufficient to disqualify film from being philosophy: the predominance of narrative, and its status as fiction.[7]

Thought experiments deal in hypothetical situations, and thus are fictions, often presented in the form of a didactic parable or an imaginary scenario. However, thought experiments are also 'What if?' conditionals, and as such they are suppositions. Conditionals and suppositions are ways of making inferences based on real world evidence, posited in such a way as to allow for deductions that can predict future outcomes.[8] On the other hand, thought experiments are invoked when trying to test a general principle that one suspects of being invalid or potentially unsound, by bringing out limits, inherent contradictions or pointing to logical paradoxes. This is where they function by way of counter-examples. As Wartenberg sums up the case he is making:

---

[3] The phrase was coined by Paisley Livingston, 'Theses on Cinema as Philosophy', *Journal of Aesthetics and Art Criticism* 64, no. 1 (2006): 11–18, part of the journal's 'Special Issue: Thinking through Cinema: Film as Philosophy' (Winter 2006).

[4] The rejectionists include, besides Paisley Livingstone, also Murray Smith. See 'Film Art, Argument and Ambiguity', in Smith and Wartenberg, *Thinking Through Cinema*, 33–42. But see also Aaron Smuts, 'In Defense of a Bold Thesis', *Journal of Aesthetics and Art Criticism* 67, no. 4 (Fall 2009): 409–20.

[5] The 'moderates' include Thomas Wartenberg and Robert Sinnerbrink, as well as Chris Falzon's entry 'Philosophy through Film' in the *Internet Encyclopaedia of Philosophy*, http://www.iep.utm.edu/phi-film/ (accessed 12 August 2013), which also includes a full bibliography.

[6] Sinnerbrink presents an informative summary of Wartenberg's arguments in *New Philosophies of Film*, 123.

[7] 'There is a well-developed philosophical technique that involves narratives, indeed, fictional ones at that: the thought experiment.' Wartenberg, *Thinking on Screen*, 24.

[8] A further use of conditionals is that they raise the issue of possible worlds, where a conditional is true in certain worlds but not others. See Warren Buckland, 'Between Science Fact and Science Fiction: Spielberg's Digital Dinosaurs, Possible Worlds, and the New Aesthetic Realism', *Screen* 40, no. 2 (Summer 1999): 177–92.

> [A] counterexample targets an important philosophical principle [such as that] knowledge is justified true belief, abortion is morally wrong, or physical facts are all the facts there are. What the thought experiment does is to present a fictional scenario in which we think that the[se] principles do not hold ... The thought experiments show that the purported universal principles do not apply in all circumstances and so must be rejected.[9]

But other kinds of thought experiments are used in mathematics and quantum physics, and they have a long history in philosophy, going back to Plato and the Socratic dialogues. In quantum physics they may contrast our common-sense view of the world with the counter-intuitive findings, especially when challenging our understanding of such basic categories as time, space, infinity, identity, past and future, mind and consciousness. Albert Einstein used a thought experiment to explain relativity ('Einstein's elevator'),[10] while Erwin Schrödinger tested quantum indeterminacy ('Schrödinger's cat').[11] Other famous thought experiments are Galileo's leaning tower of Pisa (proving gravity) and Maxwell's demon (the possibilities of defeating the second law of thermodynamics).[12]

Among the different types of philosophical thought experiments Wartenberg lists are thought experiments as counter-examples, that is, when targeting an important philosophical principle by imagining at least one exception; thought experiments as establishing possibility, by imagining something as conceivable, and thus as possible, even if not realizable in practice; thought experiments as establishing necessary connections, often in order to decide whether it is the brain or the body that constitutes the locus of identity; and thought experiments as positing an idealized state of things, in order to derive from it valid principles for a less perfect state of things – a type frequently found in Plato.[13]

The special or specifiable conditions of the thought experiment can be summarized as follows:

---

[9] Wartenberg, *Thinking on Screen*, 59.

[10] On Einstein's Elevator, see http://www.pbs.org/wgbh/nova/physics/einstein-thought-experiments.html (accessed 12 December 2016).

[11] See https://en.wikipedia.org/wiki/Schr%C3%B6dinger%27s_cat (accessed 12 December 2016).

[12] See https://en.wikipedia.org/wiki/Galileo%27s_Leaning_Tower_of_Pisa_experiment and https://en.wikipedia.org/wiki/Maxwell%27s_demon (both accessed 12 December 2016). The Wikipedia entry on 'Thought Experiment' lists an impressive number of thought experiments in physics and philosophy, http://en.wikipedia.org/wiki/Thought_experiment (accessed 12 December 2016). See also the entry on 'Thought Experiment' in the *Stanford Encyclopedia of Philosophy*, http://plato.stanford.edu/entries/thought-experiment/ (accessed 12 December 2016), which includes an extensive bibliography.

[13] Wartenberg, *Thinking on Screen*, 58–67.

- Thought experiments formulate a proposition that cannot be tested in reality or in situ, but is taken to its logical – which usually means paradoxical or impossible – conclusion, thus trying to break a sort of glass ceiling of our 'normal understanding' of how the world works.
- Thought experiments depend on someone setting up specific rules which, insofar as they venture into unknown territory, can be considered arbitrary, or as I shall argue, tend to be self-limiting constraints.
- Thought experiments often involve a 'What if' situation: they can take the form of a fictional scenario, they can suppose a set of conditionals, or they can *simulate* a real-world situation.

Wartenberg's examples of films as thought experiments include such popular mind-game films as *The Matrix* (1999) and *Eternal Sunshine of the Spotless Mind* (2004), but also more mainstream classics, such as *The Man Who Shot Liberty Valance* (1962) and *The Third Man* (1949). In each of them he identifies a specific philosophical issue that the film in question not only illustrates, but enacts or pushes further. Yet while certain films can be described as narratives presenting a single hypothetical case (rather than putting forward a general argument), there is still quite a high bar in philosophy itself for something to count as a valid thought experiment, which means that the idea of films as thought experiments might have to remain more of a metaphor, and merely function by analogy. In an illuminating chapter, entitled 'Scenes from a Marriage: On the Idea of Film as Philosophy', Robert Sinnerbrink has aptly summarized the arguments on either side:

> Defenders of the 'film as philosophy' thesis have argued that certain kinds of film are capable of screening philosophical thought-experiments (Wartenberg 2007); that film can philosophize on a variety of topics, including reflection on its own status, in ways comparable to philosophy (Mulhall 2002, 2008); or that film has its own affective ways of thinking that alter the manner in which philosophy can be experienced (Frampton 2006). Critics of the film-as-philosophy idea, by contrast, have argued that such claims are merely metaphorical: for these critics, film, as a visual narrative art, does not give reasons, make arguments, or draw conclusions, hence it cannot be understood as 'philosophical' in the proper sense (Baggini 2003; Russell 2006); or, given the ambiguity of film narrative, if there are philosophical aspects to a film, these are usually subordinate to its artistic and rhetorical ends (Smith 2006).[14]

---

[14] Sinnerbrink, *New Philosophies of Film*, 117.

Tom McClellan has added to this a further clarification. Rather than pointing out (as, for instance, Chris Fallon does) that one of the most famous thought experiments – Plato's parable of the Cave – has had an all-but foundational role in film theory, thanks to its use by Jean-Louis Baudry in his (second) essay on 'The Apparatus',[15] McClellan refers to Plato's *Meno*, and shows how Socrates more generally uses thought experiments in order to draw his interlocutors into a dialogue that leads to new knowledge. He concludes:

> Instead of claiming that film can implicitly present precise philosophical positions I suggest that proponents of 'film as philosophy' should adopt a more modest position. Perhaps a film can behave as an *invitation* for its audience to engage in a philosophical inquiry that treats events in the film like thought-experiments. On this picture there is a kind of mutual co-operation between the film and its audience. The film contributes a salient narrative in a manner that sheds light on a philosophical issue, while the audience is left to contribute the kind of explicit formal argument and articulate conclusion that integrates that narrative into a full philosophical exercise . . . In a philosophical discussion, someone can present a salient thought-experiment without elaborating on its implications. It is clear that they present the scenario as something that has philosophical ramifications, and it is even clear roughly what kind of philosophical conclusion it encourages. If such a speaker invites others to develop a rigorous and precise position on the basis of their thought-experiment, they are nevertheless making an active contribution to the philosophical activity . . . There is something deeply Socratic about this way of contributing to philosophy – without stating any philosophical conclusions, one can cleverly stimulate an audience into achieving their own insights. I claim that the voice that film can have in philosophical debate is analogous to this Socratic voice.[16]

It is this possibility of film to become a 'midwife to philosophical knowledge' that seems worth pursuing, notably when thinking about how such a Socratic method might provide the model for interpretation. In this case, neither the film nor the spectator would occupy the position of the master, that is, would be in prior possession of this knowledge, which each then tries to elicit from the other: a major problem with close textual readings that try to reconstruct authorial intentions. The same applies to the hermeneutics of suspicion that makes the text say what it either does not know or refuses to admit. By contrast, the increasingly popular practice of the video essay – re-editing a film or body of work to highlight certain (formal or thematic) features –

[15] Jean-Louis Baudry, 'The Apparatus: Metapsychological Approaches to the Impression of Reality in Cinema', *Camera Obscura* 1 (Fall 1976): 104–26.
[16] McClellan, 'Philosophy of Film and Film as Philosophy'.

might have a positive Socratic effect, when used as a pedagogical exercise to stimulate students' primary engagements (thanks to digital editing tools), or when deployed as a way of enabling the film to speak about itself in the 'language' of cinema, thus adding a reflexive dimension that could be called 'thought', made visible in and through montage and re-editing, now understood as a form of dialogue.[17]

More generally, film as thought experiment asserts the value of film as knowledge because its mode of thought, even where it does not depend on propositional thinking, that is, verbal language, is still a form of reasoning. It is the claim that film-philosophers are making (the bold hypothesis discussed earlier), but it is also shared by narratologists when they argue that narrative is a form of reasoning. The precedent would be the fact that in the continental philosophical tradition (from Hegel to Heidegger), poetry has often been accepted as a form of philosophy, even though poems do not necessarily make propositional statements.[18]

European films as thought experiments

As indicated, my reasons for adopting 'film as thought experiment' have less to do with wanting to rescue or validate 'film as philosophy', and more with understanding the particular historical conjuncture addressed above, where the status of film and cinema seems in need of being reconsidered in a specifically European conjuncture of political crisis and continental philosophy. Initially, this was prompted by the realization that many of contemporary cinema's critically and commercially successful films – across the mainstream/art cinema/avant-garde cinema divides – have found a new way of interrogating their own status as real/virtual within their fictional diegesis, which sometimes obliges the viewer to substantially revise an initial premise in order to grasp what is happening (such as the mind-game films briefly discussed in the previous chapter). They sometimes leave both protagonist and audience in the dark about the reality status of what they are seeing, effectively collapsing the subject–object divide, along with the distinction between a case study of mental breakdown and split personality disorder or the schizo-double as the new normal, while scrambling sequential time, character consistency and linear causality.

[17] See, for instance, Cristina Álvarez López and Adrian Martin's video essay on Polanski's *Repulsion* (1965), an essay described as a thought experiment: http://www.filmscalpel.com/bela-tarrs-repulsion/ (accessed 12 December 2016).

[18] The debate between philosophy and poetry has a long tradition, going back to Plato. For a very useful collection of contemporary essays, see John Gibson (ed.), *The Philosophy of Poetry* (Oxford: Oxford University Press, 2015), notably the essay by Roger Scruton, discussing Heidegger's views on poetry and truth (Roger Scuton, 'Poetry & Truth', 149–61).

In my earlier study of such films, I called mind-game films a new meta-genre (giving a twist to time travel, science fiction, film noir and the thriller, but occasionally also inhabiting melodrama and even romantic comedy). Part of its destabilizing effects were what I called 'productive pathologies', designating a new socially useful form of agency and identity that was predicated on states of body and mind that are usually considered pathologies or afflictions.[19] In the present context, mind-game films could conceivably qualify as contemporary Hollywood versions of the Socratic voice and thus as thought experiments, engaging the spectator in 'What if' situations or starting from impossibly fraught or antagonistic situations, while trying to craft narratives that 'perform' these contradictions in what I have called 'parapractic' or self-contradictory modes, but which a Deleuzian scholar might identify as a logic of inclusive disjunction.[20]

Given the broader epistemological-ontological context of the changes in cinema's reality status that I am charting, it is not surprising that European cinema's thought experiments share features with other types of contemporary cinema, such as the mind-game film, and there is indeed a certain amount of crossover, for instance, if we think of *Open Your Eyes* (1997), remade in Hollywood as *Vanilla Sky* (2001) as such a 'What if' film. However, mind-game films are first and foremost concerned with the individual, and with epistemological questions about the nature of perception. They may take place in science-fiction settings (*A Scanner Darkly*, 2006) and other Hollywood films based on Philip K. Dick stories, for example *Minority Report* (2002), or use a film noir atmosphere (*Memento*, 1999), whereas European cinema's thought experiments are above all concerned with ethical choices, the body politic, the collective and the community, and they usually draw their strength from realist story worlds and settings (see below: Lars von Trier, Michael Haneke, the Dardenne Brothers). In short, they touch on political philosophy and ethical dilemmas, more than they deal with parallel worlds and alternative universes.

If I am right, and a change has taken place, making the digital both the technical and the conceptual default value of all cinema ('digital cinema: everything is the same/ nothing is the same'), then commonalities (or inclusive disjunctions) may also appear between European thought experiments and Hollywood mind-game films, even if the former do not challenge sequential time, spatial contiguity and linear causality as drastically

---

[19] See Thomas Elsaesser, 'The Mind-Game Film', in Warren Buckland (ed.), *Puzzle Films: Complex Storytelling in Contemporary Cinema* (Hoboken, NJ: Wiley-Blackwell, 2009), 13–41.

[20] If disjunction refers to two divergent or unconnected parts, then an inclusive disjunction requires us to bring these into convergence without eliminating their diverging force. For Deleuze, inclusive disjunction is a logical operator. An extended definition can be found in Francois Zourabichvili, *Deleuze: A Philosophy of the Event; Together with the Vocabulary of Deleuze* (Edinburgh: Edinburgh University Press, 2012), 170–1.

as some of the latter. This hypothesis is based on several additional considerations: first, given that both contemporary philosophy and the neurosciences are extensively involved in revising classical accounts of the mind–body split, and, with it, are redefining what parts of consciousness or self-presence to call 'mind', 'brain', 'body' or 'environment' (eliminating both 'soul' and 'psyche'), it is not inconceivable that cinema should emerge as a major field where the demonstrably complex relations between perception, action, body, consciousness, projection, retroaction, memory, trauma and fantasy can be freshly examined, once the proper test conditions are in place, or rather, once we are able to perceive a film as such a test bed or experimental platform.

Second, among cognitivist scholars, for instance, tracking eye movement has emerged as a major new field of analysing films, in the hope of finding some empirical basis for deciding how our attention is directed and distributed as we 'follow' the action or how and why we engage with certain characters.[21] The intention is to develop a more plausible theory of identification than the suturing effect of shot-reverse shot, or the gender-biased asymmetries of looking and being looked at. Eye-tracking has also appealed to art historians, notably following on from the work done in the 1960s by the Russian behavioural psychologist Alfred Yarbus.[22] However, eye-tracking is also an analytical technique widely used in advertising and marketing, in order to optimize the display of merchandize in department stores and to design the architectural layout of shopping malls, as the filmmaker and installation artist Harun Farocki dryly documents in his *The Creators of Shopping Worlds/Die Schöpfer der Einkaufswelten* (2001). The question then arises whether we are interpreting films in order to learn about cinema, or about us the viewers, and if the latter, might we be doing no more as film theorists than proving our usefulness as unpaid labour for the marketing departments of the Hollywood studios? Which poses the additional question, whether it is the film itself that is the thought experiment or the interaction of the film with its audience that constitutes the object of the experiment, thereby crucially relocating the initiator or author of the experiment? This problem is hinted at by one of the critics of the claim of art in general and films in particular qualifying as thought experiments: he argues that 'a crucial part of the defense of this claim turns on a shift that

[21] See Tim J. Smith, 'Watching You Watch Movies: Using Eye Tracking to Inform Cognitive Film Theory', in Arthur P. Shimamura (ed.), *Psychocinematics* (Oxford: Oxford University Press, 2013), 165–91, and Jennifer Treuting, 'Eye Tracking and the Cinema: A Study of Film Theory and Visual Perception', in *SMPTE Motion Imaging Journal* 115, no. 1 (January 2006): 31–40.

[22] See also David Bordwell's 'Observations on Film Art' blog for historical context and contemporary application: http://www.davidbordwell.net/blog/2011/02/06/the-eyes-mind/ and http://www.davidbordwell.net/blog/2011/02/14/watching-you-watch-there-will-be-blood/ (both accessed 12 December 2016).

treats our watching of the film as the thought experiment, instead of the film itself, since this defense requires that the verbal mediation or rational assessment "necessary for bringing the film into the philosophical arena" be part of the thought experiment (rather than something external to it)'.[23]

Third, the key point about the methods of analysis that have arisen around films that can be considered thought experiments pertains to another aspect of the 'film as philosophy' discourse, namely the role that philosophical scepticism plays in this debate. Scepticism, as a philosophical issue involving the Cartesian mind–body split, has come widely under review (not least thanks to the popular reception of Antonio Damasio's *Descartes' Error*). But it is also an issue at the heart of the new ontology of film (under the heading 'trust in the world/ belief in the world', briefly mentioned in the preceding chapter). In the first chapter I discussed how philosophical scepticism, in the tradition of Kant and Hegel, and including Nietzsche's nihilism as well as Derrida's deconstruction, can be aligned with the specific historical situation of Europe, caught in a philosophical crisis as much as in a political one. No longer confident of the Enlightenment values that sustained the political project of democracy, the (self-)critical spirit of scepticism is also reluctant to defend these values philosophically: a point I shall argue more fully in the next chapter. My argument here and in the second part of this book is that surprisingly many films made in the past decades in Europe are at once symptom, response and contribution to the crisis, many in the form of thought experiments.

What, then, are some of the specific problems to which 'film as thought experiment' is proposed as an answer? As so often, the notion of 'crisis' is a convenient placeholder when trying to think transformation, continuity and change within a single conceptual framework, so I shall name three crises that seem to me to characterize our present moment: the crisis in *representation*; the *crisis of evidence, reference, data* and their respective forms of visualization; and the crisis in *temporality, causality and history*.

All of these crises have variously been identified with the digital turn, and are widely discussed under such headings as 'simulation and virtual reality', the 'loss of indexicality' and 'random access', 'timeless time' or 'enduring ephemerality'. Yet I want to caution against essentializing digital media as cause, while welcoming the focus on this change in basic film technology as an overdue occasion to ask more wide-ranging questions about the nature and status of cinema today. 'Film as thought experiment' is thus a way of both addressing and acknowledging these crises, while shifting the terms of the debate to a more philosophical or epistemological ground. In particular,

[23] Mathew C. Haug, reviewing David Davies, 'Can Philosophical Thought Experiments be Screened?', *Analysis* 74, no. 1 (2014): 169, in Melanie Frappier, Letitia Meynell and James Robert Brown (eds), *Thought Experiments in Science, Philosophy, and the Arts* (New York: Routledge, 2012).

the crises are brought into focus through the lens of thought experiments, because thought experiments are a) simulations (a crisis of representation), b) suppositions and thus either not based on observable evidence, or they lack a referent, and c) counter-factual histories, including conspiracy theories, addressing the crisis of history, both of which redraft what might once have passed for factual history.

Least controversial among these crises is the truism that the nature and status of cinema has changed considerably over the past thirty-odd years, due to the transformations of cinema as a photographic medium which has multiplied its technical platforms and access-points; second, due to changes in geopolitical power relations that have globalized cinema's audiences, while at the same time localizing production, by lowering the barriers of entry; and last but not least, the altered status of cinema is due to changes in intellectual priorities, reflecting the formidable challenge presented by evolutionary biology, cognitivism and the neurosciences to the value assumptions and core arguments of the humanities, traditionally the most welcoming academic host of cinema studies. As a consequence, film studies has begun to adopt quite different vantage points and methods, abandoning hermeneutic strategies and adopting analytical tools that together are reshaping the object of study that is or was cinema and film.

My own investment has been twofold. First, the different priorities have encouraged a new film historiography. In light of a changing present, film historians have been massively recasting the past. They have done so by reinvestigating early cinema and pre-cinema, discovering new genealogies for the moving image, or reinstating the function and topicality of 'forgotten' imaging technologies, such as the stereoscope or dioramas.[24]

Second, such historical perspective corrections have had consequences also for film theory. Shifts of emphasis have become evident: less and less is the creative process or intention of the filmmaker the object of study; it is the spectator's experience that has emerged as central.[25] 'Experience' is now more important than 'effects': in place of a sociological communication studies approach targeting 'the mass audience', 'experience' signals a more respectfully holistic approach to the spectator, whose mind and body are imagined as an integral perceptual organ, and whose senses, in the process of viewing, are redistributed across the surface of the film and its different

[24] Elsaesser, *Film History as Media Archaeology* (Amsterdam: Amsterdam University Press, 2016).

[25] One of the most widely used textbooks in film studies is Timothy Corrigan and Patricia White's aptly titled *The Film Experience*, 5th edn (New York: Macmillan Learning, 2017). But see also Miriam Hansen, *Cinema and Experience: Siegfried Kracauer, Walter Benjamin, and Theodor W. Adorno* (Berkeley: University of California Press, 2011), for another genealogy of the concept of 'experience'.

tactile or auditory registers.[26] For every cognitivist, relying on the neurosciences, who appears to be reverting to a stimulus-response model of the spectator, there are two for whom embodiment and the emotional brain have replaced anxieties over mass media effects.

As argued earlier, it was under the dual – but diametrically opposed – impact of Deleuze's *Cinema* books, and the critical offensive against *Screen* theory (launched mainly by cognitivist scholars in the US), that film studies turned to philosophy. From this turn I derived my preference in the preceding chapter for breaking down the object of study into the two fundamental questions we can bring to cinema – each as valid as the other, each as necessary as the other. First, *questions of epistemology*: what kinds of knowledge does the cinema convey, or promise to deliver (and then, as seemed mostly the case, *fail to deliver*), and what is the epistemological faith we are willing to invest in cinema, when believing in its political effects or emancipatory potential? Following on from this, to ask what kind of agency do films have, what forces do they activate or set in motion, what energies do films possess, what interaction do they initiate with bodies and entertain with the different senses? Second, *questions of ontology*: how does cinema distribute and divide differently what is animate and inanimate, what is object and what is subject, what is matter and what is mind, what is human and what is machine, what is sentient and what is inert – in short: what is alive and even, 'what is life', which I would characterize as belonging to ontology, since it touches on *our very being in the world*, even before we try to make sense of the world. Both questions take as given the importance of moving images, as an already present interface to our modernity, regardless of whether we go to the movies or not, whether we prefer Hollywood movies or art cinema, whether we only watch television or never watch television, whether we take selfies or hate the very idea of Facebook, Snapchat and Instagram.

My tentative answer to the ontological question was cinema's indifference to human intentions or goals, thanks to its automatisms that so much preoccupied theorists from the 1920s to the 1950s and now seems central to philosophers since the 1980s and 1990s. This very indifference vis-à-vis hierarchy and narrative, teleology and meaning (to which I associated the economic and ideological irrelevance of European cinema), is the negative ground, from which arise the ethical questions one must now address to cinema: films make us part of and participate in worlds and in lives for which we do not have to take responsibility, making of us not only spectators, voyeurs and onlookers, but bystanders, witnesses, without the obligation or indeed the ability to act, assist or intervene – however much a certain idea

[26] Thomas Elsaesser and Malte Hagener, *Film Theory: An Introduction through the Senses*, 2nd edn (London and New York: Routledge, 2015).

of political cinema wants us to, or believes it can shame or encourage us into taking action. On the other hand, if cinema is potentially a great leveller and equalizer (indifference's verso: radical equality), it can give us the world as if reborn, making it strange and unfamiliar, and thereby renewing a kind of faith or trust in the world, beyond set conventions, fixed categories and established meanings – even beyond the very impulse towards 'meaning-making', as proposed for the cinema of Abbas Kiarostami by Jean-Luc Nancy in his book *The Evidence of Film*.[27] Thus voided of interiority and subjectivity, based on an ethics I shall define (in a subsequent chapter) as 'abjection', a different politics can emerge, which has relevance for the post-heroic state that Europe finds itself in: *but it is a politics that can only be tested and implemented in the form of a thought experiment.*

Thus, the turn to issues of epistemology and ontology of cinema, is one of the possible responses to the crisis of representation, suggesting that we have to re-examine the reality-status of films, not (only) as representations of pre-constituted reality, not (only) as windows on the world, not (only) as mirrors to the self – the latter two often used, as noted earlier, as the distinguishing metaphors between classical realist and modern auto-reflexive cinema. So much of our reality – both external and internal, that is: how we perceive the world, how science understands the world, and how we experience ourselves and interact with others – is now mediated through imaging techniques and other representational technologies that it may no longer make sense to posit an a priori 'reality' of which images are a more or less accurate representation, or whose relation to reality can be denounced as an 'illusion' or 'false'. Images now function, exist, affect, circulate, mediate, provide evidence, elicit actions, have consequences or simply come and go in ways for which we – film and media scholars, historians and art historians – have yet to find an appropriate vocabulary or agree on stable concepts and binding categories.

The quick answer to this crisis of the representational (or 'realist') paradigm was what is known as constructivism. Constructivism comes in many forms, but in the humanities (and film studies) it was often radical versions of cultural constructivism that prevailed, arguing that perception of reality is determined by the language and symbolic systems in use, to the point that 'language speaks us, rather than we speak the language' (the linguistic turn). Not only is meaning something not fixed, and dependent on the inherent properties of the different representational systems, but reality – and even a scientific 'fact' – is something discursively constructed, arrived at through human and social interactions, and marked by the power relations that obtain in a given social situation, or disguising the uneven distribution

[27] Jean-Luc Nancy, *L'Evidence du film: Abbas Kiarostami/The Evidence of Film*, edition bilingue français-anglais (Brussels: Yves Gevaert, 2001).

of power (as 'representation') among classes, genders and races.[28] But as one of the major proponents of social constructivism, Bruno Latour, put it in what he calls his autocritique:

> While we spent years trying to detect the real prejudices hidden behind the appearance of objective statements, do we now have to reveal the real objective and incontrovertible facts hidden behind the *illusion* of prejudices? Entire Ph.D. programs are still running to make sure that good American kids are learning the hard way that facts are made up, that there is no such thing as natural, unmediated, unbiased access to truth, that we are always prisoners of language, that we always speak from a particular standpoint, and so on, while dangerous extremists are using the very same argument of social construction to destroy hard-won evidence that could save our lives. Was I wrong to participate in the invention of this field known as science studies? Is it enough to say that we did not really mean what we said? Why does it burn my tongue to say that global warming is a fact whether you like it or not? Why can't I simply say that the argument is closed for good?[29]

It is against the intellectual background of the different status of representation between realism and constructivism that I am testing the possibility that cinema – certain films, which I, perhaps wrongly, treat as both representative and symptomatic – can be usefully understood, precisely, as tests, as trial balloons or experiments rather than as realistic narratives, science fiction fantasies or self-referential allegories. Conversely, the idea of the thought experiment could help recast this very opposition of realism versus constructivism. With film as thought experiment we are on the terrain of social reality, yet it does not depict a single pre-existing social reality (or mindset), but instead admits multiple social realities with their own logics (rules, conventions) to coexist or compete with each other: thinking in terms of another set of cultural values (than my own) would be a thought experiment. It covers the fact that films do not necessarily 'reflect' social reality but construct alternative realities (this is their fiction effect or confirms their hypothetical status as fictions), while nonetheless looking and feeling 'real'. It also allows didactic parables or allegories to be thought experiments, when one concedes that allegories are based on drawing analogies through

---

[28] The literature on the 'politics of representation' is extensive and crosses the disciplines. See Robert Hodge and Gunther Kress, *Language as Ideology* (London: Routledge, 1993); Michael Shapiro, *The Politics of Representation* (Madison: University of Wisconsin Press, 1988); Michael Ryan and Douglas Kellner, *Camera Politica: The Politics and Ideology of Contemporary Hollywood Film* (Bloomington: University of Indiana Press, 1988).

[29] Bruno Latour, 'Why Has Critique Run out of Steam? From Matters of Fact to Matters of Concern', *Critical Inquiry* 30 (Winter 2004): 225–48 (227).

which an abstract process, usually at another scale, can be embodied. Even paranoia films or conspiracy theories are thought experiments (where it is a mind presumed to be 'outside' or 'alien' that sets the conditionals, while using the 'real world' selectively, that is, didactically, as evidence).

Film as thought experiment is thus a provisional proposition, insofar as such tests and experiments presuppose certain premises, posit 'What if' scenarios, or involve procedures based on rules. This puts the thought experiment squarely between the realist-representational paradigm and the constructivist-representational paradigm, between real-world situations and abstract or hypothetical 'models'. Thought experiments declare themselves, on the one hand, as constructs and on the other, their goal is to interact, affect and impact on a certain reality. They also accommodate fictional scenarios, and they are obligated to speculate: *speculation* being a term now loaded with contradictory and morally ambivalent connotations, given its association with financial transactions, its proximity to games and gambling, but also its use in a new tendency in philosophy, namely *speculative realism*. In other words, the *proposition to consider film as thought experiment is itself a thought experiment*: about both the nature of cinema, and about our capitalist societies, or as in the case of Europe, about political projects for whose constitutive ungroundedness the thought experiment serves as the unacknowledged ontological support. The Enlightenment project, and thus Western democracy, is the very embodiment of the thought experiment we call 'modernity'.

Film as thought experiment, strictly speaking, is neither a descriptive label nor does it have a prescriptive agenda. The term's indeterminacy and fuzziness tries to install a certain tentativeness and to signal cautious scepticism at the heart of 'what is (European) cinema (today)'. On the other hand, key to the thought experiment is the hypothetical tense and the gesture of 'What if' – both stances that apply to many of the ways we now approach reality itself. 'Let's assume that . . .' has become almost a default modus operandi, thanks to the computerized technologies of statistics, probability calculus and the extraordinary advances made in mathematically modelling the physical world in real time. They allow for data-mining, pattern-recognition and risk-assessment – practices that have turned out to be not only enormously profitable to companies owning these technologies (like Google) or that have access to big data to be mined (Facebook, Amazon, Netflix), but also form habits of mind and foster tacit assumptions that are seeping into what we understand by research and interpretation even in the humanities. They are transforming our notions of what is 'history': data to be extracted or extrapolated from the past and projected along a linear trajectory into a future we thereby hope to *pre-empt* of accident and risk, which is to say, we project a future we inadvertently try to *empty* of possibility, of contingency, of chance and radical change.

But thought experiments in mathematical modelling also affect how we conduct 'hermeneutics'. For instance, 'distant reading' (Franco Moretti) is challenging close or deconstructive reading,[30] while thinkers like Deleuze or Kittler are dead set against 'interpretation', so that strong currents in both philosophy and the humanities in general are contesting the mainstay of film classes since they entered the academy in the 1970s, definitively cutting the umbilical cord that had tied film studies to literary studies.

Film as thought experiment in this sense situates itself between (but also engages with) digital humanities at one end of the spectrum and at the other end the increasing use of imaging techniques and data-visualization as deployed in the areas of science, medicine, the military, security and surveillance, not to mention data mining for tracking stock market fluctuations, weather predictions or making purchase recommendations. Film as thought experiment also provokes the historical question I have already hinted at (and have discussed elsewhere),[31] namely whether cinema has helped or hindered such developments, whether it is (from the perspective of interactivity, instantaneity and ubiquity) an evolutionary dead end, which survives as an emergency break (standing for engagement and empathy, rather than interaction; relying on absence as presence rather than instantaneity; and insisting on the irreversibility of time's arrow in the film experience, rather than the rewind and the replay). Or on the contrary, has cinema acted as the accelerator, having been an agent of modelling the world in its own image – given that the reverse side of cinema's equal opportunity indifference would be its role of relentlessly idealizing and aestheticizing the world? As Farocki – to whose work I would readily apply the term 'thought experiment' – once put it, 'reality is no longer the measure of the always imperfect image; instead, the virtual image increasingly becomes the measure of an always-imperfect actuality'.[32]

The always imperfect actuality: *Melancholia* and *The White Ribbon* as thought experiments

To return to the question posed earlier, namely, whether film as thought experiment applies to the film itself, its relations to the viewer, its author's persona, or instead must encompass all of these relations, I want to offer three specific cases, in one instance anticipating points made in greater detail in one of the chapters devoted to individual films, and in the other instances mentioning films and directors not discussed in separate chapters. The filmmaker whose work has undoubtedly inspired me most in thinking about

[30] Franco Moretti, *Distant Reading* (London: Verso, 2013).

[31] Thomas Elsaesser, 'Media Archaeology as Symptom', *New Review of Film and Television Studies* 14, no. 2 (2016): 181–215.

[32] As cited by Anselm Franke, 'A Critique of Animation', *e-flux* 59 (November 2014), http://www.e-flux.com/journal/59/61098/a-critique-of-animation/ (accessed 10 October, 2016).

film as thought experiment is the Danish director and *enfant terrible* of European cinema, Lars von Trier, whose 2011 film *Melancholia* is discussed in the chapter titled 'Black Suns and a Bright Planet'. There I make it a test case for a thought experiment around two related issues. First, von Trier aligns a typically European 'sense of an ending' – about the (un)sustainability of a certain way of life, and by extension, of a certain economic system – with epochal shifts also in cinema's self-understanding as a realist medium, now 'in collision' with the cold and lunar images of digital cinema. In a second move, *Melancholia* plays out this 'end of our world' crisis – however we specify it – across a paradoxical sense of hope (the final image of two women and a child bravely facing the inevitable and the inconceivable), as well as on the meta-cinematic level, proposing this altered status of European cinema as thought experiment, after realism (the window) and auto-reflexivity (the mirror), by referencing precisely the universe's (the planet's) indifference in order to remind us of cinema's indifference, from which derives an ethical demand vis-à-vis the other.

Melancholia's narrative premise – that the earth is being destroyed by a collision with a hostile planet – only makes sense as a hypothetical case. It poses the problem of the 'What if' in such an extreme manner, that it thereby directly challenges the idea of cinema as a mode of representation, because it purports to represent the very epitome of the unrepresentable: the extinction of the planet itself and thus of any possible subject that could witness or observe it. To paraphrase Jean-François Lyotard's remark about what until now has counted as the epitome of the unrepresentable, the Holocaust, *Melancholia*, too, assumes the destruction of the very instruments able to record it. Putting it in these terms raises the stakes, and asks us to consider what 'limits of representation' von Trier's film invokes, or whether it sets out to deploy the means of digital cinema: now understood as post-cinema, as non-cinema, or as cinema 'probing the limits of representation' and of visualization – digital cinema as the hope to represent the unrepresentable.

Consequently, when understood as thought experiments, many of von Trier's films rely on situations that at first sight seem improbable or arbitrary, but are set up in order to examine the consequences of taking extreme positions, without deviation, compromise or hesitation (this is notably the case in *Breaking the Waves* (1996), *Dancer in the Dark* (2000) and *Dogville* (2003)). Insofar as these are versions of 'What if' scenarios, they are in line with (and a response to) the typical feature of contemporary social life that I have already hinted at, namely the *general tendency towards testing*: we have become used to running tests and simulations in order to determine possible outcomes on every conceivable topic, be it in matters of health or finance, of policy calculations or insurance risks, of weaponry or consumer products. What is special and perhaps unique about von Trier is that he takes moral dilemmas and intractable personal relations, such as gender asymmetry or couple relations, but also concepts such as liberty, the social contract, equality, justice, trust or key social roles such as motherhood, and puts them to the test, by running them through his lab procedures, in order to observe the outcome.

A director whose films are also strongly crafted around moral dilemmas is Michael Haneke, whose style combines elements of didactic parables (reminiscent of Brecht's plays, only more cruel and visceral, e.g. *Benny's Video* (1992) and *Funny Games* (2007)) with psychological realism (reminiscent of Ingmar Bergman's 'middle period' – *The White Ribbon* (2009), for instance, alludes both directly and indirectly to *Winter Light* (1963)). I have already discussed his films' pivotal role in reshaping European cinema in a contribution to a collection of essays on Haneke, and in *Film Theory: An Introduction Through the Senses* Malte Hagener and I align his work specifically with the 'mind-game film', claiming that one finds in Haneke referential images that are neither 'framed' by point-of-view structures nor 'sutured' by shot-reverse-shot editing:

> Such images bypass and exceed both the modernist paradigm of self-reference and reflexivity and the 'constructivist' paradigm of post-modernity. One could ascribe to them a . . . ['spectral' presence], in the sense that the cinema itself has a mind 'outside' or in excess of the narration or the characters, the auteur or the spectator, that eludes any fixed positionality (as in the unclaimed authorship of the video tapes in Haneke's *Caché*). Mind-game films implicate the spectator in ways that can no longer be accounted for by classical theories of allegiance and alignment, or empathy and identification, because the default value or degree zero of normal human interaction and interpersonal perception are no longer in operation. In this way, any inner framing (film-within-a-film, mental disturbance) or outer perspectivism (auteurist reflexivity, Brechtian distanciation, Russian formalist estrangement) is lacking, or can be overturned and revised, leaving the spectator in a state of irreducible uncertainty and ambiguity, as in David Lynch's *Lost Highway* (US/FR 1997), *Mulholland Drive* (US/FR 2001) or *Inland Empire* (FR/PL/US 2006) and in many of the films of David Fincher.[33]

I am quoting this passage because it forms the initial entry point to an essay by James Pearson about Haneke's *The White Ribbon* as 'Thought Experiment'.[34] Pearson starts by arguing that while the film poses enigmas and leaves many of them unanswered, it is in many ways still very classical, that is, a linear,

---

[33] Elsaesser and Hagener, *Film Theory*, 176.

[34] James Pearson, 'Interpreting Disturbed Minds: Donald Davidson and *The White Ribbon*', *Film-Philosophy* 16, no. 1 (2012): 1–15.

'chronological narrative [that] exhibits none of the twists or self-corrections' and is thus 'essentially a realist film whose story happens within our own world'. And yet, by using the philosopher Donald Davidson's theory of other minds, one can 'gain traction upon the sense in which *The White Ribbon* has a 'mind "outside" or in excess of (the narration or the characters)'.[35] Davidson's thought experiment concerns the choice that an outside observer has about the meaning of words uttered by a group of foreign language users. When these users reference words in unexpected ways, or behave in a manner that gives the lie to their words, the choice is to either revise what the observer previously surmised was the meaning, or assume that the mistake is with the language users. Davidson's point is that what he calls 'charity' demands that the observer, if truly interested in understanding the Other, is willing to revise her initial interpretation, rather than seek the mistake with the Other. The reason that Pearson thinks this helpful to understanding *The White Ribbon* is because the enigmatic behaviour of the village community requires not only this charity from the spectator, but to entertain both hypotheses:

> In Davidson's view, it is only in the process of interpreting others that we are able to make sense of ourselves as subject to the central normative standard of epistemology: objective truth. It is only through grasping that someone else might be mistaken about the world . . . that we acquire the objective/subjective contrast that is recorded by our concepts of 'truth' and 'belief'.[36]

The advantage of the thought experiment is that, according to Davidson, the content of other minds, their reference, truth and meaning, can be established by observing the behaviour and beliefs of a community (of language users), rather than as Descartes did, by starting with his own mind and then surmising about the mind of others (and thus doubting the possibility of knowing other minds). What Pearson suggests, by applying Davidson's thought experiment to *The White Ribbon*, is that because throughout the film, Haneke makes us surmise and then revise our view especially of the adults' behaviour, we gradually construe a 'mind' external to the individual characters, but belonging to the community as a whole, economically and socially interdependent as they are and existing in a kind of antagonistic mutuality, or what I called, following Kant, 'unsocial sociability', here based on suspicion, distrust, hearsay and betrayal, that is, the negative cement of a functioning community. As Pearson sums up his essay:

> To form anything worth calling a community, individuals must choose to engage in relationships with each other. But Eichwald's [the fictional name

[35] Pearson, 'Interpreting Disturbed Minds', 1
[36] Pearson, 'Interpreting Disturbed Minds', 4

> of the village] oppressive, authoritarian structure deprives its members of any choice. The villagers who have chosen . . . to be deprived of choice have reneged their own agency. The 'mind' of the film is disturbed because its very identity – the communal mind of a non-community – is paradoxical. This disturbance is made manifest by the minds which arise in the village . . . They serve as a locus for our interpretative effort, a puzzling product of the film's 'mind' that demands we carefully revise our first attempts at interpretation.[37]

One may dissent from this particular interpretation (and Pearson explicitly allows for this) and still find the conceptual framework of the thought experiment illuminating, as a way of explaining the process by which the spectator comes to make the transition from the individual psychology of the protagonists to inferring the 'mind' of the community. It nonetheless leaves open what exactly the film as thought experiment is trying to test: how the villagers' mindset (according to some, proto-Fascist; to others, murderous violence fed by authoritarianism, resentment, exclusion and rebellion) metastizes and becomes viral when 'baron', 'pastor', 'doctor' and 'teacher' (and the powers they stand for in a given society) are locked into antagonistic interdependency.

From the perspective of film-philosophy, however, I would argue that *The White Ribbon* confronts us with another paradox: the unresolved enigma of who is finally responsible and where to locate agency. The misdeeds and disasters that visit the village community also teach the spectator a meta-cinematic lesson, namely that despite the intense indexicality suggested by the film's searing black-and-white photography, there is no ontological ground on which the referentiality of these images can rest. The suspended narration, the floating points of view, the frequent pronouncements of doubt and indeterminacy (the very first words spoken into the black screen are, 'I am not sure whether the story I want to tell you is entirely true') all warn the spectator to trust neither the words nor the images. It is a message deliberately at odds with Haneke's intensely visceral and tactile *mise en scène*, lingering on physical details, concentrating on close-ups of faces and gestures, creating breathtaking compositions while giving added attention to a soundscape that dispenses with music, but where every creaking floorboard but also every silence registers as the sensory presence of menace. In other words, the thought experiment may not (only) be political, but epistemological and ontological, insofar as 'to see' here taunts and derides the desire 'to know', but neither can our other senses or bodily responses serve as reliable guides to what is the case and what exists. *The White Ribbon* as thought experiment demonstrates that in the cinema we have no choice but to trust our

[37] Pearson, 'Interpreting Disturbed Minds', 12

perceptions and sensations and yet we also must distrust our perceptions and sensations: this paradox (which could be read as the paradox of the digital image) makes the film a mind-game film as well as a thought experiment, and therefore of special interest to film philosophy.

The Dardenne Brothers

My third example of a body of work best understood as a series of thought experiments are the films of the Belgian director-duo Jean-Pierre and Luc Dardenne, better known as the Dardenne Brothers. I shall return to them in a subsequent chapter, when discussing how their films are based on moral dilemmas treated as thought experiments, but also how they address and position the audience at once close and distant, 'with' the characters and separated from them by what Luc Dardenne calls 'the secret'.[38] The secret is the gap of 'unknownness' (to use a term of Stanley Cavell) that opens up between the characters, their motives and us as spectators: a gap that the directors themselves also want to respect vis-à-vis their characters. Such unknownness leaves the spectator – comparable to Haneke's cinema, but achieved by different filmic means – in an ungroundedness that aims at insinuating a more general epistemological doubt (about other minds) than merely about the motives of (fictional) characters.

The Dardenne Brothers' credentials as practitioners of the thought experiment rest on their films creating – also not unlike Haneke and yet with very different kinds of stories – situations that are clearly devised by the director-as-God (who, regarding humanity, is of course the ultimate thought experimenter). Once set up, the implications and consequences of these 'What if' situations unfold for the protagonists with a relentless (and in the course of the narrative ever more evident) inevitability. They prove that, as thought experiments, they probe the limits of individual agency, solidarity and what it means to be a member of a community in today's Europe. To take the example of *Two Days, One Night* (2014), Sandra, recovering from a nervous breakdown, is about to lose her job at a small solar panel factory. Because of European labour laws, her colleagues have to agree first before she can be fired, but the boss has already offered the other employees a cash bonus. Desperate, Sandra is persuaded by her husband to personally visit each of her co-workers over the weekend before the decision is taken, begging them to forgo the bonus and allow her to keep her job.

Even if the film were to be based on an actual case, the emotional power of *Two Days, One Night* does not so much derive from its documentary realism. Its inner logic and narrative construction is such that it sets up the

---

[38] Luc Dardenne, *Au dos de nos images, 1991–2005* (Paris: Editions du Seuil, 2008), 130–1.

perfect conditions for testing the nature of solidarity in today's post-Fordist workplace, where job security is increasingly precarious, where trade unions are either weak or non-existent, and where the most vulnerable members of the workforce are the first to be pushed out when, as in this case, globalization, 'free trade' and the competition from China threatens the survival of an enterprise. Each of the co-workers has a different reason for clinging to the bonus, so that Sandra's plea, going door to door, doubles as a social experiment or research exercise conducted in order find out about citizenship, community values and solidarity.

The Dardenne Brothers' films have been the subject of innumerable essays, articles and books: their stories, taken from everyday life, but shaped as parables with ambiguous endings and an enigmatic moral, have invited intense hermeneutic activity among film scholars, especially those interested in film and philosophy. Consequently, the contours of a certain consensus-in-dissent, or agreement-in-disagreement, can be made out regarding the uniqueness and idiosyncrasy of their filmmaking, with interventions, among others, by Sarah Cooper, David Walsh, Lauren Berlant, Robert Pippin, Joseph Mai and Daniel Frampton. Richard Rushton, putting forward his own counter-proposal, conveniently summarizes the debate so far around the Dardenne opus:

> *Daniel Frampton* claims that the films of the Dardenne brothers 'almost entirely reject some key conventions of fiction filmmaking . . . in favour of a close and empathic form' . . . [This empathic relationship] is created for the most part by the camera placing us very close to the characters . . . *Joseph Mai* claims [that] we are drawn into a bodily relationship with the characters in the films: 'vision is not an independent entity, but is reseated in the body, or rather in two bodies [i.e. camera and protagonist], involved in a dancelike movement through other bodies'. Mai thus claims that the Dardennes offer a vision that is not merely optical but also, or predominantly, bodily and 'haptic'.

Extrapolating from these and other views, Rushton concentrates on what, borrowing from Stanley Cavell, he calls 'empathetic projection': 'essentially the imaginative act of putting yourself in someone else's shoes: that is, not *being* in someone else's shoes, but imagining what it *might be like*; to try to think what another person is thinking, to feel what another is feeling. These issues are central to the Dardennes' stylistic concerns.'[39] For Rushton, one of the points of empathetic projection is that it situates the Dardennes' work between realism and modernism, neither engaging us in the kind of illusionism of classically realist cinema, nor distancing us in the manner of modernist estrangement or auto-reflexivity. As Rushton puts it:

---

[39] Richard Rushton, 'Empathic projection in the films of the Dardenne brothers', *Screen* 55, no. 3 (Autumn 2014): 306.

> At the level of narrative, realism gives us something that seems realistic – the handheld camera, its shakiness that appears to place us 'on the scene of reality', the chronicling of the details of everyday life and the struggle to stay alive – while the generic elements also make the narrative mannered, as though we were being exposed to morality tales or fables rather than to realist narratives.[40]

What intervenes is the medium itself, which in the case of the Dardennes is the very palpable presence of the (hand-held) camera, assuming the role of an additional character, but one that is neither fully 'on the side' of the protagonist, nor a mere bystander or an antagonist. However, the same definition of empathetic projection could also be used to make the case for the films as thought experiments, notably the notion that such empathy teaches us 'what it might be like' to be in this situation, without ever giving us the sort of privileged access to a character's inner states that we would expect from an identification with the character, or outright sympathy.

In the case of the Dardennes, therefore, it is possible to redefine not only empathetic projection but also sympathy and identification in terms of a thought experiment: empathic projection would be supported by an imaginary scenario that addresses hypothetical 'What if' situations. Their quality of 'morality tales or fables' would be due to us being able to imagine what we see as conceivable, and thus as possible, even if we clearly realize that the situation is a 'set up', that is, constructed to elicit questions, or make plausible the protagonist's different options, each one with particular implications and consequences. This hovering – between hesitancy and holding back – so typical of their *mise en scène* would thus also connote the hypothetical status of the situations, allowing us to construe them as test cases of more general principles, often involving either acts of solidarity (or lack of them) or moral choices (or enigmatic refusals to make such choices).

The negative example that may yet prove my argument is *Rosetta* (1999), a film that raises the issue of the boundary between thought experiments and social reality: how are the consequences of a thought experiment carried over into social reality? For *Rosetta* gave rise to the Plan Rosetta, a law adopted by the Belgian legislature to help just-out-of-school teenagers find their first employment, which suggests that a film can cross the boundary and produce real social consequences. Whether these consequences are implicit in the film, if considered as a thought experiment, or whether they are more or less arbitrarily (or opportunistically) extrapolated from it, is a moot point. In another chapter I shall try to show that its apparent success

[40] Rushton, 'Empathic projection in the films of the Dardenne brothers', 310. Rushton goes on: 'Because we very rarely get to see characters face-on . . . our access to them – to their "insides" – is very deliberately blocked. In general terms this is a feature of the combination of realism and modernism: realism gives us detail, while modernism delivers a certain abstraction.'

as activist propaganda may actually rest on a misreading of the film's status (and the function of the protagonist as a moral agent), but even if it were a case of a 'productive misreading', it would still make *Rosetta* a thought experiment: this time about the withholding of sympathy as a turn from ethics to politics.

Conclusion

What I am suggesting is that not only are von Trier's films 'end of the world' narratives, but that Haneke and the Dardennes, too, are setting up their films as thought experiments, that is, as 'What if' situations, because they either assume that the (human, moral) catastrophe has already happened, or that we have arrived at a certain deadlock, so that there is no other position than an impossible, paradoxical or perverse vantage point from which to examine what is left of human agency and humanity, of cooperation and community, of dissidence and resistance, of solidarity and social justice.

They implicitly ask, what if we have reached not the end of history, but instead the end of the future, looping us into a perpetual replay of the past, in the hope of thereby bootstrapping us into a future? Or to put it yet another way, returning to the meta-cinematic level of redefining what is cinema, film as thought experiment knows about the 'death of cinema', it even takes the death of cinema as its starting hypothesis, so as to play through the consequences and thereby discover the conditions of breaking open the loop that keeps the cinema going as if nothing had changed, when in fact everything has changed. When all utopias have failed, and dystopias merely confirm what we already know, then maybe film as thought experiment discovers in the present deadlocks and impasses not simply data to be extracted and aggregated, but narratives that imagine the inconceivable as something conceivable, and thus as possible, leaving in suspense but also open whether anything can be realizable in practice.

To summarize, the idea of film as thought experiment is meant to raise quite diverse issues, not all of which it can as yet answer satisfactorily. First of all, it has arisen, in the film-philosophy debate, as a possible candidate to bridge the gap between the bold hypothesis ('film as thought') and the moderate hypothesis ('film as instantiation of a philosophical problem'). Within the field of film theory, it might be said to take 'apparatus theory' into Deleuzian territory ('cinema as mind and brain'). More specifically, I wanted to argue that a) it forms the European pendant to the Hollywood mind-game film; b) it confronts, even if it does not resolve, the three crises of representation, evidence and history; c) it tries to resolve the realist/modernist, identification/distanciation divide in its mode of address; and d) it accounts for the allegorical-didactic tendency in the films of von Trier, Haneke and others, while e) instantiating the ungroundedness (or indifference) of cinema in the digital age without making the digital itself the issue.

As an additional feature, in relation to the European Union as a political experiment, some of the films deemed to be thought experiments can be seen as helping to 'reboot' the European political project, by pushing its core values of liberty, fraternity and equality to their limits where they reveal their mutual incompatibilities. This, then, is the situation that makes 'Europe – a Thought Experiment'.

4

'Europe'

A Thought Experiment

The real must be fictionalized in order to be thought.

JACQUES RANCIÈRE

Political Europe as a philosophical issue

In the introductory chapter I argued that, viewed from a certain perspective, European politics and European cinema can be understood as the recto and verso of each other, on condition of 'enlarging the problem'. That is, by opening up a wider horizon: this would include both internal and external factors, such as the purportedly diminished sovereignty of the nation state, alongside continental philosophy's radical scepticism regarding Europe's value foundations, a vastly diversified and expanded mediascape alongside the much-debated 'death of cinema' generally, and – since the 1990s – the changing power relations of Europe within the globalized world, in addition to a surge of filmmaking talent especially in China, South Korea, the Philippines and Thailand.

These globalized power relations, for instance, have marginalized Europe politically vis-à-vis both Asia and Latin America (for instance, when seen from the United States' security concerns and self-interests), while redefining it (for the Middle East and North Africa's poor, persecuted and destitute) as a refuge from oppression, war and poverty, and (for Asia's aspiring middle classes) as a quaint old-world tourist destination. Such potentially colliding versions of Europe and the European Union 'from the outside' are not entirely at odds with Europe's own self-image (as seizing the moral high ground while digging away at its Enlightenment foundations). Yet any 'heroic' vision of itself is somewhat tarnished by the persistent gap between

North and South, as well as increasingly tense exchanges between West and East, following the EU's extension towards formerly Soviet-controlled countries in Central and Eastern Europe. As a result, the decentring of Europe within the contemporary world *politically* is asymmetrical in relation to both its self-ascribed *ethical* mandate and its *economic* importance, as one of the world's largest trading blocs, including its *financial* importance, thanks to the single currency, the Euro: troubled, but still traded as one of the world's two or three reserve currencies. Due to the social safety net, and more evenly spread prosperity (in neoliberal terms: thanks to Germany's industrial might, as a leading exporter of high-value goods, and to London and Frankfurt serving as the banking hubs providing financial services to the world), Europe remains the poster child for a capitalism with a social democratic face: avoiding the 'race to the bottom' of all-out laissez-faire economics, by trying to strike a balance between the growth-and-production model (mostly viewed as unsustainable and obsolete) and an ecologically sustainable economy-and-energy policy.

However, it is the asymmetries and internal contradictions that might explain why export successes in machine tools, motor cars, design, fashion and software have not been matched in the sphere of culture. There, Europe presents itself in many fields with much diminished cultural power and prestige, nowhere more clearly than in the loss of status suffered by its respective media entertainment productions. With very few exceptions, the nations of Europe do not have global media companies producing television programmes the world wants to see,[1] yet – on a smaller scale – the decline is also evident in the area of art-and-auteur cinema, where France, Italy, Sweden, Germany and Poland with their respective 'new waves' were once leading by example and excellence, certainly from the late 1940s to the mid-1970s. No longer competing with Hollywood on either economic and technological terrain or by virtue of aesthetic and formal innovations, European cinema is visible only on the festival circuit and its affiliated exhibition sites, where it competes with other national or transnational cinemas within the broader category of (non-Hollywood, non-commercial) world cinema – a category where Asian and Latin American countries are now leading.[2]

In the present chapter, I want to examine this paradoxically precarious state of Europe, but now as also an issue of political philosophy, in order to draw out the possible parallels between its politics and its cinema – preferably under the aspect of the 'thought experiment', as defined in the previous

[1] The possible exception are the Netherlands, Norway and – if counted as part of Europe – Israel.

[2] See Thomas Elsaesser, 'European Cinema as World Cinema: A New Beginning?', in *European Cinema Face to Face with Hollywood* (Amsterdam: Amsterdam University Press, 2005), 485–513.

chapter. I start by specifying some of the most common *political* dilemmas facing contemporary Europe, often articulated across a threefold lack, absence or 'deficit': the democracy deficit, the multicultural diversity deficit and the social justice deficit.

The *democracy deficit* is felt with regard to the relation between the citizens of the individual nation states and their own government, and by extension, widespread dissatisfaction and deep disaffection with the centralized bureaucracy mostly referred to as 'Brussels', which appears to decide on the larger questions without transparency or accountability, while interfering in the minutiae of daily life, usually above the heads of those directly affected. Second, the *multicultural diversity deficit* refers to the unsolved problem of Europe becoming a continent of immigrants and population mobility, both East to West and South to North, with migrants, refugees and mobile labour turning the nineteenth century European nation states into multicultural, multi-denominational and multi-ethnic communities which have not yet found a modus of how to live together (for the guests to 'assimilate' and for the hosts to 'tolerate', in the cliché vocabulary of everyday politics). Finally, there is the *social justice deficit*, that is, the growing gap in wealth but also in job opportunities, environmental protection and lifestyle between Northern Europe and parts of the South, but also between classes, and between generations within individual national entities – and this despite the welfare provisions, health insurance and free education for almost everyone within the European Union.

While these are often-voiced complaints, discussed by journalists and academics as deficits to be remedied (and providing the talking points among political parties, across the left all the way to the radical right), I want to reverse the perspective and make the wholly counter-intuitive suggestion that these *deficits*, once looked at in an enlarged context and across a different timescale, could actually be seen as *assets*: as indices and symptoms of a much more positive scenario for Europe and, maybe even more importantly, for the practice and future of democracy worldwide. In order to make such a case, the 'deficits' and what they stand for need to be re-evaluated also against the foil of what have become of the three signature virtues of the Enlightenment: liberty, fraternity, equality.

By probing the status and legacy of these ideals across three tropes that have played an important part in contemporary philosophical discourse, I intend to use them as my exploratory/experimental lens. These tropes are 'the empty centre of sovereignty' (lack of accountability and crisis of authority), 'stranger/neighbour/other' (multicultural diversity/xenophobia), and 'equality is only possible in death' (equality before the law and the limits of social justice). In subsequent chapters, they will allow me to focus on certain European films, analysed not as reflections of these deficits, documentary depictions of current ills, or activist alternatives, but considered as part of a cinema of thought experiments, combining real-world reference with 'as if' scenarios, often in order to explore and expose intractable ethical dilemmas. My experiment is to hypothesize that certain films – usually implicitly and obliquely – ask 'What if we imagine a scenario that enacts one or several of these core values of democracy, by putting them to the test in contemporary Europe?'[3] For my specific concerns – to identify certain European films as thought experiments, so as to enable them to enter into a dialogue with contemporary European political thinkers – these films (an easily expandable corpus of possible examples) hopefully serve my purpose well enough.

The 'experimental' perspective is therefore not formal, but political, requiring me to pay attention to the current debates among philosophers regarding the very definition of 'the political', and how it differs from day-to-day 'politics'. These debates are not about parties and policies, but involve the general state of (Western) democracy, and thus go beyond Europe: can liberal democracy still be considered a viable form of government, now that global capital (and sizable numbers in Italy, France, the Netherlands, Hungary and Poland, not to mention Russia, Turkey and the United States) prefers autocratic rule? Have national parliaments been fatally weakened less by supra-national technocracies and more by globalized finance capitalism represented by armies of lobbyists? Or does globalization merely bring out their inherent flaws and the inconsistencies of bourgeois liberalism?

How do the prescriptions for the social contract, say, respectively by Thomas Hobbes, John Locke and Jean-Jacques Rousseau, look from our present-day position? At stake is not only the desirability of a social contract, that is, a state, a constitution, supra-national organizations, but also these classic philosophers' underlying assumptions about human nature, as either inherently bad, so that good government means protecting citizens from themselves and each other, or are humans essentially good, and good government means helping them to perfect themselves, both morally and materially? Do contemporary philosophers even have a view on these once so momentous questions, or are they implicitly assuming a post-human condition, where 'human nature' no longer exists, at least not as a philosophical problem?

As to the question of whether contemporary philosophy still finds a relevant place for the three goals of the French Revolution – liberty, fraternity, equality – one could, for instance, ask, what are current views on *liberty*, in the wake of John Stuart Mill, and after Friedrich Hayek's *The Road to Serfdom*? Does John Rawls still have the last word in the discussion on social

[3] As a study of European cinema, this is clearly taking an arbitrary perspective, and the directors I have chosen for my case studies (among them, some very well-known names) are 'representative' only insofar as they are exceptional: most scholars of European cinema would neither count them as typical, nor – given their familiarity – as adding to our knowledge of the breadth and depth of filmmaking in Europe today.

justice and *equality*, and how has Charles Taylor redefined *individualism*, so as to bind individuals into the community, the nation or humanity as a whole? What crucial contribution has Richard Rorty made to our thinking about *fraternity*, that is, the priority he gives to consensus with others, or is it rather to Jürgen Habermas, with his notions of the public sphere and of communicative rationality, one would turn for a reinterpretation of fraternity for the present age?

These thinkers can be said to broadly continue the traditions of the Enlightenment, and remain, as pragmatists, within the liberal consensus (in North America) and social democratic politics (within Europe), defending the role of government for bettering human lives, and defending the welfare state as both a right and a necessity. Insofar as the democracy deficit is for these thinkers also an issue, they imagine democratic renewal to emerge from a more active and direct involvement of citizens, a revival of communitarian ideals and a strengthening of civil society, to counteract bureaucratic rigidities and the tendencies towards technocratic decision-making in the management of such highly complex forms of governance as the European Union or the United States.

Given my agenda of rethinking European cinema for the twenty-first century as a series of thought experiments, I have, however, chosen to concentrate on a different set of philosophers – the so-called continental philosophers – several of whom, as it happens, include the cinema in their political thinking. This is the case with Deleuze, Badiou, Nancy, Rancière, Agamben and Žižek, though not Levinas.[4] Just as importantly, however, these philosophers, often but not always within a Marxist tradition, are engaged in rethinking democracy from a more radical standpoint, with an urgency of imminent crisis, as well as the conviction that a more fundamental reorientation is needed of what we understand by politics, sovereignty, citizenship, community and social justice. Their willingness to challenge the very foundations of democracy is indicative of a radicalism that does not necessarily propose concrete political alternatives, but thinks through the consequences of the present conditions: in my view, they too conduct thought experiments on the body politic of contemporary Europe, against the background of globalization and neoliberal capitalism. Their thought experiments are about the self-governance of individuals beyond the usual bonds of belonging, by reinventing new modes of sharing, giving and distributing (Rancière), of the face-to-face (Levinas), of being-with (Nancy),

[4] There have, however, been important studies of contemporary European cinema explicitly referring themselves to Levinas' ethics and philosophy. The most notable are Sarah Cooper's *Selfless Cinema? Ethics and French Documentary* (Oxford: Legenda, 2006), and a special issue edited by Sarah Cooper, 'The Occluded Relation: Levinas and Cinema', *Film-Philosophy* 11, no. 2 (August 2007), http://www.film-philosophy.com (accessed 4 September 2017).

sometimes expressed as the idea of 'commons' (Žižek); it means extending but also challenging the discourse of human rights (Agamben) and countering but also recasting the idea(ls) of communism (Badiou). My hope is that from their thought experiments something can in turn be learnt about European films as thought experiments, so that what Žižek names 'the absent centre of political ontology' becomes indeed the recto to the verso of what in previous chapters I have called the indifference (that is, the absent centre) of 'film ontology'. Žižek refers to Heidegger's key distinction between ontic and ontological, and 'not to confuse ontological horizon with ontic choices'.[5] If the ontic is about 'what is' in the here and now, the ontological tells us how it is possible that what is can be. Thus, when applied to politics, there isn't – and never will be – an actual community (ontic) that embodies or expresses the 'truth' (ontological) of democracy. In this sense, the political project of the Enlightenment will have to stay a thought experiment (how it is possible), with an empty centre, lest it be betrayed by its concrete instantiations, whether these are communism, fascism or liberal democracy. Put differently, the truth of the ideals of the French Revolution – liberty, equality, fraternity – is that they are mutually incompatible, and thus preserve their ontological horizon.

Three Colours: Blue, White, Red

Before elaborating on these philosophical positions in more detail, I want to turn to a film, or rather, a trilogy of films that – in the early 1990s – explicitly set out to thematize the crisis of equality, liberty and fraternity in post-wall Europe: Krzysztof Kieslowski's *Three Colours*, where *Blue* (1993, standing for Liberty), *White* (1994, Equality) and *Red* (1994, Fraternity) take their titles from the colours of the flag of the French Republic. Each film – involving a woman and a man and their fraught relationship – explores these republican ideals in what at first seem uniquely personal, intimate, indeed a-political situations. In *Blue*, Julie, a Parisienne (played by Juliette Binoche) survives a car accident that kills her celebrated composer husband and her only daughter. After an attempted suicide, she decides to leave behind almost everything that reminds her of her previous life, and shuts herself off in an apartment. Liberated from ties and obligations, she comes to realize how precarious, if not illusory, such freedom is, not least because her past turns out to be full of unfinished business. Olivier, a colleague and disciple of her late husband, is determined to complete the composition the composer was commissioned to produce for a celebration of European unity. He tracks her down and ardently woos her, while she learns of an

[5] Slavoj Žižek, *The Ticklish Subject: The Empty Centre of Political Ontology* (London: Verso, 1999), 14.

affair that her late husband had with Sandrine, a woman who is expecting his child. Shocked at first by this betrayal, she eventually helps Sandrine to inherit her husband's house and have his paternity posthumously recognized. She also assists Olivier in completing the score, but he demands that the composition be known as his, and his alone. In the end, she attends the premiere of the concerto, which includes a soprano recitative of passages from Paul's Epistle to the Corinthians. Realizing that true freedom might involve self-sacrifice and self-imposed constraints, as well as commitments to others, she starts to cry, as she did at the beginning, but now her tears are liberating, perhaps freeing her from selfhood.

In *White*, equality is examined in a more explicitly 'European' context, since it concerns Karol Karol, a young Polish hairdresser who follows his newly-wed French wife (played by Julie Delpy) to Paris after the fall of communism, but finds himself not only marginalized and humiliated, but literally impotent. His wife sues for divorce, and Karol – penniless and destitute – manages to smuggle himself back to Poland, where he finds a world he barely recognizes, given that everyone has turned capitalist and entrepreneur, clumsily in pursuit of quick money and a fast lifestyle. By underhand means, like double-crossing his boss, Karol also amasses a fortune, which he uses to hatch a plot in order to get even with his wife, whom he still loves. He wins her back, makes love to her, but then feigns his own death, in order to have his wife convicted of his murder, whereupon he visits her in jail but only looks at her from afar. As she notices him, responding with a reciprocating glance and gesture, Karol starts to cry.

Equality in *White* becomes a complex network of give and take, of injury and revenge, of getting on and getting even, of being alive and playing dead. In short, we witness all manner of transfer and exchange, taking place on a generalized black market of human values, commodities and currencies that no one seems eager to contain or to control. Yet the trade-off of incommensurate entities also knows moments of energizing potential, even creating unexpectedly level playing fields for unevenly matched players, thereby infusing a strange sense of hope and possibility into a story that otherwise accumulates mostly moments of desperate slapstick, nihilism and sick humour. As with *Blue*, tears in *White* stand for a bodily affect that serves as a moment of recognition and personal redemption, but it is left open whether such moments are sharable, and what they might mean for a community to come. On the other hand, the black market of all values (material as well as spiritual) that *White* both celebrates and excoriates is an aspect of radical equality that resonates with the idea of a 'common' for a community aspiring to a different 'ontology'.

Red is set in Geneva and its theme of fraternity unfolds across a story of accidental neighbourliness, brought about by Valentine, a young model, hitting a dog with her car on her way home. She takes in the dog and manages to track down its owner, a disgruntled former judge, living by himself as a recluse and misanthrope, shamelessly eavesdropping on the telephone conversations of his neighbours. Across the dog, whom the Judge wants Valentine to keep, the two form a sort of confiding companionship, where they discuss matters of law and ethics, and whether one's life is determined by accidents or has a predetermined course after all. In a parallel narrative, the camera also follows Antoine, a law student, who crosses Valentine's path several times without her being aware of it. Valentine is at first shocked when she realizes the Judge's intrusive spying, but colludes with it, as she becomes vicariously involved in the life of the Judge's spied-on neighbour, Karin (who happens to be Antoine's girlfriend). While Valentine still hesitates about what to do, the Judge turns himself in to the police, and Valentine decides to take a trip to England, to track down her elusive boyfriend Michael. Antoine, too, is on the boat. The ferry is caught in a violent storm, and as most of the passengers perish, only Valentine, Antoine, Julie and Olivier from *Blue* and Karol and Julie from *White* survive. The Judge watches the report of the accident on television and also starts to cry, while the screen freezes on Valentine's profile from the model shoot we saw at the beginning of the film.

Fraternity is themed in *Red* in several ways, first as contacts between neighbours that are either fraught and intrusive, or consist of indifferent and overlooked contiguity. But it is also a reaching out, by way of different encounters, where recognition, substitution across time and place can bring people into tender yet tenuous contact with each other. The Judge's bitterness, for instance, nurses past betrayal and revenge, putting Valentine in a position where, unbeknownst to herself, she can make good, or make up for, something that happened a long time ago. Time shifting also ties the Judge to Antoine the aspiring lawyer, who becomes the Judge's younger self, so that spying on him and his girlfriend does not merely repeat an earlier constellation, but is almost like a desperate attempt at rewinding his own life, or undoing across another pair of lovers what undid him, when the woman in his life left him for another man. This man he later sentenced for a crime he might not have committed, an act of revenge that the Judge paid for with guilt, cynicism and self-recrimination.

In each of the three films, lives are enfolded into each other, pasts return in the guise of an alternate reality or a parallel present, and chance, accident and contingency underscore the arbitrary turns, the bitter setbacks and the general meaninglessness of life. Yet just as persistently they hint at the possibility of grace, of a divine plan we are just too close to things to apprehend or too engrossed in ourselves to experience. But where, one might ask, is post-wall Europe in this? Even *White* – most explicit in its satire of consumerism and cupidity, and of the mutual disappointment between East Europeans (feeling humiliated and rendered impotent by a triumphalist West) and West Europeans (having fantasized brave dissidents or corrupt apparatchiks, now fearing 'Polish plumbers' who take away jobs and undercut wages) – is finally more about the cruel mysteries of love and humans' perverse ways of making amends, where you have to lose or betray the object of desire, before you can prove your fidelity and restore a form of trust. Recurring motifs, repetitions, mutual interferences and even identical acts, gestures and situations bind the trilogy together and ensure that each previous film reverberates in the subsequent ones, which – when read allegorically – might suggest that Eastern and Western Europe, like these improbable couples in *Blue*, *White* and *Red*, have both much in common and nothing in common, are dependent on each other, but seem to come together more by accident than by design and yet might nonetheless share a common destiny, however little grasp they have of what this destiny entails or reveals.

This would be the – politically rather bleak, but philosophically quite cogent – basis for a different sense of community, which recognizes how each is fated to be the other's Other; what they share is not the social contract of citizens of a single nation-state, nor of being bound by belonging to a faith-based community, a tribe or a family, but rather the next-to-each-other of contiguity, chance and contingency, and the solitude that comes with being human and sharing the knowledge of being mortal.[6]

Yet there is another way of looking at the trilogy, and its views on liberty, equality and fraternity. Discussing Kant's notion of freedom, Žižek points out:

> Freedom is not simply the opposite of deterministic causal necessity: as Kant knew, it means a specific mode of causality; the agent's self-determination. There is in fact a kind of Kantian antinomy of freedom: if an act is fully determined by preceding causes, it is, of course, not free; if, however, it depends on the pure contingency which momentarily severs the full causal chain, it is also not free. The only way to resolve this antinomy is to introduce a second-order reflexive causality: I am determined by causes (be it direct brute natural causes or motivations), and the space of freedom is not a magic gap in this first level causal chain but my ability retroactively to choose/ determine which causes will determine me.[7]

In his book on Kieslowski (and the chapter on the *Three Colours* trilogy), Žižek outlines one way of understanding the moment of retroactive recognition which concludes *Blue*. Insofar as Julie achieves her inner freedom, it is by retroactively choosing to make her own all the contingent

[6] Slavoj Žižek, in *The Fright of Real Tears: Krzysztof Kieslowski between Theory and Post-Theory* (London: British Film Institute, 2001), opts for a more 'Catholic' reading, arguing that Kieslowski intends us to see these characters form a community based on the 'solidarity of sinners'.

[7] Slavoj Žižek, *The Parallax View* (Cambridge, MA: MIT Press, 2006), 203.

accidents that brought her to this state: freedom becomes 'the subjective necessity of objective contingency'.[8]

Yet this would be the 'classical', even 'idealist', reading, which remains at the level of a personal crisis and credo. What strikes me is that in all three films the protagonist goes through a devastating experience of destitution and self-abandon, of traumatic loss and an erasure of everything that had hitherto sustained them. Julie's loss is that of her husband and child, but also of her trust and belief in her marriage. Karol is humiliated by his wife, he loses all his worldly possessions, and with this, his self-respect. Early on, he is literally shat upon, in a drastic illustration of his predicament. In *Red*, it is the Judge who carries the anger of betrayal and the trauma of loss into the story, but Valentine's attachment to Michael makes her equally vulnerable to bitter disappointment. Each, in other words, is forced to stare into an abyss of self-loss, of which accident and chance are the external manifestations. From the perspective of my project, Julie, Karol and the Judge are de facto, even if temporarily, such 'abject subjects' as my case studies will highlight and examine.

It therefore seems possible and even appropriate to consider – retroactively as it were – Kieslowski's *Three Colours* trilogy as also a thought experiment, positing several scenarios of the 'zero-degree' of the symbolic order, and the potential for a radical reboot of the protagonist's subjectivity. In each film, characters experience a kind of symbolic death, which leaves them in a state of abjection. Through external circumstances, which are shown to be accidental rather than providential, they undergo a form of resurrection, or at any rate are left by the film in a suspended state of animation (literally, in *Red*). The fact that Kieslowski associates these very personal stories with the values of the French Revolution can be seen as either an endorsement or a critique of the European Union and the end of communism. Read from an auteurist perspective, critics have commented on Kieslowski's pessimistic view of consumerism and Western-style capitalism, especially in *White*, while Žižek mocks what he regards – in *Blue* – as a naïve endorsement of the European Union, that is, the musical commission of her late husband that Julie helps to complete:

> This ridiculous and flat political background of a unified Europe cannot be dismissed as a superficial compromise, of no importance in comparison to the intimate process of trauma and gradual recuperation of the heroine: the post-political notion of a unified Europe defines the only social co-ordinates within which the 'private' drama of the heroine can take place; it creates and sustains the space of such an 'intimate' experience. One is

[8] Slavoj Žižek, interview in Levi Bryant, Nick Srnicek and Graham Harman (eds), *The Speculative Turn: Continental Materialism and Realism* (Victoria: re.press, 2011), 410. The phrase is from *Nihil Unbound* by Ray Brassier (London: Palgrave Macmillan, 2007).

> thus tempted to claim that the ideal public of *Blue* is the Brussels European Union *nomenklatura* . . . it is the ideal film to satisfy the needs of a Brussels bureaucrat who returns home in the evening after a day full of complex negotiations on tariff regulations.[9]

Yet the meaning of the ending in each film is far from self-evident, since the tears in each case are highly ambiguous, separated as the characters are at that moment from the object of their look by different kinds of screens, hinting at endings that could just as well be either wholly imaginary or a reassuring if also self-deceiving fantasy. In which case, the allegorical reference to Europe and politics would also take a different shape, and the thought experiment of how to 'reboot' post-Cold War Europe remains inconclusive. Not only does it suggest that there is no gradual growing together, or a united Europe one can celebrate; the film insists that the rupture is both absolute and necessary, that not just selfhood and identity, but also the core values of European democracy, have to be, as it were, ungrounded, made empty or voided: confronted with the harshest of contingencies, before a different kind of belief or contract can emerge to sustain them.

Democracy deficit, liberty and the empty centre

The open-endedness of Kieslowski's trilogy is a useful entry point for looking at the more directly political critiques of democracy, namely the first of my three often-voiced complaints about Europe as a political entity, namely the democracy deficit: what is meant by this is that in the process of delegating certain aspects of decision-making and thus parts of national sovereignty to unelected bodies of the European Union, a general lack of accountability has been institutionalized, which not only has disempowered national parliaments, but even more so, has alienated citizens, who no longer feel they have any influence – not even through the ballot box – on crucial legislation affecting their lives and work-conditions. The sense of disempowerment is aggravated by obscure decision-making processes that resemble cabals of back-room deals and horse-trading among heads of state, engineered by their respective technocrats and 'experts'. Perry Anderson summed up the democracy deficit with reference to the 'no' vote in the referendum in France and the Netherlands, which he described as 'a popular repudiation of the charter for a new Europe, not because it was too federalist, but because it seemed to be little more than an impenetrable scheme for the redistribution of oligarchic power, embodying

[9] Žižek, *The Fright of Real Tears*, 176–7.

everything most distrusted in the arrogant, opaque system the EU appeared to have become'.[10]

Thus, the general disaffection with politics, ranging from apathy and cynicism to reactionary nationalism and active dissent ('Brexit') is explained by the democracy deficit, which undermines the EU's political legitimacy, and thus in turn discourages citizens from feeling either loyalty to the transnational community that Europe is inexorably becoming, or solidarity with the less well-off South, not to mention with economic migrants, refugees and asylum seekers.

Such a critique has both a political-cultural dimension, and a more formal-philosophical one. The political-cultural case is made, for instance, by Wendy Brown. She argues that the democratic deficit (not just in Europe) stems from the corruption of the ideals of democracy by market criteria. Neoliberalism and finance capitalism have undermined 'the basic principles of constitutionalism, legal equality, political and civil liberty, political autonomy, and universal inclusion'[11] and replaced them with criteria of cost/benefit ratios, efficiency, profitability, and efficacy: a programme that since the 2008 banking crisis is usually subsumed under the term 'austerity'.

Behind her critique stands a perhaps even more fundamental one, namely the erosion of the very concept of citizenship, increasingly replaced since the 1970s by the suggestions that even with respect to their government, people are first and foremost consumers, which also means that they relate to the state by way of rights and entitlements more than in acknowledgement of duties and obligations. Given the dependence of virtually all governments in the West on the growth of consumption as the motor of economic stability and fiscal solvency, the processes which have turned citizens into consumers are probably irreversible, and are, if anything, strengthened by a dependence on privately owned but publicly inspected infrastructural services such as water, electricity, roads, transport and the internet, whereby citizens are encouraged to trade in democratic rights (such as privacy) for convenience of access, mobility and ease of communication, thus further helping to hollow out democracy, but allowing a public–private surveillance state to install itself virtually unchecked and unchallenged. This 'convenience capitalism' thus promotes a form of democratic disenfranchisement with which citizens-turned-consumers actively collude.

Yet there is also another way of looking at the democratic deficit: what I called the formal-philosophical one. This aspect is most clearly formulated

---

[10] Perry Anderson, 'Depicting Europe', *London Review of Books* 29, no. 18 (20 September 2007), http://www.lrb.co.uk/v29/n18/perry-anderson/depicting-europe (accessed 4 September 2017).

[11] Wendy Brown, 'We Are All Democrats Now', in *Democracy in What State?*, trans. William McCuaig (New York: Columbia University Press, 2012), 47.

by the French philosopher Claude Lefort, who is cited or expanded upon by many others, notably Rancière, Badiou and Žižek. Lefort makes the crucial distinction between *le politique* (the political) and *la politique* (politics), a distinction that Rancière, for instance, radicalizes into one between 'the political' and 'the police', while Žižek comments on it as follows: 'One can put it in terms of the well-known definition of politics [*la politique*] as the "art of the possible" [while] authentic politics [*le politique*] is, rather, the exact opposite, that is, the art of the *impossible* – it changes the very parameters of what is considered "possible" in the existing constellation.'[12]

Compared to the opposition between liberal and neoliberal democracy, Lefort's distinction is more fundamental. He locates these transformations and divisions and the resulting democracy deficit in the constitutive contradiction of democracy itself, which derives from the distinct and peculiar nature of authority in any democratic systems of government.[13] This authority, according to Lefort, is ungrounded, or, more precisely, is from the very beginning organized around an *empty centre*. Since democratic legitimacy arises from the people, the people must have absolute authority. But because the people are inherently plural, diverse and multiple, there can be no single body or source that incarnates 'the people', other than by way of a formal abstraction. Historically, the modern idea of democracy emerged when, with the French and American declarations of the rights of man at the end of the eighteenth century, the power of the state was no longer attributed to a transcendent source, such as God, Nature or Divine Law, but manifested itself in a purely performative gesture ('We, the People, hereby declare'). Thus asserted (and subsequently delegated), power and authority is located within the social world, and yet it is meant to transcend the community from which it emerges, in order to be binding, enduring and universal. Given this doubly reflexive origin of democratic authority, its legitimacy is always fragile, encircling an empty space, filled either with the formalism of the law and of state institutions, or with whatever a given group, at a given point in time, determines to be a higher authority, such as Reason, the Proletariat, or the 'Common Good' that can be appealed to. But this externalized authority must remain an abstraction, the cover for a void, and thus is inherently contingent – which means that democracy can never be foundational or grounded, but remains relational and performative. Lefort draws from this some far-reaching consequences. While 'politics' will always try to disguise the void of legitimacy, 'the political' must make us mindful of the gap between the empty place of power (Žižek's absent centre) and that which fills it with authority. Lefort, borrowing from Lacan, designates this gap as the one between the Real and the Symbolic. Given that the Real, that is,

[12] Žižek, *The Ticklish Subject*, 199.
[13] Claude Lefort, *Essais sur le politique* (Paris: Seuil, 1986).

power, in this formulation, cannot be symbolized, but nonetheless makes itself felt, especially whenever the Symbolic or authority ceases to function (even in ordinary parlance, one speaks of a 'power vacuum'), the role of the political (and thus of every true democrat) is to challenge all attempts to appropriate power through symbolization, and instead, to further its dispersal across micro-manifestations, in order to forestall interpellation and subjectification, in the double meaning of the term, be it as the split subject in the psychoanalytic sense, or as the subject of the state, the nation and the law. These acts of marking the gap, of keeping the space empty, of voiding the symbolic order, are what in Rancière come to constitute *dissensus*. Forms of totalitarianism or autocracy are thus an inherent tendency of democracy, tilting the balance towards filling the empty space with the figure of the authoritarian leader, the charismatic personality, who not only embodies the authority of the state, but 'symbolizes' the power that belongs to the people, by claiming, for instance, the 'legitimacy' of an election. Autocracy thus closes the gap between the Symbolic and the Real that is both the glory and the curse of democracy, but which it is the task of *the political* to prevent from being sealed.[14]

Lefort's insights, as indicated, have been echoed by others: Agamben, for instance, taking his starting point from the well-known debate between Carl Schmitt and Walter Benjamin around sovereignty, the law and 'divine violence', summed up the dilemma when he argued that democracy's deficit derives from the very words we have inherited from the Greek language, where there is a slippage between *constitution* and *government*. For Agamben these terms represent two distinct rationalities – the legislative power of the body of citizens and the executive power of government: 'What if [democracy] were just a fiction . . . a screen set up to hide the fact that there is a void at the center, that no articulation is possible between these two elements, these two rationalities?'[15]

Yet whereas Badiou thinks (for much the same reasons as Agamben) that a 'democratic government' is either democratic or a government but cannot be both, because democracy, understood as 'the power of peoples over their own existence' can only be achieved in the withering away of the

[14] Žižek reminds us of Claude Lefort's insight that 'totalitarianism is an inherent perversion of democratic logic' (*The Ticklish Subject*, 192). For an elaboration, see *The Ticklish Subject*, 192–3.

[15] G. Agamben, in *Democracy in What State?*, 4. In the same collection, Daniel Bensaïd notes the fact that even in the case of revolutionaries like Che Guevara or Fidel Castro 'the "force of heroism" and virtue of example were not enough to bridge the tragic gap between the constituent power and instituted democracy' (31), and he concludes that no socialist leader has managed 'this mysterious democratic equation', and no radically democratic state has solved 'the puzzle which they have handed on to us' (32).

state,[16] Žižek wants to retain and even strengthen the state, not just as safeguarding certain formal rights, but as an instrument whose inner contradictions can be used strategically by taking the state by its word. In *The Ticklish Subject* he commends Étienne Balibar, another philosopher participating in the debate over democracy, for trying to rescue citizenship in the form of 'civility', understood as the civic space of dialogue in which something like the demand for human rights and other values of universal application can be articulated: 'Balibar resists the anti-State rhetorics of the New Left of the 1960s (the notion of the State as a mechanism of "oppression" of people's initiatives) and emphasizes the role of the State as the (possible) guarantor of the space of civic discussion.'[17]

Such advocacy of the state, however, would find itself on the wrong side of Rancière, for whom – as for Badiou, if for somewhat different reasons – the state is always a betrayer of democracy. What Agamben calls 'government' and Žižek calls the state, Rancière simply calls 'police' and contrasts it to 'the political', which, very much in the spirit of Lefort, is for him crucially manifested by 'dissensus'. Government is 'the police' because in most advanced democracies, politicians seek power mainly as technocrats and administrators, but when faced with difficult ethical issues or competing rights – for Rancière the very stuff of democracy, as we shall see – governments tend to hide behind formal law, and thus politicians become, even at the theoretical level, nothing but law-enforcement agents. This, too, applies *mutatis mutandis* to all those who, for instance, in the integration and assimilation debates of migrants or refugees, argue for equal rights, but define these equal rights by the canons of existing law, that is, 'the law of the land'. By maintaining that people of different faith, ethnicity and provenance can do what they like 'in private', but are obliged in public to obey the laws as they find them, they advocate the position of the police, and the very opposite of the political as Rancière understands it.[18]

Comparing these philosophical conceptions of Europe and the crises of democracy with the everyday scenarios that have been offered in the wake of the various crises since 2008 (Greece and the Euro-crisis), 2014 (Syria and the refugee crisis) and 2016 (Britain and its plebiscite to leave the EU)

---

[16] Alain Badiou, 'The Democratic Emblem', in *Democracy in What State?*, 15. See also Peter Hallward on Badiou and democracy: 'The problem with democracy is that, the moment it is established as a positive formal system regulating the way a multitude of political subjects compete for power, it has to exclude some options as "nondemocratic", and this exclusion, this founding decision about who is included in and who is excluded from the field of democratic options, is not itself democratic.' Peter Hallward, *Think Again: Alain Badiou and the Future of Philosophy* (London: Continuum, 2004), 180.

[17] Žižek, *The Ticklish Subject*, 173.

[18] See Jacques Rancière, 'Ten Theses on Politics', *Theory & Event* 5, no. 3 (2001), http://muse.jhu.edu/article/32639 (accessed 4 September 2017).

is to realize that the philosophical discourses are indeed akin to thought experiments, in the sense that they are not primarily concerned with practical solutions, but are identifying inherent paradoxes, constitutive dilemmas and contradictions, which engage the day-to-day reality (the ontic choices) mainly in the mode of 'as if'.

In this scenario, the role of 'Brussels' as the very epitome of the democracy deficit is surprisingly apt. For if the essence of democracy is to keep the centre 'empty', then Brussels emerges indeed as its necessary correlative. Since the decisions implemented in Brussels are in fact taken by the governments of the nation-states that make up the EU, blaming Brussels becomes a strategic tool of deniability of each government's own role in reaching compromises.[19] By acting as a scapegoat, Brussels 'manages' the inner contradictions between the nation-states; by acting as a placeholder, it keeps open the possibility of a closer union of federal states. What the studied blandness of Angela Merkel is to Germany, 'Brussels' is to the EU: the embodiment of the empty centre that safeguards the people's sovereignty.

If the sovereign is the people, then the people can only lend this sovereignty temporarily and in symbolic fashion to a government, a parliament or a single politician. On the other hand, the people must lend it to some symbolic instance, otherwise it is chaos. Representative democracy is the tool to exercise this periodic transfer, and by this reasoning, referenda are the wrong way of asserting sovereignty, just as authoritarian rulers, however benevolent, are the wrong way of appropriating sovereignty. In subsequent chapters, I shall argue for yet another way of conceiving sovereignty, by suggesting that at another level, sovereignty – so closely bound up with liberty and autonomy – can translate itself into the freedom that comes with divesting oneself, with having nothing (more) to lose: another way of understanding liberty as a negative category (as did Kant: see above), requiring a voided space. This space of another kind of liberty and autonomy I associate with the term 'abjection'.

The multicultural deficit

Given such radical conceptions of *the political* with their categorical rejection of *politics* as currently practised anywhere in the world, and given the insistence on the fundamental contingency of all action (leading to yet another affirmative negativity, such as 'the political is everywhere but this is

---

[19] See Caroline de Gruyter, 'Wat is er mis met Europa, en wat doen we er an?', *NRC Handelsblad*, 13 February 2016, http://www.nrc.nl/nieuws/2016/02/13/wat-is-er-mis-is-met-europa-en-wat-doen-we-er-an-1587839-a850793 (accessed 4 September 2017).

a place that nobody has ever seen'),[20] there is reason to believe that the political in this debate stands for a (post-metaphysical) political theology – a term that refers back to one of the key thinkers of 'the political', namely Carl Schmitt. Indeed, the insistence on contingency on the one hand, and the performativity of sovereignty on the other, resembles the 'leap of faith' that traverses both the history of Christianity and its obverse, post-metaphysical ungroundedness. It is therefore not surprising that the assertion of 'the political' often takes on elements of a *religious conversion experience*. It presupposes – for thinking 'the political' – a radical break in the order of things, either articulated as 'revolution' and 'messianic' (as in Benjamin), or as 'event' (Badiou). Philosophers such as Badiou, Agamben and Žižek (and in a different context also Nancy) frequently invoke concepts drawn from (early) Christian theology. Notably the many commentaries in recent years on the teachings of St Paul confirm that new thinking about democracy, legitimacy, divine violence and the formation of the community has returned to the roots of theology in European culture, at the crossroads of Judaism, Greek philosophy and Christianity. In this militant tradition, too, 'the political' emerges as the opposite of politics, now in the sense that only a community of believers based on faith, commitment and a shared doctrine can be authentically engaged in the political, and that the political, however local or historically specific this community might be, must be able to claim universal truths.

This provides a different, and in its own way, illuminating entry point to the philosophical dimension of the second political complaint about Europe I mentioned earlier: the multicultural deficit. The underlying assumption, again mostly voiced from the liberal left, is that the European Union has a double task and obligation vis-à-vis all its citizens. The first is to create an obligation of solidarity that goes beyond the nation state, bonding the different peoples of Europe around a common ideal or goal. Freedom of movement for goods, people, money and services, the abolition of border controls among most countries of continental Europe, and the common currency were all meant to give this sense of belonging to an entity that is larger than the country one was born in and the nation to which one belongs by virtue of language, ethnicity and custom. Europe would be this entity distinct enough by the diversity of history, geography and religious faiths, but united enough by a democratic political culture to engender feelings of belonging. The common past (however catastrophic in the twentieth century) could also generate the belief in a common destiny, when contrasted with other continents or parts of the world. Catastrophes such as the two World Wars

[20] The political is 'everywhere', but this is a place 'nobody has ever seen', Oliver Marchart, *Post-Foundational Political Thought: Political Difference in Nancy, Lefort, Badiou and Laclau* (Edinburgh: Edinburgh University Press, 2007), 174.

and the Holocaust can in actual fact create a common bond: nations have often rallied and rebuilt around their greatest defeats, on the anthropological ground that great common sacrifices act as strong attachment.[21] It is what I call the heroic vision of Europe.

The other task, in some sense running counter to the first, is for Europeans to recognize that they are not a separate entity, but in so many ways connected and interdependent with the rest of the world, with obligations and benefits that go beyond the borders even of Europe – wherever one determines to draw these borders: itself a somewhat arbitrary, historically variable and politically motivated decision. This means to accept that most European nation states have become not just multicultural and multi-religious, but also multi-ethnic and multilingual countries, and this for historical reasons (the colonial legacy in France, Britain, Spain, Belgium, Portugal and the Netherlands, for instance), for economic reasons (West Germany's need for skilled and unskilled labour bringing in a large contingent of Turks, Yugoslavs and Iranians in the 1960s) as well as for geographical reasons (Italy and Spain's proximity to North Africa, Greece's proximity to Turkey and the Middle East). The tensions and resentments against 'foreigners', in the wake of economic migration, political asylum and immigration, seem to have grown in direct proportion to the asymmetry in wealth and welfare that divides the continents. Pressure has furthermore mounted as a consequence of the 2008 'economic crisis', which – as many have pointed out – was also an engineered crisis, with 'austerity' part of a tactic of top-down moves that Naomi Klein memorably called 'disaster capitalism'.[22]

For Žižek, multiculturalism is the new form of European racism:

> [M]ulticultural tolerance and respect of differences share with those who oppose immigration the need to keep others at a proper distance. 'The others are OK, I respect them,' the liberals say, 'but they must not intrude

---

[21] Defeat as nation-building: if I am right that the Holocaust has been used (not entirely successfully) to create a European identity around a collective disaster, and analogies with the nationhood of Serbia (Kosovo), Israel (Massada, the Shoah), the American South (the Alamo), Germany (the Nibelungen) have some merit, this would seem to be confirmed by both Darwin and newer evolutionary theory: 'Most cultures celebrate costly collective commitments as morally good and glorious. Commemorations of collective sacrifice are timeworn rituals with proven success in fostering cooperation within the group and making it more competitive with other groups.' Scott Atran, 'Religion in America', *Huffington Post*, US edition, 25 May 2011, http://www.huffingtonpost.com/scott-atran/religion-in-america-why-m_b_126225.html (accessed 9 January 2017). Atran also responds in a similar way to Jonathan Haidt, 'What Makes People Vote Republican?', *Edge.org*, 9 October 2008, https://www.edge.org/conversation/jonathan_haidt-what-makes-people-vote-republican (accessed 4 September 2017).

[22] Naomi Klein, *The Shock Doctrine: The Rise of Disaster Capitalism* (Toronto: Random House, 2007).

> too much on my own space. The moment they do, they harass me ...' What is increasingly emerging as the central human right in late-capitalist societies is the right not to be harassed, which is the right to be kept at a safe distance from others.[23]

Why the disenchantment with the multicultural project in Europe? The United States, although built by a slave economy and brutal land grabs, managed to fashion a (left-liberal) ideology that claims that the nation thrives both economically and demographically on welcoming immigrants into the 'melting pot'.[24] This ideology of inclusiveness functioned in part because it was based on other forms of exclusion (unacknowledged racism, genocide of indigenous populations), and in part because of a fervently nationalistic patriotism, disavowed by claiming for itself the possession of universal principles. Europe, by contrast, has since the nineteenth century had to suppress tribalism and regionalism in order to create the nation state, and therefore has tended to downplay diversity within its borders, either in the name of (right-wing) racial purity or (on the left) in the name of civil society, citizenship and universalism (social democracy), or by claiming primacy of the class struggle over cultural, religious or ethnic difference (socialism and communism).

There is a general sense that here, too, the Enlightenment has left Europe with an unresolved legacy, when it comes to how the continent deals not only with the many nationalities – that is, culturally, territorially and linguistically distinct entities – but with migrants, immigrants, refugees who come to Europe either to escape poverty and persecution in their own countries, or to offer their labour power in exchange for what they hope will be a better life, if not for themselves then for their children. Added to the racial prejudice, the resentment and outright hostility often shown towards these guest workers by parts of the host population, tensions have especially focused on one particular religious group, namely Muslims. Their faith appears to oblige them to moral conduct, daily observances, attitudes to sexuality and the position of women that are at variance with Enlightenment values, notably when it comes to such basic rights as freedom of speech, education for all, or to the strict division of 'church' (i.e. religion) and 'state' (i.e. politics, public life and a secular judiciary). In the European countries that are home to substantial Muslim populations, such as France, Germany,

---

[23] Slavoj Žižek, 'Liberal multiculturalism masks an old barbarism with a human face', *Guardian*, 3 October 2010, https://www.theguardian.com/commentisfree/2010/oct/03/immigration-policy-roma-rightwing-europe (accessed 4 September 2017).

[24] Europe this time around lacks both the socio-political flexibility and the moral stamina to 'either give the newcomers a decent economic life or to confront extremism successfully'. Hent de Vries and Lawrence Eugene Sullivan, *Political Theologies: Public Religions in a Post-secular World* (New York: Fordham University Press, 2006), 5.

Britain, Belgium and the Netherlands, it seems that neither assimilation nor autonomy and separate development has been a 'successful' model of multicultural coexistence.

Jacques Derrida has argued – in the spirit of Kant – for a radical version of 'hospitality' as the stance from which to evaluate the competing claims, as does Levinas in his writings on alterity (see below). Discriminated against in education and job opportunities, especially young men with a migration background, so the 'class' argument would go, find their way barred to work, family life and recognition, taking to crime and 'terror' instead. Discrimination and desperation makes them fall back on radical versions of their religion, not the other way round: their religion does not necessarily make them radical. Others point out that 'assimilation' actually considers the person not as a full human being, but as somehow lacking a dimension, which he or she has to acquire in order to adapt to the somehow fully constituted cultural set of values owned by the host.[25] The debates confirm the dual character of both religion and ethnicity: they can be effectively deployed as political tools of exclusion and yet they are also a source of meaning by offering the grounds for solidarity and belonging, especially in minority situations, becoming the identity of last resort.

Inclusion/exclusion

Part of the problem, then, is that 'multiculturalism', when positively used, in the sense of showing respect and recognition for the 'other', *also on the other's terms* – is both descriptive and normative, but it is also self-contradictory. As a descriptive term, it refers to the ability of groups and communities of diverse origins, language, race and religion to live together in ways that allow them to manage their differences peacefully. When used normatively, or with an activist agenda, it implies a more proactive endorsement of such diversity, including legislation to bring about what is called 'affirmative action' in the US, or 'positive discrimination' or 'quota' in Europe, along with a celebration of 'cultural identity' over the claims of other forms of self-ascription of identity and belonging. Multiculturalism gained ascendancy in Europe during the 1970s and 1980s, when the failures and disappointment of left-wing politics led to the 'cultural turn', of which feminism and multiculturalism were the most enduring manifestations outside the academy, managing to enter the social and political mainstream. Multiculturalism is, however, self-contradictory when its opening towards

[25] See, for instance, Sabine Hess, 'Gerade 'Leistungsträger' treten nach unten', interview with Gitta Düperthal, *junge Welt*, 7 September 2013, http://www.jungewelt.de/2013/09-07/062.php (accessed 4 September 2017).

multiplicity is couched in the semantics of tolerance. As something that is extended to the Other, it implies the speaker's superior position, which the term renders, as it were, unassailable and unquestioned, thus giving with one hand what it takes away with the other. The change of vocabulary to 'diversity' and 'inclusiveness' would seem to be a well-intended verbal cosmetic that may only harden the counter-stance of an identity politics based on Christian fundamentalism or populist nationalism.

Underlying Europe's populist right-wing retrenchment is also the more anthropological-philosophical question of inclusion and exclusion. What is a border and what is it for? A boundary and dividing line, to keep some out and others in, a liminal space of transition, or a semiotic marker of difference, and thus the very condition of signifying? Does a border outline a territory or act as a container, establishing what is inside and what is outside, prior to raising questions of the politics of (not) belonging?[26] And what are the terms of this (not) belonging, when one is in a situation of proximity and propinquity with others, even before s/he becomes 'the Other'? Furthermore, is this problematic propinquity a consequence of specific political events (the creation of the state of Israel for the Palestinians, the enlargement of the European Union for Russia) or, more generally, a consequence of globalization, where anyone might find him/herself sharing contiguous proximity with anyone else? Does democracy itself require limits to inclusion and diversity, in order to function as a way of generating citizenship, lest it becomes a mere service provider for a nation of customers and consumers?

The Greeks and Romans, as first philosophers and founders of what we understand by the state, democracy and politics, knew about exclusion from the polis: slaves, women, 'barbarians' were all excluded, and their exclusion stabilized societal norms and not only provided the labour force for the *res publica*, but also defined what was law and what was not. In other words, the community of the polis defined itself as much by what it was not and what it excluded as it did by what it was, or rather, what it believed itself to be. At the larger scale of international relations, a 'state', in order to function, requires recognition from others, while 'nation' and 'ethnic community' are self-defined, sustained by 'belief' – and thereby are much closer to religion. In the case of the Palestinians, for instance, the debate over the two-state solution is already hampered by such disagreements over the Palestinians as a 'nation' or a 'state', and of Israel as a state of ethnic diversity, but unified and defined by its religion: consequence of the very conflation of religion and the state, which European democracies have fought against.

[26] See Friedrich Balke, 'Tristes Tropiques: Systems Theory and the Literary Scene', *Soziale Systeme* 8 (2002): 27–37.

The Other, the stranger, the neighbour

The anthropologist Claude Lévi-Strauss, when studying different tribes in his South American fieldwork, came up with a distinction between two ways communities respond to people from outside, that is, strangers or barbarians. According to him, there are anthropophagic societies (eating the stranger) and anthropoemic societies (isolating the stranger):

> If we studied societies from the outside, it would be tempting to distinguish two contrasting types: those which practise cannibalism (anthropophagy) – that is, which regard the absorption of certain individuals possessing dangerous powers as the only means of neutralizing those powers and even of turning them to advantage – and those which, like our own society, adopt what might be called the practice of anthropoemy (from the Greek émein, to vomit); faced with the same problem, the latter type of society has chosen the opposite solution which consists in ejecting dangerous individuals from the social body and keeping them temporarily or permanently in isolation, away from all contact with their fellows, in establishments specially intended for this purpose.[27]

For instance, the United States across the twentieth century has known phases of both: bulimic-anorexic when pursuing 'isolationist' policies or when at war (e.g. Japanese-Americans were put in detention camps during the Second World War), and cannibalistic when absorbing (the preferably white) immigrants, by 'Americanizing' them, that is, incorporating them through a type of patriotism that rewarded conformity and homogenization – with the result that its own indigenous population as well as blacks and Hispanics have continued to find themselves marginalized and excluded.

However, such a binary presentation of inclusion/exclusion can also be misleading, since identity politics tends to be an arena of shifting adherences and strategic alliances. As Žižek cautions:

> [T]here is an inherent split in the field of particular identities themselves caused by the onslaught of capitalist globalization: on the one hand, the so-called 'fundamentalisms', whose basic formula is that of the Identity of one's own group, implying the practice of excluding the threatening Other(s): France for the French (against Algerian immigrants), America for Americans (against the Hispanic invasion) . . . on the other hand, there is postmodern multiculturalist 'identity politics', aiming at the tolerant coexistence of ever-shifting, 'hybrid' lifestyle groups, divided into

[27] Claude Lévi-Strauss, *Tristes Tropiques* (New York: Penguin, 1992), 287–8.

> endless subgroups (Hispanic women, black gays, white male AIDS patients, lesbian mothers . . .).

Yet, the only link between these subgroups, Žižek argues, is that they all represent niche production and consumption opportunities (gay tourism, Latin music, ethnic cuisine). Žižek concludes that the 'separation between multiculturalist identity politics and fundamentalism is [ultimately] purely formal; it often depends merely on the different perspective from which the observer views a movement for maintaining a group identity'.[28]

The inclusion/exclusion argument is, of course, intimately connected to the question of 'tolerance/ assimilation' and social justice, going beyond equality before the law to include the virtue of solidarity – a value nominally inscribed in the concept of the welfare state as part of the social contract. Implied in the welfare state is the consensus that no one is to be excluded, a consensus that in recent decades has come under pressure from opposite ends of the political spectrum, as it were. An ageing population, increasing mobility of the workforce, outsourcing and downsizing has put pressure on jobs and wages for the less skilled. Along with the influx of migrant populations and refugees it has given rise not only to xenophobia and racism, but also to a more fundamental weakening of the social contract, understood first as the handing over of the people's sovereignty to the nation state (or its supranational surrogate), and second as the willingness of citizens to pay taxes in order for the government to redistribute benefits and services also to the weakest and neediest. But behind this so-called rise in populist chauvinism lies also a philosophical issue, which can best be encapsulated in the concept of the 'neighbour'.

The neighbour intersects with the challenges facing Europe in the twenty-first century: first, because it touches on the political dimension of the European Union regarding federalism: while the richer regions make separatist demands in Spain and northern Italy, the new populist Eurosceptic nationalisms are fed by resentment against their own metropolitan 'élites' and against 'foreigners stealing jobs' and 'scrounging benefits'; and second, because love-thy-neighbour has such a long history at the interface of religion, ethics and politics, when put to the test at the supra-national (European) level, it puts pressure on the political ideals of fraternity and solidarity. If solidarity is no longer secured by class consciousness and does not even cover the members of the same nation, how can it extend to other nationals either within Europe or beyond? Is it a failure of the political imagination, or is even the religious command of neighbour-love flawed?

---

[28] Žižek, *The Ticklish Subject*, 209–10.

One can recall the relatively benign remark by the social philosopher of the risk society, Ulrich Beck, who in *Cosmopolitan Europe* has called it a 'miracle' that Europe has turned 'enemies into neighbours',[29] referring mainly to France and Germany, Germany and Poland, but implying also the bonds between other nation states formerly at war with each other. Yet as became clear during the Balkan Civil War, the miracle clearly did not include the countries of former Yugoslavia, the most egregious failure of multi-ethnicity and multinationalism on European soil since the fall of communism. The formula 'enemy into neighbour' may sound both reasonable and desirable, but in ex-Yugoslavia it became 'neighbour into enemy' – with terrible consequences, which in turn have left their traumatic mark on the very discourses around hospitality, fraternity and solidarity, as indeed has the Israeli–Palestinian conflict (which applies especially to Levinas). Why is the term 'neighbour' a problem in itself? The commandment 'thou shalt love thy neighbour as thyself' has always puzzled both Christian and Jewish commentators, including Sigmund Freud. In *Civilization and its Discontents* (written under the then traumatic impact of what Freud calls 'the horrors of the last [i.e. First] World War') he states:

> The commandment, 'Love thy neighbour as thyself' . . . is impossible to fulfil; such an enormous inflation of love can only lower its value, not get rid of the difficulty. Civilization pays no attention to all this; it merely admonishes us that the harder it is to obey the precept the more meritorious it is to do so. But anyone who follows such a precept in present-day civilization only puts himself at a disadvantage *vis-à-vis* the person who disregards it.

Freud concludes that,

> . . . at this point the ethics based on religion introduces its promises of a better after-life. But so long as virtue is not rewarded here on earth, ethics will, I fancy, preach in vain . . . The recognition of this fact among socialists has been obscured and made useless for practical purposes by a fresh idealistic misconception of human nature.[30]

Freud is sceptical about this precept advanced by religion (as an ethics of love) and by socialism (as class-based solidarity), because he sees aggression

---

[29] Ulrich Beck and Edgar Grande, *Cosmopolitan Europe* (Cambridge: Polity, 2007), 224. See also the transcript of a lecture (2011), 'Time to Get Angry, Europe', http://globernance.org/ulrich-beck-time-to- get-angry-europe/ (accessed 5 September 2017).

[30] Sigmund Freud, *Civilization and its Discontents*. Quoted in *Social Theory: The Multicultural, Global, and Classic Readings*, ed. Charles Lemert, 6th edn (Boulder, CO: Westview Press, 2017), 117–18.

'at the bottom of all the relations of affection and love between human beings'. From a psychoanalytical point of view, then, the commandment is intentionally self-contradictory, alerting us to one of the tragic paradoxes of human existence, namely that love and aggression are two sides of the same coin.[31]

This paradox, focused on the stranger and the neighbour, has in turn inspired two of the most influential philosophies of the Other: Levinas' notion of ethics as alterity (centred on 'the face of the other'), and Derrida's concept of conditional and unconditional hospitality.[32] The reason why Levinas is such an important figure in the debate over fraternity (and by extension, multicultural Europe) is that he starts from the ineffable strangeness of the Other, to the point that the most basic or primordial reaction to the encounter is to 'kill' the Other, that is, to consume, absorb, ingest the Other, and to make him/her 'the same' (i.e. the 'anthropophagic' response, in Lévi-Strauss's terms). This is in stark contrast to our common-sense idea prompted by custom, civility and politeness (morality), where our first response is to give the stranger the benefit of the doubt and assume the Other is a friend, even a 'brother'.[33] Ethics, according to Levinas, however, begins with the recognition of the traumatic nature of such an encounter, which is a challenge and interrogation of my being rather than its confirmation. Ethics is the 'calling into question of my spontaneity by the presence of the Other . . . his irreducibility to the I, to my thoughts and possessions, his transcendence, his absolute and irrecuperable alterity'.[34] Starting from such a deconstructive position of negativity and radical otherness, Levinas then builds a relation ('a relation without a relation') with the Other across the 'face-to-face', 'responsiveness', 'responsibility', the

[31] '"Thou shalt love thy neighbour as thyself" is from Freud's perspective an ethical ideal that reveals the depth – and the desperation – of civilization's need in this respect. For on its face the rule makes no sense. Indeed, it seems clearly enough an idea that runs exactly counter to the self's interest. But civilization insists upon it as part of its program to promote aim-inhibited libido, and it does so in spite of the unreasonable and happiness-killing sacrifices people must make in order to follow the precept.' John Webster, 'A Map to Freud's *Civilization and its Discontents*, Especially with Respect to Spenser's *Faerie Queene*', http://faculty.washington.edu/cicero/Freud.htm (accessed 5 September 2017).

[32] Emmanuel Levinas, *Otherwise than Being or Beyond Essence*, trans. Alphonso Lingis (Dordrecht and Boston: Kluwer Academic Publishers, 1978); Jacques Derrida and Anne Dufourmantelle, *Of Hospitality*, trans. Rachel Bowlby (Stanford, CA: Stanford University Press, 2000).

[33] The most thorough discussion of Levinas' notion of fraternity can be found in Howard Caygill, *Levinas and the Political* (New York: Routledge, 2002). The neighbour as both Other and brother is discussed on p. 136.

[34] Emmanuel Levinas, *Totality and Infinity: An Essay on Exteriority*, trans. Alphonso Lingis (Pittsburgh: Duquesne University Press, 1969), 43.

'welcome' and 'proximity'. These terms turn out to be further obstacles: despite appearances, they raise the bar rather than bring the Other closer. Yet therein precisely lies their potential usefulness for rethinking what fraternity, solidarity and 'being with' might mean in a Europe bracing itself to become thoroughly multinational, multi-ethnic and multi-denominational.

Derrida has been an eloquent, if cautious advocate of Levinas, explicitly discussing his idea of the ethical relation in *Violence and Metaphysics* (1964), and paying tribute to Levinas in *Adieu* (1999). Most relevant, however, in the present context are his published lectures *Of Hospitality* (2000), written also with Levinas in mind. For Derrida, there are two kinds of hospitality: the conditional one, which applies to fellow citizens and is regulated by the laws protecting property but also ensuring basic welfare provisions for the needy, and unconditional hospitality, which is an ethical command that requires a radical openness: 'If there is pure hospitality, or a pure gift, it should consist in this opening without horizon, without horizon of expectation, an opening to the newcomer whoever that may be.'[35] One can regard this unconditional hospitality as the negative foil and necessary 'remainder' to conditional hospitality: extending hospitality to the guest and the foreigner, the stranger and the immigrant, the intruder and the refugee, whatever his/her needs, motives or intentions, is to show the limits of altruism, but also requires one to retain mastery and remain in control, if one wants to play host. Here hospitality is almost in the anthropological category of potlatch, the gift, and of 'exuberant expenditure' as advocated by Georges Bataille, that is, unconditional hospitality as the founding gesture of an alternative economy. Or – making hospitality and hostility the two sides of the same coin – one can see it as a thought experiment: what would it mean to be radically open, to the point of having not only no prejudice or demands, but also no anticipation or expectation, including no notion of sacrifice or self-sacrifice? Such 'ethical' openness would be 'tested' by the neighbour, as the figure of perilous proximity, of fatal interdependence, but also as that part of myself that I disavow and project onto the Other.

Žižek, having grown up in the former Yugoslavia, also insists on the latent aggression and actual violence of the neighbour, who is a permanent threat to my peace of mind, since he is the potential intruder who never goes away, whom I cannot exclude, and from whose contiguity I cannot keep a proper distance, not least because he is too much like me. As a Lacanian, Žižek's notion of ethics, however, is quite different from Levinas

[35] Jacques Derrida, 'Hospitality, Justice, and Responsibility: A Dialogue with Jacques Derrida', in Richard Kearney and Mark Dooley (eds), *Questioning Ethics: Contemporary Debates in Philosophy* (New York: Routledge, 2002), 70.

or Derrida, since ethics is defined by Lacan as 'not giving up on one's desire'. Ethics seeks the authenticity of the singular act, while its alterity is the fidelity to the self's otherness (as manifest in the death drive) and thus ethics may well be at the expense of the Other *and* the self. As 'subjective destitution', the ethical act necessarily ruptures the social contract, rather than building the community, which makes Antigone defying Creon, the law and the community, at the risk of her own death, the epitome of the ethical act.

Žižek is particularly troubled by Levinas' quasi-sacralization of the 'face', disclosing the Other in his/her humanity and thus extending the primordial ethical demand: that I take responsibility for the Other, prior to my even knowing it, as the only way of being a 'self' in relation to others.[36] In Levinas' later work, notably *Otherwise than Being*, in the ethical relation, my subjectivity is constituted by being 'taken hostage', thus defining my belonging to a community across a complex web of (heteronomous and potentially also hostile) obligations and demands. Since the face of the Other condenses these relations, and makes them present, Žižek asks:

> [What if . . .] we restore to the Levinasian 'face' all its monstrosity: face is not a harmonious Whole of the dazzling epiphany of a 'human face,' face is something the glimpse of which we get when we stumble upon a grotesquely distorted face, a face in the grip of a disgusting tic or grimace, a face which, precisely, confronts us when the neighbour 'loses his face'[?][37] . . . [F]ar from displaying 'a quality of God's image carried with it,' the face is the ultimate ethical lure . . . The neighbour is not displayed through a face; it is in his or her fundamental dimension a faceless monster.[38]

Yet Žižek seems to take the Levinasian face too literally in its frontal gaze: as a composite and a condensation of a mutually sustaining but also antagonistic (non-) relation, the face does not even have to be an actual face. One of the most eloquent defences in this respect comes from David Wills, author of a book on 'Dorsality', that is, the back as 'face':

---

[36] Judith Butler has similar doubts: 'It is not enough to say, in a Levinasian way that the claim is made upon me prior to my knowing and as an inaugurating instance of my coming into being. That may be formally true, but its truth is of no use to me if I lack the conditions for responsiveness that allow me to apprehend it in the midst of this social and political life.' Judith Butler, *Frames of War: When Is Life Grievable?* (London: Verso, 2010), 179.

[37] Slavoj Žižek, 'Neighbors and other Monsters', in Kevin Reinhard, Eric Santner and Slavoj Žižek, *The Neighbor: Three Inquiries in Political Theology* (Chicago and London: University of Chicago Press, 2006), 162.

[38] Žižek, 'Neighbors and other Monsters', 185.

> We have to imagine that it is by hearing the eyes speak rather than by looking at them – or seeing them look at us – that we understand the vulnerability of the other, and hence the possibility of and prohibition against murder. In fact, late in *Totality and Infinity* [Levinas] writes that 'the whole body – a hand or a curve of the shoulder – can express as the face'.[39] It is as though the space of the face were being extended up the arm and over the shoulder to the back. And indeed, the encounter with the other and the naked revelation of vulnerability results when 'the face has turned to me', making the interpersonal relation an 'asymmetrical' one . . . Thus there is ample scope for interpreting the face in Levinas as something other than what is simply frontal.[40]

Does ethics precede politics or does politics exceed ethics?

Wills' argument is a point worth bearing in mind for two reasons: it suggests that Levinas outlines an interpersonal asymmetrical *formal* structure that applies to other fields as well, and it cautions against too easy an association of Levinas' face-to-face with the revelatory, epiphanic encounter that Žižek has in mind when he sarcastically speaks of Levinas' 'gentrification' of the Other, of the 'decaffeinated' Other, or when he suspects that religion is being smuggled in through the back door.

At stake in the dispute are thus three terms – the 'Other', the 'stranger' and the 'neighbour' – that may overlap, but in other respects should be kept distinct, especially insofar as they belong to different discourses: the psychoanalytical, the ethical, the religious and the political discourse. For instance, the stranger is also the opposite of the neighbour: if the *neighbour* is the figure of the Other, with whom I share an uncanny familiarity and disturbing proximity (a psychoanalytic trope), the *stranger is* the Other, from whom I am separated by all the particularities of otherness that I fear or desire (with political implications). Nonetheless, Levinasian ethics of the Other obligates me to engage with both stranger and neighbour, while in the political realm it is only the neighbour with whom I have to arrange myself, while the stranger elicits my hospitality or hostility, and needs to redefine himself as refugee, foreigner, migrant, tourist and so on, before he falls under

---

[39] Levinas, *Totality and Infinity*, 262.

[40] David Wills, 'Dorsal Chances: An Interview with David Wills', interviewed by Peter Kilroy and Marcel Swiboda, *Parallax* 13, no. 4 (2007): 4–15 (5).

the responsibility of the state (or myself as citizen). It highlights the difficulty of grounding universalist claims, obligations and rights – about liberty, fraternity, equality – in a purely political interpretation of society and sociability, but also the dangers of not doing so, for my ethics and my psyche.[41]

What is thus once more at stake in Žižek's critique of Levinas is the relation between ethics and politics quite generally, insofar as both the neighbour and the stranger raise questions that go to the heart of the European project, not least because the 'heroic' version of this project sees Europe as occupying globally the moral high ground, especially with regard to human rights and their universal applicability. The question then becomes: do ethical precepts precede and exceed politics, or is it – in the absence of God – politics that ultimately ground and justify universal principles such as human rights? It is a key issue among continental philosophers, putting, for instance, Derrida and Levinas on one side and Badiou and Rancière on the other. One version has it that for Levinas, ethics precedes politics, and in another version, ethics is opposed to politics. Žižek once again helpfully summarizes the issue:

> Far from preaching an easy grounding of politics in the ethics of the respect and responsibility for the Other, Levinas rather insists on their absolute incompatibility, on the gap separating the two dimensions: *ethics involves an asymmetric relationship in which I am always-already responsible for the Other, while politics is the domain of symmetrical equality and distributive justice* . . . One is tempted to say that, far from being reducible to the symmetric domain of equality and distributive justice, politics is the very 'impossible' link between this domain and that of (theological) ethics, the way ethics cuts across the symmetry of equal relations, distorting/displacing them.[42]

[41] It is a point made forcefully by Žižek when he says that Freud and Lacan, discussing the problematic of the neighbour, are 'not just making the standard critico-ideological point about how every notion of universality is coloured by our particular values and thus implies secret exclusions; they are making a much stronger point on the *incompatibility of the Neighbour with the very dimension of universality*'. Žižek, 'Neighbors and other Monsters', 162.

[42] Slavoj Žižek, 'Smashing the Neighbor's Face: On Emmanuel Levinas' Judaism', *Lacan.com* (2006), http://www.lacan.com/symptom/?page_id=91 (accessed 10 January 2007) (emphasis added). Also: '[T]he true ethical step is the one beyond the face of the other, the one of suspending the hold of the face, the one of choosing against the face, for the third' (Žižek, 'Neighbors and Other Monsters', 183). Žižek develops this line of critique, taking issue with what he sees as the Levinasian fascination with the Other, which blinds one to the suffering of concrete others. True ethics, then, necessitates a move away from the dyadic moment of the face-to-face encounter (the ethical proper) to an incorporation of the Other's others (the political proper).

Human rights: beyond politics or bound by politics?

This suggests a potential opening, provided we redefine what we mean by politics: the grounds on which Levinas' ethics and (say, Rancière's) politics[43] might usefully be comparable is their respective *asymmetry* in relation to conventional notions of *morality* on the one hand, and conventional notions of *politics* on the other.[44] I shall try to show why such a comparison might be useful at the end of this chapter, but want first to examine more fully the historical background to the foundational or anti-foundational arguments concerning human rights. This debate goes back to the origins of the modern secular state, the 'will of the people' and beginnings of parliamentary democracy – whether located in England's Magna Carta, the American Constitution or the Jacobin ideals of the French Revolution. Today, human rights by their definition claim a universality that applies to all human beings, regardless of whether they are citizens of particular nation states, are stateless or are exposed to civil war. And yet, if they are grounded and justified by nothing other than a political agreement, made either under a specific form of government (e.g. Western liberal democracy) or by a world body like the United Nations (at the time, unrepresentative of large parts of the world's populations),[45] then – however well intentioned and beneficial – they can be challenged, and have been, in the name of 'cultural relativism', as an instrument of power, legitimating interference in sovereign states (traditionally a *casus belli*, a ground for war) and as the expression of a unilateral, Eurocentric imposition of values and precepts.[46]

Critiques of the inherent bias of universalist claims can be found in Europe itself, going back to Johan Gottfried Herder and Karl Marx, and including Friedrich Nietzsche and Freud. After the Second World War, one

[43] The contrast between Levinas and Rancière revolves around 'ethics' versus 'politics', and an essay by Simon Critchley tries to make this gap or difference productive for a comparison, suggesting that what in Rancière is the 'dissensus' is in Levinas the 'ethical'. Both try to keep open 'interstitial spaces' of resistance and refusal, spaces of and for the people. Simon Critchley, 'Five Problems in Levinas's View of Politics and the Sketch of a Solution to Them', *Political Theory* 32, no. 2 (April 2004): 184–5.

[44] For Levinas any self–Other relation is always (at some level) asymmetrical, involving both a joining and disjoining, proximity and distance, a 'relation without relation' (rapport sans rapport), as Levinas calls it elsewhere (*Totality and Infinity*, 80).

[45] The Universal Declaration of Human Rights was adopted by the United Nations General Assembly in 1948 at the Palais de Chaillot in Paris, with forty-eight nations in favour and eight abstentions.

[46] The controversy between universalists and cultural relativists is too complex to be dealt with here. A useful overview is Jack Donelly, 'Cultural Relativism and Universal Human Rights', *Human Rights Quarterly* 6, no. 4 (1984): 400–19, http://mym.cdn.laureate-media.com/2dett4d/Walden/PSPA/3040/02/Donnelly.pdf (accessed 5 September 2017).

of the more trenchant discussions of the problems inherent in human rights universalism, when solely emerging from political rights, can be found in Hannah Arendt's *Origins of Totalitarianism II: On Imperialism*, where she puts forward the notion that what is also needed are 'rights to have rights'.[47] Arendt points out that during the refugee crisis caused by the persecution and expulsion of Jews in Europe, the many who were refused entry in the US and elsewhere became proof that 'the conception of human rights, based upon the assumed existence of a human being as such, broke down at the very moment when those who professed to believe in it were for the first time confronted with people who had indeed lost all other qualities and specific relationships except that they were still human'.[48]

Arendt's argument is taken up and developed further in Agamben's writings, notably in *Homo Sacer: Sovereign Power and Bare Life* (1999) and *State of Exception* (2005).[49] There, he acknowledges that 'the so-called sacred and inalienable rights of man show themselves to lack every protection and reality at the moment in which they can no longer take the form of rights belonging to citizens of a state'.[50] His thinking, however, takes a somewhat different direction from Arendt's, in that, citing Michel Foucault's notion of bio-politics and bio-power, Agamben sees the primacy given to human rights, especially in Europe's conflicts and dealings with the rest of the world, as *depoliticizing* public life not only in international relations, but in domestic affairs, so that 'protecting freedom' and human rights has been used to justify a vast expansion of the state's security apparatus, reintroducing practices of inclusion and exclusion, based on disguising power-political objectives and limiting internal dissent, in the name of human rights and the delivery of humanitarian aid.

The politics of victimhood

One consequence of prioritizing human rights and humanitarian aid is that it has given prominence to one particular figure: the victim. Among the signs

---

[47] See Hannah Arendt, 'The Decline of the Nation-State and the End of the Rights of Man', in *The Origins of Totalitarianism* (New York: Harcourt, 1951), Part II (Imperialism), Chapter 9. Important writings discussing the different versions of universalism are Michael Walzer, 'Two Kinds of Universalism', in *Nation and Universe: The Tanner Lectures on Human Values* (1989), http://tannerlectures.utah.edu/_documents/a-to-z/w/walzer90.pdf, and Étienne Balibar, 'On Universalism: In Debate with Alain Badiou', *European Institue for Progressive Cultural Policies* (2007), http://eipcp.net/transversal/0607/balibar/en (both accessed 5 September 2017).

[48] Arendt, 'The Decline of the Nation-State', 299.

[49] Giorgio Agamben, *Homo Sacer: Sovereign Power and Bare Life*, trans. Daniel Heller-Roazen (Stanford, CA: Stanford University Press, 1999), and Giorgio Agamben, *State of Exception*, trans. Kevin Attell (Chicago: University of Chicago Press, 2005).

[50] Agamben, *Homo Sacer*, 75.

that there has been a move from agency as heroic and proactive to post-heroic and reactive is the shift of emphasis to the victim as the emblem of authenticity, with trauma as one of the strongest affects by which to assert one's identity and claim one's unique subjectivity. Asserting victimhood has become more than being the aggrieved or injured party to a dispute or a conflict. It has become a way of making one's voice heard, in a public sphere that does not recognize all that many legitimate speaking positions. On television, for instance, the 'victim' or 'survivor' not only has assigned to him/her a certain circumscribed role (for instance, to produce affect and emotion, and to refrain from having an opinion or promote a political cause), but the survivor also has a certain negative agency, namely – besides 'authenticity' – that of righteousness and subjective truth, *but only on condition of consenting to being a victim*, testifying to powerlessness and pure need.

Reflected in the gradual detachment of the victim from the causes and particular context of his/her condition, and its slippage into a surreptitiously universalizing category, is also a shift from 'politics' as party politics and organized militancy to politics as crisis management and security operations. It parallels an understanding of 'ethics' purely as 'living in the shadow of death and disaster'. Under these conditions, victim status highlights a philosophical problem, since it places those who seek freedom and equality at the receiving end of aid and humanitarian support, making helplessness the primary definition of their humanity. It seems that only as victim or survivor – of discrimination, of oppression, of harassment, of military or domestic violence – do I have the public credibility to claim rights and entitlements. Such rights used to be the result of political struggles and often costly collective action, but are now more a matter of self-presentation, and increasingly of self-presentation on social media.

Homo sacer and bare life

Agamben also takes up where Foucault and his later work on bio-politics/bio-power breaks off. Foucault rewrites nineteenth-century demographics and state programmes for health, hygiene, education and so on, but he also implies that in the twentieth century, what takes over from discipline is 'self-control', which in the later part of the century has become the 'care of the self'. This 'care of the self' has contributed to weakening the social bond and the evisceration politics (by making politics seem mainly to be about health-care provision, pension rights and 'security'), and has been turned into a hugely profitable consumer industry (because such 'care of the self' is liberty without any obligation to the Other). Commodified as an array of service industries, care of the self can tolerate disease and poverty elsewhere; indeed it uses poverty and disease (the argument for the need for 'security', i.e.

exclusion) as a justification and a self-fulfilling prophecy, as the motor for ever-tighter cycles of exclusion (based on the 'politics of fear'). As Žižek sums up Agamben's position, 'for Agamben, the implication of his analysis of homo sacer is not that we should fight for the inclusion of the excluded, but that homo sacer is the "truth" of all of us, that it stands for the zero-level position in which we are all placed'.[51] Once again, what emerges is the 'absent centre' and 'empty space', now at the personal level and involving the individual fate, which for these philosophers is the locus of (ontological) truth.

Zygmunt Bauman sees a continuous logic between the ghettos of Renaissance towns for Jews (needed as moneylenders, but excluded from civic rights), the concentration camps of the colonial period (South Africa), the extermination camps of the Nazis to the Gulags of Stalin, the no-go areas of contemporary metropolitan cities and the 'gated communities' in the wealthy parts of the globe. For Bauman this exclusionary trait has intensified since the colonial period, undoing many of the gains of the French and American revolutions, and the ideals of liberty, equality and fraternity. The Industrial Revolution, which could only happen because of colonialism and slavery, was thus also a counter-revolution (with respect to the ideals of the Enlightenment). If globalization is another version of colonialism, then more production of humans as 'waste' will be inevitable.

Bauman in some ways also follows Arendt's argument, when she makes the case that the camps were either sites where redundant people could be usefully employed (and worked to death), or that they served as laboratories (extra-territorialities) where the extremes and the limits of what is human were tested. Bauman extends this thought by turning it around: economic progress as such (technology) produces camps, and with them, redundant people. These are what he calls 'concentrationary spaces', and they emerge whenever humans are set to create (a new) order and improve the world:

> The production of 'human waste', or more correctly *wasted humans* (the 'excessive' and 'redundant', that is the population of those who either could not or were not wished to be recognized or allowed to stay), is an inevitable outcome of modernization, and an inseparable accompaniment of modernity. It is an inescapable side-effect of order-building (each order casts some parts of the extant population as 'out of place', 'unfit' or 'undesirable') and

[51] Slavoj Žižek, *Living in End Times* (London: Verso, 2011), 124–5. He also comments: 'The distinction between those who are included in the legal order and *homo sacer* is not simply horizontal, a distinction between two groups of people, but is increasingly also a "vertical" distinction between two (superimposed) ways in which *the same* people can be treated. Put simply: at the level of Law, we are treated as citizens, legal subjects; but at the level of its obscene superego supplement, of this empty unconditional law, we are treated as *homo sacer*' (*Living in End Times*, 124).

of economic progress (that cannot proceed without degrading and devaluing the previously effective modes of 'making a living' and therefore cannot but deprive their practitioners of their livelihood).[52]

Mutual interference in the internal affairs of the Other

The discussion about the radical separation or all too convenient conflation of ethics and politics has brought us to a point in the argument where the core values of Europe, its Jacobin heritage of liberty, equality and fraternity, seem to have been tainted if not perverted, so that 'liberty' either means (neo-)liberalism, where politics is entirely in the service of economics, or 'claiming rights and entitlements without duties and obligations'; 'fraternity' produces new tribal and nationalist forms of inclusion/exclusion; and 'equality' connotes either the purely formal equality before the law, or the egalitarian individualism of consumption. Such devaluation also reinforces the sense that the three ideals are fundamentally incompatible with each other, producing deadlock and self-cancellation. However, their mutual incompatibility could also prove their resilience as the aspirational ideals they were meant to be, encouraging not only Europe to continue endeavouring to fulfil their promise.

The latter is the possibility I would like to entertain and expand on further, returning to a political strategy briefly pursued by European thinkers who wanted to make sovereignty and fraternity conditionally interdependent, by balancing the antagonistic mutuality of their incompatibilities. In the context of proposing the idea of 'double occupancy' as an alternative to identity politics in an earlier essay I introduced what I thought of as the 'political' version of double occupancy, namely the doctrine of 'mutual interference in the internal affairs of the other'. Politically, it was a way of opening up the deadlocks of delegated sovereignty, which the European Union encountered in the run-up to enlargement in 2004. What makes the US Constitution a unique document is not only the division of powers between the executive, the legislature and the judiciary (European democracies have these checks and balances as well), but the singularly powerful performative act enshrined in its wording: 'We, the People hereby Declare . . .'. This performativity derived its self-assurance from moments of decisive rupture: the secession from the British Crown in the case of America, the guillotining of the king in the French Revolution. In the case of the European Union, the moment of

[52] Zygmunt Bauman, *Wasted Lives: Modernity and its Outcasts* (Cambridge: Polity Press, 2004), 4.

rupture symbolized by the defeat of Nazism does not seem to have had the same legitimizing effect in the transfer of authority and the grounding of sovereignty.

Although retaining the status of a thought experiment, 'the right of mutual interference in the internal affairs of the other' represents perhaps one of the most consequential and challenging ways of thinking about nationhood since the Treaty of Westphalia in 1648 and the Congress of Vienna in 1815, which enshrined non-interference as one of the ways of defining nationhood, and thus the principle of mutual recognition of sovereign states in international relations, precisely the point where human rights can seem to be transgressing or overriding such sovereignty.

Rephrased as a political principle adopted by the EU, it allows 'Brussels' to tell a member state (or a state seeking to become a member) how to change not only national laws, economic rules and environmental regulations, but also how to adapt typically national practices or uniquely national values. To quote myself:

> Yet the principle remains transgressive, and that is probably how it should be, especially given the uneven and asymmetrical power relations which obtain, when it is being applied by 'us' on the inside, telling 'them' on the outside: either you do as told, or else you stay outside. On the other hand, it does allow individual citizens of a nation-state to take their own government to court if national laws appear to infringe rights granted by the laws of the Community, or indeed when challenging such laws in the name of human rights. In other words, the right of mutual interference could be seen as the beginning of a new social contract, by which parties with grievances against each other, can seek redress, justice and negotiate a consensus, as well as establish a mutually confirming sovereignty based neither on divine right nor on a performative speech act.[53]

My added contention is that the *mutual interference* model is in some sense quite Levinasian, if one compares their respective formal structures, based as they both are on antagonistic mutuality. Mainly concerned with the delegation or distribution of sovereignty, 'mutual interference' nonetheless accepts a fundamental asymmetry involved in the quid pro quo, a destabilizing moment inherent in any exchange. It recognizes that – contrary to the heroic version of the nation state and its sovereignty – Europe has to start from the weakness of the nation state as a political entity, and build on democracy's vulnerabilities, in much the way that the precariousness of the Other inspires and necessitates the ethical response: that is, calls me to my own vulnerability.

---

[53] Thomas Elsaesser, 'Real Location, Fantasy Space, Performative Place: Double Occupancy and Mutual Interference in European Cinema', in Temenuga Trifonova (ed.), *European Film Theory* (New York and London: Routledge, 2009), 54.

However, it is the *formal* structure of Levinasian ethics, prior to any specific ethical imperative, that I want to highlight. As possibly similar to the political model of delegated and distributed sovereignty, it might provide the ungrounded foundation of the community – recognizing the mutual incompatibility of liberty, fraternity and equality while still insisting on the validity of their ethical-political promise and the productiveness of their internal antagonisms.

I noted the asymmetry involved in mutual interference, as well as the transgressive and destabilizing momentum it relied on. This asymmetry is important also in Levinas, as is the grounding of his ethics in a negativity (what he calls 'a relation without relation'). If Levinas insists on the face-to-face as the basis for the ethical relation, we saw that this need not connote an actual face. Furthermore, the encounter initiates a process that is explicitly designed to deconstruct any stable subject–object, self–Other relation based on exchange or equivalence: the asymmetry is in fact a double asymmetry, in which inequality runs from Other to self and from self to Other: not only is the face-to-face asymmetrical, there is also a spatial gradient (above/ below the Other). Put in different terms, the encounter installs a kind of relay of substitutions, and a transfer of functions: in the ethical act, I delegate to the Other my power of decision, a power which then returns to me, negatively, by way of an obligation (making me 'hostage' to my own self). This delegation of ethical agency to the Other, in order for me to derive *from* the Other my responsibility *for* the Other, is not without its risks: the self outsources itself to the Other, who is unknowable, and whose unpredictability (or monstrosity, if he is Žižek's 'neighbour') 'grounds' my ethical relationship in a kind of asymmetrical exchange that is clearly not reciprocal, but skewed into a shared and precarious *im*balance.[54] In fact, insofar as it presupposes a voiding (or 'calling into question') of the self in the face of the universality of the Other's demand, the encounter is mediated by processes of delegation and substitution which place the face 'above me', establishing a relation of force that is not reversible. In other words, the face-to-face does not oppose me to the Other, nor does it mirror me in the Other. It allows for no meeting of equals, but establishes the fraught relationality between self and Other which Levinas calls 'alterity'. In discussing Derrida's *Adieu à Emmanuel Levinas*, Simon Critchley draws out the political implications:

> [T]he hiatus between ethics and politics permits Derrida to make an absolutely crucial move in his reading of Levinas . . .: on the one hand, it enables him to accept the *formal* notion of the ethical relation to the

[54] It's the opposite of holding the other responsible, but it resonates with Žižek's and Robert Pfaller's notion of 'interpassivity': delegating to the other beliefs one does not hold, but nonetheless needs.

> other in Levinas whilst, on the other hand, refusing the specific political *content* that Levinasian ethics seems to entail, namely, the question of Levinas's Zionism, French Republicanism, Eurocentrism, or whatever. Derrida writes that 'the formal injunction of the deduction remains irrefusable . . . ethics entails politics and law . . . But, on the other hand, the political or juridical content thus assigned remains indeterminate, to be determined beyond knowledge and any possible presentation, concept or intuition, singularly in the speech and responsibility taken by everyone in each situation.[55]

When Derrida goes on to say that we would need 'another international law, another politics of frontiers, another humanitarian politics, even a humanitarian engagement that would hold itself effectively outside the interest of nation states',[56] does he not outline the mutual interference principle established as 'another international law'? Thus, one way of envisaging the European Union's internal managing of liberty, fraternity, equality, would be in this distinctly post-heroic form of institutionalizing instability, antagonism and mutuality. What Derrida (and Critchley) call the formal terms of an ethics that 'entails politics and law', and which they see as impossible to achieve in the present, corresponds more or less exactly to what I call the European thought experiment.

To return to our question – *Does the formal structure of Levinasian ethics allow for a politics, and if so, what kind of politics?* Would it be a politics that already presupposes citizenship, some sort of social contract, that is, an already legal framework of adjudicating conflicting claims? Or does the formal structure of such 'ethics into politics' precede and supersede the attainment of citizenship, allowing even those outside (the nation) and without (citizenship) a form of existence: not the 'right to have rights' but the 'right to be', while not obliging them to be 'inside', to integrate or to assimilate? Europe as thought experiment would suppose the latter: it acknowledges the force of Agamben's '*homo sacer*/bare life' argument, but differs from the 'can be killed but not sacrificed' injunction by establishing a *positive* relation of inside and outside, yet based on *negative* criteria (along the lines of Bartleby the Scrivener's 'I prefer not to', intriguingly invoked by the pro-Levinasian Agamben and the anti-Levinasian Žižek as the emblem of today's 'passive resistance').[57]

---

[55] Critchley, 'Five Problems'.

[56] Jacques Derrida, *Adieu à Emmanuel Levinas* (Paris: Galilee, 1997), 176.

[57] Michael Hardt and Antonio Negri, *Empire* (Cambridge, MA: Harvard University Press, 2000), 203–4; Žižek, *The Parallax View*, 381–5. On the significance of Bartleby for contemporary dissidence, resistance and protest movements, see Jonathan Poore, 'Bartleby's Occupation: "Passive Resistance" Then and Now', *Nonsite.org* (1 May 2013), http://nonsite.org/article/bartlebys-occupation-passive-resistance-then-and-now (accessed 5 September 2017).

However, I would like to make a further step and take both 'mutual interference' and the Levinasian ethical relation into another register, and recast the relation of non-relation, of alterity and of 'the right to be' as a relation of *abjection*. Levinas' formal structure, which ties me to the Other in the intimate/extimate way of positing a radical break while nonetheless eliciting from me a responsibility that leaves me dependent on the Other, is a description of abjection, insofar as in the ethical act, I make myself abject in relation to the Other, rendering the Other both sovereign and abject, outside the law but also above (or below) the law. The 'mutual interference in the internal affairs of the other' thus generates a relation of equality after all, but on a condition of mutual abjection – a thought (experiment) to which the next chapter is devoted.

The third deficit: equality – social justice or radical equality

With a detailed discussion of abjection – and its strategic role in relation to Europe and its cinema – deferred to the following chapter, some further thoughts on the question of equality are necessary in order to conclude the present one. The debate about fraternity, the neighbour, the Other and their ethical as well as political ramifications has shown how difficult, indeed impossible, it is – both in the encounter with the Other and in thinking about a new social contract of distributed sovereignty – to assume any kind of natural or spontaneous equality. On the contrary, the insistence on antagonisms and asymmetry as *a priori* givens are emerging as critical elements also for assessing equality as the relation between individuals, and of social justice as the relation of individuals to society in the political realm.

If the republican right of 'equality' is enshrined in Western democracies as 'equality before the law', this does not automatically guarantee 'social justice': on the contrary, it is formal, in the sense that justice as a legal concept in a democracy is supposed to be kept separate from the realm of politics (impartiality, division of powers). Social justice, on the other hand, is typically a matter of specific political struggles around the distribution of wealth, education, opportunities for work, health and other 'benefits and burdens' of being a member of society. What is at issue are the limits of the distributive model: the growing inequality in prosperity within Europe itself, aggravated by the scarcity of meaningful work for the following generation, as well as the disparities of wealth, governance and welfare between Europe and the rest of the world. These evident injustices – and the resulting guilt feelings, philanthropic acts and humanitarian interventions – have put a different idea of equality on the agenda of a new democratic mandate for Europe.

Yet how can these deficits in democracy I have been detailing be assets for Europe, or for the 'community to come'? They are assets, first of all, insofar as they oblige one to rethink what is meant by 'liberty, equality, fraternity' today, whether these are mere words, sounding antiquated and obsolete, or can be infused with new life and urgency. Secondly, they are assets in the light of my earlier assertion, namely that I consider the three republican ideals of the French Revolution to be both necessarily complementary *and* mutually incompatible. This is the reason they have endured as basic values over the centuries, but also why their realization has so far eluded us. Yet rather than consider it an inherent failure or shortcoming, their incommensurability is their ethical strength, their revolutionary legacy, their utopian promise and their political value as transgressive instruments in the struggle for unattained but nonetheless attainable ideals. Their promise and potential stand under somewhat different conditions than those obtaining in the United States where an 'ever more perfect (religio-political) union' is ritually invoked by every president as proof of American exceptionalism.[58]

European thinkers struggle with the question of how equality and, by extension, the republican ideals either validate themselves through Christianity or are sustained through the tensions of their inherent incommensurability. For instance, Howard Caygill highlights the dilemma experienced by Levinas around being both French and Jewish, between equality and fraternity. Levinas' solution, it emerges, was to see these ideals not as 'one dimensional' (and thus in competition with each other) but in terms of a three-dimensional topology, a Euclidian space that finally depend on a fourth, the religious dimension that stabilizes the others.[59]

In a similar vein, Eric S. Nelson, writing on the political implication of 'asymmetrical ethics', considers 'whether social-political equality necessarily requires presupposing the moral symmetry of subjects of classical liberalism'. He refers to Levinas to argue that 'social-political equality is compatible with and, more radically, can only be adequately developed in relation to the moral asymmetries between self and other. Levinas reframed questions of equality, justice, and solidarity in relation to the interruptive encounters between inherently asymmetrical subjects.' Such an asymmetrical ethics and humanism, he concludes, 'is most appropriate for confronting contemporary moral and social issues involving unequal situations, opportunities, and

[58] In a different but nonetheless relevant context, this idea is taken up by Stanley Cavell in his combination of 'perfectibility' and 'praise' as the ethical core of (Emersonian) democracy.

[59] Caygill maintains that 'The possibility of events of injustice . . . was nested in the revolutionary trinity itself. Liberty, equality and fraternity . . . remains an equivocal formula susceptible to a host of interpretations . . . Throughout his writings Marx, for example, showed the contradiction that arose in bourgeois societies between liberty and equality – economic liberty producing inequality that then compromises the liberty of the disadvantaged – and pitted against it the fraternity of the international proletariat' (*Levinas and the Political*, 178–9).

resources between pluralities of non-identical concrete individuals by calling and awakening me to my inescapable responsibility to the other – regardless of and prior to any relation of mutual exchange, expectation, negotiation, or recognition'.[60]

Thus, as a philosophical issue, the question of equality is fractured between the *social democratic model* of 'distributive justice', 'negotiation' and 'recognition' (associated with John Rawls, Habermas and Axel Honneth) and the *rupture model* of equality, derived from the 'asymmetrical ethics' of Levinas. Yet there is also a third position in play, the call for 'radical equality' associated with Rancière, whose views on democracy, politics and the 'distribution of the sensible' at first glance diverge quite sharply from Levinas' ethico-religious notions, but may nonetheless be comparable, as hinted at, thanks to a shared insistence on asymmetry (Levinas' alterity) and rupture (what Rancière calls dissensus).

Jacques Rancière and radical equality

Among European thinkers on equality, Rancière stands out as the most incisive and controversial. His call for 'radical equality' in the face of the 'distribution of the sensible' has injected into these debates a new kind of urgency, but has also raised as many questions as it answered. I want to argue that in the gaps that his seemingly contradictory views on equality of individuals, just societies and community of equals have opened up, one can first recognize an intellectual style and a procedure similar to what I call the thought experiment, and second, that his apparent vacillation between individual and collective equality designates a space that in my argument is occupied by the concept of abjection.

Rancière first developed the idea of radical equality as a premise and tool of pedagogy.[61] Drawing on the educational writings of a French teacher, Joseph Jacotot, working in Flemish-speaking Belgium in the 1820s, Rancière outlines 'five lessons in intellectual emancipation', among which are that 'all men have equal intelligence', that 'every man has the faculty of being able to instruct himself', and that 'we can teach what we do not know'. Central to these lessons is that all men have equal intelligence, which becomes, in Ruth Sonderegger's review of Rancière,

[60] Eric S. Nelson, 'Who is the other to me? Levinas, Asymmetrical Ethics and Socio-Political Equality', *Mono Kurgusuz Labirent* 8–9 (2010): 454–66, https://www.academia.edu/756166/Who_is_the_other_to_me_Levinas_Asymmetrical_Ethics_and_Social-Political_Equality (accessed 5 September 2017).

[61] Jacques Rancière, *The Ignorant Schoolmaster: Five Lessons in Intellectual Emancipation*, trans. K. Ross (Stanford, CA: Stanford University Press, 1991).

> . . . a paradoxically anti-foundational fundament of political action. According to Rancière, equality is not a (utopian) goal or a principle that could be grounded ontologically, transcendentally, anthropologically, or otherwise. Rather, it is a precarious presupposition, a presupposition, moreover, that is first of all demonstrated and verified temporarily by those who claim equality, although they are denied the status of candidates for equal treatment. Or, in Rancière's deliberately paradoxical wording: equality is verified when those who have no part, claim and take their part. Radical equality, in other words, needs to be taken rather than (condescendingly) given or granted . . . Whereas equality within the confines of an institutionally and hierarchically structured world can be distributed, radical equality cannot be granted or distributed as it cannot be perceived and conceptualized within the status quo (dubbed 'distribution of the sensible' by Rancière) and by those who represent the order of the status quo and claim that 'there is no alternative.' As a consequence of this, the unequal equals who are not visible within a particular status quo . . . need to act as if they were already visible. *They need to perform their equality to make it real.*[62]

There are three aspects to the proposition: first, equality is asymmetrical: those who claim it do not have any positive or secure ground to claim it from, while those who may be in a position to grant it, cannot see or grasp what is being claimed. Second, equality is the outcome of an active struggle and a politics of dissent: you assert and gain it, rather than receive it as a gift or have it conceded as entitlement. Third, it is a performative act, where you 'presuppose': you act *as if* you were already equal, which is to say, you place yourself on the inside even though you are outside, suspending or rendering immaterial any division or boundary line.[63]

Rancière can define equality in this way because of how he perceives the dominant order: parliamentary democracy under the sway of neoliberalism, with its priority given to economics; the European Union with its technocrats and crisis-managers; the French state with its centralized bureaucratic cadres drawn from the same elite schools and universities. This is politics as police: enforcing, patrolling, managing 'the distribution of the sensible', making sure that a contradiction, an injustice or any other kind of incommensurability

---

[62] Ruth Sonderegger, review of *Jacques Rancière and the Contemporary Scene*, by Jean-Philippe Deranty and Alison Ross (eds), *Constellations* 20, no. 2 (2013): 365–7 (366).

[63] An example of what Rancière's notion of equality might mean in practice is a movement calling itself Critical Mass. These are cyclists who on a specific day and an agreed time ride en masse through city streets, asserting their presence and protesting against pollution and congestion. Their motto is what makes them equal: 'We aren't blocking traffic, we are traffic'. Cited in Todd May, *The Political Thought of Jacques Rancière* (Edinburgh: Edinburgh University Press, 2008), 174.

is translated into problems that can be solved, or be resolved – in the case of conflicting claims – by a negotiated settlement, a consensus. By contrast, politics in Rancière's sense is not, in Ruth Sonderegger's account,

> struggles for, or negotiations about, getting more of this or that property, be it power, sovereignty, money, influence, rights or whichever other goods or positions that are available within an established community. For all these struggles do not challenge the existing orders of properties, powers, positions etc. . . . Such orders define and secure what counts as property, knowledge, or right, and who is entitled to claim the goods and positions just mentioned.[64]

As becomes evident, what is at stake for Rancière, when contrasting radical equality to the distribution of the sensible that marks our present order (which he also names the 'aesthetic regime'),[65] is not just the more or less equitable distribution of goods and services, wealth and welfare, but also the mental categories and discourses by which we perceive, describe and order the world – much in the way Foucault had argued in his *Archaeology of Knowledge* and *The Order of Things (Words and Things)*. But where Rancière differs is in his method or intellectual style. As he puts it:

> [The challenge to the usual] distribution of roles [of teacher and pupil, of intellectual and philosopher] concerns the status of my own assertions as well. I have tried to offer them as probable assertions, to avoid a certain affirmative, categorical style which I know is elsewhere encouraged in philosophy, but which I have never been able to assimilate . . . [So] it is true that we don't know that men are equal. We are saying that they might be. This is our opinion, and we are trying, along with those who think as we do, to verify it. But we know that this 'might' is the very thing that makes a society of humans possible.[66]

What is of note in this self-description is that Rancière's method as philosopher is not only performative but also probabilistic, which is to say, the 'as if' status of equality is repeated in Rancière's style of arguing for it, suggesting that his 'radical equality' is – as a politics – a 'thought experiment'. Equality is not the *telos* you want to reach or make real (as in the case of a utopia), but the point from where you start a process: it is your hypothesis,

[64] Ruth Sonderegger, 'Do We Need Others to Emancipate Ourselves? Remarks on Jacques Rancière', *Krisis – Journal for Contemporary Philosophy* 1 (2014): 53–67 (56).
[65] See Joseph J. Tanke, 'What is the Aesthetic Regime?', *Parrhesia* 12 (2011): 71–81.
[66] Rancière, *The Ignorant Schoolmaster*, 73. Also cited in Jean-Philippe Deranty and Alison Ross (eds), *Jacques Rancière and the Contemporary Scene* (London: Continuum, 2012), 3.

which you proceed to try and 'verify', which is to say, to examine its implications and explore its consequences.

Rancière's notion of a politics of 'emancipation into equality' is different from both the Marxist class struggle and social-democratic battles for workers' rights because of his insistence on the fundamental non-communication between rulers and ruled.[67] Such a radical exclusion of the ruled points in the direction of the '*homo sacer*' and of 'bare life', with a significant difference: Rancière assumes that striving for equality 'emancipates' the excluded and brings them (back) into the community, whose 'distribution of the sensible' as consensus thereby becomes the 'dissensus' of 'the part that has no part', installing the principle of antagonism and negativity at the heart of the social symbolic. The problem is twofold. Does the very term 'emancipation' not run the risk (not unlike 'tolerance') of implicitly assuming (and speaking from) a position of superiority, and therefore needs itself to be deconstructed in view of its own lack of equality?[68] Secondly, following Jacotot, emancipation is strictly an individual act, even a kind of face-to-face between the 'ignorant' schoolmaster and the 'intelligent' pupil. It suggests a structural inversion and imbalance of power relations that parallels Levinas' ethical version of the same asymmetry of the encounter with the Other, where I am nothing until constituted as 'obligation' by the Other's 'demand'.

Sonderegger, as one of Rancière's most astute but also critical commentators, finds it difficult to reconcile Rancière's assumption of universality with regard to the equality of intelligence with his resolute stand against any form of collective emancipation. She notes that Rancière wants to distance himself from both Hardt/ Negri's faith in the power of the 'multitudes', and from any kind of networked community constituting itself through social media or online activism:

> However, without further clarification *Rancière's concept of a collective or communist intelligence remains rather opaque*. It is difficult to see more in Rancière's kind of communism than, on the one hand, the universal intelligence of all speaking beings; or, on the other, *the possibility*

[67] 'Instead of addressing the representatives of the status quo, Rancière's account of equality therefore puts the emphasis on encouraging those who are so radically excluded from equal treatment that their claims appear as incomprehensible, as mere noise, gibberish, or nonsense. By expecting substantial changes from the demanding party instead of the wrongdoers who represent the status quo Rancière emphasizes the demanding party's capacity to learn, to speak (up), and to change the distribution [of the sensible] in place.' Sonderegger, 'Do We Need Others', 57.

[68] Sonderegger makes a similar point: 'The moral and political implications of Rancière's claim that the subalterns who have no part, can under all circumstances speak for themselves if they only want to and try hard enough, are anything but unquestionable. For this seems to imply that those (without a part) who do not emancipate and subjectivize themselves are morally and politically inferior.' Sonderegger, 'Do We Need Others', 60.

> *of a succession of individual acts of emancipation [whose] connection [to each other] appears as arbitrary.* But why then should one call such succession collective or even communist intelligence?[69]

Sonderegger's solution is to return to the vulnerability and fragility (what I called the inversion and imbalance of power relations) of Jacotot's universal intelligence, which cannot be shored up and stabilized by

> . . . an individual or a collective that speaks with one voice but, rather, an inter-active communality of mutual encouragement as far as faith in equality is concerned. Such communality would allow us to envision an emancipatory communality that no single individual or collective subject could ever establish and that, therefore, actually goes beyond a concatenation of individual acts of emancipation . . . [It] would enable us to invest concepts like 'collective intelligence' or 'communism of intelligence' with meaning and liberate Rancière from undecidedly oscillating between an almost empty communism and an individualistic account of emancipation.[70]

Such a solution finally proceeds from the notion that equality should after all be something to strive after and to realize in the 'here and now' of the given world order, rather than be considered as a thought experiment that tests the relations of individual and society, the inside and the outside, what is human and what is not (or no longer), by extrapolating their extreme or radical consequences. Perhaps Rancière's 'undecided oscillation' is the better part of the bargain, calling to mind another philosopher's struggle with equality. In his *Works of Love*, Søren Kierkegaard takes up the 'love thy neighbour' conundrum, and surmises that the ideal neighbour to love is the dead neighbour, because, other than in the case of lovers, where the loved one possesses uniquely distinguishing qualities, 'to love one's neighbour means equality, [and thus you have to] forsake all distinctions so that you can love your neighbour'.[71] As Žižek remarks, quoting this passage, 'However, it is only in death that all distinctions disappear, since as Kierkegaard avers: "Death erases all distinctions, but preference is always related to distinctions".'[72]

Thus, an alternative to Sonderegger's 'puzzle' regarding Rancière's oscillation would be to consider radical equality as a form of 'positive undeadness' suspended between not altogether dead and not fully alive,

---

69 Sonderegger, 'Do We Need Others'.
70 Sonderegger, 'Do We Need Others'.
71 Søren Kierkegaard, *Works of Love*, trans. Howard V. Hong and Edna H. Hong (New York: Harper, 1994), 74.
72 'Introduction', in Reinhard, Santner and Žižek, *The Neighbor: Three Inquiries in Political Theology*, 3.

which would correspond, without coinciding, to Agamben's *homo sacer*, but even more so with my idea of *abjection*: as we shall see, it can be both singular and collective, it is both obstructing and empowering, it is both an equalizer and a universalizer. In other words, the concept of the abject reworks and opens up, or rather 'redistributes' the valencies of the living body and the corpse. But it also traverses, transgresses or negates notions such as the boundary between inclusion and exclusion, between the external and the internal, and challenges other seemingly foundational categories. Therefore, whatever we may finally make of Rancière's views of 'radical equality' in the realm of the political, their implication (and his own film-philosophical arguments) for a different conception of cinema, as the next chapter shows, are crucial for both my concept of 'film as thought experiment' and for European cinema as a 'cinema of abjection'.

Summary: what is Europe as a thought experiment?

The chapter argues that the much-criticized 'deficits' of Europe (as a political entity) are in fact assets when seen from another perspective. This other perspective is informed by a number of assumptions, which together constitute the 'thought experiment' of the title. First of all, the perspective is that of political thought, rather than sociology or economics, refiguring 'democracy' around the question of sovereignty, which in the European Union has to be distributed between the nation states – a process that in actual fact brings back the essence and origin of democratic sovereignty : the empty centre, confirming that it cannot be either conferred on an individual or distributed evenly. Second, the other perspective includes a different take on Europe becoming multi-ethnic and multi-denominational, discussed under the heading of 'the other as neighbour and stranger' and the dynamics of inclusion and exclusion, also from an anthropological perspective that asks who or what are the masses, the migrants, the refugees, the multitudes – as the boundaries of inside and outside are being defensively redrawn by globalization, fuelled by a retribalization that not only affects the break-up of (artificially created) nation states in the Middle East, but also Europe's post-nation state nation states.

This in turn raises the question of the relation between ethics and politics, as debated among Levinas, Derrida, Agamben and Žižek around the ethical act as either foundational or as dependent on religion or politics, with the corollary of human rights as either universal and above politics, or an instrument of power politics and an excuse for intervention and interference. The perspective finally taken is that the ethical act, as conceived by Levinas, has a structure similar to the political model of distributed sovereignty as 'mutual interference' (creating equality out of mutually antagonistic asymmetries). It is at this level that ethics and politics can be aligned together, in the form of a thought experiment that redefines Europe as an ethical as well as a political project, unique and exceptional in that it builds on the *constitutive weakness* of democracy (the ungrounded performativity of sovereignty) and on the *inherent vulnerability* (i.e. the mutual incompatibility) of its ethico-political core values: liberty, fraternity, equality.

What the thought experiment proposes is to adapt one of the more extreme perspectives discussed, namely Agamben's *homo sacer* as the ground zero of this vulnerability, but to modify his 'bare life' by making it relational. The name given to this relationality is 'abjection' – a term which hopefully also brings us back to the cinema, as one of the prime sites where the consequences (of pushing to such apparently extreme negativity the perceived deadlocks of European democracy) are given bodies and scenarios that situate themselves as thought experiments between realistic narratives, performative enactments and didactic parables.

Abjection defines this negative relationality as a form of agency and it is such abject agency that may 'reboot' Europe, in the sense of returning us to the roots of democracy, reviving it and keeping it alive, at a time when democracy does not seem to be the form of self-government either needed by the dominant economic model of global growth-oriented capitalism, or supported by an absolute majority of citizens.

5

A Cinema of Abjection?

Two films from Cannes

Two films that prompted much discussion at the 2016 Cannes Festival were the Palme d'Or winner, Ken Loach's *I, Daniel Blake*, and the surprise of the festival, Maren Ade's *Toni Erdmann*. One is an impassioned attack on the bureaucratic inhumanity of the British welfare system, humiliating the vulnerable in order to enforce the state's austerity targets, thereby driving a good man to his death. The other is a serio-comic father–daughter story, where a high-flying but stressed-out female business consultant, whose firm specializes in making 'inefficient' East European workers redundant, is possibly brought back to her humanity through the antics of a father who is grieving about the loss of his dog.

At first sight, these two films have little in common, since *I, Daniel Blake* is a social melodrama – a kind of Charles Dickens *Hard Times* for the twenty-first century, complete with single mother of two driven into prostitution and a tearful funeral scene – while the other could be taken for a contemporary version of the sort of hard-edged comedy that in Germany made another female director famous in the 1980s: Doris Dörrie's biggest hit, *Männer/Men* (1985) features a man in a gorilla suit, which in Maren Ade's *Toni Erdmann* becomes a man's shaggy dog-face and a furry Kukeri costume.

Yet *I, Daniel Blake* and *Toni Erdmann* (besides having male proper names as titles) have deeper similarities. These relate to a central topic of this study, namely what neoliberalism does to human beings and the social contract, the symptoms of which can be traced in what I am calling 'cinema of abjection'. Each film features one or several potential 'abjects', embodying a tendency or turn among (mainly, but not uniquely) European cinema since the 1990s. And yet each of the two films narrowly misses the ethical implications and political stances I also detect in this phenomenon.

What prompted the label 'cinema of abjection' is the surprising number of films with protagonists trapped in a seemingly relentless downward spiral, until they 'hit bottom' or realize there is no bottom at all. A prototypical early example is Mike Leigh's *Naked* (1993), which might as well be called *Abject*.[1] Towards the end, Johnny – the arrogantly anarchic, oversexed, unemployed, dead-beat wise guy – is thrown out of his on-off girlfriend's flat. It is clear that this is not the first time he has been thus evicted by a woman, making one wonder whether the end returns to the beginning, where Johnny has brutal sex in a rain-soaked back alley near a dumpster. Although *Naked* is an extreme – and extremely harrowing – example, Leigh's film is not exceptional as a study in abjection: a state of mind and body that this chapter both tries to define and to defend, by aligning it with the idea of cinema as thought experiment as discussed in Chapter 3. Abjection in everyday parlance is often used synonymously with dejection and despair, but in the humanities it is best known as a psychoanalytical concept introduced by Julia Kristeva, where it denotes the infant's desire, need and dread to have to detach from the (body of the) mother.[2] As such, it represents a painful and violent expulsion from a familiar space. One way of understanding the protagonist of *Naked* is to see him compulsively repeat cycles of attachment and ejection, vehemently refusing to become a social being, even – shockingly – raping the mother (substitute) in order to return to and retain her.

Over the past thirty-five years, Kristeva's ideas have been several times reformulated: for instance, the concept has extended beyond the specifically psychoanalytic realm, gaining critical traction in feminism and the art world, but also in social and cultural studies, as a mode of defiance beyond victimhood.[3] Building on these changing semantics of abjection, I want to give the term a further philosophical dimension and political application. Following the counter-intuitive claim, proposed in Chapter 1, that European cinema's weaknesses compared to Hollywood and Asian cinema may be the reverse side of its philosophical acumen and freedom to experiment, abjection enters the discussion about European cinema as part of another horizon for thought: rethinking the politics and ethics of being European *within* the post-secular and *after* the post-human. In view of my polemical definition of 'European' as the appropriate designation for films that stress-test the core principles of *liberté*, *egalité*, *fraternité*, abjection would be the fulcrum and defiantly radical vanishing point of these values.

The problem that a cinema of abjection addresses is that – confronted with the many crises the world faces – the present way of life is unsustainable. Yet rather than illustrate the devastating consequences of global warming,

[1] Michael Coveney, speaking of 'the nauseating nineties', comes close to using the term 'abjection', in *The World According to Mike Leigh* (New York: Harper Collins, 1996), 19.

[2] Julia Kristeva, *Powers of Horror: An Essay on Abjection*, trans. Leon S. Roudiez (New York: Columbia University Press, 1982).

[3] See, in this context, Imogen Tyler, *Revolting Subjects: Social Abjection and Resistance in Neoliberal Britain* (London: Zed Books, 2013).

the growing disparity between rich and poor, the social injustices through discrimination on the basis of gender and race, or the suffering inflicted on people through civil wars, corruption or the remnants of colonialism, a cinema of abjection takes these evils almost as given, as the natural state of the world, in order to intimate a different kind of 'reboot of the system'. Challenging the idea of us humans as the pinnacle of creation, rather than a mere accident of evolution, abjection gets us back to basics: to what it means to be part and not part of a community, what it means to be 'singular' in the plural multitudes, what it means to 'opt out' without being 'left out' – in short, what remains of us as human beings when none of the traditional bonds (marriage, family, clan, civil society, profession, nation, law, religion, language) can be relied upon to support a sense of self or identity other than the power of negativity itself. Cinema of abjection says, 'What unites us are the spaces that separate us.' It is radical, but also hypothetical (a 'thought experiment'), and it aligns itself neither with the humanism of identity politics, nor with its opposites, the philosophies of the post-human, whether in the name of object-oriented ontology or speculative realism. The 'abject' positions itself between the 'subject' and the 'object': as an intermediary category, it is a relational term, designating not a fixed state, but what emerges at moments that suddenly strike or confront an individual in a given situation. It is relational also in the sense that an asymmetrical reciprocity binds the abject to the force or instance that abjects and ejects. In the films I am concerned with, *abjection* can be the state of characters or of the main protagonist; the director can be *an abject* in relation to the institution cinema (as 'servant of two masters' – see Chapter 12), but *abjection* can also be *the position that the spectator* is put in by a film's mode of address, which bars both the role of the voyeur (in fiction films) and of the witness (in documentary).

Cinemas of abjection: Béla Tarr, Pedro Costa – Michael Haneke, Agnès Varda

Two examples of films whose characters can be described as abjects are Béla Tarr's *The Turin Horse* (2012) and Pedro Costa'a *In Vanda's Room* (2000). These are directors whose work exemplifies some of the aesthetic virtues, as well as the ethical seriousness and deep humanity, that such a cinema of abjection can bring to our notice. This includes their uncompromising reduction of narrative and spectacle, their focused concentration on the sacred moments of the ordinary, their close attention to the everyday, their steadfast gaze on characters who want neither sympathy nor do they open themselves to empathy, since we know so little about them. The films' attention to the materiality of objects and the figures' rapport with the spaces they inhabit, physically specific yet universal in their minimalism; and finally the characters' refusal to be treated as either victims or case studies, however peculiar their way of life and however severe their bodily afflictions – all this designates them as protagonists of a cinema of abjection and epitomizes what can be at stake: not only are their characters abjects, and the directors themselves marginal even in the festival system, but the length of their films obliges the spectators to recalibrate their own presence, oscillating between a kind of spectatorial of entropy and intense, trance-like involvement.

However, while Tarr and Costa can serve as a benchmark, their films by no means exhaust or even explain what is meant by the cinema of abjection. In what follows, I want to focus not on their work (or on directors who share a similar aesthetics), but on narratives or moments of abjection in films made right across Europe over the past two decades. They feature characters – not necessarily migrants or homeless, not outcasts or marginals, but ordinary, sometimes well-to-do and seemingly established members of the community – who either find themselves falling out of their habitual lives for no special reason other than chance and bad luck, or who lose their footing in their social and domestic lives under abrupt but barely explicable circumstances. They encounter a moment of radical point zero – often paired with an ethical crisis, the unravelling of social bonds or the return of a past long forgotten and/or repressed.

For instance, in Michael Haneke's *Code Inconnu* (2000), the careless tossing aside of a crumpled paper bag sets off a chain reaction that all but destroys the lives of three characters from very different walks of life, and one of several harrowing scenes has the heroine trapped in a seemingly bottomless void of anguish and abjection. A different moment of abjection – the abrupt shattering of middle-class existence – is at the centre of Haneke's *Caché* (2005), when a videotape, anonymously pushed through the letterbox in a bourgeois couple's home, causes the settled life of a Parisian literary talk-show host to precipitously unravel.

A genealogy of such cinema of abjection in Europe would go back to Chantal Akerman's *Jeanne Dielman* (1975) and Agnès Varda's *Vagabond* (1985). Varda's masterpiece, *The Gleaners and I* (2000), also qualifies: it is a more stoic-humorous, but also more acerbic-autobiographical version of abject moments, shared with others whose lives have to be lived beyond the pale. Other French directors' films that know moments of abjection are Matthieu Kassovitz' *La Haine* (1995), Gaspar Noé's *Seul Contre Tous* (1998) and *Enter the Void* (2009), Claire Denis's *Beau Travail (*1999), Catherine Breillat's *A Ma Soeur* (*Fat Girl*, 2001) and Leos Carax's *Holy Motors* (2012), as well as almost every other film that features Denis Lavant, the very face of abjection in French cinema. In Britain, apart from Mike Leigh's *Naked*, it is Danny Boyle's *Trainspotting* (1996) and David Mackenzie's *Young Adam* (2003) that come to mind, not forgetting the films of Lynn Ramsay, especially *We Need to Talk About Kevin* (2011). In Scandinavia, there is Roy Andersson's *Songs from the Second Floor* (2000), Lukas Moodysson's *Container* (2006), Joachim Trier's *Oslo 31 August* (2011), Thomas Vinterberg's *The Hunt* (2012) and Ruben Östlund's *Force Majeure* (2014), where the avalanche is a moral catastrophe more than a natural one, turning the father of the family into an abject: abandoning his family to save his mobile phone. All these films put their protagonists in extreme or exceptional situations, but these situations are situated at the bottom of what is human, as if to test what remains in an emergency, when protective conventions and symbolic mandates are stripped away, and what survives when dignity evaporates and the 'ethical self' disintegrates.

In Belgium, the Dardenne Brothers' *La Promesse* (1996) and *Rosetta* (1999) inaugurated a cycle of abjection that also includes Bruno Dumont's *L'Humanité* (2000), while in Germany abject subjects haunt Christian Petzold's *The State I'm in/Die innere Sicherheit* (2000), *Ghosts/Gespenster* (2005), *Barbara* (2012) and *Phoenix* (2014), as well as Tom Tykwer's *Winter Sleepers* (*Winterschläfer*, 1997) and *The Princess and the Warrior/Der Krieger und die Kaiserin* (2000) and Fatih Akin's *Head on/Gegen die Wand* (2004). Directors whose protagonists are especially liable to a sudden loss of ground are, besides Haneke (*Funny Games*, 1997, *The Piano Teacher*, 2001, even *The White Ribbon*, 2009 and *Amour*, 2012) and the Dardenne Brothers (besides *La Promesse* and *Rosetta*, one must also mention *Le Fils*, 2002, *L'Enfant*, 2005, *Le Silence de Lorna*, 2008 and *Two Days, One Night*, 2014), Aki Kaurismäki (*Drifting Clouds*, 1996, *The Man without a Past*, 2002 and *Le Havre*, 2011) and especially Lars von Trier (*Breaking the Waves*, 1996, *Dancer in the Dark*, 2000, *Dogville*, 2003, *Antichrist*, 2009, *Melancholia*, 2011 and *Nymphomaniac*, 2013).

If at one end of the spectrum are the films of Béla Tarr and Pedro Costa, and at the other end, Lars von Trier and the Dardenne Brothers, my own interest in states of abjection in cinema began with Rainer Werner Fassbinder. Figures such as his Fox in *Fox & his Friends/Faustrecht der Freiheit* (1975) and Erwin/Elvira in *In a Year of 13 Moons/In einem Jahr mit 13 Monden* (1978) provided templates for the abject heroes of the 1990s and beyond, insofar as Fassbinder's characters are different from the outsider hero of previous European art cinema. It is as if the alienated men and women of Ingmar Bergman, Robert Bresson and Michelangelo Antonioni, the rebel outsiders of Jean-Luc Godard and François Truffaut, the lost souls of Wim Wenders and Jim Jarmusch had at some point in the 1990s flipped over into descendants of Fassbinder's affectless but driven, sullen but restless post-mortem creatures (a state literalized in Noé's *Enter the Void*).

Fassbinder's abjects were made more dire and precarious because they were exploited or discriminated against for being gay or transgender. Yet, in retrospect the Klaus Kinski figure in some of Werner Herzog's films, notably the overreaching hubris of Aguirre at the end of *Aguirre Wrath of God*

(1972), might qualify as abject, as does Bruno S., the underdog in Herzog's *Stroszek* (1977), and even Timothy Treadwell in *Grizzly Man*. On the other hand, the protagonist of Cristi Puiu's *The Death of Mr Lazarescu* (2005) – resurrected and saved from a blood clot in the brain, merely in order for him to die of liver cirrhosis – while in many ways a typical abject, is depicted more like a victim: one's response to his absurd plight is pity, while anger at 'the system' is actively solicited, as is identification with the nurse who refuses to abandon him.

Such emotions tend to be blocked or made more complicated in many of the films I have listed, because abjects are neither victims nor saints. What is most enigmatic (and most threatening) about them is that, by having lost or given up much, they gain a strange sort of freedom, which renders their pain less pitiable but also their character less likeable. Abjection can make someone uncanny: such is the case of Johnnie in *Naked*, such is the case with Majid, the Algerian in *Caché*, and also with Pierre, Anne Laurent's son in Haneke's *Happy End* (2017), a director especially adept at making audiences 'uncomfortable'.[4] Johnnie, Majid and Pierre are, in psychoanalytic terms, (death) drive creatures rather than desire creatures, hence their negative power over others, a state not unrelated to Giorgio Agamben's *homo sacer*: they embody a truth about society or about the world that has to be sacrificed.

Abjection defined and retained

Abjection, as mentioned, is a concept that comes to us via Kristeva's *Powers of Horror: An Essay on Abjection*, influenced by among others Jean Paul Sartre's *Nausea*, as well as Georges Bataille's *The Accursed Share*. Since the book's publication in 1982, there has been a lively and controversially fought debate over the term's history, definition, fields of applicability, critical traction and affirmative uses.[5] Points of contention have focused on its origins: while Bataille's concept of the *informe* is crucial here,[6] so is

[4] See Scott Roxborough, 'Michael Haneke on "Happy End" and the Art of Making Audiences Uncomfortable', *Hollywood Reporter*, 30 November 2017, https://www.hollywoodreporter.com/news/oscars-michael-haneke-happy-end-art-making-audiences-uncomfortable-1062407 (accessed 1 December 2017).

[5] For a highly critical overview of the debates, see Martin Jay, 'Abjection Overruled', in Martin Jay, *Cultural Semantics: Keywords of Our Time* (Amherst: University of Massachusetts Press, 1998), 144–56.

[6] '. . . on the other hand, affirming that the universe resembles nothing and is only formless (*informe*) amounts to saying that the universe is something like a spider or spit'. Georges Bataille, 'Informe', *Documents* 7 (December 1929): 382. See also Yves-Alain Bois and Rosalind Krauss, *Formless: A User's Guide* (New York: Zone Books, 1997).

anthropologist Mary Douglas's seminal *Purity and Danger*,[7] also cited by Kristeva.[8] She gives these thinkers an explicitly feminist and psychoanalytic turn: everything emphatically excluded from the self, such as bodily waste and bodily fluids, becomes abject, whenever it acts as a reminder of the threat to the integrity of the self, imaged and figured through the body. Since the most traumatizing detachment for the subject-to-be is from the mother, her body and its secretions are especially liable to abjection, with the detachable skin of boiled milk a particularly irrational but potent object of this disgust.

However, it is the corpse that above all exemplifies the abject, since it literalizes the breakdown of several boundaries that assure identity and personhood since infancy. What a corpse confronts us with is not only our own mortality made palpably real. The corpse's lifeless objectness while still reminding us of the living being that was, also makes us doubt the very possibility of being a subject. As Kristeva writes, 'The corpse, seen without God and outside of science, is the utmost of abjection. It is death infecting life.'[9] What attracts and repels in equal measure is the proximity and familiarity of an abject object or person, which means that the abject is something or someone whose trace as waste returns as a traumatic memory. The abject marks also the narrow gap that separates the useful from the useless, signalling the point when humans are seen or treated as material objects. The negativity of the abject thus paradoxically functions as an affirmation of the human. It is as much a perspective and a perception as it is a situation and a state.

For Kristeva, the abject can also manifest a form of female empowerment, suggesting that there is the possibility of a reversal of perspective, where the abject derives power from being excluded or expelled. For if Kristeva is right, then what she calls the 'powers of horror' of the abject derive from the other's fear of fusion or contamination, giving the abject not only the license to defy those societal norms that treat such 'natural' bodily manifestations as spittle, sweat, semen or blood as disgusting, obscene or inappropriate, but 'your' disgust also empowers 'me' over 'you' who rejects and abjects 'me', since the violence of your gesture of expulsion, that is, disgust, is the clearest admission that I am – or was – part of you, and that something in you knows it. It is this secret knowledge of what we share, but cannot admit, that makes the abject relevant also for analysing genocidal hatred, racial prejudice or other forms of discrimination that depend on a

[7] Mary Douglas, *Purity and Danger: An Analysis of Concepts of Pollution and Taboo* (London: Routledge & Kegan Paul, 1966).

[8] Keith Reader, in *The Abject Object: Avatars of the Phallus in Contemporary French Theory, Literature and Film* (Amsterdam: Rodopi, 2006), 39–42, has also put forward another possible influence, Marcel Jouhandeau's *De l'abjection*, first published in 1939.

[9] Kristeva, *Powers of Horror*, 4.

troubled self–other dynamic.[10] Acts of exclusion, however, are apt to produce empowered abjects only when such acts – or more often words – of racial or sexual abuse can be appropriated and turned into a badge of honour (as in 'black', 'punk' or 'queer'). This manifests the power of the abject in the social and political sphere, highlighted by the dual meaning of the English word 'revolting': an act of rebellion by some, it induces disgust in the others.[11] The powers of horror (or of 'revolting') also mark the crucial distinction already mentioned: the abject is different from the victim.

The abject in art

Throughout the 1990s, the concept of the abject was widely discussed (and used) in art history, theory, curating and art making.[12] The landmark for such an *aesthetics* of abjection – where artworks immerse themselves in abject materials, or try to evoke disgust – was the show organized by the Whitney Museum of American Art in 1993 called *Abject Art: Repulsion and Desire in American Art.*[13] In the debate that accompanied this art world event – organized by the editors of the art journal *October* – one can identify several clearly articulated, but internally antagonistic positions, of which the two most important ones were the *substantive* definition of the abject (i.e. material, embodied, attached to a specific referent) and the *structural* definition (semiotic, differential and symbolic), focused more generally on

---

[10] 'The abject', in Kristeva's vivid and evocative language, refers to 'my loathing an item of food, a piece of filth, waste, or dung. The spasms and vomiting that protect me; the repugnance, the retching that thrusts me to the side and turns me away from defilement, sewage, and muck; the shame of compromise, of being in the middle of treachery; the fascinated start that leads me toward and separates me from them.' Kristeva, *Powers of Horror*, 2.

[11] This is the key argument of Imogen Tyler: '*Revolting Subjects* explores the dual meanings of "abjection" and "revolt": the processes through which minoritized populations are imagined and configured as revolting and become subject to control, stigma and censure, and the practices through which individuals and groups resist, reconfigure and revolt against their abject subjectification.' Tyler, *Revolting Subjects*, 4.

[12] Examples of abject art prior to the 1990s are the performances of the Viennese Aktionskünstler (Hermann Nitsch, Otto Mühl). Their arrival in New York in 1964, on the invitation of Jonas Mekas, was crucial for artists of the abject such as Carolee Schneemann. She was influenced more by Nitsch and Mühl than by Kristeva. See Thomas Nesbit, 'Otto Mühl and the Aesthetics of Seduction', paper for the Institut für die Wissenschaft des Menschen, Vienna (2005), http://www.iwm.at/publications/5-junior-visiting-fellows-conferences/vol-xviii/thomas-nesbit/ (accessed 26 November 2017).

[13] The Whitney Museum in New York staged *Abject Art: Repulsion and Desire in American Art* in August 1993. It was preceded by another exhibition, called *Dirt and Domesticity: Construction of the Feminine*, in June 1992, also at the Whitney.

processes of rupture and disorientation.[14] The round-table participants were not involved in curating the Whitney exhibition, but some had more of a stake in the debate than others, notably Rosalind Krauss and Denis Hollier, editors and commentators on Bataille and his concept of *The Informe*.

Consequently, part of the *October* discussion turned on the question of whether Kristeva had misunderstood or misused Bataille, and whether Bataille's *informe* was compatible with Kristeva's *abject*. Krauss and Hollier contested this, which led to a joint effort on the part of the participants to arrive at a more precise definition and to differentiate between these distinct meanings of abjection, when applied to art objects, their display and their reception. While the *substantive* is prominent in Kristeva and aligns the abject with psychoanalysis and the immediate pre- and post-natal states of human development, the *structural* belongs more to an aesthetic discourse, and features mostly in the art world. The *structural* version of the abject, prior to any specific bodily substance or physiological response, insists on the radicality of rupture, on unsettling transgressions of any kind, on disorder and disorientation. The abject object or substance is then merely the contingent instance or occasion through which the act of separation, exclusion, but also of redistribution and dispersal, makes itself known and manifest. The overlap or confusion between the two types made the abject productive for artists, because it opened a semantic field where the *abject* meets the *informe*, and the visceral becomes both visual and conceptual.

This led Hal Foster and Benjamin Buchloh to propose the distinction that while Kristeva's *abject* is 'scatological', Bataille's *informe* is 'scatterological':[15]

> 'Scatterological' points to a discrepancy we should deal with: are these notions about subject or structure? 'Scatter' suggests structure, and points to the *informe*. 'Scatological' involves the subject, and points to the abject. Rosalind Krauss confirms this distinction, when she says: 'Kristeva's project is all about recuperating certain objects as abject-waste products, filth, body fluids, etc.' These objects are given an incantatory power in her text. I think that move to recuperate objects is contrary to Bataille.[16]

---

[14] The occasion for drawing these distinctions as sharply as possible was a two-part round-table discussion organized by the editors of the New York-based art journal *October* in 1994, whose second part, entitled 'The Politics of the Signifier II: A Conversation on the *Informe* and the Abject', brought together Hal Foster, Benjamin Buchloh, Rosalind Krauss, Yves-Alain Bois, Denis Hollier and Helen Molesworth, mainly to reflect on the Whitney exhibition, which was seen by the participants as symptomatic for wider tendencies in end-of-the-century art.

[15] 'In a given work of art that has been grouped into this category, some critics argue that the abject component of the work is its subject matter, the real-world referent it employs or emulates, while others argue that it is the process it reflects, the act of exclusion, which makes it pertinent to the concept of abjection.' Hal Foster, 'A Conversation on the Informe and the Abject', *October* 67 (Winter 1994): 3–21.

[16] Foster, 'A Conversation on the Informe and the Abject', 3–21.

The *October* panel discussion, besides vividly illustrating – with the *scatological* versus the *scatterological* – the difference between the substantive and structural meaning of abjection, also underlines that in Kristeva, as in Bataille, the abject is subversive in its negativity. Provoking the abjecting instance or agency by an ineradicable contiguity and abiding relationality, it recalls (from Chapter 4) the problematic proximity of the 'neighbour' who (according to Žižek) can provoke not only disgust but the sort of visceral hatred that leads to murder.

The abject in political theology and ethics

If, on the other hand, abjection can also take the form of provocative self-abasement, it becomes political as well as philosophical in a different sense, namely as a gesture and an act that challenges the other to respond to the abject's particular kind of 'embodied truth'. For instance, in Peter Sloterdijk's *Critique of Cynical Reason*, Diogenes of Sinope's abject life in a barrel is used as an example of 'cynical' politics, in which *personal degradation is used for purposes of challenging or castigating the community*. As a form of tactical abjection, the cynical philosopher lives and thus embodies the message he is trying to convey.[17]

Agamben's version of abjection, the *homo sacer*, is different from, yet can be related to, Sloterdijk's cynical abject. Taken by Agamben from Roman law, the *homo sacer* stands for a form of existence in which certain human beings cannot be addressed socially and are thus reduced to their bodily presence or subsistence. As discussed in the previous chapter, the abject for him is an ethical rather than a political category, hence his philosophy must oppose the separation of the ethical from the political since the ethical operates outside the law and the state, and thus in the 'state of exception'. It makes the abject the mirror image of the sovereign, in a process that follows the same logic as that of the concentration camps: first stripping persons of their citizenship (or civilian status, e.g. the Nuremberg race laws); then reducing them to bare life (in the camps), obliging them to live without a *telos* or goal other than survival (turning them abject, i.e. making them, according to Primo Levi, into *musulmans*), while investing an arbitrary someone (a bureaucratic nobody like Adolf Eichmann) with the sovereign power over their life and death. Even if such abjects are subsequently rescued from death by being given food, medicine and shelter, their personhood is reduced to the status of 'survivor', a category that does not represent citizenship or legal due process. If Jewish prisoners are abjects, then one

[17] Peter Sloterdijk, *Critique of Cynical Reason*, trans. Michael Eldred (Minneapolis: Minnensota University Press, 1987), 101–4.

understands why Agamben is against the notion of the Nazi genocide being called the Holocaust (fiery sacrifice), because the *homo sacer*, the category to which the Nazi declared/reduced the Jew, is someone who cannot be sacrificed but who can be killed.

It is possible to argue, therefore, that Giorgio Agamben's reintroduction of *homo sacer* and 'bare life' into the contemporary debate was such a powerful intervention because it addresses an urgent problem of today: the shifting terrain of the social around inclusion and exclusion, which our present predicament has inherited from Nazi ideology and the perverse shadow of an as yet incomplete enlightenment.

Put differently, the political background to both the abject and bare life is the crisis in what we understand by human, which in turn is related to what is left of the social when under the sway of bio-power. Both the human and the social have been dramatically upended by neoliberalism and global capitalism, creating new fault-lines of inclusion and exclusion, above and below the nation state. *Inclusion* once operated on the basis of social conflicts seeking consensus by 'agreeing to disagree', whether in national parliaments and local communities ('tolerating difference') or in international forums and power-bloc rivalry ('mutual deterrence'). *Exclusion* functioned by territorial markers, by language and nationality. Now, both migrants and élites cross borders, but under radically different conditions: the EU passport holder or cosmopolitan multilingual traveller has protection wherever s/he goes; the migrant, the undocumented or the refugee has no protection, even when s/he stays – with no option other than to become a victim, in order to claim human rights, or be abject and have none at all. Asymmetric warfare is the name for a related shift: war used to be conducted by national armies, identified as such by the insignia of state (uniforms) and the monopoly on violence (the right to kill). Now, on both sides, we have non-state combatants: militias, army sub-contractors, terrorist groups, special forces, sleeper cells, black operations. We also have war on terror, states of emergency, civil war, insurrections, abductions, piracy on the high seas, armed raids on civilians. Socio-economic conflicts 'solved' by unsocial means create their own non-persons.

Agamben's concepts added historical, philosophical and political dimensions to Kristeva's literary and psychoanalytical derivation of abjection, addressing but also reframing several of her underlying themes. Yet 'bare life' all but eclipsed 'abjection' and in the process mostly stripped it of its feminist connotations, while foregrounding different kinds of transitional or liminal states of 'bio': man/animal, man/machine, man/revenant. Hence the usefulness of Michel Foucault's term 'bio-politics', which references similar shifts in the social and the body politic.

Homo sacer/bare life does, however, usefully address the ongoing crisis in the foundations of democracy and the modern nation state. Globalization, corporate multinational capitalism and the attendant mobility of people, goods and services have led to a weakening of the social contract and have intensified the precariousness affecting work and labour, but also access to citizenship and recognition of civic responsibility.[18] The paradox – namely that the introduction of human rights in place of political activism and civic engagement may actually have weakened the state (with the consequence that not only the consumer but also the 'survivor' and the 'victim' are replacing the citizen) – means that there are fewer options for locating identity, and no safe zones for a sense of belonging. The return of religion, the rise of philanthropy and the declining legitimacy of the welfare state can all be read as symptoms of the retreat of democracy and the entrenchment of bio-politics, making bare life seem the appropriate description for the contemporary human condition.[19]

Thus, while bare life touches on some aspects of the situation I am concerned with, it lacks one crucial aspect: the uncanny effects of the excluded, the power of those who do not claim power, and the power that an existence which merely insists on being can exert over those that exclude them. On the other hand, an Antigone-like rigour of the 'ethical subject as abject' makes such politics almost indistinguishable from cynical desperation, especially where the ethical abject is prepared not only to persist, to the point of self-destruction, but is prepared to take everything and everybody down with them, as is potentially the case with any individual who thinks they have nothing more to lose. It is the state of mind and body from which derives the terrifying power of the suicide bomber – considered (maybe only in the context of this argument) as an ethical subject, turned 'abject object', and 'becoming corpse'. A similar argument might apply to US mass shootings.

There is thus a problematic *ethics* of abjection: the abject is beyond victimhood, because she or he has no claims to make, which means that the abject commands a particular kind of freedom that probes the limits of *both* freedom *and* the law. This ethical dimension of abjection – as a freedom that *requires* the other, but is *indifferent* to the community constituted as nation or state – is one of the several reasons I want to revive the term, as is implied in my discussion of the victim turned abject, which will be expanded further and will lead me to a reconsideration of spectatorship in the cinema. As these are tentative and exploratory connections being drawn between different discourses and fields of endeavour, I will add another extension to abjection, not least because the film example discussed in Chapter 11 explicitly thematizes it.

---

[18] Few politicians seem to seek election because they want to serve the common good. The daily corruption scandals, bribery, lobbying, the cheating on expense accounts in Britain and Brussels speak volumes, not to mention the United States Congress and its open pay-for-play politics.

[19] See Peter Sloterdijk's intervention on behalf of philanthropy and against taxes.

Abject nations?

The other – very problematic – area where the abject can also be invoked is in competing claims to land, property and nationhood, touching also memory and trauma.[20] In other words, can there be a *history of mutual abjection between peoples and nations*? In one of the more tragic ironies of history, the most intractable of political conflicts – that between Israelis and Palestinians – has cast these two peoples and their histories as each other's abjects, and this in several senses:

- an intimate relationship (you share the same soil, often the same food, you 'know' each other), but it is an intimacy that is fed by hatred, not love;
- horror and disgust: to the Israelis, the Palestinians are the very embodiment of the terrible power of the abject, and the Israelis are to the Palestinian the very embodiment of their powerless rage and daily humiliation;
- a relationship where a subject is treated as an object, and responds by assuming his/her object-state, but as a subject, that is, with all the singularity and life force of the animate: a corpse that always comes back to life;[21]
- the abject knows that the other is somehow dependent for his identity on this exclusion;
- a heteronomous relationship (both are pawns in a wider game, and servants of their respective – regional or global Superpower – masters);
- abject whenever Palestinians find themselves addressed as victims/ terrorists, or refugees/ displaced persons/nomads, but not as individuals, civic persons, citizens;
- the sense that the Palestinians, in their state of destitution, constantly remind Israelis of their own past, the precariousness of their former stateless existence, their fragility as a nation, as well as their duties towards the neighbour, and the endlessly deferred, endlessly complicated feelings of guilt, along with the disavowal of such guilt, mingled with the originary trauma of the Zionist pioneers, who were in search of 'a land without people for the people without land';
- under the general category of (Nazi) occupation and persecution, each is the other's Other: while the Israelis see in the Arab refusal to

[20] See Dan Rabinowitz, 'The Right to Refuse: Abject Theory and the Return of Palestinian Refugees', *Critical Inquiry* 36, no. 3 (Spring 2010): 494–516.

[21] Such a corpse more than metaphorically coming to life gives the title to an Israeli film about female soldiers, Tamar Yarom's *To See If I Am Smiling* (2007).

> grant them the right to exist the resurrection of Nazi genocide, the Palestinians also invoke Nazism, seeing themselves in the position of the Jews, held captive by the oppressed turned oppressors.

This problematic idea of not only individual subjects but whole peoples being each other's abject is a conceit that several filmmakers have toyed with, notably Jean-Luc Godard, as well as Israeli filmmakers in (French) exile, such as Amos Gitai and Eyal Sivan. Chapter 11, on Christian Petzold's *Barbara*, touches on a similar constellation, taking the case of former East Germany which figures as both abject and superior in relation to West Germany, at a time when the GDR had not yet become the historical 'corpse' that refuses to disappear or be buried.

Abject reciprocity as 'relations without relations'

Even more than the usual figures of precariousness and vulnerability (the child, the victim and the survivor), the abject emerges in the gap that opens up between the 'useful' and the 'superfluous', the 'online' and 'offline'.[22] Furthermore, if as person or individual one relates to the community, the nation and the social symbolic only by way of bureaucratic routines and technocratic dispositifs, then one is in the space of the abject, or as Emmanuel Levinas might put it, in 'relations without relations'.[23] It makes abjection once more *structural*: the historically determined consequence of the situation diagnosed by Foucault's bio-power, a point touched on and thematized in *I, Daniel Blake*.[24]

The point to remember is that the abject subject is not a recipient of philanthropy, nor the object of pity or compassion: these affects establish a *positive* relation to the other, precisely what abjection suspends. It is important to note that the idea of the abject is also different from 'precariousness' – a term that might seem cognate and is often used synonymously with abject and bare life. At the root of 'precarious' is a relationship of pleading and entreating, that is, the appeal to a higher entity

[22] See Zygmunt Bauman, *Wasted Lives: Modernity and its Outcasts* (London: Polity Press, 2004), and especially Manuel Castells, *End of Millennum – Vol* II *The Information Age Rise of the Network Society* (Oxford: Blackwell, 1996), 72–3.

[23] See the discussion of Levinas and 'relations without relations' in Chapter 4.

[24] Sometimes the objectively weaker position contains strengths, embodied in a presence that does not seem to contest the dominant social order, other than by its presence alone. Hence the abject is different from the victim who still has claims to 'belonging' and is acknowledged as belonging to the social symbolic. See my further comments on *I, Daniel Blake* below.

and thus, by inference, the acknowledgement of a positive link to power, even if formulated from its negative state. As Hal Foster argues:

> Precarious: from the Latin precarius, obtained by entreaty, depending on the favour of another, hence uncertain, precarious, from precem, prayer. This implies that this state of insecurity is not natural but constructed – a political condition produced by a power on whose favour we depend and which we can only petition . . . The note of entreaty is largely lost in the English word, yet . . . in all instances this importunate quality implies that the entreaty carries the force of accusation as well – an attesting to the violence done to basic principles of human responsibility.[25]

Since Foster hints at both the asymmetrical power relations and the reciprocity across violence and disavowal, the difference between 'precarious' and 'abject' is finally one of degree rather than kind. However, abjection in its *structural* sense (which is how I use it almost throughout) is above all the vantage point from which to conduct a *thought experiment*, making it an ethical-political construct that in the chapters that follow (Chapters 7–11) takes the form of a number of exemplary cinematic fictions. In none of the films discussed is abjection a sociological category, descriptive of a particular person, let alone a group of actual people.

The thought experiment in which abjection plays a role is, as indicated, aimed at testing what remains and what persist of the human, by way of situations, events, actions, gestures, choices and affects when the social contract has been damaged or dissolved, and the category of 'human life' (bio) is no longer fixed but in flux. In this sense, the abject would be the contemporary figure (of thought or the imagination) that corresponds to the 'noble savage' of the eighteenth century, also a thought experiment. The abject reopens but also undoes the Enlightenment philosophers' project of pre-empting the decision of whether human nature is good or evil, by first binding 'man' into the social contract. Today, we no longer talk about 'human nature' but about DNA, genes and cognitive processing, but the question of what is species (hard-wired) and what social (acquired) persists: the abject in this context can serve as the inside/outside figure emerging from the various pressures the post-human makes on traditional (European) definitions of the human in social and interpersonal situations.

Clearly there are ambiguities and slippages in such a use of abjection, not only in the oscillation between the structural and the substantive meaning of the term, as argued by Krauss, Buchloh and Foster. There is also the possible conflation of the ethical with the political, and the political with the aesthetic. For instance, Mark Greif aptly summarizes the danger of all too readily politicizing and aestheticizing abjection:

---

[25] Hal Foster, 'Precarious', *Artforum*, December 2009, 297–9.

> I do think there's something powerful about the notion of a manifest abjection, an incomprehensible and visible refusal of power, a pure gesture. But it has no place in politics except as the sort of aesthetic symbol that mobilizes those who know how to read it. It is still the merely human or merely bodily who are most invisible to fellow citizens as well as to leaders; only when the abject have a means of redress within the law can they be seen. Dull as it may seem, the withdrawal of law has to be opposed, the protections of law retained. Fantasies aside, all we really have are rights.[26]

Point well taken. The notion of the abject as asserting a freedom outside the law, while still bound to the community by a pure negativity, is thus open to several kinds of challenge. What I am arguing is that the abject – as that which is outside or expelled, whether it is because of a physical border, social ostracism or a verbal act of exclusion – does not thereby disappear: it still sustains a form of reciprocity, however hidden, unconscious or self-divided, with the expelling instance. Mutual interference, of the kind identified in the previous chapter, may be the structural equivalent of the involuntary physical reaction provoked by Kristeva's abject object: disgust, vomiting, horror. The abject is always something that does and does not belong to me, and whose presence can act as (ethical) demand or (political) interpellation.[27] What appears to be external, while also intimate and internal, has a way of returning, of interfering, of persisting even as one tries to resist it. The key difference would be that the abject, as a 'relation without relation', exacerbates the uncanny sense of return or persistence, because it is *something that first must be actively cast out, before it can become visible*.

The abject in American cinema

I am not the first to speak of abjection in reference to the cinema. Indeed, given the very diverse scope of the notion of abjection in psychoanalysis, philosophy, ethics and political thought that I have briefly sketched, it would have been surprising had it not been applied to cinema as well. Also not surprisingly, given cinema's sensory appeal and visceral effects, the *substantive* version has been more prevalent than the *structural* one. One finds abjection above all applied to the horror film and melodrama predominantly in American cinema, where it names either physical spaces as

[26] Mark Greif, 'Apocalypse Deferred', review of *State of Exception*, by Giorgio Agamben, *N+1* 2 (2005), https://nplusonemag.com/issue–2/reviews/apocalypse-deferred/ (accessed 26 November 2017).

[27] This is a feature of a 'cinema of abjection' when considered under the aspect of spectatorship. See section below.

'abject' or identifies the position of women as 'abject', in, for instance, Gothic melodrama. Abject spaces in films are often discussed with direct reference to Kristeva, but the argument tends to regard abjection as synonymous with repression and its violent return.[28]

Most feminist critics also cite Kristeva's views of the maternal body and the corpse as the emblematic signifiers of the abject body, which the symbolic order (including religion) attempts to repress, or purify: 'The various means of purifying the abject – the various catharses – make up the history of religions, and end up with that catharsis par excellence called art, both on the far and near side of religion.'[29] The fact that Kristeva adds 'art' was a welcome opportunity to also include the cinema, which is the most mimetically immediate art (thanks to its sensory-visceral impact), but also the most precariously exposed site (censorship, scandal, public outcry) for the body as a locus of abjection that cinema deals with. If most genres can indeed be said to try to 'purify and repress' – feminist film theory has made it its task to demonstrate what is being repressed, how and why – there are films that explicitly start with attempts at purging of the abject, only to violently stage their failure to do so. The genre of the 'body horror' comes to mind, and it has indeed been one of the preferred genres of analysis when speaking of abject bodies, abject spaces or abject spectatorship.

The films of Eli Roth, David Cronenberg or Abel Ferrara are notorious, for instance, for crossing the line between pornography and horror, but they are only one index of the 'powers (of horror)' that Kristeva's substantive version of the abject body can attribute to cinema. Cronenberg is known for celebrating the sublime beauty of raw, quivering flesh, seemingly detached from and yet part of body and personhood.[30] Similarly, Ferrara's best-known film, *Bad Lieutenant* (1992), although not a horror film, has Harvey Keitel

---

[28] The exception is Victor Burgin, who already in 1988 was proposing the notion of abject space in the structural sense. Starting by also citing Kristeva, Burgin wanted to deconstruct renaissance perspective via the concept of the abject, which he treated as a category opposed to the logo-centric, 'phallic' space of the 'cone of light' of Euclidian geometry. Formulating a critique that also challenged the subject–object division underpinning monocular representation, Burgin regarded the abject, as 'the means by which the subject is first impelled towards the possibility of constituting itself as such' to be a promising alternative to the post-Renaissance articulation of space as 'horizontal, infinitely extensible, and therefore in principle boundless'. This is because abject space is layered, decentred, folded, emerging from the margins and along borderlines but above all, because it can be 'imploding' and 'corporeal'. Victor Burgin, 'Geometry and Abjection', *Public* 1 (Winter 1988): 12–30.

[29] Kristeva, *Powers of Horror*, 17.

[30] There is no shortage of essays on Cronenberg discussing 'abjection'. See, for instance, Linda Kaufmann, 'David Cronenberg's Surreal Abjection', in *Bad Girls and Sick Boys: Fantasies in Contemporary Art and Culture* (Berkeley: University of California Press, 1998), 115–45. For an appraisal of the literature on Cronenberg and abjection, see also Gordon M. Sullivan, 'Fascinated Victims: Aspects of Abjection in the Films of David Cronenberg', MA thesis, North Carolina State University, Raleigh, 2007.

play a crack-snorting New York detective who uses and abuses his body to the point of abjection through addiction and physical violence, as if to escape his body by deadening it, or through a drug kick wanting to more fully possess and inhabit it.[31]

In *Abject Spaces in American Cinema*, which deals with films set in coercive institutions such as prisons, asylums or other correctional facilities, Frances Pheasant-Kelly argues that

> . . . the excessive control that pervades the on-screen institutions leads to visual chaos and narrative disruption . . . It is therefore relevant to diverge from typical Foucauldian analyses, which tend to focus on order, regulation and panoptic modes of surveillance, to a theoretical model that centres on the implications of repression. Julia Kristeva's theory of abjection provides such a model.[32]

Similarly, in the analysis of horror films, abject spaces appear as all but interchangeable with spaces of the uncanny, especially when referring to cellars, attics, rooms with locked doors, in short, to the spaces of dread and foreboding as they feature in almost any female melodrama, such as *Rebecca*, *Gaslight* or *Secret Beyond the Door*. What prompts the term 'abject' in such cases is the evocation of the body of the mother, metaphorically if not actually present in such dark, dank spaces like crypts or cellars, which is, of course, how Hitchcock presents the archetypal horror cellar in *Psycho*, where Lila discovers the mummified body of Norman Bates's mother.[33]

Theorists of queer cinema also have recourse to abjection. Calvin Thomas's study begins with a regretful note by the author, who wanted to call the book *Adventures in Abjection*.[34] A reviewer duly praises

---

[31] Roger Ebert, in his review, while not using the word 'abject' does discuss the tension in the film between the abused body, purification and religion. *Chicago-Sun Times*, 22 January 1993, https://www.rogerebert.com/reviews/bad-lieutenant–1993 (accessed 12 November 2017).

[32] Frances Pheasant-Kelly, *Abject Spaces in American Cinema* (London: I.B. Tauris, 2013), 1.

[33] 'The Pandora myth and the examples of Hitchcock's heroines who investigate the uncanny house suggest that, although both sexes are subject to abjection, it is the heroine rather than the hero who can explore and analyse the phenomenon with greater equanimity. It is the female body that has come, not exclusively but predominantly, to represent the shudder aroused by liquidity and decay . . . The house and Mother [in *Notorious*] prefigure the cinema's most uncanny house ever: the Bates' house in *Psycho* (1960) . . . Hitchcock's mise en scene suggests that the gradual movement of the heroine towards and into the house is a movement leading to a confrontation between the body of the young woman, alluring and cosmetic, and the mother's body, redolent (especially, of course, in *Psycho*) of disintegration, decay and death. The mask of feminine beauty then takes on another level of disavowal, that is the specific, psychoanalytic, problem of the mother's body.' Laura Mulvey, 'Pandora's Box', in *Fetishism and Curiosity* (London: BFI, 1996), 53–64 (64).

[34] Calvin Thomas, *Masculinity, Psychoanalysis, Straight Queer Theory: Essays on Abjection in Literature, Mass Culture, and Film* (New York: Palgrave, 2008), 1.

> . . . the evident relish with which its author embraces all things abject. If, according to Julia Kristeva, abjection depends on excluding filth, then the logic of Thomas's project consists in getting down and dirty with the contaminants that normative masculine subjectivities constitutively exclude . . . Of the many corporeal substances that qualify as abject, Thomas is most interested in the anal and the scatological. He aspires to harness the equivocal energies of the abject for a critical project that contests normative masculinity from within – or, rather, from either side of its most vulnerable borders.[35]

Almost none of these uses of the abject in cinema are directly relevant for my project, which focuses on the structural effects of abjection, except perhaps Barbara Creed's distinction, in *The Monstrous Feminine*, between the abject and the victim.[36] For Creed, the abject can manifest a form of female empowerment, which corresponds to my claim of the uncanny power of those who have nothing to lose. However, such is the price of Creed's female empowerment that the abject subject remains tethered to the maternal body. Creed also highlights the structural meaning of abjection alongside the substantive, when she argues that the abject 'refers to that which acknowledges no boundaries, rules or fixed positions, and which upsets identity, system and order'.[37]

Abject spectatorship in European cinema

Creed's return to the distinction between the substantive and structural, between the representation of abject bodies, substances or spaces, and the function of these abjects as that which 'acknowledges no boundaries, rules or fixed positions, and which upsets identity, system and order' is therefore

[35] Tim Dean, review of *Masculinity, Psychoanalysis, Straight Queer Theory: Essays on Abjection in Literature, Mass Culture, and Film*, by Calvin Thomas, *MFS Modern Fiction Studies* 55, no. 4 (Winter 2009): 871.

[36] Barbara Creed, *The Monstrous Feminine: Film, Feminism, Psychoanalysis* (New York: Routledge, 1993).

[37] 'The horror film is important here for three reasons: firstly, because it displays images of the abject – mutilated or dead bodies, bodily secretions, discharges and waste. Secondly, the horror film combines the monstrous with the abject – the monster crosses boundaries between the human and the non-human, while the abject challenges the very idea of a boundary. And thirdly, Creed postulates (based on a number of narrative analyses of horror films) that the horror film connects the abject with the maternal, i.e. the mother in the literal sense or such instances that adopt maternal functions. It is therefore the stable symbolic order (of society, the family, and the subject) that is threatened by abject (deformed, boundless, disfigured) bodies in horror films.' Thomas Elsaesser and Malte Hagener, *Film Theory: An Introduction through the Senses* (New York: Routledge, 2015), 132.

welcome, since it is evident from what has been said so far that my concept of the abject is more structural and substantive. Yet I do not want it to be understood as just another metaphor for the 'in between' the 'disruptive', the 'transgressive', or as challenging identity and essentialism. In fact, the greatest danger for the concept of the abject when applied to cinema is that it will be (mis)taken for yet another way of marking (and occupying) the now obligatory 'deconstructive' position of 'destabilizing' existing categories, opening up binaries to their hidden contradictions, or (another frequent move) creating 'undecidability', by maintaining ambiguity and generating multiplicity. Although these connotations are unavoidable and have not altogether been circumvented in this chapter either, the heuristic value of abjection for my overall argument about film as thought experiment does demand that I distance myself from these critical and hermeneutic moves, but also that I let these moves show, because they are, as it were, the foil against which my use of the term abjection becomes visible and comprehensible.

This proves to be especially important when one moves from abject protagonists and abject spaces to what I shall call abject spectatorship, which – see below – also reconfigures the distinction between substantive and structural abjection. Once again, there exists scholarship on the 'abject spectator', especially in American cinema, where it is usually prefaced with quotations from Kristeva referencing instances of visceral abjection.[38] Under discussion are especially those horror films that put their female protagonists in extreme peril, or expose their heroines to situations likely to arouse disgust, shame or embarrassment.[39] One Kristeva citation, for instance, links abjection directly to voyeurism:

> Voyeurism is a structural necessity in the constitution of object relation, showing up every time the object shifts towards the abject; it becomes true perversion only if there is a failure to symbolize the subject/object instability. Voyeurism accompanies the writing of abjection.[40]

Voyeurism in turn tends to associate Laura Mulvey's theses on the look (or 'male gaze') and the fetish,[41] further glossed with passages from Barbara

[38] See Laura Wilson, *Spectatorship, Embodiment and Physicality in the Contemporary Mutilation Film* (Amsterdam: Springer, 2015).
[39] Heather L. E. Neilson, 'The Reluctant Voyeur: The Spectator and the "Abject" in Gillean Mears' Fineflour', *Sydney Studies in English* 21 (1995–6): 103–16.
[40] Kristeva, *Powers of Horror*, 46.
[41] See Tina Chanter, *The Picture of Abjection: Film, Fetish, and the Nature of Difference* (Bloomington: Indiana University Press, 2007).

Creed[42] and references to Carol Clover's *Men Women and Chainsaws*.[43] In other words, abject spectatorship has mainly been viewed as an exacerbating instance of female spectatorship, problematized since the mid-1970s and complicated with arguments about heteronormativity at one extreme[44] and female empowerment at the other.[45]

The more general question I need to ask is, given that a cinema of abjection is neither part of a recognized genre, nor a label that directors set out to apply, how do I know that audiences, such as they exist for European films, either comprehend or care (about abjection)? Can one as a viewer feel 'abjected' in relation to a film? What would this mean: that one is 'expelled' from the film, even as one watches, or does one feel excluded from emotionally engaging with the characters? That intellectually, one is left disoriented and morally confused? Must one feel, as people do in a horror film, disgusted and repelled: responses deliberately targeted in slasher movies, or in films of visceral brutality and extreme violence? Such provocations to the spectators' moral emotions and physiological endurance need not create abject spectators. On the contrary, if one follows Kristeva, the response to disgust is to 'spit out' what disgusts in order to protect oneself from noxious substances. Similarly, spectators may actively 'abject' the horrors on the screen, in order to retreat into the safe zones of normativity – until coaxed out again by some visual lure or narrative bait. Films that provoke but also fascinate (say, through violence, horror and pornography) may catch us in a double bind: either we go along with their visceral physicality, or we take cover, avert our eyes, or walk out in disgust. Is there not a secret contract between the horror film and its fans precisely around such conflicted emotions? Beyond the dilemmas of female spectatorship, one can imagine that a film elicits emotions of physical as well as moral discomfort: villains, for instance, may revolt by their actions and yet attract by their wit, captivate by erotic charisma but repel by their dark motives. Yet this does not in itself constitute abject spectatorship. It is part of what

[42] 'The three main "looks" which have been theorized in relation to the screen–spectator relationship are: the camera's look at the pro-filmic event; the look of the character(s) in the diegesis; and the look of the spectator at the events on the screen. In his discussion of pornography Paul Willemen (1980) has specified a fourth look, the possibility of the viewer being over-looked while engaged in the act of looking at something he or she is not supposed to look at. The act of "looking away" when viewing horror films is such a common occurrence that it should be seen as a fifth look that distinguishes the screen spectator relationship.' Barbara Creed, *The Monstrous-Feminine*, 29.

[43] Carol Clover, *Men Women and Chainsaws* (Princeton, NJ: Princeton University Press, 1992).

[44] Dawn Esposito, 'Mafia Women and Abject Spectatorship', *Melus* 28, no. 3 (Autumn 2003): 91–109.

[45] For an extensive-exhaustive rehearsal of these arguments, see Amy Jane Voster, 'Film, Fear and the Female: An Empirical Study of the Female Horror Fan', *Off-Screen* 18, no. 6–7 (July 2014), http://offscreen.com/view/film-fear-and-the-female (accessed 27 November 2017).

makes a villain a convincing villain and thus belongs to the respective genre's repertoire of conventions.

European directors already identified with the abject, such as Lars von Trier, Pedro Almodóvar and Michael Haneke have produced a number of films that play on more radical forms of discomfort. For instance, von Trier's *Antichrist* (2009) shocks with images of abject bodies also found in horror or slasher films: the viewer is confronted with a veritable catalogue of the abject in relation to gendered male and female bodies, including mutilation and self-mutilation. But von Trier explicitly mythologizes his *mise en scène* of abjection, first by including nature's indifference as that form of exclusion-in-inclusion that renders human grief as well as human joy abject almost by definition, and second, by relying on a quasi-mythological text, the *Malleus Maleficarum*: a fifteenth-century witch-hunt manual and classic document of male paranoia. Also known as the witches hammer, it violently tries to eject femininity from the social realm. What von Trier shows is how the excluded reinserts itself into masculinity with a fury of agency inhabiting the abject body in direct reciprocity to the violence projected onto it, thereby illustrating the dynamics that animate the 'powers of horror' inherent in abjection. As a contemporary story about a bourgeois couple, *Antichrist* charts an allegorical path across subjectivity, gender and the forces of social disintegration: the film starts with a woman's trauma and the (male) attempt to therapize her back into family and the middle-class community. It ends with the triumph ('chaos reigns') of the abject: taking over in the struggle for bare life and physical survival. Insofar as von Trier's film fuses substantive and structural abjection, viewers found it near impossible to reconcile their experience with any particular set of genre conventions, and therefore remained unsettled in a way that makes the secret, collusive enjoyment of *Antichrist* as a horror film all but impossible.

The violent rejection of *Antichrist* by the press at the Cannes film festival in 2009 is one indication of such a deeper discomfort: the panicky, near-hysterical response can be read as a concerted effort to make the film itself into an abject object, in order not to become an abject spectator. So unsettling was *Antichrist* and yet so intensely engrossing that the resulting double binds created for the spectators needed the voice of outrage in order to enter into the discursive symbolic of the Festival that the Ecumenical Jury awarded it a specially created anti-prize.[46] Extreme polarization of critical opinion

[46] http://www.reuters.com/article/us-cannes-antichrist-idUSTRE54G2JF20090517. 'More controversy over *Antichrist* after the festival director denounced an "anti-prize" it received as an attempt at censorship. Lars von Trier's film was declared "the most misogynist movie from the self-proclaimed biggest director in the world" by an Ecumenical Jury, which every year hands out a prize to a Cannes film that celebrates spiritual values. The jury was so shocked by Von Trier's film – which closes with a shot of a clitoris being sliced off with rusty scissors – that it felt the need to award a special "anti-prize".' Mike Collett-White, 'Lars von Trier film "Antichrist" Shocks Cannes', Reuters, 17 May 2009, https://www.reuters.com/article/us-cannes-antichrist/lars-von-trier-film-antichrist-shocks-cannes-idUSTRE54G2JF20090517 (accessed 27 November 2017).

would seem to be the necessary condition for a film *not* to create abject spectators, becoming instead an abject object, thereby once more stabilizing the spectators' mastery over the film's disturbing effects.

Appeals to potent anxieties about the body's integrity, especially when coupled with confused or fluid gender identity, speaks equally vividly to fears about becoming abject as spectator, losing one's moral bearings as well as the perceptual ground for telling male from female. Almodóvar's *The Skin I Live in* (2011) is in this respect an especially sophisticated and haunting example of an almost clinical 'cinema of abjection': exploiting uncertainties about the relation of inside/outside, such as skin to body, and body to subjecthood and identity, the film renders skin a material substance in its own right, growing and taking on a life of its own. Almodóvar, too, revives ancient mythologies of human sacrifice – now on the altar of beauty, rather than by burning witches. He blends a Pygmalion obsession about possessing the female creation with the 'mad scientist' in the Frankenstein mould, as his plastic surgeon (Antonio Banderas) takes revenge on the presumed rapist of his daughter by kidnapping him and subjecting him to skin grafts and a sex change. However, instead of assuaging his anger and grief, he manages to create an object of such desire and erotic allure that the creature overpowers him, both metaphorically and literally.

The Skin I Live in makes use of the abject in several ways, mostly to explore the indeterminate boundaries between protective cover and vulnerable exposure, human lust and animal urges. In addition, skin becomes the palpitating yet depersonalized metaphor for a cinema no longer functioning as window or mirror, but as a permanent and ubiquitous surveillance machine. It turns the watcher watched into an abject, trapped in a knowing vulnerability. To know and not to be able to act is an extreme state of abjection, and with it, Almodóvar enacts also a new paradigm also of spectatorship. *The Skin I Live in* plays with many of the conventions of the body horror genre (and thus alludes to the substantive side of abjection), as well as featuring a convincingly demonic villain (with motives we both recognize and dread). Yet its unsettling reversal of body and gender, face and surface, together with the several layers of surveillance, provoke a more profound sense of losing one's bearings: not just about male and female, but inside and outside, active and passive, hunter and hunted, shock and laughter. *The Skin I Live in* disconcertingly but powerfully 'redistributes' the attributes of the living body and yet it also activates most of the registers identified with the structural version of abjection: it manages to plant doubt and disorder about several bodily categories we normally consider foundational and indispensable.

The controversies provoked by Joshua Oppenheimer's *The Act of Killing*, or by Haneke's *Funny Games*, can be considered similar examples of films becoming abject objects in order to protect the spectators from turning abject. *Funny Games* explicitly asks what kind of contract does the viewer think s/he has with a film, and when is it broken or not honoured? If the spectatorial contract is one of voyeurism, is an abject film one that breaks this contract, in that it no longer sustains the implicit agreement that both sides of the voyeuristic bargain are in a complicit state of disavowal? The actor pretends the spectator isn't there, and the spectator pretends s/he is not there, even though what is on the screen only takes place because the film knows that the spectator is there, and the spectator also knows, but suppresses this knowledge. In *Funny Games* Haneke calls our bluff, in the most brutal and uncompromising way, but as my example of body horror shows, not every 'abject' film creates abject spectators, but *Funny Games* surely does.

The abject is not a victim

What I wish to associate with abject spectatorship in this chapter is something less visceral-substantive, and even more abstract and structural, yet by the same token, more politically relevant to my project: the *blockage of empathy*, without it being replaced either with defamiliarization and distanciation, or with horror and disgust. Such blocking of empathy is not for its own sake but has as its background the problematic subject position of the victim (of capitalism, of European history, of the vicissitudes of life) so casually adopted by people in the privileged West. This emergence of victimhood as a privileged subject position of authenticity when in need of being heard can be linked to the degeneration of 'the political' into 'the police' (see Chapter 4): what was once party politics and organized militancy has, within Western democracies, mutated into politics as crisis management and security operations. Under such conditions, victim status constitutes part of a very contemporary condition, since it is only as victim or survivor that I possess the public credibility to claim rights and entitlements: there is an increasing awareness that victims are not a category of passive subjects, but central actors, positioning themselves in political struggles over recognition and the airing of grievances.

Given the sheer scale of inequality and injustice in the world, and the massively uneven distribution of goods and of vital necessities across the globe, there are indeed victims of the depredation of life, of capitalist globalization and of proxy wars in so many parts of the world. To this victimization, we – Europe, the West, the world's so-called middle classes – have been more or less silent witnesses, if not voyeurs. Maybe one of the reasons why victimhood has become such a desirable subject position is that it helps alleviate our guilt, by indirectly acknowledging that we have been complicit beneficiaries, and making universal victimhood stand for a symbolic act of solidarity. But it is a compromise and thus also a compromised form of solidarity, allowing us to stay below the radar of personal responsibility while still staking a place in the world, even if our participation in this world merely testifies to our self-perceived powerlessness and impotence.

There are films which test this proposition about *guilt-management* by featuring perpetrators. Such is the case in Ari Folman's *Waltz with Bashir* (Israeli soldiers involved in the massacre of Palestinians at the Sabra and Shatila camps outside Beirut in 1982) and Joshua Oppenheimer's *The Act of Killing* (Indonesian thugs reminiscing and re-enacting how they killed thousands of people during the 1965–6 massacres of 'Communists'). In both cases, the directors seems concerned neither to denounce the protagonists as perpetrators, nor to deconstruct them into victims, but to depict them as abjects: only as abjects, in a creaturely condition, can they communicate with each other and the audience, fugitively constituting the 'inoperative community' where all that unites protagonists and spectators are the spaces that separate them.

If empathy is no longer an ethically feasible gesture of solidarity, then the rapport we can have with certain protagonists on the screen will have to change as well. Beyond sympathy, empathy and identification, films may be able to evoke these spaces for the abject spectator. Such a spectator would then be one who, without holding a pre-existing, conventional 'contract' with the film, is nonetheless bound to the film, but in a proximate relation, made neither complicit nor put 'in the know', yet nonetheless aware of being (and acknowledged as) present.

Abjection as withdrawal: the cinema of the Dardenne Brothers

Such a cinema of foreclosed empathy, in which the protagonists do not solicit the spectator either by offering themselves as spectacle or by eliciting compassion and demanding understanding, seems to me par excellence that of the Dardenne Brothers. Their films are perhaps the prime examples of a 'cinema of abjection' as I envisage it in the form of thought experiments. This applies in the first instance to their narratives, where characters are set up for major moral dilemmas, which they resolve by decisions that seem contingent, enigmatic and ambiguous, at times putting them beyond the pale among their fellow human beings, often their nearest relatives. As the film follows the protagonists' abjected state, they undergo a transformational process that makes their initial decisions seem retrospectively 'right' – mostly in light of the radically revised premises we are encouraged to discover, sometimes along with the protagonists, sometimes by drastically shifting our own point of view. Igor, the male lead of *La Promesse* (1996), after following his father's orders throughout, eventually (and seemingly out of the blue) betrays him, in order to keep the promise that he made to a dying illegal immigrant, even though no immediate gain can be expected to accrue to him. Rosetta, the eponymous heroine of *Rosetta*, decides to denounce her potential employer, the only person ever to have shown her love and affection. In *Le Fils* (2002), Olivier, a father whose life, marriage and career have fallen apart after a senseless murder, decides to all but adopt the boy who brutally strangled his son. In *L'Enfant* (2005), Bruno, a shiftless drifter who got his girlfriend pregnant, decides to sell the newborn child for cash, only then to try and buy the baby back from a dangerous gang of people traffickers. *Le Silence de Lorna* (2008) is the story of a legalized immigrant in a sham marriage to a drug addict who colludes with her boyfriend to divorce her husband, in order to marry another foreigner for money, but after the sham husband's sudden death decides otherwise, putting herself in mortal danger.

What has been said so far gives an indication of how the individual characters become – within the world of the story – abject subjects in relation to the community, to their nearest and dearest, or to the persons they are most dependent upon or beholden to. They usually do so with a decision they themselves take, rather than through something that befalls them from outside. This complicates above all the moral attitude we as spectators may have towards them. If in the case of Igor (from *La Promesse*), betraying his father can still be regarded as both ethical (the father let the immigrant die for fear of being prosecuted) and as an act of Oedipal revolt (the father is arrogant and authoritarian), it shocks us to see Rosetta rat on her friend. It pains us because of the immense empathy we have developed for her plight, but this is precisely the point: it unambiguously releases her from the status of the victim and makes her visible as an abject, since the abject, as indicated above, is someone who first must be cast out before becoming visible. The peculiarity of the Dardennes' films is that often the characters themselves do the casting out, thereby raising the moral stakes, but not changing the basic constellation. Once the stakes are made visible, we as spectators are obliged to reassess the premises of our allegiance to the characters: they become (once more) enigmatic. In *Le Fils*, Olivier's decision to take into his workshop the callous murderer of his son appears scandalous to his ex-wife and to us inexplicable (or rather: open to multiple explanations). In response to her incredulous 'Why did you do it?' he says 'I don't know': a scene that Luc Dardenne cites in his *Au dos de nos images* ('Behind the back of our images') by commenting 'and we [i.e. he and his brother] don't know either'.[47] Were one to ask Bruno (of *L'Enfant*) or Lorna (of *Le Silence*

[47] 'Il y a quelque chose d'impossible dans ce que fait Olivier. Magali a sans doute raison de lui dire: "Pourquoi tu le fais alors?", et il a sans doute raison de lui répondre: "Je ne sais pas." Nous non plus, on ne sait pas', Luc Dardenne, *Au dos de nos images, 1991–2005* (Paris: Editions du Seuil, 2008), 127.

de Lorna) or Samantha (of *Le Gamin au vélo*) the same question, one would surely receive exactly this answer: 'I don't know.' In other words, these protagonists are abject to the extent that they display *a special kind of withdrawal*. If such withdrawal is the very opposite of coming towards us, whether to gain our sympathy or to earn our respect, it puts us on notice that nonetheless something is stirring that deserves our utmost attention.

In the discussions around the Dardennes the name most often mentioned is that of Robert Bresson, and indeed Bresson's characters, too, defiantly display a similarly outright withdrawal. Yet there is also an important difference: Bresson's protagonists are often 'angels of sin' wrestling with their God,[48] while the Dardennes' characters' withdrawal usually makes something visible that is closer to the specifically human condition in the here-and-now of the Belgium of today, and with it, of contemporary Europe in the world. One way of defining this withdrawal more closely is to say that the Dardenne brothers position their characters neither inside the action nor external to it, but on a threshold which they cross and transgress, as well as withdraw and hide behind. Rosetta, for instance, often appears at the edge of a frame (or opening) as if she was leaning into a space, much as we as spectators might wish to lean into the film. When she finally enters, it is as if she is bolting, running away even more than running towards, already on her way out, even before she is fully inside. What makes the threshold an important marker is not only the reversibility of direction and the liminal as the permanence of transition, but also the way it problematizes the relation being-for-another/being-for-oneself as the ideal condition of a self-within-a-community, of which the abject now embodies the definitive impossibility. It also puts the spectator in a new situation, insofar as it introduces the notion of 'being-with the characters' which is distinct from either empathy or identification, but reproduces, at the level of spectatorship, the 'relations without relations' noted as typical of the abject.

To take the example of *L'Enfant*, at first, Bruno, the principal protagonist, does not seem to share the emotional responses of ordinary humans. He treats others like objects, things among things, including his own newly born son. He lies and cheats whenever he has to, and seems to have nothing one would call a conscience. Yet he is neither a sociopath, nor is he evil, however wicked and cruel may be his acts (and they are). There is a self-sufficiency, a compactness and brazen directness in his mode of being which qualifies him as abject: to the degree that he reproduces so precisely – by way of mimicry rather than mimesis – the forces that have acted upon him.

In one sense, Bruno is abject because he is nothing but a labouring animal, looking for money and food, for sustenance and survival, twenty-four hours a day. He, too, is not a victim, nor is he alienated; rather, he is entirely native

[48] Robert Bresson's first film was called *Les Anges du péché* (1943).

to his environment. Foraging in the urban wilderness of a working-class suburb of Liège makes him treat as given the need for cigarettes and a cell phone as equal to the need for food and shelter, and it puts a fashionable jacket he cannot really afford on a par with a baby pram he cannot really afford. At the same time, his tireless cunning as petty thief and street hustler makes him the mirror image of the self-made entrepreneur constantly on the go, cell phone clamped to his ear. Bruno is the abject perfectly adapted to the flexibilized labour market, but also to its counterpart, the bureaucratically administered welfare state, with its unemployment benefits and child welfare office. His story is furthermore symptomatic for how babies in Europe have become hyper-emotional objects for the state, because of their relative scarcity and thus increased demographic value: this is due to the declining birth rate in Europe, a fact that Bruno acknowledges by monetizing not only his baby but the social situation which makes trafficking babies both necessary and lucrative. As he says to his distraught girlfriend when she realizes what he has done, 'Never mind, we'll make another one.'

How can we be engaged with this creature who is so Other that he might as well be an animal or a machine? Do we approach him like a biologist observing a rare species in its natural habitat? It is here that the Dardennes' cinematic technique generates a particular kind of *proximity in separateness* that is disconcerting even as it reassures. *L'Enfant* subverts identification quite radically, as did *Rosetta*, but with different means: the latter, famously, had the camera constantly at Rosetta's back, following her as she scurried from place to place, also a kind of feral animal, both tracked and hunted, both tagged and tethered. By contrast, Bruno mostly faces us frontally, yet by a curious trick he has a way of not 'looking at' but 'seeing through' us – much as he does with passersby or fellow passengers in the bus. We are thus aware of being very much 'present' in his field of vision, but absent in relation to his actions and their consequences – his casual indifference to our presence is quite distinct from the voyeur's contract as described above. There is no suturing element of shot-reverse-shot, yet we know we are *excluded* even as the camera insists on us being also *included*. The different means, however, highlight contrasting but complementary ends: Rosetta's *idée fixe* of a proper job and a proper home contrasts with Bruno's freedom to live without home, conscience or guilt, and yet they are both outstanding examples of a self-sufficiency radicalized to the point of becoming abject, while maintaining their power over that which excludes them – and this includes us.

From such a perspective, the films of the Dardenne Brothers are indeed a series of variations on the themes of liberty, equality, fraternity, now as values neither subsumed under the heading of citizenship (as in the motto of the French Revolution) nor reserved for a Puritan elite that believes itself 'predestined' (as in the American Declaration of Independence). Instead these values must appear in abject form as the condition of their universality, given that the very idea of 'humanity' has become double-edged. Double-edged because upholding a classical 'humanism' (on the basis of 'human rights') while also cognizant of the post-humanism of bio-power and by extension, aware of abjection as a defence and a weapon: it strategically upholds the human against the post-human, but it also accepts that there is no return to bourgeois-liberal citizenship. It de facto positions the self 'post' and past any consumerist individualism but also 'post' and against any collective 'we' proposed by either socialism and communism, or any of the current populist European-based nationalisms.

It is illuminating to contrast such a vision with the one present in *I, Daniel Blake*, a film that wholeheartedly solicits our empathy. Ken Loach wears his political heart on his sleeve: he strongly believes in the values of the community, the social contract, the nuclear family as a nurturing unit, good neighborliness across the racial divide, the dignity of work – and the director shows how all these civic virtues and Enlightenment values are combined in the eponymous hero. *I, Daniel Blake*'s moral ground and political perspective, in other words, is a classically social-democratic value system, and by today's standards it is quite obsolete (as can be seen by the collapse of the left in virtually all Western countries). But when Blake is being addressed and interpellated by the state and its representatives no longer as a citizen or an individual, but only by way of bureaucratic routines and technologies, such as the computer he cannot handle in order to fill in his claim forms, he (briefly) becomes an abject. His abjection is the politically motivated response to a situation not dissimilar to Michel Foucault's bio-politics. Yet the point where Blake actively assumes and inhabits this abjecthood as a weapon is not when he protests and demands his rights at the Job Centre, but when he paint-sprays his name on the wall of the self-same Job Centre and then sits down on the pavement, cheered by the crowd until hauled off by the police.

At these moments, Daniel Blake reminds me of a homeless man I observed one winter morning near Washington Square in New York, whom a film crew was asking to move. The man refused; he also could not be bribed with a hot drink or with money. The director eventually gave up, saying, 'It's impossible to negotiate with someone who has all the time in the world, and no place to go,' and so the homeless was eventually incorporated into the shot. Homeless people are rare in New York these days, and this one would have been an example of the ethical power that the abject can exert. Another version of the position of the abject, it aligns the man with the figure of Herman Melville's *Bartleby the Scrivener*, whose 'I prefer not to', as mentioned in the previous chapter, has become the philosophers' motto of an *ethics of withdrawal* rather than of militant resistance or open refusal. Manifesting presence and nothing more was also what was said to have lent power to the Occupy Wall Street movement, whose participants – like Daniel Blake in front of his graffiti signature – protested merely with their *thereness*, without articulating any demands. If society 'casts out' what it considers useless or 'spits out' what is inconvenient, the abject may still have the choice to 'opt out' while refusing to move.

Abjection: a Europe on the verge of a nervous breakdown

So why are both *I, Daniel Blake* and *Toni Erdmann* symptomatic and yet not quite the thought experiments of a cinema of abjection? Daniel Blake is clearly a victim of the system, and he is such a good man that one's heart goes out to him. But there is also reason to be relieved that he is allowed to die when he does, because he is, after all, too good for this world, and thus the protagonist of melodrama. In the final scenes, he becomes part of the precariat rather than remain an abject: a supplicant pleading for readmission into the community as is, rather than 'preferring not to'. As a human being, of course, I wish him to get his benefits and live happily ever after as the grandfather of his surrogate family. But as the protagonist of this film – if considered as a possible thought experiment with its own kind of truth – his death does not come a moment too soon, before some of the more problematic premises of *I, Daniel Blake* became too obvious to ignore. For instance, had he stayed alive, Blake may well have been a disaffected Labour voter supporting Brexit: that is, he would have been one of those angry ones who act against their own self-interest.

The problem is different with Toni Erdmann, who outwardly looks and acts like an abject. But Erdmann is a hippie dropout (rather than an outcast). Grief for his dog, the onset of old age and parental phantom pain make him emotionally bereft, but in fact he merely 'plays at being an abject' – drawing on his pension or welfare cheques in order to do so. Abjection is one of his tragicomic turns. He does not test what is human today: he still presumes to know what is human. At most, he is the abject as anarchic provocateur, freed of social decorum and norms, the id in the land of the repressive superegos. However, what makes the film symptomatic is that Toni Erdmann's pseudo- or para-abjection actually steers his daughter – across shame, embarrassment, regret and guilt – to the point of her becoming abject: and it is there – in the last image, with her grandmother's silly hat and her father's set of false teeth – *as abject* that the film leaves her, as if to suggest that we are only able to regain or redefine our humanity by first becoming abject, not by presenting ourselves as victims (or even dropouts).

Therefore, in the films I have in mind, abjection functions as an ethical foil and a political vanishing point, testing real-life situations and pushing them to the point where they become deadlocked. A cinema of abjection conducts typically European thought experiments of the post-heroic: wanting to know *not* whether the sky is the limit and what goal can we reach as individuals, but how and when do we hit bottom, regardless of whether we eventually touch the ground or stay suspended and just keep falling. The post-heroic – as the next chapter will argue – is the return to something more basic and more modest, when the traditional ways of imagining change, of believing in progress, or of overturning the given order, by a revolution from the bottom or the top, have either already happened or have become unthinkable and unimaginable.

If we can no longer believe in progress, if the efforts over the past sixty-odd years to make of Europe a community of freedom, social justice and good neighbourliness have become imperilled or are being undone, then maybe we need to go low rather than aim high, find equality at the bottom rather than expect it at the top, find fraternity in acknowledging the spaces that separate us rather than endlessly seek what unites, and redefine freedom not as 'I do as I please' but as the negative freedom of having nothing to lose, that is, a *divested*, *disjunctive* freedom (freedom from) rather than an *invested*, *acquisitive* one (freedom to).

The abject subject, I insisted, is a theoretical construct. Within the discursive field of subjectivity and the social symbolic, it is a suspended state, suspended between the power that accrues from 'wanting nothing' and the power that derives from 'having nothing (more) to lose'. Because the abject is cast outside without being separated from the inside, the power it wields has the force of a critique, but implicit and by default, because it cannot set itself apart from that which it challenges by its very existence. But there can be no misunderstanding: in real life the price of abjection would be steep indeed: to not own anything, and to not owe to anybody, to not demand anything, to not desire anything and to not aspire to anything.

In this situation, the figure of the abject opens up a space for thinking. Even if it is not philosophy, this thinking is in the service of a thought experiment: what would it mean – what would be the consequences – of placing oneself outside the existing symbolic order? How low can one go? What freedom does it expose? But the abject also exerts a fascination on others: refusing the position of the victim, s/he asserts a stance of radical equality, which endows the abject with the power of negativity, resistance and refusal, but especially *the power of withdrawal*. The abject is thus also the post-political agent of a politics that is neither utopian nor socialist, that neither accepts nor 'fights' the capitalist system. The abject – as thought experiment – is the 'thinking through' of some of the deadlocks that liberal democracies are left with at the beginning of the twenty-first century.[49]

[49] In the present state of capitalism, where we tend to outsource so many of our jobs, tasks and even faculties (including memory and feelings), concepts like 'the abject' gain new traction and relevance, because there has emerged a peculiar relation of what is ours (inside) and what is not ours (outside). We can be 'abject' to ourselves: not quite separate from us and yet not quite belonging to us either.

Hence one finds it as a conceivable, thinkable option among certain philosophers, but one also sees it performatively asserted in those protest movements that put no positive demands. There, bodies merely insist on making their presence manifest: they refuse to go away, but they also refuse to be co-opted into any pre-exiting agenda or ideology.[50]

The philosophers' vision of Europe, I argued in the previous chapter, is centred on a thought experiment of how the world might run differently and still be governed by democracy. The purpose of the experiment is to test the 'commons' after both liberal democracy and communism, via the notion of the abject. The abject subject would be a cleansed subject, freed from uneven exchange – indeed from any kind of actual or symbolic exchange: this is its ethical value. Thus, by becoming 'common' the abject also signifies a political value: it can be a placeholder for a revised 'economy' by first living a 'no-economy' – a necessary first step past capitalism, but only possible as a thought experiment, albeit tested in some of the 'real' situations of the present.

Instead of the libidinal economy that now underpins our economic system, by way of desire/lack, drive/desire, addiction/compulsion, the abject prepares an ethical economy of gift and sacrifice, of which transgression is the ethical wager.

Conclusion

My hypothesis has been that the different states or moments of abjection one can identify in contemporary cinema are not the result of the multi-cultural pressures on European societies due to an influx of migrants, nor to the presence of the undocumented 'foreigners' or groups of different faiths. Instead, abjection emerges from the conflicted states of Europe itself, designating in oblique fashion also the about-to-be-discarded residue of the positive values once associated with the European Enlightenment and the ideals of the French Revolution: equality, liberty, and fraternity – human rights, equality before the law, individual freedoms. These values are threatened even more from within than they are from without, and therefore necessarily appear in *abject* form, as the negative reminder not only of their former universality, but of a once precious part of us. Given the degree to which the very ideas of 'humanity' and 'humanism' have become contested, abjection strategically upholds the human against the post-human, but also accepts there is no easy return to the inclusive ideals of bourgeois-liberal

[50] Imogen Tyler's *Revolting Subjects: Social Abjection and Resistance in Neoliberal Britain* details several of these occupy movements in Britain, including sit-ins and youth riots, all of which she convincingly defines as 'social abjects', with reference to both Kristeva and Rancière.

enlightenment. The abject is thus a placeholder for democracy: something we suspect is now a mere crinkly skin on the surface of global capitalism and thus probably dead matter, but still too much part of us and too deeply needed to be buried yet. Therefore, to vary Kristeva's definition of the corpse, 'Democracy, seen without the Sovereign and outside of party politics, is the utmost of abjection. It is death infecting life.' A cinema of abjection sets out to keep this particular corpse alive.

6

Post-heroic Narratives and the Community to Come

The preceding chapters have laid out the general philosophical and political terrain on which Europe might reassess (and one day even reassert) its 'Europeanness' as a value-based political entity. The chapters have also offered an analysis of European cinema since the 1990s, highlighting certain tendencies and focusing on those possibilities that outline a new ethical cinema, conceived neither around documentary realism nor didactic parable, but proposing films as thought experiments. The project I distil from these thought experiments is to test the values of the Enlightenment and to imagine a 'reboot' of the implicit social contract of Western democracy, which has been fraying under the onslaught of globalization and the neoliberal rollback of the welfare state. This reboot I call 'cinema of abjection', conceived of as a critical vantage point, hypothetical in its radicalism, but designed to examine how individuals may live and interact as a community under conditions of *antagonism*, rather than presuming unity and yearning for belonging. What, in other words, could constitute the bonds of common humanity when communities are no longer held together by family, ethnicity, religious belief or the nation state?

The chapters that follow present individual case studies meant to exemplify the diversity of this 'cinema of abjection' as thought experiment. They are offered as proof that such a cinema has been, if not exactly 'on the minds' then 'in the works' among some of the most recognized directors of European cinema. The constellation being identified as 'cinema of abjection' is furthermore confirmed by the fact that (as laid out in Chapter 12) the director-auteurs whose films serve the festival circuit are themselves, despite their privileges, structurally positioned as 'abjects': at once inside and outside, obliged to make outsider films in order to be recognized inside, while still asserting their autonomy. Abjection can thus signify at several levels: protagonists that find themselves abject in a film, spectators made abject by a film that gives them no ready entry points, and directors placed abject by making films that have to serve several masters.

The present chapter briefly recapitulates the external conditions of such abjection in European cinema, suggesting how our critical thinking might understand these conditions more productively. I argue that this necessitates a change of default values, that is, the shift from what I call a 'heroic' to a 'post-heroic' narrative about Europe itself. In the second half of the chapter I examine what such a post-heroic narrative entails from a philosophical perspective, drawing especially on Jean-Luc Nancy's thoughts regarding the community to come, predicated on the *inoperative community*.

European cinema does not exist

To begin with the external conditions of European cinema as an abject subject, it is difficult to argue that European cinema exists, other than as a bureaucratic dream, a subject taught in film studies, and as a promotional tool for national producers and distributors of art house films. Insofar as these bodies will it into existence, European cinema has over the past three decades been funded mainly by governmental subsidy schemes, public service television or via the European Union's various MEDIA initiatives, that is, by the public purse. Such largesse is politically justified in the name of either preserving a national cultural heritage or promoting European integration, the latter obliging recipients of such funds to enter into transnational co-production agreements or joint distribution arrangements. It is not unusual, for instance, to find up to a dozen different funding bodies and production companies listed in the credits of a Michael Haneke or Lars von Trier film. Cinema risks becoming the means to an end rather than being an end in itself – the paradox being that the means – promoting European cinema – only work if the end is kept in place: the auteur as autonomous artist.

Two further factors are indicative of the decentring and marginalization of European cinema. Since the end of the Second World War, national new waves or film movements (along with the auteurs associated with them) have been created by Europe's leading festivals, such as Cannes and Venice (and to a lesser extent, Berlin and Rotterdam), rather than emerging from their national film cultures, where all too often such auteurs and new waves have been viewed by the general film-going public as too difficult or elitist, with even successful auteurs being shunned or ignored in their own country. Finally, European cinema today, whether considered as counter-Hollywood, as avant-garde or auteur cinema is best subsumed under the umbrella categories of 'world cinema', 'global art cinema' or 'international festival cinema'.[1]

[1] Thomas Elsaesser, 'European Cinema as World Cinema: A New Beginning?', in *European Cinema Face to Face with Hollywood* (Amsterdam: Amsterdam University Press, 2005), 486–513.

These arguments are laid out in more detail in *European Cinema: Face to Face with Hollywood*. There, I show, inter alia, that the favoured view, namely regarding European cinema collectively as the good object (connoting 'art', 'originality' and 'cultural value') against the foil of Hollywood's bad object ('commerce', 'formula' and 'box office'), has become untenable. Not only does it fail to recognize the determining conditions mentioned above – the role played by film festivals, publicly funded television and government agencies – it also ignores that festival films are niche products serving the cultural tastes of privileged minorities. In short, it is these external conditions that make (national as well as transnational) art cinemas aesthetically possible, economically viable and ideologically necessary, rendering the notion of 'independence' performative rather than substantive: even a misnomer if such films are indeed serving several (pay-)masters, agenda setters and taste makers.

In the process, European directors and festivals have also established many kinds of indirect cooperation, invisible interfaces and covert complicities with Hollywood: ranging from stars on the red carpet in Cannes or Venice to Cannes' promotion of American directors such as Woody Allen, Martin Scorsese, David Lynch or Quentin Tarantino as (European-style) auteurs. Above the line, film festivals are all about art, but what sustains them is their market/industry component. The Hollywood interface also includes talent transfer from Europe to the United States (Roman Polanski, Louis Malle, Volker Schlöndorff, Wolfgang Petersen, Paul Verhoeven, Bille August, Tom Tykwer – to name just a few) and US distribution deals for European films, with Miramax (for *Amélie*), Sony Picture Classics (for *The Lives of Others*) or the Weinstein Company (for *The Artist*).[2]

Because these (and other) forms of cooperation and collusion are necessary at the structural level, while often negated or disavowed at the level of discourse, they survive and thrive by a kind of 'antagonistic mutuality', while European cinema – no different from the nation states that make up the European Union in this respect – is 'doubly occupied'. That is to say, it always already contains what it considers its 'other', while stabilizing its identity by suppressing difference, and by trying (in vain) to exclude that which is already part of its own internal make-up.[3]

A further, more pro domo reflection can be added. Given the pressure to incorporate film and media into the curriculum of European literature and modern language departments at universities, especially in the United States and United Kingdom, there have, in recent years, been notable attempts to forge something like a consensus around how to study and teach European

---

[2] On Hollywood talent transfer, see Melis Behlil, *Hollywood is Everywhere: Global Directors in the Blockbuster Era* (Amsterdam: Amsterdam University Press, 2016).

[3] Thomas Elsaesser, 'Real Location, Fantasy Space, Performative Place: Double Occupancy and Mutual Interference in European Cinema', in Temenuga Trifonova (ed.), *European Film Theory* (New York and London: Routledge, 2009).

cinema, and how to coordinate the appropriate research networks.[4] Dozens of readers and as many monographs with 'European' and 'cinema' in their titles are competing for attention on students' reading lists.[5] Whether these bring us closer to a new definition of European cinema for the twenty-first century is a matter for dispute. What is clear is that – just as in the European Union – there are federalists among scholars and transnationalists, either emphasizing common elements or insisting on diversity. Given that Europe encompasses more countries than are members of the European Union, notions of national cinemas prevail (backed as they are by policy-makers in charge of culture, tourism and heritage, as well as the rising tide of populist nationalism). The result is another paradox, insofar as the top-down directives and economic underpinnings of European cinema are integrationist and favour ever-closer union, while scholars tend to concentrate on individual auteurs, specific films and national cinemas, also in order to retain governmental funding and to serve institutional agendas.

The present study tries to resolve the paradox by simultaneously enlarging the context and assuming a more oblique entry-point, which invokes auteur cinema as the site where the inherent contradictions can best be grasped. On the one hand, I build upon the arguments aired more fully in *European Cinema: Face to Face with Hollywood* where one of the key entry-points was the film festival network as index of the precarious and problematic self-construction of European auteur and national cinemas. On the other hand, I am changing – as should be evident from the preceding chapters – the main terms of the debate. For instance, in *European Cinema Face to Face with Hollywood* I made the argument that European cinema was a symbolic construction, in the sense of Claude Lévi-Strauss's symbolic efficacy, which I paraphrased by saying that the structuring effect of symbols ensures that even if there is no such entity as European cinema, we still believe in it.[6] This symbolic efficacy has now become the case for regarding '(European)

[4] What comes to mind is the very successful 'Network of European Cinema and Media Scholars' (NECS), established in 2006, publishers of a journal and drawing several hundreds of their 2,700 members to their annual conferences. https://necs.org/ (accessed 24 October 2017).

[5] Elizabeth Ezra (ed.), *European Cinema* (Oxford: Oxford University Press, 2004), Catherine Fowler (ed.), *European Cinema Reader* (London: Routledge, 2002); Mary P. Wood, *Contemporary European Cinema* (London: Bloomsbury, 2007); Mary Harrod, Mariana Liz and Alissa Timoshkina (eds), *The Europeanness of European Cinema* (London: I.B. Tauris, 2015), Wendy Everett (ed.), *European Identity in Cinema* (Bristol: Intellect Books, 2005). Everett and Axel Goodbody (eds), *Revisiting Space: Space and Place in European Cinema* (Brussels: Peter Lang, 2005); Rosalind Galt, *The New European Cinema: Redrawing the Map* (New York: Columbia University Press, 2006); Myrto Konstantarkos (ed.), *Spaces in European Cinema* (Exeter: Intellect Books, 2000); Jo Labanyi, Luisa Passerini and Karen Diel (eds), *Europe and Love in Cinema* (Bristol: Intellect Books, 2012).

[6] See Claude Lévi-Strauss, 'The Effectiveness of Symbols', in *Structural Anthropology*, trans. Claire Jacobson and Brooke Grundfest Schoepf (New York: Basic Books, 1963), 181–201.

film as thought experiment' (Chapter 3), while the idea of 'double occupancy' has been radicalized into a 'cinema of abjection' (Chapter 5) and into directors as 'servants of two masters' (Chapter 12), while 'mutual interference in the internal affairs of the other' has been re-examined as part of an ethics of equality under conditions of asymmetry (Chapter 4). These concepts are ways of putting forward a change of model, internal to Europe's self-understanding as to its future role in globalization, which at the same time proposes a more philosophical case for why and how cinema might indeed be an important, if not indispensable, agent in bringing about such different self-understanding, not *in spite* of having lost some of its cultural prestige, but *because* of it: its newly 'abject position' vis-à-vis Hollywood and Asian cinemas.

The 'European' community: heroic and post-heroic narratives

What emerged from my earlier discussion about the binaries that used to structure the symbolic relations between European cinema and Hollywood is that a similar rivalry *mutatis mutandis* also structures the respective understanding of political values and democracy. Both Europe and the USA consider themselves the birthplace of modern democracy, and especially France and Britain fashion a heroic narrative around their 'birth of a nation'. The disasters of the twentieth century have tempered this self-image (not only in Germany), but the United States' understanding of its own exceptionalism and the kind of democracy flowing from it is still fully invested in the heroic accounts of how to think of the nation politically. The heroic version will always promote identity and purity over diversity and thus maintains the self–Other boundary drawing, embodied in the US by the intractable issue of race and exemplified by its black population, on whose discrimination and exclusion the heroic narrative depends. Countries like Hungary and Poland, out of multiple defeats and occupations are now trying to reconstruct a heroic national narrative with the same results: racism and xenophobia – the heroic narrative, in other words, cannot but create 'abjects'.

For Europe, the heroic narrative is no longer an option. The challenge therefore is to imagine a post-heroic version of democracy, of the colonial legacy, more appropriate for our age as well as the continent's different history, in order to deal with diversity, multiculturalism and the consequences of the free movement of goods, services and people. In the post-heroic narrative, the notion which must prevail is that antagonisms, dissensus and disagreement can still be mutually beneficial, for the asymmetries of globalization are the realities which both Europe and its cinema are part of.

What do I mean by a post-heroic narrative? There is a widely shared conviction that the fall of communism, the unification of Germany and the subsequent enlargement of the European Union since 1990, instead of strengthening Europe in the global context, has accelerated the decentring of the continent in relation to the Americas, China and other Asian nations. Now that the various European nations have come (or been made) to realize how much their heroic narrative of self-identity was based on the colonial legacy and centuries of Eurocentrism, not only politicians are beginning to reassess Europe's present predicament. Yet, so far, there is little sign of a readiness to adopt or accept a more pragmatic narrative about Europe's place in the world. On the contrary, nation states are clamouring to reclaim their sovereignty, and a rift has opened up in almost every country between those who embrace a populist nationalism that seeks drastic measures of exclusion and those who want to occupy the moral high ground of making Europe the last defender, if necessary, of human rights and the welfare state. Both versions are, in their way, still heroic narratives, however diametrically opposed they are in their values and outlook.

At the same time, European intellectuals, mostly on the left, who have cast a more critical eye on the Enlightenment and liberal democracy, find themselves accused of having helped to undermine Europe philosophically. By challenging the values of Enlightenment humanism, they risked promoting forms of social constructivism that ended up distrusting the legitimacy of its political institutions, breeding both cynicism and apathy.[7]

These supposedly corrosive effects of post-metaphysical philosophy could, however, be the starting-point for post-heroic narratives, which accommodate both Europe's much diminished role in the age of globalization, and formulate a different basis for a social contract on the far side of either nostalgia or nihilism, of either resurgent nationalisms or fundamentalist religions.

In a short but often cited text called 'Idea for a Universal History With A Cosmopolitan Purpose', first published in 1786, Immanuel Kant speaks of 'the unsocial sociability of man' ('die ungesellige Geselligkeit des Menschen'), which, I think, opens up a pertinent perspective on a very contemporary dilemma:

[7] Leading spokespersons for this view in Germany are the philosophers Peter Sloterdijk and Norbert Bolz, both prominent public intellectuals on the (centre-) right of the political spectrum. But see also Helen Pluckrose, 'How French "intellectuals" ruined the West', *aeromagazine*, 27 March 2017, https://areomagazine.com/2017/03/27/how-french-intellectuals-ruined-the-west-postmodernism-and-its-impact-explained/. As a long-standing complaint, it has its own history. See the overview by Jan-Werner Müller, 'The Failure of the Intellectuals', *Eurozine*, 11 April 2012, http://www.eurozine.com/the-failure-of-european-intellectuals/ (both accessed 24 October 2017).

> . . . the unsocial sociability of men, i.e., their propensity to enter into society, bound together with a mutual opposition which constantly threatens to break up this society. Man has an inclination to associate with others, because in society he feels himself to be . . . more than the developed form of his natural capacities. But he also has a strong propensity to isolate himself from others, because he finds in himself at the same time the unsocial characteristic of wishing to have everything go according to his own desires . . . He expects opposition on all sides because . . . he knows that, for his own part, he is inclined to oppose others. This opposition . . . awakens all his powers, brings him to conquer his inclination to laziness and, propelled by vainglory, lust for power and avarice, [leads him] to achieve a rank among his fellows whom he cannot tolerate but from whom he cannot withdraw . . . Man wishes concord; but Nature knows better what is good for the race; she wills discord . . . [Thus,] the sources of . . . mutual opposition from which so many evils arise, drive men to new exertions of their forces and thus to the manifold development of their capacities.[8]

Kant's brief text is one of those seminal 'anthropological' statements on which much of Europe's political and social thinking has been based. Its idea of a providential world history, using men's moral weakness rather than their moral strength, provoked Hegel into developing his own dialectic of the world spirit. It in turn inspired Marx's thinking – very much with Kant in mind – about the struggle of antagonistic forces in society leading to greater perfection of the human race. But I return to Kant's passage at this other political juncture, not in order to revive his teleological schemas of progress, but to derive from it useful concepts, such as 'antagonistic mutuality'. Kant's 'unsocial sociability' also anticipates Rancière's 'dissensus' ('Nature wills discord'), and Kant also directs our attention to the dynamics of the singular and the plural, a key to Nancy's thinking, as detailed below, where the individual does not merge or fuse with the community, while still dependent on and part of the collective. Finally, Kant's proposal makes room not only for perfectibility, but also acts as a reminder of immanence and our finitude, and thus provides the horizon for 'abjection' to be considered both as an ethical stance and a political vantage point.

Such thinking appears to inspire many of today's leading political philosophers, notably Nancy, Rancière, Agamben, Balibar and others. By reviving Kantian notions of 'cosmopolitanism', with its recognition of the

---

[8] Immanuel Kant, 'Idea for a Universal History with a Cosmopolitan Purpose', first published in 1784. First English translation in *The London Magazine* (1824), 385–93. See also James Schmidt and Amélie Oksenberg Rorty (eds), *Kant's 'Idea for a Universal History with a Cosmopolitan Aim': A Critical Guide* (Cambridge: Cambridge University Press, 2009).

paradoxical 'unsocial sociability of men', Balibar redefines citizenship, and Nancy proposes new thinking about singularities and collectives. Nancy in particular has explored notions of community and multitudes, after the demise of the great utopian, millennial, totalitarian and progressive social projects that have dominated European political thinking over the past 200 years. Reconceptions of 'what is a community' such as these are far from accepted wisdom among policy-makers of the European Union, but in the meantime they help delineate at least a perspective towards a post-heroic narrative for a post-national Europe: a project that could find in the cinema its imaginative test-bed or research and development lab, in the combination of what I am calling 'the cinema of abjection' and 'film as thought experiment'.

The argument would be that the renewed concern with the idea of community, as reflected by very diverse thinkers, has several driving motives, some of which come from an awareness of global citizenship and a shared sense of mutual interdependence and responsibility not only for our fellow humans, but for other sentient beings in nature (animal studies), for the environment and the planet (anthropocene studies), leading, among others, also to the idea of a 'parliament of things' (Bruno Latour).[9]

Yet it is also the case that the evacuation of traditional party politics, the uneven distribution of job opportunities across North and South, as well as the continuing reliance on the nation state for cultural identity, solidarity and historical cohesion has made the concept of a post-national Europe a difficult sell, leading to a return of chauvinism, xenophobia and racism, rather than a revival of trans- or international solidarity. On the other hand, the crisis of legitimacy and sovereignty of the nation state has also given rise to the centrality of human rights as the foundational logic that legitimates political action – including external interference and military intervention. This logic implies that we delegate to supranational bodies the task of prosecuting political crimes, negotiating over minority rights or seeking justice for 'crimes against humanity'. It has led to the so-called 'ethical turn': the return to religion and the emergence of a post-ideological politics of the moral emotions. Double edged as its grounding in religion might be, the ethical turn is indicative, it can and has been argued, of the failed or exhausted politics of representation and of identity politics,[10] whose horizon was recognition in a world of difference, rather than social justice and the assertion of a common humanity in a world of disparity, antagonism and inequality.

[9] Bruno Latour, *We Have Never Been Modern*, trans. Catherine Porter (Cambridge, MA: Harvard University Press, 1993). See also *The Parliament of Things*, http://blog.theparliamentofthings.org/ and http://parliamentofthings.info/ (accessed 16 December 2016).

[10] See Mark Lilla, 'The End of Identity Liberalism', *New York Times*, 18 November 2016, https://www.nytimes.com/2016/11/20/opinion/sunday/the-end-of-identity-liberalism.html (accessed 15 December 2016).

If human rights are now the platform for the articulation of universally agreed values in the political sphere, then the popularity of neurobiology, evolutionary psychology and cognitivism would indicate that the search is also on for a new set of innate universals, tempering the Enlightenment belief in reason with the 'emotional brain', replacing the mind–body split with the 'embodied mind' and challenging rationality with the 'mirror-neurons' of hardwired empathy.

A post-heroic narrative – in contrast to recovering such old or new universals that seek to find common ground between the different religions, or posit shared mutual responsibilities and interests – is more likely, in the spirit of Kant, to affirm incompatible interests, dissensus rather than consensus, and incommensurable values, while still insisting that there are things that bind singularities into a community. As already suggested, much of contemporary European philosophy is concerned with foundational questions, including the foundations of democracy and the social contract. This concern has rightly been expressed against the background of the failures of socialism, of communism and the disaster of the fascist communities of male bonding, as well as the failure of other theories of the 'we', such as the Marxist revolutionary subject of history and the working class as a collective agent of struggle and change.

In light of tribalism, sectarianism and communities based on race, religion and ethnicity, which seem to have re-emerged on the back of these failures, the question of whether there are different ways of relating to one another has become urgent, and highly political: 'How can we manage to be together? What do we share and how? What is our common ground and what our isolation? What does it mean to touch one another?'[11] This new thinking of the 'we' *after* both the collective *and* the individual subject is what these philosophers are concerned with, while at the same time accepting and acknowledging the necessary but insufficient basis of 'human rights' as a foundational gesture of this 'we'.[12]

For instance, a new idea of community, widely embraced in cultural studies, was the adoption and appropriation of the analyses of Benedict Anderson, who – after seeing how the idea of community began to separate from the nation state – launched the term 'imagined communities'.[13] Anderson's main

---

[11] Anja Streiter, 'The Community according to Jean-Luc Nancy and Claire Denis', *Film-Philosophy* 12, no. 1 (2008): 49–62 (50), http://www.film-philosophy.com/2008v12n1/streiter.pdf (accessed 9 January 2017).

[12] See the discussion on Hannah Arendt, Agamben and human rights in Chapter 4.

[13] Using Indonesia as his chief example of postcolonial nationhood, Anderson describes the nation as a cultural and political artefact that provides a previously heterogeneous collectivity with a sense of geographical unity, historical continuity and emotional consistency, through media such as print journalism or disciplinary regimes such as universal schooling. Benedict Anderson, *Imagined Communities – On the Origins of Nationalism* (London: Verso, 1983).

thesis was that nationalism was a project developed and understood not simply through political systems of power, but rather through cultural systems of sign- and image-production. Although anthropological in its initial formulations, Anderson's concept of imagined communities was avidly seized upon by cultural critics and media scholars in order to validate the new media of the late twentieth century like television and the internet, with their transient but intense, volatile but ubiquitous, communities. If anything, this thinking of communities as self-generated and culturally constructed has grown in recent years, wherever online or virtual communities of social networking are promoted as the natural successors to the bourgeois public spheres of the eighteenth and nineteenth centuries. As the new global cultural avant-gardes, they are said not only to demonstrate the wisdom of crowds, but also understand themselves as a politically progressive force – as seen in the Facebook and Twitter communities during the unrest in Iran in 2012, or the even more intensely mediatic 'Arab Spring' in 2013. But the internet also allows for the gathering of less desirable communities: reactionary, bigoted groups – whether they are neo-Nazis, jihadists, paedophiles or white supremacists of the alt-right.

These ambiguities or contradictions inherent in the concept of imagined communities, once taken out of Anderson's anthropological-historical framework and applied to swarm phenomena or social networks in general, have in turn prompted intense scrutiny and critique. More philosophical and sceptical rethinking of the idea of community has been proposed by Wendy Brown, Judith Butler, Slavoj Žižek, Michael Hardt and Antonio Negri (as well as Habermas, Luhmann and Sloterdijk), while prominent among the (mainly French) philosophers who are rethinking 'community' are several former Marxists: Rancière, Balibar and Badiou, but also a 'libertarian socialist' thinker such as Claude Lefort, and the philosopher most closely allied with the Heidegger-Derrida tradition, Jean-Luc Nancy. Thanks to two of his books, *Being Singular Plural* and *The Inoperative Community* (as well as his writings on the cinema), Nancy is the thinker I want to concentrate on, by way of introducing the individual case studies. Together with Blanchot's *The Unavowable Community* and Agamben's *The Coming Community*, Nancy's work has opened up the concept of community into a broader politico-ethical and philosophico-ontological context.

In what ways, then, are any of these reconstruction efforts – whether the post-Marxist (Anderson) or post-Heideggerian (Nancy) theories of community that have emerged since the 1980s and been under discussion since the 1990s – relevant to my inquiry into post-national Europe and its cinema? In *European Cinema: Face to Face with Hollywood*, I may have been too optimistic in suggesting the formation of new communities when discussing the crucial importance of film festivals for the survival of European cinema as part of world cinema. Wanting to construct a bridge between the idea of the post-national and its echoes in the cinema, I put forward the point that at film festivals, films address themselves to a community, which is no longer either the national audience of popular genre cinema, nor the art cinema audience following the careers of the great auteurs, but an international, transnational festival audience, made up of very different segments and constituencies, from critics and fellow filmmakers to cinephiles, local audiences, buyers and sellers and agenda-setting interest groups. As I suggested, such a festival audience might be addressed by a film which 'performs' its own version of the 'national' to the exoticizing (curious, voyeuristic) gaze of the Other, in a gesture of ingratiation, by giving the Other what it thinks the Other wants or expects. Alternatively, however, a film or auteur might also be able to present and promote issues for which the context of a festival offers not a 'window on the world' but a unique 'window of attention' and a serious forum for debate. Which is why I put forward the idea of the film festival potentially serving as a surrogate NGO, an alternative public sphere, or at least as a kind of placeholder for an 'agora of a community to come'.[14]

But if I am right in arguing that a post-heroic European cinema would have to liberate itself from self–Other schemata in whatever form, in its thematics as well as its modes of representation, then the cinema for the community-to-come would not only have to think its way past traditional notions of identity and difference, but also have to rethink itself in cinematic terms and no longer assume the screen to be functioning as either 'window' or 'mirror', and it would have to forgo both 'identification' and 'distanciation' as the two poles that have defined the spectator–film relationship.

In the meantime, the Hollywood mainstream ever more determinately 'works though' the surveillance paradigm and reconstructs 'cinema as two-way mirror' – whenever we look at and interact with the world on the screen, another eye emanating from the screen is looking at us. We are always already enfolded in a look that never meets our eyes. If Hollywood is emulating the two-way mirrors of social media, a cinema of abjection, by contrast, deploys the screen as a surface that is neither transparent nor reflecting back, deconstructing identification, by resisting sympathy and blocking empathy. It features protagonists whose subjectivities are sealed off, whose goals are minimal, whose presence is distinct and singular, even in the act of withdrawal, yet who testify by their very separateness from us to a common humanity of ultimate solitude. Nancy, with his idea that what we share are the spaces that separate us (see below), is the philosopher whose thought rises to the challenge of such a cinema.

---

[14] Elsaesser, *European Cinema Face to Face with Hollywood*, 103.

Jean-Luc Nancy and the inoperative community

Speaking of 'imagined communities', social networks or an 'agora of a community to come' would, I imagine, be anathema to Nancy. His ideas, difficult though they are, and bound up with an entire philosophical system, might nonetheless prove quite productive for thinking the aesthetics of specific films in the post-heroic mode of what he calls 'being singular plural'.[15] By this, Nancy calls for the disbanding of any kind of substantive community (such as nation, ethne or faith-based community), but has also dismissed as naïve and utopian their opposite, the swarm communities of technological mediation. According to him, community as the dominant Western political formation is founded upon a totalizing, exclusionary myth, basing itself on a presumed national, racial or religious unity. It must be 'unworked' (made inoperative) in order to accommodate more humbly inclusive, but also dissensual, forms of being-in-common, of dwelling-together in the world, under the present conditions of *mondialization* – French for globalization, but also 'world-making'.[16] Coming from the Heideggerian tradition, it is evident that Nancy argues within a very complex and precise field of conceptualization, which I can only sketch and paraphrase here. But I take the core statement of his work to be a critique of Heidegger's notion of Dasein, conceived primarily around the singular being, against which Nancy pleads for an extension of Dasein towards plurality and the multiple, understood as what comes after 'nation' and 'the people', but also what can counter globalization as homogenization. This community is thus founded not on the immanence of individuals being-in-common (Dasein), but on an 'unworking' (desoeuvrement) of togetherness into a being-with (Mit-sein): making the inescapable solitude and finality of 'Da-Sein' the very ground for the commonality of 'Mit-sein'. This Mit-sein, also taken from Heidegger, is explicated by Nancy as follows in a roundtable discussion with fellow philosopher Avital Ronell:

> The 'with' is a quasi-empty category for all philosophy. The whole scheme of our culture knows very well what is to be in or out, to identify with something or to be totally exterior to it, to be homogeneous or to be heterogeneous. But to Be-With, this is the same thing as to say that the glass is with the pen on the table and [that] to 'be on' (the table) is a way to 'be with' . . . What is that? In a certain way this is nothing, because . . .

[15] Jean-Luc Nancy, *Being Singular Plural*, trans. Robert D. Richardson and Anne E. O'Byrne (Stanford, CA: Stanford University Press, 2000).

[16] This is how Jean-Luc Nancy introduces the term (as distinct from globalization) in *La Création du monde ou la mondialisation* (Paris: Galilée, 2002).

> 'the glass and the pen' . . . have nothing to do with the other . . . If the pen is hidden behind the glass, you can't say that they are 'with.' Or if I hide myself behind [you] there is no longer ['me' 'with you.'] So, 'With' implies proximity and distance, precisely the distance of the impossibility to come together in a common being. That is the core of the question of community; community doesn't have a common being, a common substance, but consists in 'being-in-common.' From the starting point it's a sharing, but sharing what? Sharing nothing, sharing the space between.[17]

With these thoughts, which posit at once a radical contiguity-in-commonness and a radical separateness-in-singularity, Nancy is yet another thinker at the forefront of the philosophical debate against multiculturalism and any kind of identity politics, where a group can speak for individuals or constitute itself as a fusion of tolerated differences. In line with my own questioning of the 'face-to-face' as a stabilizing construction of identity, Nancy acknowledges, like Levinas or Derrida, the inherent violence of any face-to-face.[18] Yet Nancy also generally defends a position similar to that of Alain Badiou – that radical Otherness or alterity, such as advocated by Levinas, is caught in the same epistemological trap as the Cartesian subject/object split. The 'Other' always ends up somehow being the good Other, or the Big Other, which is to say, the same as me (or the idealized, projected-introjected 'me'), bringing us back to the mirroring dynamics of subjectivity, the very concept that *Mit-sein* is designed to do away with.

Nancy's main targets of attack, however, are the socialist-communist ideals of collectivity and the bourgeois-liberal insistence on the individual. Both of these apparent opposites are for him figures of heroic immanence, of the self-realization through work and works, through production and labour – which are to Nancy ways of trying to avoid finitude or to cheat death by sacralizing it. Hence his choice of the word *désoeuvré* (idle, out of work, inoperable, unproductive) for the true community.

As the byline of *The Inoperative Community* emphasizes: 'Contrary to popular Western notions of community, Nancy shows that it is neither a project of fusion nor production.'[19] Needless to say, Nancy also avoids thinking in terms of binary oppositions or contrasting pairs. Conceptions of community, nation or individual that work on the divide of self/other, me/you, I/thou, subject/object are inimical to the Mit-sein, as defined by him. Mit-sein would thus be a constantly shifting relation of distance and proximity, of

---

[17] See www.egs.edu/faculty/nancy/nancy-roundtable-discussion2001.html (accessed 23 September 2017). Jean-Luc Nancy, 'Love and Community: A Roundtable Discussion with Nancy', Roundtable Discussion, European Graduate School, August 2001.

[18] See my discussion of Levinas and Derrida in Chapter 4 ('"Europe": A Thought Experiment').

[19] Jean-Luc Nancy, *The Inoperative Community*, ed. Peter Connor (Minneapolis: University of Minnesota Press, 1991), back cover.

contiguity and presence, of the field of vision and its effacement or invisibility, of the single point of view and its multiple, impossible refractions. Mit-sein would be a way of being in the world and among human beings, but stopping short of any suggestion of mutuality, reciprocity or cooperation, as well as any necessary interdependence along the lines of Hegel's master–slave dialectic. As Nancy points out, in the West we operate with the categories of inside/outside, before/after, up/down, in front of/behind (all the spatial body-based 'container' metaphors that regulate our epistemology and our language – if we believe Lakoff and Johnson's *Metaphors We Live By*).[20] But we have little experience of what 'being-with' means and what it does not mean, and how it is more than in-between, and less (that is, more specific) than 'entanglement', 'hybridity' or other metaphors of choice in postcolonial and multicultural discourses.

The 'inoperative community' means, in other words, that a community is not the result of a production, be it social, economic or political. It is neither constructed and a work, nor a discourse and a creation, whether heroic and man-made or natural and God-given. Nancy thus opposes the idea of the state as a work of art, or even the nation as either chosen or self-created. As Christopher Fynsk formulates it in his preface, 'The community that becomes a single thing (body, mind, fatherland, Leader. . . .) necessarily loses the "in" of *being-in-common*. Or, it loses the "with" that defines our *being-with*. It gives up its being-together to a being of togetherness.'[21] In view of the imagined communities of the media, one might add that they give up their being-together in exchange for a being of togetherness, with all the temptations of fusion, merging or the ecstasy of communion that reaches from popular culture to political activism – American Idol to Occupy Wall Street; and from ecstatic communalism to demagogic populism – Bruce Springsteen rock concerts to Donald Trump rallies.

These are harsh injunctions, and at first sight, they sit uneasily with any idea of a more perfect, that is, politically integrated, European Union, and they seem equally hostile or inapplicable to any concept of European cinema as the expression of creative endeavour or aesthetic autonomy. And no doubt Nancy has little patience for the ways in which European summits try to patch together 'rescue packages' for debtor nations and preach austerity to their citizens, while being held hostage by banks and corporations, whose loyalty is neither to a government, state or nation, but to their bonuses and perhaps to their shareholders. No doubt the entire ideology of a common market, of fiscal union or moral hazard and debt mutualization, would strike Nancy as the very perversion of his idea of community.

[20] George Lakoff and Mark Johnson, *Metaphors We Live By* (Chicago: University of Chicago Press, 1980).

[21] The phrase *être-en-commun* in French corresponds with *being-in-common* in the English translation. See Nancy, *The Inoperative Community*, xxxix.

Nancy's definition of modernity is the classically modernist one: *we have no God as a measure of transcendent truth, we no longer have tradition (or history) as a measure of value, and we no longer have 'nature' to give us a measure of things*. This could be seen as the heroic, 'Nietzschean' stance, or that of a more humble 'nihilist': for instance, Nancy derives the word 'rien' from rem (res, a thing), and 'nothing' from no-thing: that is, he insists on the materialism of nothing, nothing is no-thing, which would be a double-negative definition of a human being, as neither a thing nor a 'not nothing'.[22]

However, as with Kant, one senses an anthropological dimension to his rethinking of the foundations of democracy and politics: in particular, the idea of the 'sacred' plays a central role, opening up its full ambiguity. On the one hand, the sanctity of life is associated with irreducible, but also meaningless, 'singularity', and on the other, it is seen as the main ideological bastion of bio-politics, associated with the 'care of the self' that for Foucault ushered in a new phase in the disciplinary regimes of modernity, where bourgeois self-control and sublimation hands over to auto-regulatory self-monitoring. Against this, thinkers like Agamben have reclaimed the other meaning of sacred, as in *homo sacer* or 'bare life', redefining also the idea of the abject as not only a term of exclusion and casting off, but one where the excluded and abjected gains and retains power over that which excludes, by its proximity and contiguity.[23] Sanctity thus becomes a complex relation where one either uses the Other's exclusion as a 'foundational' moment for one's own inner consistency, reminiscent of the scapegoat theory of René Girard, or it connotes the back-and-forth between sacred and abject more generally (the abject-as-sacred/the sacred-as-abject), held in trust as that which can one day found the 'new community', albeit by acknowledging its actual impossibility. Nancy, I imagine, is here in dialogue with both Bataille and Blanchot.[24]

When it comes to the cinema, Nancy has named several directors in whose work he recognizes concerns similar to his own. One prominent auteur is Abbas Kiarostami, to whom – as mentioned previously – Nancy has devoted an extensive study, *The Evidence of Film*. There he develops a theory of cinema that makes much of *Mit-sein*, and that he sees translated

[22] Jean-Luc Nancy, *Dis-Enclosure: The Deconstruction of Christianity*, trans. Gabriel Malenfant, Michael B. Smith and Bettina Bergo (New York: Fordham University Press, 2008).

[23] See also Jeffrey Geller's review of Giorgio Agamben, *Profanations* (New York: Zone Books, 2007) where the function of the sacred in Agamben is aligned with his critique of capitalism: *Notre Dame Philosophical Reviews* (2008), http://ndpr.nd.edu/review.cfm?id=13409 (accessed 26 October 2017).

[24] *La Communauté inavouable* (The Unavowable Community, 1988), a short work by Blanchot, was a response to Nancy's work on community (and was inspired as well by Bataille, whose work on sovereignty is discussed in *La Communauté désoeuvrée*). The dialogue between Nancy and Blanchot continued until Blanchot's death. *The Unavowable Community*, trans. Pierre Joris (New York: Station Hill Press, 1988).

into practice especially in Kiarostami's so-called Koker trilogy, and in particular its second part, *Life and Nothing More* (1991).

The other auteur to whom Nancy has devoted both his philosophical attention and his personal friendship is Claire Denis, whose film *Beau Travail* makes up the substance of the next chapter, considered as a thought experiment of what might be an example of post-heroic European cinema in the spirit of the inoperable community. At the same time, *Beau Travail* has as its main protagonist a figure who, in an attempt to exclude and eliminate another human being, descends himself into 'becoming abject'. At the end, deprived of community, and in utter solitude, he defiantly experiences his abjection as moments of ecstatic liberation. The poignancy, however, is that he is expelled from a community – the French Foreign Legion – which is itself ambiguously positioned between the sacred and the abject, vis-à-vis the Great Nation that the men are called upon to represent and to defend.

Denis's work and *Beau Travail* in particular also fit into what earlier I called a cinema that treats the screen as neither window nor mirror, and that distributes its elements, its protagonists, their bodies, gestures and spaces differently. But *Beau Travail* also features, quite explicitly, a very unusual set of people, held together and prized apart by both mutuality and antagonism, by an imposed code of discipline and a self-chosen separateness, around which the idea of an 'inoperative community' might be probed and given shape, especially when placed against the background of Nancy's notion of 'being singular-plural'.

7

Claire Denis, Jean-Luc Nancy and *Beau Travail*

Claire Denis is both marginal and central to French cinema as a national cinema. Marginal, in that her autobiographical background is quintessentially postcolonial; she was brought up in the parts of North Africa that feature in *Chocolat* (1988) and *Beau Travail* (1999), the area around the Horn of Africa. But she is also central to French cinema, thanks to her stints as an assistant director to several of the canonical directors of the *nouvelle vague*, notably her friendship with Jacques Rivette, and with the *ciné-fils par excellence*, Serge Daney. Yet Claire Denis is also in between two generations of French filmmakers: she came too late onto the scene to be part of the generation that rejected the *nouvelle vague* in the 1970s, but she is too old to belong to the *cinéma du look*, or the more recent New French extremity cinema (though a case can be made for her setting that movement's agenda).[1] Because of her personal background, she also is in tune with the more recent, hyphenated generation of filmmakers that touches on the topics of multiracial Europe and postcolonial France.

French cinema, until the late 1980s and early 1990s, when Denis made her first film, *Chocolat*, had had relatively little to say about either postcolonialism or the ideology of multiculturalism. Since the Third Republic generally considered its colonial past as part of its 'civilizing mission' and downplayed its consequences for the nation's self-image even after the protracted and very brutal Algerian War of Liberation, the cinema rarely broke this consensus, with the possible exception of Jean-Luc Godard's *Le Petit Soldat* (1963), to which *Beau Travail* explicitly refers. As to the question of national identity and national community, the French state's approach to having immigrants from Africa and the Maghreb region come to France either as cheap labour or as permanent immigrants had been treated predominantly as a matter of assimilation. As long as immigrants learnt

[1] Martine Beugnet, 'The Wounded Screen', in Tanya Horeck and Tina Kendall (eds), *The New Extremism in Cinema* (Edinburgh: Edinburgh University Press, 2011), 29–42.

French and abided by French laws, there was officially no discrimination: you're welcome, as long as you speak, behave and preferably think like the French.[2] Hence no real discussion about 'melting pot' or 'salad bowl' or 'separate development' or multicultural and multi-ethnic society such as raged in Britain, Germany or the Netherlands. To vary a famous saying, the motto in France seems to have been 'You can be whoever you like to be, as long as you're French.' France's strongly centralized educational system, its fierce belief in republican *laicité*, in the strict division of Church and state, for a very long time shaped attitudes to both immigrants and to the narratives of French colonialism, which may also explain why the debates about the Muslim headscarf have been so bitter, but also why there have been comparatively many films about schools and school life, now that multiracial society is being taken seriously: they provide a kind of microcosm of the current state of French thinking about its republican values.

Successful on the festival circuit (it garnered many prizes, e.g. at the Berlin Film Festival, Rotterdam Film Festival, Chicago Film Critics' Award and many more nominations) as well as when released on DVD, *Beau Travail* has been a favourite on the academic circuit, being written up and analysed by virtually everyone working in French cinema.[3] Without going into the various stances taken by the critics, one can nonetheless identify recurring critical positions: thus US critics (Jonathan Rosenbaum, Jim Hoberman)[4] saw it as a poetic masterpiece, highlighting the body paradigm of skin and touch, the military drill as dance ritual of strange insect-like creatures, the landscape, the indigenous women as 'chorus' commenting on the action, while exposing the viewer to archaic forms of communion and communication beyond language. Also mentioned was the layering of cinephile references to Godard's *Le Petit Soldat* (via Bruno Forestier), to Alain Resnais' *Muriel* (1963) (the flashback structure) and to the few other films that reflected the

[2] 'The true 'French ideology' . . . [lies] in the idea that the culture of the 'land of the Rights of Man' has been entrusted with a universal mission to educate the human race. There corresponds to this mission a practice of assimilating dominated populations and a consequent need to differentiate and rank individuals or groups in terms of their greater or lesser aptitude for – or resistance to – assimilation. It was this simultaneously subtle and crushing form of exclusion/inclusion which was deployed in the process of colonization and the strictly French (or "democratic") variant of the "White man's burden".' Etienne Balibar, 'Is there a Neo Racism', in Étienne Balibar and Immanuel Wallerstein, *Race, Nation, Class: Ambiguous Identities*, trans. Chris Turner (London: Verso, 1991), 24.

[3] See special issue of *Studies in French Cinema*, and especially Martine Beugnet and Jane Sillars, 'Beau travail : time, space and myths of identity', *Studies in French Cinema* 1, no. 3 (2001): 166–73, and Sarah Cooper, 'Je sais bien, mais quand même . . .: Fetishism, Envy, and the Queer Pleasures of Beau travail', *Studies in French Cinema* 1, no. 3 (2001): 174–82.

[4] Jonathan Rosenbaum, 'Unsatisfed Men: *Beau Travail*', *Chicago Reader*, 25 May 2000, https://www.chicagoreader.com/chicago/unsatisfied-men/Content?oid=902343 (accessed 21 August 2017); J. Hoberman, 'Work in Progress', *Village Voice*, 28 March 2000, https://www.villagevoice.com/2000/03/28/work-in-progress/ (accessed 21 August 2017).

French colonial experience.[5] Amy Taubin spoke admiringly about the drama of desire and repression, the strange post-Oedipal rivalry between two 'sons' over the love of the father, calling it a ballet of homoeroticism observed and filmed by the female gaze, at once tender and curious, eroticized and stylized.[6]

Another critical approach has been to explore the complex relation that the film entertains with Herman Melville's novella *Billy Budd* and Benjamin Britten's opera by the same name based on Melville. Is it an adaptation, is it an interpretation, is it a counter-Melville, or is it translating the paradoxes and opacity of Melville's prose into paradoxical and enigmatic images?[7] Perhaps the most consistent line of analysis has been to examine the complex weaving of the narrative, with respect to the temporal structure, mingling flashback, time-present, as well as flash-forwards and also scenes that seem both timeless in their pictorial beauty and a-temporal in relation to the narrative intrigue. These differential temporalities are motivated by the inner and outer world of a former officer of the French Foreign Legion, now living in Marseille. A brief encounter in the streets with a detachment of legionnaires reminds him of his past in the legion, which ended ingloriously with his discharge after jeopardizing the life of one of his subordinates in a premeditated plot to have him die in the desert.[8]

Equally as disorientating as the temporal structure is the optical and aural point of view that the film adopts. Like many French films, *Beau Travail* has a voice-over commentary, as well as a hero who seems to be

---

[5] Peter Bradshaw, 'Beau Travail', *Guardian*, 14 July 2000, https://www.theguardian.com/film/2000/jul/14/1; Hannah McGill, 'Blood and Sand: Beau Travail', *Sight & Sound*, May 2012, http://old.bfi.org.uk/sightandsound/feature/49855 (both accessed 21 August 2017).

[6] Amy Taubin, 'Under the Skin', *Film Comment* 36, no. 3 (May/June 2000): 22–8.

[7] Denis herself has said that she was more influenced by Benjamin Britten's opera than by Melville's text: 'One of the cast had actually been in the Legion, so we took all their real exercises and did them together every day, to concentrate the actors as a group. We never said we were going to choreograph the film. But afterwards, when we started shooting, using Britten's music, those exercises became like a dance.' 'Film-makers on film: Claire Denis', interview by Sheila Johnston, *Daily Telegraph*, 16 August 2003.

[8] A more complex plot summary might go something like this (taken from Wikipedia): 'Back in France, master sergeant Galoup (Denis Lavant) remembers the time in the desert, where he led his men under the command of Bruno Forestier (Michel Subor). His life there consisted mostly of routine duties like supervising the physical exercise of his men. One day, his troop is joined by Gilles Sentain (Grégoire Colin), whose physical beauty, social skills, and fortitude make Galoup envious. Repressed homosexual feelings on the part of Galoup are suggested. When Sentain helps another soldier, violating previous orders by Galoup, Galoup sees a chance to destroy Sentain. As a punishment, he drives him out into the desert to make him walk back to the base. But Sentain does not return because Galoup has tampered with his compass, and Sentain cannot make his way out without it. Even though Sentain is later found and rescued by a group of Djiboutis, Galoup is sent back to France by his commander for a court martial, ending his time in the Foreign Legion. The final scene suggests the possibility of his suicide.'

keeping a diary (think Bresson's *Diary of a Country Priest*): we therefore assume that the perspective of the camera is not only that of the central protagonist, but also of the story's hero. Yet the opening scenes quite specifically undermine any such perspectival alignment, and even when the voice and the body are introduced, we are made aware that the point of view we are sharing is not straightforward: our officer-hero, named Galoup, turns out to be the 'bad guy', in that he took revenge on another soldier, possibly out of unrequited homosexual love, possibly out of rivalry over the attention of his commanding officer, possibly because he took his duties too seriously. At the same time, we are also party to many scenes that could not have been witnessed by Galoup.

This modernist flouting of the sequential temporal register – one thinks of Gilles Deleuze's crystal image – and the unlocalized and unlocatable point of view of many of the scenes has been discussed by several critics. Christine Noll Brinckmann, for instance, has pointed out that these features are the strong personal signature of Denis's regular camerawoman, Agnès Godard, and has demonstrated how images in the film respond to each other, how they build up subtle patterns, visual rhymes and unexpected correspondences in a way that might not have been possible if the images were more directly subservient to either the narrative or to Galoup's point of view.[9]

Yet, these same stylistic features could also be read as making a quite persuasive case for Denis's *mise en scène* as teaching the audience what it might mean to be with someone, the *Mit-sein* discussed by Nancy, as neither identification nor projection, neither inside nor outside, neither in front of nor hierarchically organized or fixed along perspectival sight-lines. One of the remarkable features of *Beau Travail* is the fact that, as spectators, we are uncannily (and sometimes uncomfortably) close to the main character (and not only to him), but without thereby having access to any kind of interiority. Even where we do share Galoup's point of view, and even when we hear his voice-over or read his diary entries, he remains contiguous but distant, close but closed off. As with Albert Camus' *L'Etranger* (though we are also in the world of Jean Genet's *Querelle de Brest*), one gets to know very little about this person's inner life. Yet the camera also keeps us very close to his body, his pockmarked skin and unruly hair. We are with him during banal everyday actions like washing his clothes, ironing his shirt, pruning a tree, writing in his notebook, cooking; we see the veins on his muscles – in short, we share a close physical intimacy without getting to know him. Especially the ending of *Beau Travail* is a careful study of ambiguity: is Galoup going to commit suicide, has he already committed suicide, or has he found some self-liberation in his final ecstatic dance, which releases his pent-up energy and

[9] Christine Noll Brinckmann, 'Die Arbeit der Kamera', in Isabella Reicher and Michael Omasta (eds), *Claire Denis: Trouble Every Day* (Vienna: Filmmuseum-Synema, 2005), 18–33.

aggression but also leaves him vulnerable in his solitary singularity, making his acceptance of death the condition of re-entry into the community that expelled him? In other words, Galoup would be something of an 'abject' hero, while we, the audience, have to experience a sometimes awkward, sometimes bewilderingly intimate and sometimes bafflingly remote condition of Mit-sein: a 'being with' that breaks with almost all the conventional spectator positions, such as voyeur or invisible fly on the wall, participant observer or aggressively implicated addressee. Instead, all possible forms of affective and perceptual responses to the protagonist have to be reassessed by the spectator.

Confirming this impression of a different way of spectators 'being with' the characters in the film is the space and the contact zone that the men share and occupy. What is striking is that the legionnaires, who hardly speak, often touch each other, bump into each other and make physical contact with each other and the earth, as if to emphasize a certain direct sensory materialism in their lives, where people and things, object and gestures have equal weight and valency. Such moments would seem to illustrate Nancy's point about humans in the inoperable community being both not-things and not-nothing: the film is going to some length to build into the space and camera movements a strong lateral axis, in contrast to the usual top-down structure of a regimented military hierarchy. The community, where all the passions of love, admiration, jealousy seem to be alive, is shown as one where bodies inhabit the same undifferentiated space – whether water, desert, the exercise yard, or their living quarters – and make physical contact, without any special meaning being attached to it or manifesting any particular inner emotion that might lead to thought or action: they neither fuse nor do they participate in a common project.

Interestingly enough, Nancy himself, in his article on *Beau Travail*, also comments on the physicality and the men's bodies, but takes a quite different line of argument, speaking as much if not more about Herman Melville and *Billy Budd* as he does about Claire Denis's film. Nonetheless, what he says is fascinating.[10] He uses the occasion to develop further his concern with what he calls 'the deconstruction of Christianity', coining the phrase 'a-religion'. He first of all points to the film's almost insupportable literalness and physicality, which he interprets as a bold and resolute refusal to interpret or to allocate sense. According to Nancy, while the phrase 'beau travail' comes from Melville, and is said spitefully and ironically by Claggart ('nice work'), when Billy spills the food, in Denis's film it becomes a kind of credo: *beau travail* becomes *travailler le beau*: work on beauty, which is to say,

[10] See also Laura McMahon, 'Deconstructing Community and Christianity: "A-religion" in Nancy's reading of Beau travail', *Film-Philosophy* 12, no. 1 (2008): 63–78, http://www.film-philosophy.com/2008v12n1/mcmahon.pdf (accessed 21 August 2017).

make the images so beautiful that they stand as a kind of defiant answer to the moral iniquity of the story of jealousy, passion and betrayal:

> C'est le film lui-même qui l'est: voici un beau travail. De fait, c'est un travail sur la beauté: corps, lumière, apparence, harmonie, majesté, rythme sévère du montage, qui tient la narrativité en respect, au second plan, en faveur d'une ostension des images par quoi la caméra se signale ou se signe. (It is the film itself which is this: here is a beautiful piece of work. Indeed, it is a piece of work on beauty: body, light, appearance, harmony, majesty, severe rhythm of montage, which keeps narrative at bay, in the background, in favour of showing images through which the camera is highlighted or identifies itself.)

In other words, what we have is not the aesthetization of naked bodies à la Leni Riefenstahl or the fascist mass ornament that Siegfried Kracauer detected in Fritz Lang's *Nibelungen* (1924), but more the cinematic work on the physical materiality of sand, sea, body surface, texture – in a kind of grandiose reduction of the soldiers' lives and fates to a rhythm that both encloses them and exceeds their understanding and participation, that of the stark indifference of nature and the cosmos, once more the 'groundless ground' of the community.

But why a-religion? For this we have to make another detour, bringing us to where I started from: the present state of Europe in the globalized world, now within the philosophical–ontological–religious framework of scepticism, self-reflexivity and deconstruction. Nancy's notion of Europe as a philosophical entity is characterized not so much by secularization and disenchantment, but by the self-deconstruction of Christianity, in its trajectory from Judaism via Greece and Rome to the Enlightenment – Kant, Hegel – to Nietzsche and Heidegger, culminating in the latter's attempt to make philosophy or thinking 'overcome' (Christian) religion, by returning it, as it were, to its 'Greek' state – a trajectory that one can follow in many of the late twentieth-century thinkers: Foucault's reinvention of Greek sexuality, Badiou's return to St Paul, and Friedrich Kittler's quest for the common origins of mathematics and music in a resurrected Greece.

Nancy is very specific: Christianity for him is characterized by the fact that it no longer knows a God outside man, as it were, but within: the triply divided god, the dying God in Christ.[11] Perhaps one can understand this as

---

[11] Melville's *Billy Budd* story is often interpreted allegorically, not least by Jean-Luc Nancy, who claims that 'Melville's tale is a tale of a Christic passion whose iniquity leads to no salvation . . . A ship called the Athée (the Atheist) leaves no room for doubt: the tragedy of Billy is that of Christ in a world without God.' Jean-Luc Nancy, 'A-religion', *Journal of European Studies* 34, no. 1/2 (2004): 15.

meaning that Christianity deconstructs itself (hence a-Christianity) because it is the only religion that thinks the infinite within the finite (the fact that 'life goes on' – no Messiah to come, eternal repetition), in that it posits that the moment of salvation is already behind us. Christianity, taken literally, is the end of life making 'sense'. Nancy can thus argue that Christianity is the religion on the way of departing from religion (as a binding to a higher order and to a power outside man). In Nancy – echoing Heidegger citing Hölderlin – man has the privilege to save himself, which is why the Gods remain far.[12]

But while on the one hand, salvation is behind, Christianity is an opening up (in Heidegger's term): but what is it to open up, if there is no boundary, border, not even a horizon? We are constantly trying to reinsert boundaries and limits and horizons in our thinking and our being: setting targets, goals, frames of reference.[13] The paradox is not only that Christianity – faithfully understood – has done away with these; insofar as Christianity inscribes human beings into history as a journey, its horizonlessness is a self-undoing: it constantly restates the paradox that life goes on, but we do not. This groundless ground (of our epistemology) and this horizonlessness (of our teleology) Nancy calls a-Christianity, which is not post-Christianity, and not anti-Christianity, but the self-manifestation-as-self-undoing of Christianity itself, as the dynamics of the West, of technology, capitalism and thus also of globalization – an endlessly self-defeating telos, rather than a deferred telos of shifting goalposts. Here Nancy's critique of the classic ideals of community, based on the heroic narrative, sets in: if Christianity is necessarily self-creation, but also self-resorption and self-overcoming, then its narrative is the heroic-tragic one of man-God and God-man, where faith and nihilism stand back to back with each other.

We can now see how such a reading of Christianity fits in with an analysis of Europe in the post-national era of globalization, where our territorial boundaries, our state sovereignty and our national identity have also deprived us of horizons, limits, boundaries. And it was deconstructionism that provided us with the appropriate philosophy of not only the groundless ground, that is, no foundational moment for our being and knowing, but also with the promise and terror of limitlessness. We neither have ground 'beneath' us, nor a horizon 'in front of us': the hubris of the twentieth

---

[12] 'Christianity is from the outset a self-overcoming: first Jewish Christianity, then Greek Christianity, and then Roman Christianity – in each case, a split which is also a self-overcoming/self-creation out of its own negation/sublation. Old Law into new law, logos into The Word, civitas into civitas dei.' (Like other religions, Christianity becomes orthodox by fixing 'heresies' and 'apocrypha'.) Jean-Luc Nancy, 'L'areligion', *Vacarme*, 14 January 2001, http://www.vacarme.org/article81.html (accessed 21 August 2017).

[13] See my discussion of 'creative constraints' and 'performative self-contradiction' in Chapter 12 as versions of the same dilemma.

century carried into the twenty-first – except that in a Europe that turns only to the past and closes its borders, there is a shrinking from this limitlessness of expansion, but the borders and boundaries are mere paranoid fictions, supported by neither creative constraints nor ecological sustainability.

Beau Travail would then be the film that shows what such a world without a ground or horizon might look and feel like, and the fact that Denis makes it so breathtakingly beautiful is yet another aspect of its terror. In this sense, the cinema – of identification, of participation, of interaction – would then be profoundly Western, in that it wants the image to function as window or door or mirror – entities that are bounded and circumscribed – rather than simply opening up to the 'beyond-sense', to the (liberating, renewing) meaninglessness of the world, and our being-in-it.[14] Such a reading would modify or even counter the generally preferred one, where *Beau Travail* is seen as a celebration of touch and tactility, of haptic vision and skin, of sensory plenitude – which sometimes veers dangerously close to a post-postcolonial version of the Orientalist seductions of Africa, with its colours, sounds, textures, tastes and smells.

While Nancy has more to say, for instance, about the all-male community in the film, which, in a short essay, he likens to the monastic orders of medieval Christianity, even more appropriate for his notion of 'being singular plural' would be the constitutive paradoxes at the heart of this uniquely French community: not only a military unit and an all-male community, but the French Foreign Legion. To conclude by briefly examining what Denis may have had in mind when tackling the French Foreign Legion, and magisterially sidestepping the usual Legionnaire clichés in films (think Gary Cooper and Marlene Dietrich in *Morocco* (Josef Von Sternberg, 1930), Gary Cooper again in *Beau Geste* (William A. Wellman, 1939), or Jean Gabin in *La Bandera* (Julien Duvivier, 1935), etc.). What emerges instead is an astute commentary on a French dilemma, but also on a typically 'European' situation, where the very 'successes' of the EU in overcoming the old nationalist enmities have also disarticulated the homology of state–nation–territory and military, where each could 'stand for', 'reflect' or 'represent' the other, and which together made up the strength of the nation state. Now, of course, the state has handed over much of its power to Brussels, with the consequence that civil society has been depoliticized, the state increasingly relies on culture and ritual to maintain a semblance of authority, and governments are mostly management teams that administer

[14] See also Nancy's essay on the cinema of Abbas Kiarostami as a non-Western cinema dedicated to such an 'opening-up of the image' into a freedom from meaning. Jean-Luc Nancy, *L'Evidence du film: Abbas Kiarostami/The Evidence of Film*, bilingual French–English edn (Brussels: Yves Gevaert, 2001).

capital and the economy, while bureaucratically distributing welfare, health care, education and other social services.

The nation has become post-national, in that the media and popular culture recycle the folkloric, culinary and touristic markers of nationhood, most visible in sport, the arts, the countryside, heritage and history. The territory has become permeable: Germans are buying up the border regions of France and the Netherlands, while the British buy second homes in the abandoned peasant *terroirs* of France, and Swedes, French, Germans and Britons buy up farmhouses in Tuscany. Finally, the military, that is, the formerly conscripted national armies, are delegated to the North Atlantic Treaty Organization, where they are used as peacekeeping forces, to deliver humanitarian aid to stricken areas, or to lend logistic support to the US combat troops in Afghanistan. In other words, the military (in Europe, but also within NATO generally) no longer knows its purpose and function: it no longer seizes enemy land or defends national territory, it no longer knows whether it is an army or a police force, it is engaged in asymmetrical warfare with enemies where combatants are indistinguishable from civilians, it is involved in counterterrorism (traditionally handled by intelligence agencies), it is asked to help in nation building but has to blow up family homes, or it deals in counterinsurgency where the aims are vague, the legality doubtful and no exit strategy is given by politicians. While soldiers who died in battle were once heroes who gave their lives for a just cause and thus sacralized war with their blood, now they are merely casualties that need to be hidden for fear of bad publicity at home. Indeed, one might venture the definition that a heroic war narrative is one in which the dead sacrifice themselves and thus empower you, while a post-heroic war narrative is one in which the dead are casualties, and they have power over you.

Within this post-national, European perspective, the French Foreign Legion is especially symptomatic. In one sense, it is a mere remnant of an earlier, colonial age, replete with the paraphernalia of France's heroic self-celebration. Yet from another vantage point, it can also be regarded as a vanguard for a new kind of community – one befitting a post-heroic national narrative. Recall the ritual of initiation and entry: those enlisting in the Legion change their names, they leave behind their previous identity, their nationality, their religion. In exchange for erasing their previous selves, they not only gain a new name, but they are also sworn to serve and die for the glory of France, to become members of France's elite corps, defending the Grand Nation, but also doing its dirty work, as it were, on the margins of the law and legality, just as they often come from the margins of their society, with criminal records or worse. In other words, they enter the Legion as bodies without inner substance in order to become the sacred body – the corps – of the republic. A curious and deliberate transubstantiation takes place, which we could describe as the taking in of the world's outcasts or abjects, in order to give them a sacred mission – to uphold the glory of

France – but where, when required, they become once more France's own abject, whenever the Legion has to carry out missions that the regular French Army either cannot or does not want to engage in. *Beau Travail*'s French Foreign Legion is made up of such bodies without subjects, who, once 'inside' the Legion, connect and collide, but do not fuse or form a single body. The tensions, jealousies, ways of being together and separate begin to form patterns of contact, touch, routine, but there is nothing beyond in the way of sharing or give-and-take or mutuality or reciprocity. Without inwardness or subjectivity, they are the test case of Nancy's *communauté désoeuvrée*, but they are also a test case for a new cinema: neither mirrors to our subjectivities nor windows opening up on an exotic other world/world of the Other.

Beau Travail then becomes a meditation on the many paradoxes of the sacred and the abject, as it manifests itself in this very unique and peculiar French institution, but which – anachronistic in one sense, topical-utopian in another – appears to allegorize the situation that increasingly applies to soldiers elsewhere[15] as well as to many of us in the West, given over as we are to the care of the self, which means worrying about our bodies, our health, subjecting ourselves to treadmills and physical exercise, neither young nor old, neither in time nor out of it.[16]

Becoming abject

Such a reading clarifies some of the ambiguities surrounding Galoup, and also justifies him as the film's hero. His trajectory through the narrative is that of learning to become abject, half sacrificial, half self-elected, in that he opens himself up to the full contradictions of the Legion, as made up of bodies that are at once abject and sacred, and to whom he initially does not belong, being a French officer rather than a legionnaire. Whereas his superior, Bruno, keeps himself separate and aloof, being a more ordinary cynic and nihilist who 'doesn't care' and who survives by chewing hash or cocoa-leaves,

---

[15] Soldiers are, as I tried to indicate, no longer quite sure if they are combat troops or policemen, if they carry the nation's honour or merely dispose of the nation's garbage (corps – corpse).

[16] The relationship between the body and the abject (the corps and the corpse as it were), as described by Julia Kristeva in her essay 'Approaching Abjection', is a concept relevant to the depictions of the body in both Denis's *Beau Travail* and Kaurismäki's *The Man without a Past*. As stated by Julia Kristeva, the abject is neither subject nor object,: it 'has only one quality of the object – that of being opposed to I'. Julia Kristeva, 'Approaching Abjection', in *Powers of Horror: An Essay on Abjection*, trans. Leon S. Roudiez (New York: Columbia University Press, 1982), 1. What is abject, Kristeva explains, is that which is 'radically excluded and draws me toward the place where meaning collapses . . . And yet, from its place of banishment, the abject does not cease challenging its master' (2).

Galoup is 'touched' by the beauty and grace of Sentain, the Billy Budd figure of the film, whose simultaneous intrusion and aloofness provokes Galoup into an obsession with his singularity that has him punish Sentain and send him to his death. But this deep engagement with Sentain's radiant self-sufficiency and 'not-belonging' also awakens Galoup to the reality of the Legion's ontological mission, making his actions, despite their apparent criminality, once more 'ethical' in relation to the full contradictions embodied in the Legion.

Nancy, in his comments, seems to recognize the affinity of Denis's legionnaires with his *communauté inemployée* when he describes them as existing 'between having nothing to do and being constantly on guard', suggesting that their enforced idleness and disjointed existence is their salvation. It explains why Sentain, the beautiful intruder, does not belong, because he is too active, too much in-the-world without being with-the-world: a saviour who can be sacrificed (or rescued) but not an abject who can become, in Giorgio Agamben's terms, a *homo sacer*, like Galoup.[17] While the latter suffers a solitary entry into the post-heroic, Sentain is someone who is finally still too much part of the heroic project of self-creation and self-sacrifice. The paradox is underlined by a scene that acts as a foil to the Galoup–Sentain opposition: a soldier who dies in a helicopter crash is immediately reclaimed as 'heroic' and given a burial with all the military honours, even though he died neither in combat nor by sacrificing himself, but through a stupid accident. By contrast, Galoup's particular 'heroism' (if that is what it is) cannot be recuperated: his is a singular and unremarked death, but for all that, perhaps more authentic and ethical. Galoup's journey would then embody the contemporary complement to the heroic – and increasingly phony – narrative of the soldier's accident-turned-sacrifice for and on behalf of the nation. He would be the one whose exclusion saves and purifies the community from which he is excluded, in sync with the larger narrative that allows the Legion to both perpetuate French colonialism and to cleanse it, by a form of sacralized disavowal. On the other hand, Galoup's becoming abject in relation to the Legion would be an act of auto-sacralization, with his final dance a radical opening up, a voiding that is usually foreclosed by the telos of goals and projects that has had such an ideological hold on the Western political imaginary. Galoup, who appeared to us at first as the inscrutable antihero, or even the non-hero, of *Beau Travail*, turns out to have been the post-hero of a community both exceptional in its extraterritoriality and exemplary in its paradoxes and contradictions: a community that is in transition between the old nation state and the yet to be defined post-national community, where individuals

[17] For an extensive discussion of Agamben's notion of *homo sacer* and bare life in relation to the idea of abjection, see Chapter 5.

share a common space, but only on condition of their final, irremediable singularity.

Beau Travail is thus delicately poised between the nostalgia for noble sacrifice, for a pure gesture of erasing yourself in order to serve and die ('Sers la bonne cause et meurs' is the official motto of the Legion), and the realization (in the figure of Galoup) of a state of 'abjection', where the Legion functions as that in-between space, where a different kind of singularity in plurality can emerge, thereby prefiguring a post-heroic community. What the Legion and Galoup's trajectory demonstrate would be the zero-degree of a 'Mit-einander' prior to all mutuality and reciprocity.

Although not unique among the films of Claire Denis, *Beau Travail* is nonetheless an exceptional case within European cinema in thematizing the idea of a community-to-come, its internal dynamics and its relation to others as explicitly as it does. Nonetheless, an important constellation of figures and tropes has emerged that can also be fruitfully explored in other films whose provenance is the European subsidy-cum-co-production system, and whose directors try to come to terms with what I have called post-heroic narratives of identity, nationhood and community. I am thinking in particular of the tropes around the figure of the abject, briefly outlined above, as both outcast and sacred, as both singular and saviour, as both no-longer-alive and not-yet-dead. By marking the margins of the community such a figure is nonetheless an essential part of the community.

These abject bodies, as discussed in Chapter 5, are predominantly indigenous, white and even often middle class, but they stand for the 'other' within the self, thereby avoiding the mirroring divisions and overcoming the dichotomy of self and other. They not only challenge the old ideas of progress and telos, but they also resist narratives of 'bureaucratic federalism' as practised by politicians and Euro-elites (and criticized by Habermas and Balibar). Similarly, abjects in their implacability also stand apart from the online fusion of multitudes, as celebrated in sporting events and Eurovision song contests. Abjects are not victims, nor are they perpetrators; they do not embody power but neither are they powerless, and their singularity and sacredness could once more reveal the mysterious wisdom and hope that Kant identified in the unsocial sociability of humanity, and that Nancy envisages with his 'Being Singular Plural'.

8

Hitting Bottom

Aki Kaurismäki and the Abject Subject – *The Man Without A Past*

Post-human, posthumous and post-mortem agency

Crucial to our idea of Hollywood cinema is the action hero. Audiences love American films for their practical problem-solvers, their gangster-mafia entrepreneurs, their world conquerors, their reluctant but ruthless avengers, sly and wily detectives, law enforcers, wilderness-civilizing pioneers or their child heroes and young men, initiated into manhood by proving themselves against human adversaries and cosmic adversity. So strong has been the reliance on the action hero that such single-source agency as he displays has become one of the bases for defining not only the classical 'Hollywood' cinema, but also the European cinema as its inverted mirror image. While Hollywood narratives are character-centred, with their protagonists goal-oriented autonomous agents, motivated by rational choices and committed to a linear time frame proceeding by a logic of cause and effect, the typically European film narrative features an indecisive, troubled central character, lost in an urban labyrinth or traversing a desolate landscape of the mind. The action is open-ended, the causal nexus is weak, the plot episodic, and time – even if linear in its overall sense – dilates, runs backwards or simply stands still.

A whole ideology of 'can-do' pragmatism is embedded in the American action hero, and also in his negative counterpart. Is such trust in individual agency not counter-intuitive, when despite philosophical assumptions of source–path–goal schemas, everyday experience suggests that in its very embodiedness, the action hero's modus operandi is abstract, selfish and even autistic? Are there not other – cooperative, diplomatic, collusive, negotiated – ways of solving problems or getting things done? Is not the European attitude much more 'realistic', seeing that as individuals we very rarely 'come, see and conquer', but bungle our way through life with indecisions, rash moves we come to regret, and the knowledge that the chaos we have created for ourselves defeats our best efforts to control it?

The European imagination (and its cinema) is resigned to and even proud of its Hamlet heroes, doubters and procrastinators, who 'probe dilemmas' rather than 'solve problems'. Think of the protagonists of Bergman, Antonioni, Wenders or Angelopoulos: plagued by hesitation and rumination, they are drifters, knight errants, men of God who have lost their faith, or self-exiles forever trying to return home, driven by inner demons as well as lofty but unattainable ideals.

Given what in earlier chapters I have invoked as the end of the Europe–Hollywood divide and the desirability of a transnational world cinema perspective, I am suggesting that it makes sense to classify different types of cinema not in terms of classical and post-classical, mainstream or auteur cinema, not even into categories of auteur, genre, narration or mode of production, but instead around different action scenarios. Such a classification schema in which 'agency' plays a major role has of course been advanced by Deleuze, who identifies what he calls the 'motor-sensory schema' of the 'movement image' (which to him signals the embodied agency of perceiving, feeling, comprehending and acting) in order to distinguish classical (American) cinema from modern (European) cinema. The movement image places the emphasis on the (large) sensory motor schema of 'disclosure' (of the world as to be acted upon) and 'adequacy' (to the milieu, capacity, event), so that a character's look and what he 'sees' provides him with a vantage point whose truth is its degree of adequacy to the situation perceived and thus indexing his ability for taking action. Contrasting such motor-sensory alignment of body, agency and identity with its rupture in the 'crisis of the movement image', Deleuze posits the emergence of a new type of cinema, organized around the 'time image' where vision, affect and agency are split, pointing to the incommensurability of the situation or event, and thus 'explains' the typically European inaction hero.[1]

This is a helpful, but as I argue elsewhere, also an incomplete categorization. Especially in the way it is generally applied, it becomes a rigidly binary scheme that ultimately more or less reproduces the Hollywood–Europe divide. We need to add to the action/inaction oppositional pair also reaction, the delayed action of trauma, the posthumous agency of *The Sixth Sense* (M. Night Shyamalan, 1999) or *Abre los ojos/Open Your Eyes* (Alejandro

[1] Gilles Deleuze, *Cinema 2: The Time Image*, trans. Hugh Tomlinson (Minneapolis: University of Minnesota Press, 1989), 40–1.

Amenábar, 1997), the random reaction of certain male rampage films, the emphasis on running, in films as diverse as *Forrest Gump* (Robert Zemeckis, 1994) and *Lola rennt/Run Lola Run* (Tom Tykwer, 1998), *Trainspotting* (Danny Boyle, 1996), *Cidade de Deus/City of God* (Fernando Meirelles, 2002) and *Slumdog Millionaire* (Danny Boyle, 2008); or the strategic use of car rides as the static vehicles of suspended but consequential agency in Wenders and Kiarostami, Jarmusch and Petzold.

In Chapter 1 I discussed several European films since the 1990s in terms of the way they address three traumas of Europe. In the same films we find significant variations in the concept of agency. These narratives feature the modern global city or the urban sprawl that surrounds it, which act as the site of multi-ethnic and subcultural desire, violence and power (often symbolized by drugs, music, intense sensations, and out-of-body experiences). These films imply a more dispersed, randomized, intermittent agency of unintended and unpredictable consequences (multi-strand movies are generally symptomatic of this trend towards different forms of agency). Other films focus on immigration, usually through a female heroine from somewhere in Eastern Europe who is forced into prostitution or has to fend for herself and her child in a hostile, not to say predatory environment. Yet other films – by Scottish, French, German, Italian, Danish or Dutch directors – could be said to explore the idea of interference agency or agency at cross-purpose. They concern relations of interdependence, of parasite and host, of heteronomy (i.e. where initially antagonistic parties are obliged to cooperate because both are responding to outside forces over which they have little control). A further group of films that could be classified in terms of agency focuses more specifically on the dynamics of inclusion and exclusion, of which one example, along with Lars von Trier's *Dogville* (2003), Danny Boyle's *Trainspotting* and Fatih Akin's *Gegen die Wand/Head On* (2004), is Aki Kaurismäki's *Mies vailla menneisyyttä/The Man without a Past* (2002), to which I will return.

Mutual interference

In order to be able to address the issues of agency that these films raise, with all the ramifications they have for the changing connotations of private and public, for the new permeability of 'I' and 'we' in the social network society, and for the new relationality of distance and proximity, I make a case for a concept developed in Chapter 4 via the ethical relation (Levinas) and abjection – 'mutual interference'. Mutual interference is meant, first of all, to displace the discourse of identity in the direction of Self-and-Other; second, to attend to the different valences of 'action' beyond active/passive; and third, to relate agency to the micro-level of affective and cognitive engagement, of immersion and interaction in the post-cinema, moving-image experience.

With respect to the problematic ideology of multiculturalism, 'mutual interference' is meant to highlight a certain, fully intended transgressiveness, not only because it signals reciprocity, but because it implies spaces to be redistributed, egos to be dissolved, identities to be questioned and power relations to be renegotiated. Thus, 'mutual interference' designates a complex, multilevel and possible confusingly inclusive semantic field; one where, with respect to the social contract, such 'soft' *ethical* demands – as the need for 'dialogue' with the Other, for 'tolerance' and for 'trusting the Other' – are understood not so much as 'requiring direct action', but more like 'hold open a space', or hint at the possibility for a much 'harder' *political* mandate, one that does not come for free, but at a cost, namely of action as 'interference', but under conditions of being 'implicated'. In other words, I am trying to include the active part of 'in betweenness', of 'entanglement' and of 'hybridity' (to name some of the terms of the postcolonial discourse) and to emphasize the risks to selfhood and autonomy, when talking of embeddedness, embodiment and situatedness (to name three terms much in use in contemporary theory and cultural studies).

Mutual interference ideally holds out hope for a utopian option for the problems of democracy, the failing social contract and the community to come, discussed at length in previous chapters: taking responsibility for the Other, while neither imposing on the Other nor forsaking self-interest, but acting out of 'enlightened altruism'. If on the one hand, this notion is very different from the 'inoperable community' of 'being singular plural' that Jean-Luc Nancy argues for (discussed in Chapter 7), mutual interference nonetheless leaves room for antagonism and dissensus, as advocated by Jacques Rancière and insisted upon by him as the minimal condition of 'the political' (as shown in Chapter 4).

Thus, besides the generic or rhetorical implications, a reason for choosing the term has to do with the changing nature of agency not only with respect to the Europe versus Hollywood divide, but also in view of the changing character of cinema itself. While cinema is still part of a recognizable public sphere (where the 'I' of the singular spectator interacts and mingles with the 'we' of the spectatorial community), film viewing has nonetheless become an increasingly privatized activity. Yet home cinema or downloading movies are privatized experiences often in such interpersonal modalities and under such technical conditions that they in turn lead to the 'private' becoming once more 'public', as on the internet, among gamers, via YouTube or on Facebook, where 'sharing', 'liking', 'friending' and other forms of exchange and interchange resurface as viable and desirable, if highly problematic, forms of agency in the public domain.

However, my main reason for choosing the term 'mutual interference' brings me back to the specifics of Europe and its internal debates around nation, state and sovereignty. In particular, there is one version of the political objectives of the European Union in which mutual interference plays a crucial role. As is well known, very different agendas circulate among the political elites as to how the European Union might evolve in the twenty-first century – from no more than a trading bloc held together by free-market principles and possibly a common currency, to the United States of Europe – a unified confederation bound to each other, via checks and balances, on the model of the Federal Republic of Germany if not the United States of America.[2]

After the failed referendum in France and the Netherlands for a European constitution, one commentator, the American sociologist Benjamin Barber, opined that what Europe needed was not, like the United States of America, a 'Declaration of Independence', but a 'Declaration of Interdependence'[3] which echoes the idea of mutual interference as a productive move for fostering a post-national form of solidarity.

The term 'mutual interference' actually comes from a book by the diplomat and writer Robert Cooper, *The Breaking of Nations* (2003). Cooper argues that the present world order – based on liberal democracy – will come to an end, since, as everyone readily acknowledges, we are currently in the middle of a major reconfiguration of geopolitics. He distinguishes four state forms: the hegemonic state or contemporary form of imperialism (USA), the post-modern state (EU), the modern (nationalist, authoritarian) state (Pakistan, Iran) and the pre-modern (failed) state (Sudan, Congo). Cooper maintains that the European system of nation states and their concept of sovereignty as non-interference in matters of state and religion by outside powers, as formulated in the Treaty of Westphalia in 1648 and reaffirmed by the Vienna Congress in 1815, will have to give way. According to this view, the old balance of power system has been superseded, because the European Union has institutionalized the mutual interference in domestic affairs between nation states as its modus operandi. Cooper's model of the European Union as a conglomerate of nation states that are connected with each other through the right and necessity of mutual interference contrasts with the Franco-German notion of a European superstate, but it was also intended as part of a damage-

[2] When inventorizing these big ideas of Europe, one realizes just how many different scenarios for the geopolitical future of the Union exist. Focusing on just some of them, for instance, one can distinguish the hope for a European Union as a multicultural melting pot along the lines of the former Austro-Hungarian Empire; the ideal of a Christian Europe; Europe as the super-nation of the United States of Europe; the Europe of the strong nation states, ceding as little of their sovereignty as possible; Real Europe, i.e. an association of largely economic interest groups under a common legal framework and binding rules of the game.

[3] See Benjamin Barber and Sondra Myers, *The Interdependence Handbook: Looking Back, Living the Present, Choosing the Future* (New York: International Debate Education Association, 2004).

limitation argument against the Bush doctrine of pre-emptive strike and unilateral interference in the internal affairs of another country.[4]

Cooper wrote in the wake of the accession talks with the post-communist states of Central and Eastern Europe, as well as in view of the talks about membership with Turkey and Serbia, where it very much seemed that it was the European Union interfering in the sovereignty of these nations, but with very little mutuality in return – with the consequence that several of these countries have reverted to forms of ultra-nationalism and to such strict non-interference, for instance, regarding refugees, that they are in danger of contravening European law.

Staying outside without stepping outside

Here, I want to discuss European anti-heroes, distributed agency and interference in the work of a director who focuses more on inclusion and exclusion than on *mutual* interference, and who presents a model *from the outside*, but without *stepping outside*. Aki Kaurismäki's work – *Leningrad Cowboys Go America* (1989), *Kauas Pilvet Karkaavat/Drifting Clouds* (1996) and especially *The Man without a Past* – seems to me exemplary in this respect, less as an illustration of this maxim and more as an ongoing – serious but also comic-subversive – contribution to the debate about the nature of European governmentality in the force field made up of globalized capitalism, the nation state as welfare state, and the forms of social contract or reciprocity possible when nationalism and a boom economy no longer provide the sticky glue of solidarity or kinship loyalty.

I shall concentrate on *The Man without a Past*, which I propose to look at across three possible frames of reference, all of which intersect, but also displace or modify my general argument about transnational cinema and post-national governmentality. What initially struck me about Kaurismäki is that he does not need prostitutes from Moldavia or Lilyas from Latvia, he does not need Afghan or Bosnian refugees, he does not need involuntary organ donors or exploited maids, in order to go right to the heart of the matter of what is at stake in Europe today, between globalization and outsourcing, high-tech and low wages, the social contract and the systematic production of human expendability. Rather like Lars von Trier's minimalism in *Dogville* with its chalk marks on the bare floorboards, an abandoned

[4] 'The most obvious feature of [our present] world is American power; but in the long run the most important facts may be the end of empire and the transformation of the state through globalization. The most hopeful feature is the emergence of the postmodern system of security in Europe.' Robert Cooper, *The Breaking of Nations: Order and Chaos in the Twenty-First Century* (New York: Atlantic Books, 2003), Preface, x. See also pp. 3–4 about 'interference in each other's domestic affairs'.

container by the Helsinki waterfront, a bunch of drunks, a jukebox and a few other ready-to-hand props are all Kaurismäki needs to make his points. Helped no doubt by the fact that Finland is one of the European Union countries with fewest immigrants, but with nonetheless a high incidence of xenophobia, he elegantly bypasses both the pat denunciations of racism and the pitfalls of multiculturalism. Instead, in what I take to be a typical piece of Finnish humour, Kaurismäki simply whacks his hero over the head, and hey presto, he has a perfect specimen of the 'stranger', the 'Other', the 'migrant' and the 'victim', without having to leave the country or change language.

My first frame of reference would be what one might call social romanticism. An ordinary man and citizen, minding his own business, is suddenly evicted from his no doubt comfortable surroundings and loses all items of personal identity (name, memory) and signifiers of social integration (ID papers, social security number). Now a loner, an outcast, he finds among other marginals and outcasts the rudiments of a community whose values are not those of acquisitive capitalism or even of the welfare state, but at once more archaic, more 'authentic' and more 'primitively' socialist. We can read the story like a reverse *Bildungsroman*: of an education into a happier and simpler state, where you grow your own potatoes and wash your own shirts, where simple human companionship is worth more than a house, a career and a wife. *The Man without a Past* in this respect might usefully be referenced to certain films by Mike Leigh, as examples of stories about 'losers' who seem to inspire hope by the very 'terminal' condition they get themselves into.[5] In another sense, the film 'touches bottom' by a sort of generalized state of destitution, hinting at the kinds of communities that, for instance, drug addicts form when they share needles or a hit. In *Trainspotting*, for instance, they are depicted as having some of the features of anarcho-communist utopias. In *The Man without a Past* the men and women on the breadline are the ones who most readily accept his zombie-like state, which in turn allows M, the otherwise nameless hero, to reconstruct a network of mental coordinates and points of affective contact that sustain his will to live. When once more he is attacked by the hooligans who robbed and all but killed him in the opening scene, the beggars and cripples take up their crutches and planks of wood, rescuing him: reminiscent of those Vittorio de Sica films, like *Miracolo a Milano/Miracle of Milan* (1951) where the poor of Milan's slums and *bidonvilles* also drive out the bad guys from the government, help each other and are rewarded by magic that makes them fly off into the sky and to a better life.

Such a reading of Kaurismäki's film as a therapeutic narrative of the poor with a heart of gold, of solidarity and brotherhood as the natural nobility of

---

[5] In Chapter 5 I briefly discuss Mike Leigh's *Naked*, but one could add *Abigail's Party* and *Happy-Go-Lucky*.

the deprived and exploited is inviting in these cynical times, but surely also misleading. Kaurismäki may be familiar with de Sica, but so he is with Luis Buñuel, whose vicious beggars and cruel children in *Los Olvidados/The Forgotten Ones* (1950) came onto the cinema scene in almost the same year as de Sica's film, demanding of the audience a quite different – anarcho-surrealist? – sense of solidarity through empathy with victims *and* victimizers, heteronomously intertwined and interdependent in the mutuality of their equally hopeless situation and sordid social transactions. Kaurismäki is also no doubt familiar with Rainer Werner Fassbinder's films and their victims, male or female, masochists or exploited, who feel no special obligation to be less vicious and cruel than the rest of the world when they see a chance to victimize someone else. The opening scene of M getting beaten up in the park is visibly Kaurismäki's version of the opening scene in Fassbinder's *In einem Jahr mit 13 Monden/In a Year of Thirteen Moons* (1978), with the differences as striking as the similarities.

A second frame of reference would be that of the social parable for our age: a Grimm fairy tale of banks and bankers helping themselves before serving their customers, of multinationals depending on cheap labour and job-outsourcing, and of the welfare state caught between big business privatizing the profits and socializing the losses, and a market economy which needs cycles of 'creative destruction' to foster competitiveness and 'innovation', while also needing consumers to spend the money they do not have. In this reading – as an allegory of the increasingly conflicting relations between a consumption-based 'national' market economy and the social-democratic welfare state, as both are coming under pressure from global capital flows – the film offers an intriguingly nuanced and yet sardonically apt picture. First, we see 'religion' (in the shape of the Salvation Army) step in where the state's hands are tied, as it were. As in the Middle East, where Hamas and Hezbollah provide the social services that corrupt politicians and impotent civil institutions are incapable of delivering, the Salvation Army can use unofficial circuits of distribution, acting both at sub-state local and supra-state international level. Kaurismäki here clearly indicates how (and some of the reasons why) in our post-secular society, religious influence – from all religions – is on the rise. But the film also neatly sketches the dilemma of the state: the welfare provisions it offers require workers to be 'citizens', with papers, names and addresses, and so our hero – freshly made abject by amnesia – can neither apply for a job nor receive the social benefits of the jobless.

By contrast, in today's economy, the film seems to say, a worker with a memory of the past and personal attachments is actually at a disadvantage. Amnesia – structural amnesia as well as individual amnesia – is much better for the overall system reboot, but also for making the individual flexible and adaptable. The scene in the welfare office, where M is caught in a Catch 22 situation with the bureaucracy, is matched by the scene in the shipyard conglomerate's office: global capitalism only needs raw labour power; since it does not provide benefits, it can afford to provide work, without caring if his name is Albert Einstein or King Kong. In the drive for low-wage advantage and a seasonal/flexible workforce, it does not matter what sort of past you have.

In other words, the biopolitics of casual work in Helsinki are no different from those of Nike's or Adidas's sweatshops in Bangladesh, but in the next breath, quite rightly, the film also points out that such bare labour is better than starving, no less in Helsinki than in Dacca or Bangalore. Tragic and tragic-comic dimensions come to the fore in the figure of the old-style factory owner, who would rather rob a bank and then commit suicide than be thought by his ex-workers to be a profiteer or a cheat. These scenes, too, remind me of other films (by Charles Chaplin, Frank Capra's Depression movies, Mario Monicelli's comedies), and again, Kaurismäki deftly undercuts the pathos, when in the bank hold-up, he has the woman cashier, whose last day it is, point out that the surveillance camera he has just shot is not working anyway, because the bank is actually closing the branch, as the new owner, a South Korean *cheabol*, is 'consolidating', that is, saving money by shedding jobs, with the unemployment benefits due to these employees most likely being paid out by the Finnish state. The 'solution' to these dilemmas is also presented, namely 'flexible entrepreneurship'. In one of the great scarily comic and comically scary creations of recent European cinema, Kaurismäki gives us the character of Anttila, the perfect embodiment of the 'new' capitalist (in contrast to the factory owner), who sees and seizes an opportunity to make money in the most creative manner and creates opportunities where none exist, as when he tries to charge M for the open-air concert of the Salvation Army that M himself organized:

Anttila: Tickets.
M: What do you mean?
Anttila: You haven't paid.
M: But I organized this.
Anttila: That's what you think.
M: Is that so?
Anttila: Yes.
M: Fancy that.
Anttila: That's outrageous!
M: It is, isn't it?

In fact, Anttila is a popular villain on the internet, in much the same way that Hannibal (the cannibal) Lecter is popular, in honour of whom Anttila seems to have named his dog Hannibal, who 'only eats raw meat' (at least in the subtitles; I gather that in Finnish, the dog is called Tähti, i.e. 'Star'). The Internet Movie Database dutifully lists most of his best exchanges with M:

[M is renting an abandoned shipping container]
M: When can I move in?
Anttila: As soon as I turn my back.
M: And the keys?
Anttila: You see a lock anywhere?
M: No.
Anttila: Don't go splitting hairs then, or I'll take the door, too . . . But if you don't pay, I'll send my killer dog to bite your nose off.
M: It only causes trouble, shadows the way wherever I go.
Anttila: You couldn't smoke in the shower anymore.

Again, one can see Kaurismäki's sense for, not so much the 'absurdity of existence' (as critics like to describe his deadpan humour), but more precisely, for the interdependence of opposites (and thus a form of 'mutual interference'). At first sight, M and Anttila are antagonists in this exchange: one exploited, the other exploiting. But with regard to their humour, they are complementary – parasite and host, if you like – in that the source of their wit, a self-deprecating sarcasm that escalates to nihilism, is synchronous, in the sense that each depends on the other being on cue, like performers of a duet.

This brings me to my third frame of reference for *The Man without a Past*, which I have earlier referred to as the ability to look at a given situation *from outside without stepping outside*. If my allegorical reading gives us a parable of today's global capitalism locally experienced, where M's amnesia turns out to be a blessing in disguise as well as a bitter truth about our present world, my third reading would take the same state of affairs – the 'objective' advantages of amnesia – but now from the point of view of the subject. In order to do so, however, one needs to uncouple the subject from the subject–object relationship, as it were, which also means one should not see our protagonist as 'victim' – either in the sociological sense (e.g. as a victim of urban crime) or in the personal, affective sense (e.g. as a victim of his wife's infidelity). Kaurismäki could not be clearer about this, whether after M leaves the hospital and finds a home among the containers, or at the end when he meets his ex-wife and her new man, who feels duty-bound to offer M a fight, only for our hero to dismiss any such notion of male dignity and pride. M's subjectivity, in other words, needs a new definition, or rather a space and a context in which his particular form of agency can be identified or understood.

Abjection and the abject subject

For this space and context, I draw on Manuel Castells and his vision of Europe. Castells, best known for his books on the network society, has often argued that the European Union will not be able to sustain itself as a viable political experiment if it relies on its Christian values, or even on its present understanding of liberal democracy around the notion of ethnicity and multiculturalism. Castells' main concern is to insist that the European Union cannot escape the impact of globalization dividing up the world quite differently, namely between those who are networked, connected and 'online' and those who are not.[6] Translated into slightly different terms, Castells predicts a situation where there are human beings that are useful to the world system as producers or as consumers on one side, and those who are too unskilled, too sick or too destitute to be either producers or consumers, not even consumers of health and welfare services on the other. Unable or unwilling to participate in any of the circuits of redistribution and networks of exchange – of goods, services, affective labour or needs – these human beings effectively drop out of the human race. In fact, by this reasoning, not only drug dealers, criminals, traffickers of women or refugees, but also patients in hospitals or car thieves in prison are more useful to our society than, say, someone who grows his own vegetables, is self-sufficient and never leaves his plot of land. Castells, with a sarcasm that Kaurismäki might appreciate, goes so far to speculate that to be a slave labourer or a colonial subject might come to be seen as preferable to being not even thought valuable enough to be exploited.

Similarly gloomy but less ironic, such considerations can also be found in the writings of Zygmunt Bauman, especially in his *Wasted Lives: Modernity and its Outcasts*: 'The production of "human waste" – or more precisely, wasted lives, the "superfluous" populations of migrants, refugees and other outcasts – is an inevitable outcome of modernization,' he writes.[7] To Bauman, this expendability is an unavoidable side effect of economic progress and the quest for order, which always involves a reclassification. Modernity is like a gardener who takes over a field or meadow, and now suddenly considers most of what has been growing there as 'weeds'.

> The global spread of the modernity has given rise to growing quantities of human beings who are deprived of adequate means of survival, but the planet is fast running out of places to put them. Hence the new anxieties about 'immigrants' and 'asylum seekers' and the growing role played by diffuse 'security fears' on the contemporary political agenda.[8]

What is relevant about this position with respect not just to Kaurismäki's film but to European cinema is that it alludes to a state of subjective

[6] Manuel Castells, 'The Construction of European Identity', in Maria João Rodrigues (ed.), *The New Knowledge Economy in Europe* (Cheltenham: Edward Elgar, 2002), 232–41.

[7] Zygmunt Bauman, *Wasted Lives: Modernity and its Outcasts* (Cambridge: Polity Press, 2004), 5.

[8] Bauman, *Wasted Lives*, 5.

destitution that has been thematized in many recent films from the last two decades (though they are probably not entirely confined to Europe). Two key concepts outlined in the first part of this book – abjection and bare life – explain this state of destitution. One might call this state that of abjection, to use a term made familiar by Kristeva,[9] or the state of 'bare life' in the terminology of Agamben.[10] The protagonists' stories generally take them through this progressive stripping of all symbolic supports of their selfhood: they lose their jobs, their friends, their family, their mind or their memory, as in the case of Kaurismäki's hero.

To reiterate, it is significant that most of these protagonists are not victims; at least they do not consider themselves as such. This removes them from yet another circuit of exchange and interaction – that of the victimizer or perpetrator – but also neutralizes the power of those who through tolerance and philanthropy, or in the name of human rights, implicitly or explicitly assert their moral or material superiority. Such films, in my scheme of things, are the negative equivalent of double occupancy: they may be subjects 'in circulation', but they are 'out of service'. Or, to vary the metaphor, the subjects of such narratives have been vacated, even by their oppressors, and the space they occupy has been declared a blank. 'Vacated' heroes or heroines in European cinema are not only symptomatic for what they tell us about a society and subjectivity that no longer has a social contract about what counts as the minimum conditions of value and use, labour and affective work in and for a given society or community. They may also tell us something about the conditions of possibility of a counter-image of what it means to be human, and thus they approach what could be called the utopian dimension of double occupancy.

The interesting aspect of *The Man without a Past* is that it makes us see the consequences of exclusion from the side of the excluded, not as victims or 'waste', but as the basis for a different sense of both singularity and community. The space of abjection which the film gradually establishes is the one that shows the now separate and distinct 'archipelagos' of the former unified state of the nation; the national economy and its social services come together in what is usually considered a 'non-space'. But the film indicates that this is the only space where the structure and dynamics of contemporary society can be seen in the way this society actually hangs together and its antagonisms are interrelated.

Thus, the term that comes to mind for the subjectivity of the *Man without a Past* would be that of the 'abject subject', though perhaps not quite in

---

[9] Julia Kristeva, *Powers of Horror: An Essay on Abjection*, trans. Leon S. Roudiez (New York: Columbia University Press, 1982).

[10] Giorgio Agamben, *Homo Sacer: Sovereign Power and Bare Life*, trans. Daniel Heller-Roazen (Stanford, CA: Stanford University Press, 1999).

either the way Kristeva understands it or in Agamben's sense. Instead, the abject would indicate a different, post-Cartesian as well as post-Hegelian 'subject-position', which recognizes the fundamentally if not constitutively 'traumatized' position of the global-local subject, but which is also envisaging the possibility of a liberating or utopian potential in abjection. In the context of my overall argument we need to ask what kind of agency typifies this abject subject.

This agency at first seems to approach what I earlier called 'posthumous agency' or the post-mortem agency of the corpse, of a walking dead or zombie – but a zombie with a subjective point-of-view shot! Kaurismäki has come up with an extraordinary scene to illustrate this post-mortem mode, when – with a subjective camera tracking shot – we are placed 'inside' the left-for-dead protagonist, as he staggers from the park into and through the railway station, to collapse, blood-soaked beneath his welder's helmet, in the men's lavatory, like a ghost in armour.

On further reflection, and in the course of the film, the hero's agency is less that of a ghost (he does not haunt anyone) and more that of the abject, if we can describe and define the abject subject more precisely. The agency of abjection would encompass a 'sacred space', which is more powerful in its singularity than the atomized and fragmented institutional spaces that work at cross-purposes in a society that is in denial about the degree to which parliamentary politics and the welfare state have already ceded to these different configurations of global business and the separate social formations that now wield power, with little or no contact between them.

The 'abject', as I argued, is distinct from and at the same time rearticulates the various victim discourses. There are three kinds of victims: the 'passive' ones whose suffering the mass media, notably television, 'harvests' in talk shows, or when there are natural catastrophes or man-made disasters; the victims who make themselves powerful when they decide they have nothing (more) to lose, not even their lives, because they already feel dead – suicide bombers; and the victims that become 'active' in another mode, actively passive.[11]

[11] In order to understand the latter, and to see him/her in the context of the abject, it would be useful to look at the debate between Simon Critchley and Slavoj Žižek around Herman Melville's story of *Bartleby the Scrivener*, and his famous 'I prefer not to' cited by both Critchley and Žižek as a form of 'political' resistance, which, however, does not have to manifest itself as resistance, because it is yielding. For Critchley it approximates his 'ethical anarchism' of a politics of 'infinite demand', whereas for Žižek this maximal minimalism is the very sign of a collusion with the powers that be, who are much more threatened by non-action ('Don't just do something, stand there!' is how Žižek describes Bartleby's 'activism'). For Critchley, see *Infinitely Demanding: Ethics of Commitment, Politics of Resistance* (London: Verso, 2007), critiqued by Žižek, 'Resistance is Surrender', *London Review of Books* 29, no. 22 (15 November 2007): 7. Žižek's own 'Defence of Bartleby' can be found in *The Parallax View*, 381–5.

Amnesia: a productive pathology

Amnesia becomes what I have called a 'productive pathology' not only because it adapts the 'subject' more flexibly to the cycles of creative destruction and periodic 'system reboots'. 'Amnesia' as the psychological name for 'abjection' can also be understood as the very form of non-activist protest against the 'obsolescence' discussed by Castells and Bauman, produced, according to them, as the natural effect of a certain form of modernity (in this case, global capitalism). In *The Man Without a Past*, this is made very explicit, insofar as our hero is flanked by three other males, all responding differently to the crisis in masculinity and self-value. M's friend and drinking companion leads a double life: during the day he works in the dark underground and emerges all black, while every Friday he drinks away the money he earns during the week instead of giving it to his family, whereupon he is kicked out by his wife. The more 'above ground' existences are the landlord/town official Anttila, in his vintage car, the eternal entrepreneur, the new capitalist who can 'monetarize' or 'securitize' everything under the sun: filthy containers become luxury abodes, a spontaneous concert an occasion to charge an entrance fee, the threat with a dog a way of getting the other to look after the animal for free. And on the other side, the old-fashioned entrepreneur, who robs a bank and then kills himself, all in order to be able to pay his workers after the banks forced him into bankruptcy. 'Abjection' in this sense becomes a way of escaping/overcoming/resisting the social order *through the bottom*, rather than climbing to the top by kicking those below.

Instead, the hero finds a new form of selfhood through abjection as the protesting mirror image of the respect and recognition that society is not willing to give. In this regard, abjection is not just traumatic (as it is in Kristeva), but also liberating: it 'performs' the condition of precariousness within an *ethos* of humility and self-sufficiency that can claim universality by the very fact that it has placed itself outside both marginality and hierarchy.

Kaurismäki seems to me to respond to this need for a different way to articulate opposition, resistance and critique of both capitalism and the welfare state, and to pay due attention to the inherent contradictions (positive as well as negative) of global capitalism, immigration, mobility of labour and so on. His films are about the dual image of modern-day entrepreneurism, a theme that takes over from the 'country' versus 'city' binarism of an earlier European cinema, but also supersedes the old left–right political opposition. Abjection, in the form of binge drinking and alcoholism, could also be read as manifestations of a form of 'shamelessness' within the distinct 'shame culture' still prevalent in modern-day Finland.

The classically 'abject' experience is that of the corpse, that is, something that was once a subject and is now an object, but an object to which cling all the properties, particularities, appearances and memories of a subject. In this sense, Kristeva's theory of the abject joins the 'post-mortem' subjectivity discussed elsewhere: the search for a position both outside and yet part of. In *The Man Without a Past* we have such a typically post-mortem hero.

The point about the (male) abject hero is that he is 'affectless', somehow self-enclosed and almost perfect in his abjection. But his female companion and counterpart, the Angel of Mercy, too, has this quality of the abject, which in her becomes somehow a more delicate and dignified stance, but still, in its withdrawn and self-enclosed minimalism, corresponds to the affectless neutrality of the corpse. Besides the (almost lethal) mushroom picnic, abjection is performed in two other scenes: one is the ruined steak (what should have been the date from hell becomes the 'hitting bottom' that brings the two together), and the other the used tea bag in the matchbox, in the way its abject status as a piece of 'waste' is dignified in the restaurant. The abject in our hero is what attracts the women; thus the abject makes him keep his dignity even when he has nothing at all. Translated into the theme of the 'Other', the 'stranger', it means that respect and recognition have to be renegotiated not from the Other's individual culture (as assumed by the logic of multiculturalism), but from the Other's very absence and lack of culture (or symbolic value).

Perhaps the most powerful aspect of the film is the use of music to create scenes of abjection: the music that is played on the jukebox, and then 'taught' to the Salvation Army boys, is not merely nostalgic; its obsolescence makes room for a new kind of dignity, reminiscent of the Leningrad Cowboys who want to go to America but end up in Mexico. Waste and failure become the conditions and instances of utopia: the goal which you fail to reach turns out so much better for you (more 'authentic') than had you succeeded.

Yet in relation to the dynamics of oppression/exclusion, abjection is an ambivalent term, because it returns us to our primary (pre-symbolic) selves. Also, the abject always brings back the body, and thus it is a 'living' reminder of our mortality. The abject sounds a warning note about the risk entailed by 'embodiment' and 'situatedness' when understood as unproblematic categories of a new authenticity.

Conclusion

The Kaurismäki abject subject would be the dialectic or dynamic complement of 'double occupancy' and 'mutual interference', in the sense of 'voiding' the (doubly occupied) subject in order to 'open' itself radically towards the Other (on the far side of mutual interference). Such abjection might constitute the zero degree of a new politics of the cinema, in the European transnational context, since – as Kaurismäki shows – our geopolitical position of marginality within globalization has created the conditions for a new kind of action hero, who combines great humanity and humility that can elicit empathy beyond 'tolerance'. It makes his otherness and status as a stranger in his own country the very basis of a new kind of community, which – considered against the social and political agendas of another community, that of the European Union – formulates at once a comment, a critique and a promise. Kaurismäki's film thus perfectly embodies the current potential of European cinema, now no longer just 'demoted' vis-à-vis Asian cinemas and Hollywood, but rather rising to the ethical challenge of being the 'abject subject' of world cinema.

9

'Experimenting with Death in Life'

Fatih Akin and the Ethical Turn

Prelude

For many of my generation, our love of cinema has never been just a way of enjoying our favourite form of entertainment. It has always also implied a question: what is the place of 'cinema' in the public sphere that used to be called 'progressive politics' (which was always also understood to be transgressive)? Since May 1968, and then since November 1989, this question has often resolved itself into one of two options: one was to claim 'the personal as the political' and to examine cinema's capacity for enacting the divisions of the subject, as it comes up against the limits of desire that both constitute and bar the subject's self-presence. This has been the province especially of feminist film theory, much of which was predicated on the paradox of the woman as subject of desire, without the possibility of acceding to desire other than through the desire of an other, or as Mary Ann Doane put it, 'Paradoxically, [woman's] only access is to the desire to desire.'[1]

The second option – especially since September 2001, if we want to put dates to it – has been to interrogate cinema as to its potential for opening up the equally impossible, but nonetheless always demanded, 'dialogue': dialogue with the ethnic, the religious or the national Other. Precisely because of the screen's ambiguous status as both window on the world and mirror to the self, the moving image's deceptive transparency and self-evidence always gives rise to the hope that the cinema machine can attend more closely than the human eye to all the visible phenomena in the world,

[1] Mary Ann Doane, *The Desire to Desire* (Bloomington: Indiana University Press, 1987), 9.

but also reveal the unremarked and overlooked, while freeing us from a subjectivity always already caught up in miscognition and disavowal. There lies the hope that cinema can inflect desire towards the encounter with the Other, rather than merely see the self in the guise of the Other. Beyond negotiating this difficult encounter, cinema is deemed to keep alive, by giving visible body to the democratic promise of representation, such core political issues as justice and rights, entitlements and empowerments, while attending to grief and grievances: remembering the forgotten, lending a voice to those who cannot speak for themselves, and giving a presence to those usually absent; the cinema as a powerful instrument in bringing about a juster and more equitable world.

The ethical turn

Philosophically as well as politically, the 'demand for dialogue', the question of 'the Other' and of 'alterity' have been at the forefront of the debate about the future of Europe as a multicultural and multi-ethnic continent. As questions about ethics and politics, in the form of cinematic thought experiments, they have also been a major theme in several previous chapters, most extensively in Chapter 4 ('"Europe": A Thought Experiment'). The focus has been on the potential conflict between rights, (social) justice and the law – issues that in the past two decades have been expressed in the renewed uncertainty over one of the key legacies of the Enlightenment and the French Revolution (as well as, in slightly but nonetheless significantly different terms, the American Revolution), namely the universalism of certain rights, in light of various claims for entitlements that cannot be assumed to be universal, but manifest themselves at the level of the particular. This may concern the uniqueness of an individual (the 'sanctity of life', against 'bio-politics'), the particular identity of a specific group (ethnic minorities or Diaspora communities, against the different manifestations of hegemony, assimilation and normativity), or the historical singularity of an event (the Jewish Holocaust; America and 9/11, against state-terror and terrorism as permanently hovering threats and 'states of exception').

It is in these contexts that ethics has returned as a critical issue, emerging at the juncture where the multiplicity of identities based on markers of difference defined as 'cultural' (and now subsuming nationality, ethnicity, religion, gender) no longer afford a common framework or an agreed basis on which competing claims can be arbitrated or negotiated, other than by mainly bureaucratic forms of redistribution (for instance, 'quotas' or 'affirmative action' in the US, financial grants to foster 'regional autonomy' in the EU, the expansion of the culture industries and the administration of multiculturalism at local and community level). Instead of 'Eurocentrism' and Western universalism, it tilts the balance towards regional, ethnic, tribal or religious particularism. The resulting debates around 'multiculturalism' and 'diversity' have already been addressed in Chapter 4, under the heading of 'the neighbour', but it may be worth just summarizing what is at stake.

Ideally, multiculturalism designates the different efforts to mitigate the consequences of Eurocentric essentialism, and to militate for a new tolerance, thus to lead to a levelling of hierarchies and biases. Committed to the recognition of the 'Other', however, multiculturalism is not the only politics trying to achieve this aim. There is the emphasis on human rights, as a way of reasserting universals from the bottom up, as it were, rather than top down, since Enlightenment values of democracy and rights, however desirable, have often been seen (especially by non-Western people) as imposed from above and from outside, and implemented with the force of arms: the recent history of Latin America and the Middle East are only the most flagrant examples. Thus, the contradictions between 'political' universalism and 'cultural' particularism persist: some new standard or category of conduct seems to be needed to break the deadlock. Ethics offers itself as just such a category: it, too, has been the name for this encounter with the Other, if one thinks of Emmanuel Levinas, for instance, for whom ethics connotes precisely, 'the calling into question of the Same'.[2] Yet it, too, combats relativism and sees itself as a 'politics'. As Levinas explains:

> A calling into question of the Same – which cannot occur within the egoistic spontaneity of the Same – is brought about by the Other. We name this calling into question of my spontaneity by the presence of the Other ethics. The strangeness of the Other, his irreducibility to the I, to my thoughts and my possessions, is precisely accomplished as a calling into question of my spontaneity as ethics.[3]

Levinas' notion of ethics has already been discussed in Chapters 4 and 5, and both compared and contrasted with the positions taken by Jacques Rancière. Here I want to put the emphasis on their differences, notably by aligning Rancière more closely with Alain Badiou, one of Levinas' most determined critics.[4] To this end, I shall make a rough and inexact distinction between ethics mark 1 and ethics mark 2. 'Ethics', by common definition, and thus 'ethics mark 1', would encompass both the authority and respect a person commands, on the basis of his or her actions, as well as the principles

---

[2] Emmanuel Levinas, *Totality and Infinity: An Essay on Exteriority*, trans. Alphonso Lingis (Pittsburgh: Duquesne University Press, 1969), 43.

[3] Levinas, *Totality and Infinity*, 33

[4] Alain Badiou, *Ethics: An Essay on the Understanding of Evil*, trans. Peter Hallward (London: Verso 2001), 18–23.

that govern the good life, the 'examined life' worth living.[5] But 'ethics' can also refer to the particular traditions, the customs, habits and values someone holds dear and sacred.[6] In this sense, ethics is compatible with the aims of multiculturalism, understood as the recognition as 'valuable' (if one hesitates to use the word 'equal') of different cultures or identities within a given social entity or geographical space.

However, insofar as one can speak of an ethical turn,[7] one enters the realm of ethics mark 2, where ethics emerges as the recto to the verso of multiculturalism, of which it is both the complement and the missing supplement. Sometimes also called post-ethics, it is a complement in that it seeks to identify a principle of action that goes beyond mere respect and tolerance, and it is a supplement, in that it tries to fill the perceived absence of normativity in multiculturalism. Levinas has specified the fundamental principle as follows: 'ethics' encompasses *demands that present themselves as necessarily to be fulfilled, but which are neither forced upon me [by morality], nor are they enforceable [by law].*[8] Such a definition – mapping out a complex terrain separate from, but implying law and force, individual and community, necessity and choice – usefully indicates the interdependence that exists between ethics, politics and multicultural tolerance, but also indicates (as discussed in Chapter 4) the differences, with regard to the status of the respective discourses, notably around questions of equality, equivalence, relativity, universality and justice. As I noted, Levinas has insisted that an encounter with the Other cannot be reduced to a reciprocal relationship (an exchange, a mutually agreed contract or bargain, a quid pro quo – as would be suggested when equality is identified with equivalence, rather than, say, subordinated to the law). However, if indeed ethics might well find itself responding to a demand coming from outside both law and custom, then it is in this second sense that ethics appears as a counter-term to culture: raising the bar, as it were, by pointing to the inability of

[5] 'The unexamined life is not worth living', Socrates, in Plato, *Apologia Sokratous*, 38a. Plato, *Five Dialogues: Euthyphro, Apology, Crito, Meno, Phaedo*, trans. G. M. A. Grube (Indianapolis, IN: Hackett Publishing, 2002), 41.

[6] Ethics as the authority and authenticity a person has thanks to his/her rootedness in established value- and-belief-systems. See Aristotle, *Rhetoric*, where Ethos, Pathos and Logos are the three major modes of argumentative appeal to an audience.

[7] The ethical turn in philosophy is usually attributed to Jacques Derrida's deconstruction of the ethical implications of key normative assumptions in the value systems of liberal democracies. However, it is a 'turn' since the ethical has crossed into several other disciplines, notably literary studies, anthropology, law and sociology. Besides Levinas and Derrida, major contributors to the 'turn' are (late and posthumous) Michel Foucault, Rancière and Badiou. See Jacques Rancière, 'The Ethical Turn of Aesthetics and Politics', *Critical Horizons: A Journal of Philosophy and Social Theory* 7, no. 1 (2006): 1–20.

[8] Emmanuel Levinas, *Otherwise than Being or Beyond Essence*, trans. Alphonso Lingis (Dordrecht and Boston: Kluwer Academic Publishers, 1978).

multiculturalism – as an ideal of equality, grounded in identity thinking – to specify the precise terms of such an encounter with the Other: ignoring, notably, the risks to selfhood and identity that such an encounter entails, and on which Levinas so forcefully insists.[9]

Besides involving Levinas, this ethical turn is associated with the name of Jacques Derrida, for whom ethics signals *both* an uncoupling from the traditional idea of (party) politics *and* a setting up of a critical distance from any form of culturalism, by insisting on a distinction between Law and Justice, but also refusing to pose the question of rights in the terms of identity politics, that is, either as a matter of distribution (equality) or of the collective will (democracy). Instead, as pointed out in Chapter 4, ethics for both Levinas and Derrida introduces the question of violence, usually excluded from multicultural discourse, while insisting on notions such as 'obligation' or 'demand' generally absent from culturalism, given that these terms are addressed to the individual in all his/her singularity, while culturalism addresses itself usually to some kind of group or community, that is, in the plural.[10]

'Auf der anderen Seite': Jacques Rancière

This is one possible logic of the ethical turn: it tries to address, if not resolve, the dilemmas of multiculturalism, of old-style Marxist politics and of new style NGO-type human rights, and thus it answers to the political legacy of May 1968 and to the end of the Cold War (1989), as well as to the so-called clash of civilizations (post–9/11).

The challenge is to see how such an extended framework might clarify what is at stake in those films made in Europe during the last decades that are the object of study in so many volumes dealing with immigration, globalization and multicultural identities, but also with the aporias of 'desire', such as 'deterritorialization', 'excess' and especially 'abjection' – in my reading perhaps the 'ethical' stance par excellence. From this perspective, Fatih Akin's *Gegen die Wand* (*Head On*, 2004) is appropriately symptomatic, insofar as at first glance it plays with all the clichés of multicultural and hyphenated filmmaking: Turkish weddings in Hamburg, tanbur-and-reed

[9] Kwame Anthony Appiah, when arguing for cosmopolitan open-mindedness against parochial universalism, once illustrated the latter by quoting the phrase often attributed to Fürst Bernhard von Bülow (1903): 'und willst du nicht mein Bruder sein, so schlag ich dir den Schädel ein' ('and if you do not want to be my brother, I will crack your skull'). Kwame Anthony Appiah, *Cosmopolitanism: Ethics in a World of Strangers* (New York: W.W. Norton, 2006), 209.

[10] A prominent disciple of Levinas and Derrida in this respect is Simon Critchley, notably in his book *Infinitely Demanding*.

flute music on the shores of the Bosporus (a recurring tableau-scene acting like a chorus and a framing device), arch-conservative patriarchal fathers (the angry father disowning his daughter) and male double standards when it comes to wives and sex even among the younger generation (strict separation between domestic prudery and public macho lechery).

Yet what drives the film's inner dynamic is not only this ethnic in-betweenness, the cross-cultural fusion of musical styles or inter-generational family feuds. Especially during the first half of the film, the male–female couple seem to compete with each other as to who can be more singular, more non-cooperative, more self-destructive; in short, more abject and more radically transgressive. In these moments, cultural differences or the multicultural 'dialogue' between Germans and Turks play hardly any role at all, and instead it is their sense of freedom that comes from having nothing more to lose (to misquote Janice Joplin) that the film forcefully conveys. Both characters meet when they are, in a direct sense, post-mortem creatures, having tried to commit suicide and being ready to do so again, ejected as they feel themselves to be from their respective social symbolic: a more radical ejection/abjection than either caused or cured by any reassertions of ethnic or national identity. Initially, the two do not fall in love, but enter into a contract to sustain their respective trajectories of desire, of 'personal independence' (for him) and the 'good life' (for her), trying to convert these into their 'ethics'. Akin lets the spectator see what ethics beyond identity might look like: a dangerous, violent, but also potentially liberating state, which unravels when one of them assumes that the encounter with the other can be secured by a bargain, a mutual quid pro quo, and tries to enforce the contract they concluded with the other.

The 'ethical' power of the film, to my mind, then, comes from not only *not* marking any difference between 'Turkish' and 'German' culture – and thus to forego all the dramatic (tragic as well as comic) potential that hyphenated identities usually connote in the cinema (*My Big Fat Greek Wedding* (Joel Zwick, 2002), *Monsoon Wedding* (Mira Nair, 2001), *Bride and Prejudice* (Gurinder Chadha, 2004), *Kebab Connection* (Anno Saul, 2004)) and instead emphasizes the risks that a true encounter with the other poses to all forms of identity thinking. The more each becomes aware of their 'Turkish roots', the more their bid for a new ethics unravels and collapses: Turkish cultural identity leaves them abandoned and isolated, rather than allowing them a 'homecoming' or a 'coming together'.

However, it is one of Fatih Akin's subsequent films – in German *Auf der anderen Seite* ('on the other side') (2008) and in English *The Edge of Heaven* – that may be even more symptomatic as to the consequences of the ethical turn, when explored in cinema. For this, however, I need to call on the 'new politics', the post-Marxist thinking about 'the political', here exemplified in the writings of Rancière and Badiou, two dissenting disciples of Louis Althusser. In particular, I want to introduce Rancière's critique of the 'ethical turn', what he calls the 'tournant éthique dans l'esthétique et la politique' ('the ethical turn in aesthetics and politics').[11] As a thinker who considers politics and aesthetics as two communicating vessels, Rancière sees the 'politics' of rational management and consensus (such as practised by the EU) as the very abrogation of politics. The so-called post-ideological politics, such as intervention in the name of 'world opinion', economic sanctions in the name of 'human rights', or humanitarian missions on the back of military actions, seem to him not only a negation of politics, but testimony to what he considers a deep (philosophical) nihilism. Words and actions that put victims, fatalities and survivors at the centre of a politics of rights and obligations tend to define the purpose of life as living in the presence of death, or rather, they implicitly assume that 'life' has to be rescued: from constitutive precariousness, from permanent danger, from all-enveloping death. Thus, disaster and 'catastrophe' (historically, the Shoah, the Nakba, the Armenian genocide, the Gulag; environmentally, tsunamis, hurricanes, earthquakes; militarily, 'pre-emptive strikes', 'war on terror') become the 'ground' and 'origin' of being, from which victimhood emerges as the only form of authentic agency:

> Ethics establishes its reign in the form of humanitarianism and infinite justice . . . (subject to no law) against the axis of evil. It is the Law itself which is evacuated (right of interference, targeted assassinations) by establishing a right beyond all other rights, that of the victim. The result is an ethical indistinction (a tendency towards eliminating the differences between politics and law), a new definition of human rights, and a vision of art that ties it to the social contract.[12]

This, for most of us, is a tough message, but is in keeping with the post-Nietzschean radicalism and 'anti-humanism' in French thinking, from Foucault and Deleuze to Rancière and Badiou. But perhaps even more counter-intuitive and startling is Rancière's claim that the 'ethical turn' associated with Levinas and Derrida is the complement of the same nihilism. Especially in Levinas' formulations, according to Rancière, both action and thought find themselves suspended in the face of pure otherness. Whether humanist and secular, fixated on health care, welfare and humanitarian aid (as in our Western democracies), or religious and messianic, living for the

---

[11] Jacques Rancière, *Le Tournant éthique de l'esthétique et de la politique* (2004), http://1libertaire.free.fr/JRanciere75.html (accessed 21 October 2017).

[12] 'L'éthique instaure son règne sous la forme de l'humanitaire et de la justice infinie . . . (soumise à aucune loi) contre l'axe du mal. C'est le droit lui-même qui est évacué (droit d'ingérence, assassinats ciblés) par instauration d'un droit au-delà de tout droit, celui de la victime. Il en résulte une indistinction éthique (disparition tendancielle des différences de la politique et du droit), une nouvelle définition des droits de l'homme, et une vision de l'art qui le voue au lien social.' Jacques Rancière, *Le Tournant éthique de l'esthétique et de la politique* (2004), http://1libertaire.free.fr/JRanciere75.html (accessed 21 October 2017).

sublime encounter with absolute alterity (as in Levinas), both ethics mark 1 and mark 2 are unable or unwilling to attach positive value to the present, which becomes a site of paralysis and suspension, meaningful only against the foil of death, disease or (natural/man-made) disaster. In other words, the underlying conviction of the 'ethical turn' is that – now in the words of Alain Badiou – 'the only thing that can really happen to someone is death'.[13]

Against this humanist 'state of exception' (Agamben) or Judeo-Christian ethics of alterity (Levinas), Rancière holds on to a radical conception of democratic politics as the thought and action towards equality, in the full knowledge of division, dissension and desire. Democracy for him is not 'representative' and has nothing to do with substituting or 'standing in for' the people. Predicated on notions such as the distribution of the sensible, on dissensus, on the articulation of incompatible demands, on contradictory choices, and thus on justice and on equality not as goals, forever deferred, but as the permanent, felt absences in painfully lived daily realities, or in guiltily enjoyed privileges, in the here and now, Rancière argues that these fundamental aspects of the political can nowadays be found, if at all, only in modern (ready-made, conceptual, installation) art, and there in an attenuated, often parodic form: as montage effects of juxtaposition, as the provocative display of the 'worthless', of junk and the discarded, as instances of the paradoxes and the double binds of self-reference. Politics must reclaim this territory now occupied by art alone, and with it, it must extend the public space or public sphere which art, and – as we shall see – cinema, still potentially inhabits.

In twentieth-century art it is Marcel Duchamp, not surprisingly, who is the champion of this idea of radical equality, because he has shown how it is that anything can be art if it changes place and category, and thus radically reorganizes the categories, working on a different ontology through the aesthetic. Yet for Rancière, cinema, too, has this potential to be such an art, on the point of becoming 'political', because cinema is so impure, at once so mechanical and so lifelike; in short, so self-divided (or 'thwarted' as Rancière calls it) that it can bring into being the singularity and visibility (and thus the value) of the ephemeral, the humble, the excluded and the abject. Cinema accomplishes the levelling of differences between art and life, as originally promised by the avant-gardes, but does so as its basic, 'apparatic' condition. At the same time, as the successor to the realist novel, itself the heir of the French Revolution, which first made the ordinary, the transitory as well as the abject and the obscene into suitable subjects for art, cinema has the potential to complete this move in the direction of 'radical equality' also in the political sense. Rancière makes clear how much his theory of art is tied to a theory of labour and human agency, which is why he seems to be

[13] Alain Badiou, *Ethics: An Understanding of Evil* (London: Verso, 2001), 35.

in covert dialogue with Adorno and other neo-Marxists, while objecting to their notions of reification, alienation or commodification.

It is this radical but consistent stance on the political as aesthetic and the aesthetic as political not as antinomic realms (as they are famously in Walter Benjamin) but as heteronomic relations (of mutual antagonism sustained by mutual dependence) that gives Rancière the authority and the vantage point (of 'the political') from which to deconstruct the ethical, too. In the sphere of politics, conflicts articulate themselves between different part(ie)s of the community in such a way that the antagonisms are not only external, vis-à-vis an opponent or enemy, but internal and constitutive, touching the individual as a mortal being of body and voice, of desire and its vicissitudes. As Rancière famously puts it, 'politics precisely begins when they who have no time to do anything else than their work, take that time that they do not have, in order to make themselves visible as sharing in a common world and prove that their mouths indeed emit common speech instead of merely voicing pleasure or pain'.[14] By contrast the ethical, as represented by the primacy given to human rights, as well as by Levinas' or Derrida's ethical turn, seems deadlocked between the idea of a multiply aggrieved, but ultimately unified community of victims (what Rancière calls 'l'éthique soft') and the ethics of radical alterity and the state of exception conceived from the perspective of seemingly forever deferred infinite justice ('l'éthique hard'). But as Rancière remarks, somewhat sarcastically, taking a swipe at the 'hard ethics' of Levinas and Agamben, 'a whole trend of thought today dissolves political dissensuality in an archi-politics of exception and terror, from which only a Heideggerian God can save us'.[15]

'Auf der anderen Seite': Fatih Akin

With this somewhat summary version of Rancière's thinking on ethics in mind, I am ready to return to Fatih Akin's *Edge of Heaven*. The film won a prize for best screenplay at the Cannes Festival in 2007 and has been profusely commented on and written about,[16] allowing me the shortcut of taking the plot summary from the film's own website:

[14] Jacques Rancière, 'The Politics of Aesthetics', *Mute* (14 September 2006), http://www.metamute.org/editorial/articles/politics-aesthetics (accessed 21 October 2017).

[15] Rancière, 'The Politics of Aesthetics'.

[16] To cite only three examples: Vivien Silvey and Roger Hillman, 'Akin's *Auf der anderen Seite* (The Edge of Heaven) and the widening periphery', *German as a foreign language* 3 (2010), www.gfl-journal.de/3-2010/SilveyHillman.pdf (accessed 9 January 2017); Claudia Breger, 'Configuring Affect: Complex World-Making in Fatih Akin's *Auf der anderen Seite*', *Cinema Journal* 54, no. 1 (Fall 2014): 65–87; and Dudley Andrew, 'Fatih Akin's Moral Geometry', in Seung-hoon Jeong and Jeremi Szaniawski (eds), *The Global Auteur: The Politics of Authorship in 21st Century Cinema* (New York: Wallflower Press, 2015), 179–98.

Retired widower Ali sees a solution to loneliness when he meets prostitute Yeter. Ali proposes to the fellow Turkish native to live with him in exchange for a monthly stipend. Ali's bookish son Nejat seems disapproving about his bully father's choice. But the young German professor quickly grows fond of kind Yeter, especially upon discovering most of her hard-earned money is sent home to Turkey for her daughter's university studies. The accidental death of Yeter distances father and son even more, emotionally and physically.

Nejat travels to Istanbul to begin an organized search for Yeter's daughter Ayten. He decides to stay in Turkey and trades places with the owner of a German bookstore who goes home to Germany. What Nejat doesn't know is that 20-something political activist Ayten is already in Germany, having fled the Turkish police. Alone and penniless, Ayten is befriended by German student Lotte, who is immediately seduced by the young Turkish woman's charms and political situation. Lotte invites rebellious Ayten to stay in her home, a gesture not particularly pleasing to her conservative mother Susanne. Ayten ends up arrested and confined for months while awaiting political asylum. When her plea is denied, Ayten is deported and imprisoned in Turkey.

Passionate Lotte decides to abandon everything to help Ayten. In Turkey, Lotte gets caught up in the frustrating bureaucracy of the seemingly hopeless situation of freeing Ayten. A chance bookstore meeting will lead her to becoming Nejat's roommate. A tragic event will bring Susanne to Istanbul to help fulfil her daughter's mission. Emotional moments spent with Susanne will inspire Nejat to seek out his estranged father, now residing on Turkey's Black Sea coast.'[17]

What interests me first of all is the presence of Hanna Schygulla, Fassbinder's muse in so many iconic films from the 1970s, in the role of Susanne, one of the two mothers central to the story. The plot, too, makes more than casual reference to Fassbinder's films: the initial situation is reminiscent of *Ali: Fear Eats the Soul* (1974), with a Muslim guest-worker (also called Ali) paying a prostitute not just for sex, but for making him 'proper' food. His accidentally killing her and doing time in prison recalls Franz Biberkopf and Ida in *Berlin Alexanderplatz* (1980), while the lesbian relationship has echoes of *Bitter Tears of Petra von Kant* (1972). Another significant point is that *The Edge of Heaven* was in Germany billed (retroactively) as the second film of a trilogy, meant to respond, according to the director, to Fassbinder's BRD Trilogy (*The Marriage of Maria Braun* (1979), *Lola* (1981) and *Veronika Voss* (1982)). What the troubled relationship between West Germany and

[17] http://www.auf-der-anderen-seite.de/THE_EDGE_OF_HEAVEN_presskit.pdf (accessed 15 December 2017).

its Nazi past was to Fassbinder, Akin seems to say, is to him the no less troubled negotiation between 'assimilated' Turks in Germany and their homeland.

Once more, Akin avoids the Romeo & Juliet melodramas of multicultural star-crossed lovers, nor is he interested in the comedies of mistaken ethnic or national stereotypes, also common in the 'Greek wedding' genre already referred to, though he co-wrote and co-produced a typical example of both, Saul's *Kebab Connection*, and went on to make *Soul Kitchen* (2009). The hyphenation of ethnic or religious identities in such films tends to join too comfortably what remain messy sets of generational tensions, universal moral dilemmas, emotional ambivalences and split loyalties. Instead, as in Fassbinder, perversely improbable love stories, sadistic scapegoating and suicidal sacrifices prevail. As will be recalled, the film is divided into three parts, each announced by an intertitle, with the first two equally mercilessly predicting 'Yeter's Death' and 'Lotte's Death'. The third part, with the film's title as its intertitle, sees the surviving characters arrive in Turkey, their quests intersecting without actually converging, keeping to parallel tracks and bringing more near-misses (with the coffins of Yeter and Lotte crossing at Istanbul airport in opposite directions). This stark and memorable image is a reminder that the film as a whole is conceived in the shape of the Moebius strip, or infinite loop, running between the two cities of Hamburg and Istanbul, while the six characters criss-cross each others' lives in both directions, or more accurately, have an existence on both sides of the Moebius strip: *Auf der anderen Seite* translates literally as 'on the other side', leaving open whether this refers to the other side of life/death, of political and national divides, of self/other, or – as in my reading/translation – 'on both sides of the same loop'.

The parallels, coincidences, improbabilities and dramatic ironies have irritated several critics, but in all fairness such pointed over-plotting is in keeping with the Douglas Sirk–R.W. Fassbinder genealogy of Hollywood – and maybe even Turkish – melodrama that Akin is inscribing himself into. However, in the present context, it is a perfect example of 'film as thought experiment', by setting up a calculated and controlled set of circumstances, into which certain actions and (human) agents are inserted as so many (chemical) substances poured into test tubes and heated over a Bunsen burner in order to observe their reactions (and ultimate combustions).

Schygulla as the matriarch presides over more than the film's liberal conscience: she is the guardian of a pledge to continue the generational burden of the German–German 'Hollywood' dialogue, extended now into a German–Turkish 'European' dialogue. For the ingenuity of the film's dramatic architecture is not in the plotting per se, but instead has to do with a complex moral fabric that is being spun through the story, whose overall design, however – this would be my first argument – might indeed need a third part, to carry the ethical weight the fable of these six interwoven lives claims for itself. If *Gegen die Wand* can be said to have been 'political' in Rancière's sense, in that it constantly works towards maintaining that dissensus which allows the ordinary to seem extraordinary, *Auf der anderen Seite* is – my second point – an example of 'l'éthique soft', that is, of antagonisms and dissensus working towards acquiescence and resolution, however deferred or suspended at the end.

It should be clear from the plot summary just given that 'transgressions' (of whatever kind: sexual, political, ethnic, religious) are punished. Yet equally clearly, there is a will towards sacrifice and self-sacrifice, arising in response to these violations and infractions, though not coming from the 'perpetrators' themselves. Instead, they emerge and manifest themselves by way of stand-ins, substitutes and 'representatives'. The son wants to make amends for his father's deed by continuing the payments for which a mother had sacrificed her body and honour, only to die without this sacrifice being known or acknowledged, while another mother wants to become worthy of her daughter's sacrifice, irrespective of whether she believes in the cause that the daughter's lover embraced, a cause that makes the other sacrifices (of 'son' and 'mother') seem very nearly futile. Choices are being made in the name of primary bonds, but the families are incomplete, their missing halves absent and even the dyad is torn apart: son and father, but no mother, mother and daughter, but no father, mother and daughter, but neither encounter nor recognition.

Evidently, these symmetries, repetition and parallels are carefully established and cleverly worked out. First, the opening scene and the closing one make a temporal bracket and are set during a *bayram*, the national celebration and public holiday that unites secular and religious groups, regardless of their differences. Then, placed near the beginning of the third part, but at the heart of the film and its moral fulcrum, is a scene where Nejat explains to Susanne before an open window – putting it in a frame for contour and emphasis, as it were – the meaning of the procession of young men coming down the steps outside: they are celebrating the memory of Abraham's Sacrifice, a story as important to Muslims as it is to Christians and Jews. In this and other scenes, tolerance and bridge-building, the virtues of Turkey's secular constitution, the shared beliefs of the three 'world religions of the book', the modernizing effects of possible/improbable Turkish entry into the European Union, the shadow of Sharia law on Western democracies and several other topical motifs are all closely woven into the destinies of Germans and Turks of the second post-war generations, born like Fatih Akin in the 1970s and now entering public life, often as artists, musicians, intellectuals and academics.

At the same time, Akin seems to hint that there is no easy compromise in sight, and that a price will have to be paid in this generational transfer from first to second generation, between Germans and Turks, between secular liberalism and the long memory of injustice. Since Ayten enters a plea bargain with the police to be freed, it means she is betraying her activist comrades, an act that surely cannot remain without consequences. Likewise, the ethics of the various acts of sacrifice are peculiarly New Testament (turning the other cheek, rather than an eye for an eye), based on empathetic identification with the Other and a relay of substitution and place-holding. How does this look from the point of view of the Old Law or of Islam, or indeed, how does this square with the harsher lesson that the story of God testing Abraham is meant to teach? Just as dread anticipation of pointless deaths suffuses parts one and two of *The Edge of Heaven*, at the end the viewer is poised for more dread anticipation of the third part of the trilogy announced by Akin, and dealing – after 'Love' and 'Death' – with 'Evil' (in German, *Liebe*, *Tod* und *Teufel*). More coincidences, fatal choices, ethical dilemmas and doubtful sacrifices? A ratcheting up of suffering and intransigence, of political radicalism and religious hatred? We are not told, and at the end of *Edge of Heaven*, we are left in pending expectation.

In one sense, then, the film is very much in the spirit of Levinas: it places a very high ethical value on sacrifice and substitution. The characters learn and accept their roles as they confront radical otherness; they become active – leaving their homes, their jobs, their countries – in the service of fulfilling a typically Levinasian demand, namely the necessity to define and find yourself by seeking out an ethical relation of risk and uncertainty. As Levinas maintains in *Otherwise than Being*, in this process, substitution is the very core of subjectivity in the ethical relation. In another sense, *Auf der anderen Seite* – with its implied title 'Death' – also perfectly illustrates the point made by Rancière about such scenarios of substitution and atonement. By seeking to transcend politics (those of the EU and of Turkey), religion and ethnicity (Abraham's sacrifice), such redemptive acts end up with death as the horizon of individual action and decision. The question this raises is whether the film takes such an 'ethical turn' because Akin is committed to this Levinasian ethics, no longer believing either in multiculturalist coexistence, however tragic-comic or mutually complementary (as it appeared in one of Akin's earliest films, *Kurz und schmerzlos/Short Sharp Shock*), nor putting his faith in a negotiated, consensus, EU-style 'political' solution, and therefore settles for a 'soft' version of ethical universalism. Opting for the ethics of victim and sacrifice, of substitution and delegation, the film depicts a specifically Judeo-Christian way of dealing with the issues, if not altogether New Testament-Christian.

On the other side, just as plausible is the possibility that Akin is offering a Rancièrean critique of this Levinasian ethics, by making this second film, like the slower counter-movement of a musical piece, after the *furioso* of the first movement (*Gegen die Wand*), the preparatory antithesis for a third and final part, once more to be played *fortissimo*. Are we being literally put *on the other side* if we accept *Die andere Seite* as a self-enclosed work and authorial 'statement' – endorsing what elsewhere I have called the 'Utopian' aspects of mutual interference in the internal affairs of the Other?[18]

Remembering how the acts of atonement of Susanne and Nejat are set off against the 'plea-bargaining' of Ayten, how substitution is matched by betrayal and how Ayten lives in states of exception and abjection (in Germany initially she has no money, no food, no home), while her political cell is a female 'terrorist' one, it is clear that something ominous is in the offing. It is hard not to recall that Hamburg was the home of Mohamed Atta's conspiratorial cell, prior to him setting off to fly a plane into the North Tower. Death is omnipresent; yet while the German and German-Turkish characters live under the sign of actual and symbolic death, the militants (whether belonging to the PKK or some other radical grouping), even though they are potential suicide bombers, are nonetheless full of 'life', of schemes, projected into the future. They have that fierceness of conviction and righteousness which suggests the possibility of an Antigone-style 'ethical act' (the singular conduct, the terrible choice, the decision taken in the dark night of the soul, putting you outside the Law and beyond the pale, but also dividing you against any community, fighting for the life worth living even if it means your own death). Yet, Rancière might also argue that Ayten's sullen individuality and her comrades' lethal resolve merely instantiate the recto of the verso of the 'ethical turn': the nihilistic need for a permanent state of exception and for the radical 'outside' – all taking place under the sign of death as the only positive value.

The third part(y): Alain Badiou and the nature of 'evil'

Yet if, as suggested, one considers *The Edge of Heaven* not so much as a self-enclosed work, but as part of a trilogy, a further possibility arises. Since it is already known that the first part was under the sign of 'love', the second 'death' and the third will be about 'evil', another reading of the trilogy-in-the-making also becomes possible, this time not following Rancière, but Badiou instead. In such a reading, *Gegen die Wand* becomes an example of one of Badiou's instances of the 'event' (of which there are four types: love, a scientific breakthrough, a revolution and a work of art). An event, in Badiou's sense, steals up on you, it strikes you and it changes your life. Love, in *Gegen die Wand*, is such an event: when the male hero thinks he is safe because he has a contract that regulates marriage by reducing it to its proper dimensions of sex, money and domestic service, love hits him when he least expects it and

[18] See Chapter 8 for a more detailed description of 'mutual interference in the internal affairs of the other'.

when he is least prepared for it. But once it does, he has to be true to the event, no matter what the consequences (which may include killing someone).

Badiou's concept of love as event is difficult and demanding. It is opposed to the romantic one, according to which love is the total fusion of two beings to the point of extinguishing their individual identity, symbolized in the ecstatic self-abandonment of the Wagnerian *Liebestod*. But it also differs from the sceptical or, if you like, cynical version, according to which love is pure ideology, in the sense that either it ennobles sexual desire or compensates for the lack of a sexual relation (as in Lacan's version of the narcissistic fantasy frame required to sustain sexual desire). For Badiou, on the other hand, love is about the ability to sustain separation, to think disjunction and to keep two distinct moments, two elements or two beings in mind at the same time (in other words, the highest form of dialogue). To this extent, as the 'scene of the two', love is part of the striving after truth, understood as a unique process but predicated on the acceptance of difference. What makes it so difficult, but also gives it its high ethical value, is that it commits the lover to a fidelity towards this singularity in division, which is the event, this rupture in the fabric of reality, from which alone 'change' can come.

In the case of the second part of *The Edge of Heaven*, a Badiou reading would not be that different from the one already given: with death as both palpable presence and the ethical horizon, Badiou might see the various acts of charity and sacrifice not only as the wrong kinds of love, predicated on over-identification (and thus imaginary fusion) with the Other, but as forms of self-betrayal and self-deception, whose major mistake would be to think that good comes *after* evil and that such living by proxy can be redemptive, going so far as to imagine that one's exemplary life will make the world a better place. If you cannot resist or oppose or dissent, but think you can strike a bargain with fate because you might find a meaning to your life through the manner of your death, then Akin, too, intimates the futility of such a calculus, because his film shows just how pointless and absurd the deaths of both Yeter and Lotte are.

At the same time, by deferring all these encounters – between Nejan and Ali, his father, between Nejan and Aytan, as daughter of Yeter – *The Edge of Heaven* prepares the viewer for future manifestations of life (in the third part of the trilogy) as violent, but possibly also as irredeemable, as the deaths were in part two. If indeed there should be a third part, the logic so far sketched would imply that it deals with 'terrorism', and in particular with suicide bombing, but also with the question of evil. This in turn would retroactively suggest a different reading also of part one – *Gegen die Wand* – now in the light not so much of love, but with respect to the relation between subjectivity, the body, desire and death. For Badiou, in our current debate about 'subjectivity' and 'the body', there are two, ultimately unacceptable, but also mirroring positions. One assumes that the subject is identical with body, and the other that the subject must separate itself from the body. While the former stance manifests itself in the pursuit of jouissance as the subject's self-fulfilment through the experience of the body's limits (typically, in *Gegen die Wand*, when Sibel says she wants to live, meaning drugs, dance, sex) the latter is prepared to sacrifice the body in this life for pleasure in the next (typical for the suicidal jihadist 'martyr'). In either case, however, according to Badiou, it would be death that dominates: in the first case because this testing of the body's limits in relation to technology, and the sensations as well as subject effects this produces, is a way of 'experimenting with death in life'; and in the second case, dying as a martyr is what is seen as that which gives meaning to life and recaptures agency under conditions felt to be intolerable, like the prey that launches itself into the jaws of its predator. In other words, for Badiou, sacrifice – whether as a martyr to the cause or in the spirit of atonement and redemption – is the reverse side of enjoyment, *jouissance*, the name for the death drive, that is, for seeking out fusion, and for the self in the image of the Other, to whom one hands over agency.

To return to *The Edge of Heaven*, Ayten's betrayal – not so much of her comrades, but of the political event itself, her not being true to her initial commitment to the political act: of fighting for Kurdish self-determination, or whatever her group is fighting for – is the crux of the ethical dilemma of the film, understood as the difficult journey from the self(ishness) of the individual, to the 'we' of the community, back to the 'singularity' of the ethical act, or ethical choice, which can never be any thing but singular. Yet by the same token, there must be a connection to the community in order to produce an ethics. The temptation would be for her to try and redeem the death of Lotte by being the daughter that Susanne has lost, while Susanne would be the mother, whom Ayten did not know had paid with her life for trying to support her. But the ethical act might involve another betrayal to cancel out the initial one, as a way of paying her dues to the community. This, then, would have to be the matter addressed in the third part of the trilogy, which – by this logic – is rightly advertised as dedicated to the exploration of 'evil'.

But what is 'evil' in the context of the 'ethical turn'? In the war on terror, or in humanitarian missions to Darfur or Somalia, evil pre-exists in the world and has to be fought by the forces of good. This would be the 'soft ethical' position. Rejecting such a turn and reversing its premise, Badiou would argue that for a proper ethical stance, good must be considered as logically and ontologically preceding evil. This would be in contrast to our version of Christianity, where the fact of the fallen world means that 'good' is a reactive response to preternatural evil. For Badiou, on the other hand, the good and the true belong together, which means that he associates ethics with the production of universal truths. Evil, instead of being preternatural, would be the consequence of a failure to live up to or bring into the world this particular union of the good and the true. As Michael Rothberg has pointed out, there is a substantial heuristic value, but also risk, to be gained from this stance:

> Positing evil as a derailed truth process is helpful in understanding one of the key questions of the twentieth century – how can ordinary people commit extraordinary acts of evil? – because it demonstrates evil's proximity to progressive and potentially liberating human projects. Evil is thus not easily ghettoized as the [opposite or] 'other' of reason or humanism.[19]

The term 'ghettoized' might be an unfortunate choice, because one of the tasks that Badiou sets himself is to explain Nazism:

> Evil is seen as belonging to one of three genres: it appears as terror, as betrayal, or as disaster. Terror involves the attempt to produce a truth that does not hold for all, that is, that cannot be universalized. Nazism falls into this category insofar as it constructs an exclusionary imaginary community, but so would various other communitarian, nationalist, and racist projects.[20]

When a subject does not remain faithful to a truth process, the second form of evil and betrayal results. In scenarios of betrayal, 'former revolutionaries are obliged to declare that they used to be lost in error and madness', 'a former lover no longer understands why he loved that woman' or 'a tired scientist comes to misunderstand, and to frustrate through bureaucratic routine, the very development of his own science'.[21] Disaster, on the other hand, follows from the too rigorous application of a truth, the 'absolutization of its power', such that it comes to wipe out entirely the everyday kinds of knowledge of the situation and the 'human being' that constitutes 'truth's very foundation'.[22] This would have been the tragedy of communism and Stalinism.

In this light, the 'war on terror' would have to be seen as a version of 'evil', just like the acts of the terrorists, which it claims to defeat, not only because both are grounded in fear, that is, a stance that makes death the horizon of being. But it also misses its mark as politics, because it claims to develop a positive account of the Good by an act of exclusion. In this reading, this discourse – whether instantiated in the Bush doctrine of pre-emptive action and the declaration of a de facto state of emergency that suspends the law (as in Guantanamo Bay), or embodied in its opposite, namely the struggle for the reinstatement and universal applicability of human rights, would in either event function as the ideological support for the current political status quo, by presenting as potentially evil any organized political collective that seeks to challenge the domain marked out by parliamentary democracy and neoliberal economics. In short, multiculturalism would thus be the very logic of liberal

[19] Michael Rothberg, review of *Ethics: An Essay on the Understanding of Evil*, by Alain Badiou, *Criticism* 43, no. 4 (Fall 2001): 482.
[20] Rothberg, review of *Ethics: An Essay on the Understanding of Evil*, 482.
[21] Badiou, *Ethics*, 79–90.
[22] Badiou, *Ethics*, 84–5.

democracy, rather than its counter-stance, which by contrast would have to be capable of assuming a position that 'truths are addressed equally to all'.

This absolute commitment to the ethical value of the Same – in contrast to Levinas' 'calling into question of the Same' – demonstrates, on the part of Badiou, a provocative and radically egalitarian-democratic spirit, *transgressive in its very normativity*. It seems to raise the bar to impossible heights, and indeed, when trying to reposition cinema between 'cultural studies', 'politics' and 'ethics', both Rancière and Badiou are very severe taskmasters indeed. I for one am not sure that Badiou's 'fidelity to the truth event' would help understand the scope of human agency in the mediated environment, but also in the newly politicized environment: say, between the power of the terrorist and the power of the victim, the two positions so urgently thematized in Akin's film. Who is to decide that fidelity to the event is not another name for fanaticism, or that the victim, once s/he fully assumed victimhood, does not acquire a terrible power not just over him/herself, but over others? If, however, we see cinema, as Rancière suggests, as the great democratic leveller, giving agency not just to the camera and to the characters, not just to the look and the gaze, but to the animate and the inanimate, to 'things' as well as to people, to thought as well as to action, then the notion of cinema as both progressive and transgressive, but also as both (ethically) transgressive and (politically) normative – in short, as proposing to us a new taxonomy of 'life' before death – seems at least conceivable.

It would make Fatih Akin's rejection of multiculturalism and his embrace of deterritorialization, his experimental testing of the ethics of sacrifice and his tentative exploration of evil one of the more interesting projects in contemporary European cinema. A cinema, in other words, that does not so much experiment with death in life, as it is on the way to the possibility of a European cinema of 'ethical agency', which is not thereby an 'action' cinema.

With this last thought, I have opened up quite a few further dilemmas and moved from progressive politics to something like transgressive politics, but I have also switched from an actual film (albeit one constructed as a thought experiment) to one that is more inferential than it even is hypothetical. It is thus a good moment to stop my reflections, before I also find myself on the other side: not just beyond good and evil, but in the realm of pure speculation.[23]

[23] Fatih Akin has made several films since *Auf der anderen Seite* (2007), most notably and problematically, *The Cut* (2014), a big budget, international co-production that chronicles the effects of the Armenian genocide on a young Armenian who travels the world in search of his possibly surviving family members. A critical and commercial disappointment, *The Cut* uses the broader historical canvas to examine once more what it means to live without 'roots'. In its epic sweep and meandering plot it foregoes raising the kinds of ethical dilemmas, sharp paradoxes and test scenarios that would qualify it as a thought experiment. However, his film *In the Fade* (*Aus dem Nichts*, 2017) confronts 'head on' the theme of terrorism, and the damage it does to victims and perpetrators.

10

Black Suns and a Bright Planet

Lars von Trier's *Melancholia* as Thought Experiment

End-of-the-world movies

Asked in an interview about the future of humanity, German director Werner Herzog gave a terse reply: 'I'm convinced that our presence on this planet is not sustainable, so we will be extinct fairly soon ... Cockroaches and reptiles have a much better survival chance. The human race is not sustainable and there are too many things that can wipe us out. Microbes are after us, or a meteorite hitting us, or something man-made. ... There is a wonderful thing that Martin Luther said when he was asked, "What would you do if the world were to disappear tomorrow in the apocalypse?" And Luther said, "Today, I would plant an apple tree." If I knew that tomorrow a meteorite would destroy our planet, I would start shooting a new film today.'[1]

Lars von Trier's *Melancholia* could be that movie. It, too, assumes that at least a certain form of human life is not sustainable, and from among Herzog's possibilities, the option von Trier chooses is that of a meteorite, or planet, and yet, at the same time, there is the clear suggestion in *Melancholia* that it is 'something man-made' that has the rogue planet change its course and collide with Earth.

Melancholia is only one of several films in recent years which assume that our world is coming to an end. Usually, these are hardware blockbusters, like

---

[1] Werner Herzog, 'Werner Herzog: Trust in My Wild Fantasies', interview with Sven Schumann and Johannes Bonke, *The Talks*, 30 January 2013, http://the-talks.com/interview/werner-herzog/ (accessed 10 January 2017). See also Steve Rose, 'Werner Herzog on death, danger and the end of the world', *Guardian*, 12 April 2012, http://www.theguardian.com/film/2012/apr/14/werner-herzog-into-the-abyss (accessed January 12 2017).

Independence Day (1996), *Armageddon* (1998), *The Day After Tomorrow* (2004), *War of the Worlds* (2005), *Prometheus* (2012) and *Interstellar* (2014), and the threats are natural disasters or the invasion of aliens. In Hollywood films, total extinction is usually averted at the last minute, invariably by the intrepid teamwork and infallible technology of a group of resolute Americans. But even these vestiges of can-do optimism have been on the wane in recent years, a late or latent consequence of 9/11 and its trauma-prone aftermath.

Generally, the more fatalistic outlook has been the prerogative of Europeans, and among filmmakers, one thinks of Chris Marker's *La Jeteé* (1962), Ingmar Bergman's *Shame* (1968), Andrej Tarkowski's *The Sacrifice* (1986) or Michael Haneke's *Time of the Wolf* (2003) as 'end of the world' films. They are joined by American directors with a blacker kind of humour but a European sensibility, such as Stanley Kubrick and his *Dr Strangelove* (1964), or Terry Gilliam's *Brazil* (1985) and *Twelve Monkeys* (1995). Lars von Trier aligns himself with this legacy, yet intriguingly enough, he attributes an American fear of being wiped out, or of no longer being in control, to Claire, played by the French actress Charlotte Gainsbourg, while the more overtly melancholy, but also in the end more stoical and resigned Justine is played by an actress known for airhead roles – the American Kirsten Dunst. As reviewers have also noted, there is something unsettlingly cheerful and serene about von Trier's apocalypse.

Cosmic and man-made disasters

If Hollywood tends to invoke cosmic disasters in order to distract from the man-made ones, von Trier, by calling both the film and the life-threatening planet 'Melancholia', sets out to establish an interdependence between the cosmic and the man-made. The inside and the outside, the infinitely large and the insignificantly small become 'communicating vessels': itself perhaps a sign of a melancholy but also a liberating *ruination* of differences, distinctions and hierarchies.

Melancholy, as one of the four humours, has a long history. Often now simply equated with clinical depression, it used to connote a more general, non-specific despondency, as well as mood swings or states of mind and body that we might now call bi-polar disorders. In Freud's paper on 'Mourning and Melancholia' – to which I shall return – it is not only mourning over the death of someone close, or a pervasive sense of loss, but a persistent hanging on to this feeling of loss, invested with libido, as a way of coping with unconscious ambivalence towards the lost person or object.[2]

[2] Sigmund Freud, 'Mourning and Melancholia' (1917), in *The Standard Edition of the Complete Psychological Works of Sigmund Freud*, Volume XIV (1914–16), 239–60.

But melancholy not only encompasses abnormal lugubriousness, the irrational sense of being doomed, or an inability to sustain viable human bonds. Melancholy, ever since Aristotle's *Problemata physica*, was also the hallmark of exceptional, and exceptionally creative, human beings: 'Through what cause do all those who have become eminent in philosophy or politics or poetry or the arts turn out to be melancholics?' he asks.[3] It is a question that most writers on melancholy – Erwin Panofsky and Fritz Saxl, for instance – have tried to answer, pointing out that since the early sixteenth century, Renaissance scholars tended to associate the planet Saturn with melancholy.[4] The astrologers argued – probably following Aristotle – that physicians, philosophers and scientists were born in a constellation with a strong Saturn placement, giving them the malady of melancholy, but also the blessing of special wisdom. This artistic strain of melancholy, taking its cue from Albrecht Dürer's enigmatic etching from 1514, and Robert Burton's *Anatomy of Melancholy* (1621), will become the very emblem of modernity, as reprised from Walter Benjamin in *Ursprung des deutschen Trauerspiels* (*The Origin of German Tragic Drama*) to Susan Sontag in *Under the Sign of Saturn*, and continuing from Julia Kristeva's *Black Sun* to W. G. Sebald's *The Rings of Saturn*.[5]

End of cinema?

Another 'end-of' feeling probably pales into insignificance at the very margins of such 'end of the world' scenarios, fuelled as they are by seemingly irresolvable conflicts of resources, race and religion, and imminent natural disasters like global warming[6]: that of the end of cinema, or at the very least, a melancholy sense that a certain kind of cinema is in danger of becoming extinct. 'End of cinema' scenarios have been invoked in the past, often when

[3] An alternative translation is: 'Why is it that all those who have become eminent in philosophy or politics or poetry or the arts are clearly of an atrabilious temperament, and some of them to such an extent as to be affected by diseases caused by black bile, as is said to have happened to Heracles among the heroes?' Aristotle, *The Complete Works of Aristotle Vol. II*, ed. Jonathan Barnes (Princeton, NJ: Princeton University Press, 1984), *Problemata* XXX.1 953a, 10–14.

[4] Erwin Panofsky and Fritz Saxl, *Dürers' Melencolia I. Eine Quellen- und typengeschichtliche Untersuchung* (Leipzig and Berlin: Studien der Bibliothek Warburg, 1923).

[5] For an assessment of melancholy in modernist twentieth-century thinking, see Beatrice Hanssen, 'Portrait of Melancholy (Benjamin, Warburg, Panofsky)', *MLN* 114, no. 5, Comparative Literature Issue (December 1999): 991–1013. But see also Jennifer Radden, *The Nature of Melancholy: From Aristotle to Kristeva* (Oxford: Oxford University Press, 2002).

[6] All of these are man-made calamities, to which applies Fred Jameson's apocryphal dictum that 'today it is easier to imagine the end of the world than the end of capitalism'. On the origins of this much-quoted phrase, see 'Easier to imagine the end of the world . . .', http://qlipoth.blogspot.com/2009/11/easier-to-imagine-end-of-world.html (accessed 10 January 2017).

technical changes, such as the coming of sound or video affected both the way films were made and the way they were being understood.[7] In the new century, this end is variously attributed to the digital image (signalling the end of celluloid-based film and the so-called 'loss of indexicality') and to the combined challenge of television and the internet (threatening the survival of classical filmmaking and putting an end to actual movie-going). These specific causes – including the end of European art and auteur cinema – seem almost an afterthought to the strong sense that the cinema as a distinct and autonomous art form (outside the museum) has become unsustainable.[8]

And yet films continue being made not only the world over, but also in Europe – perhaps *post festum, post mortem*, in the spirit of Werner Herzog's intuition that maybe the catastrophe has already happened. *Melancholia* is one such film-after-cinema, fully aware of its precarious status and digital hybridity, and thus invoking both realism (the 'window on the world' view of cinema) and modernism (the 'mirror to the crisis of a bourgeois subject' view of cinema) as henceforth the optional 'special effects' of digital cinema, which is now the groundless ground of images whose beauty is but the beginning of terror (to invoke the opening lines of Rainer Maria Rilke's first *Duino Elegy*).[9]

Cinema as thought experiment

In other words, I am positing a tenuous bridge between different kinds of 'the sense of an ending' by envisaging for certain films a post-cinema (ontological) status, different from the ones we usually assume in academic discussions, where we see films as individually authored statements, as belonging to specific genres or as social texts about 'representation' – symptomatic, enigmatic, illusionist and decipherable thanks to the hermeneutic procedures

[7] On 'end of cinema' prognostics, see, among others, Paolo Cherchi Usai, *The Death of Cinema* (London: BFU Publishing 2000), Jon Lewis (ed.), *The End of Cinema As We Know It* (New York: NYU Press, 2001) and, more recently, Matt Zoller Seitz, 'The Death/Decay of Cinema @15', *Rogerebert.com*, 31 July 2014, http://www.rogerebert.com/mzs/death-of-filmdecay-of-cinema-at-15-a-conversation-with-godfrey-cheshire (accessed 10 January 2017).

[8] Raymond Bellour, *La Querelle des dispositifs: Cinéma – installations, expositions* (Paris: P.O.L., 2012); André Gaudreault and Philippe Marion, *The End of Cinema? A Medium in Crisis in the Digital Age* (New York: Columbia University Press, 2015).

[9] 'Wer, wenn ich schriee, hörte mich denn aus der Engel/Ordnungen? und gesetzt selbst, es nähme/ einer mich plötzlich ans Herz: ich verginge von seinem/ stärkeren Dasein. Denn *das Schöne ist nichts/ als des Schrecklichen Anfang*, den wir noch grade ertragen,/ und wir bewundern es so, weil es gelassen verschmäht,/ uns zu zerstören.'

'For beauty is nothing but the beginning of terror which we are barely able to endure and we are so awed because it serenely disdains to annihilate us.' R. M. Rilke, *Die erste Duineser Elegie* (1912) (Berlin: Insel-Verlag, 1923).

we are familiar with from literary studies, ideological critique and from 'theory'. The altered status I want to propose for films such as *Melancholia* is that of a 'thought experiment', as outlined in some detail in Chapter 3, where I argue that a thought experiment is speculative and self-reflexive, but also driven by external necessity, permitting certain freedoms of the imagination but obeying its own internal constraints.[10] As such, it invites comparison with Dürer's *Melancholia*, showing a figure lost in thought, outwardly a picture of dejection, world-oblivion and self-abandon, but with an intense inward concentration, working on solving a problem.[11] Speaking less metaphorically, a thought experiment posits a hypothesis, a principle or a situation, for the purpose of thinking through its ultimate consequences. Thought experiments display a patterned way of thinking, designed to explain, predict or control (possible) events.

The films of Lars von Trier can serve as especially apt examples of 'film as thought experiment'. His first public statements on cinema emerged at a time and in a climate of intense speculation over the current state and future of cinema: the famous *Dogme* manifesto was launched at a conference in Paris in 1995, entitled 'Le cinéma – vers son deuxième siècle' (Cinema – towards its second century), where one of the main organizers, the critic Jean Douchet, launched a frontal attack on digital images.[12] By contrast, in a typically wily counter-move, Lars von Trier and his co-conspirator Thomas Vinterberg produced a document that could either be read as a 'back to basics' plea, in line with Douchet's conservative cinephilia, or as a bold if coded call for a new cinema fully embracing the (ontological, as opposed to technical) challenges of the digital turn.[13] Thus, von Trier was one of the first directors to intervene in the 'end of cinema' debate, by proposing a repositioning of the cinema altogether. He has been testing, refining, modifying, subverting and recasting the *Dogme* principles ever since.

---

[10] As examined in Chapter 3, the idea of films as thought experiments has in recent years been widely discussed within the 'film and philosophy' debate. See, for instance, Thomas Wartenberg, *Thinking on Screen: Film as Philosophy* (London: Routledge, 2007), 56–65, and Thomas McClelland, 'The Philosophy of Film And Film as Philosophy', *Cinema: Journal of Philosophy and the Moving Image* 2 (2011): 11–35.

[11] For a contemporary reading of Dürer's engraving, see Hartmut Böhme, *Albrecht Dürer, Melencolia I: im Labyrinth der Deutung* (Frankfurt: Fischer, 1989).

[12] 'The shift towards virtual reality is a shift from one type of thinking to another, a shift in purpose, which modifies, disturbs, perhaps even perverts man's relation to what is real. [Today] cinema has given up the purpose and the thinking behind individual shots, in favour of images – rootless, textureless images – designed to violently impress by constantly inflating their spectacular qualities.' *Le Cinéma: Vers son deuxième siècle*, conference held at the Odéon, Paris, 20 March 1995. Press handout of Jean Douchet's lecture, in English, 1.

[13] The text of the *Dogme* 95 manifesto can be found at http://en.wikipedia.org/wiki/Dogme_95. For a more in-depth analysis, see John Robert, 'Dogme 95', *New Left Review* 1, no. 238 (November–December 1999): 138–44, and Mette Hjort, *Small Nation, Global Cinema: The New Danish Cinema* (Minneapolis: University of Minnesota Press, 2005).

On the threshold of the digital, 'film as thought experiment' sets out to repudiate our way of looking at cinema as a form of representation, to which categories of truth and illusion, reality and appearance might apply. Gilles Deleuze in his two cinema books forcefully argues the thesis that the particular conjunction of temporality and movement that is cinema should be called 'thinking', provided we accept a mode of thought that is based on a logic of connection, conjunction and inclusive disjunction rather than one solely based on predication, that is on 'language' or on the binary logic of the excluded middle.[14]

In addition, thanks to philosophers like Deleuze, but also Stanley Cavell, Robert Pippin, Jacques Rancière and others, we now tend to treat films as 'strong texts', creating their own conceptual frames of reference; we interrogate them as we would a text of theory, or we regard them as allegories of their own conditions of possibility. Our readings of Lars von Trier are in some sense predicated on such a hermeneutic move – except we do not always spell out the principles we apply – but the result is that we are able to confirm to ourselves that von Trier, even when he is *spassing* us, is not only a gifted director and acute witness of the age, but also a 'thinker in cinema' who has important things to say on issues in philosophy, critical theory and ethics, or – as may be the case – on 'gender, power and politics'.

In this context, the thought experiment intervenes as a different kind of entity: its realism, such as it is, is of a stylized kind, its narrative situations are often schematic or inherently implausible or far-fetched, the characters' psychological make-up is extreme or borders on the pathological, and their motivation is either left obscure or is manifestly perverse. All this applies to von Trier's films and shifts the critical focus to character configuration and the structure or dynamics of a given situation, often set up early in the film, across which the rest of the film tests the variations and permutations. Perhaps the tenth commandment of the *Dogme 95* manifesto – 'the director must not be credited' – can also be read in this way, as indicative that the director has merely prepared the conditions and set the rules: the situation and constellation then take their own course, with a kind of unpredictable but relentless momentum.[15]

Lars von Trier's films would be an instance of one version – the European version – of a specialized kind of thought experiment, which I have called – following Trier himself but more often applicable to American and Asian

[14] Gilles Deleuze, *Cinema I: The Movement-Image*, trans. Hugh Tomlinson (Minneapolis: University of Minnesota Press, 1986), and *Cinema II: The Time-Image*, trans. Hugh Tomlinson (Minneapolis: University of Minnesota Press, 1989).

[15] For more on von Trier's films as thought experiments, see Chapters 3 and 12.

films – 'mind-game films'.[16] Mind-game films often feature protagonists who are in some ways marked by what the rest of the world sees as a disability, an illness or affliction, but which these characters experience as a special gift or distinction. Von Trier's female protagonists – from Beth in *Breaking the Waves* to Selma in *Dancer in the Dark*, from 'She' in *Antichrist* to Joe in *Nymphomaniac* – would be examples of such characters with 'productive pathologies'.[17]

'What if . . .'

Among these several options from von Trier's films, I have chosen *Melancholia*, because its narrative premise only makes sense as a hypothetical case. It poses the problem of the 'what if' of the thought experiment in such an extreme manner, that it thereby directly challenges the idea of cinema as a mode of representation, because it purports to represent the very epitome of the unrepresentable: the extinction of the planet itself and thus of any possible subject that could witness or observe it. To paraphrase Jean-François Lyotard's remark of what until now has counted as the epitome of the unrepresentable, the Holocaust, *Melancholia*, too, assumes the destruction of the very instruments able to record it. Putting it in these terms raises the stakes, and asks us to consider what, if any, 'limits of representation' von Trier's film invokes, or whether it sets out to deploy the means of digital cinema – now understood as post-cinema, as non-cinema, or as cinema 'probing the limits of representation' – precisely in order to represent the unrepresentable. A critic who comes close to making this point has noted:

> The extreme slow motion shots are as if carved in hyper-real temporality, suggesting a journey into dead time, a time frozen in eternity. This opening implies that the story is to be understood as a flash back, but strangely without a point of view, other than that of Justine's face in close up with her jelled locks fashioned as thorny outgrowths, framed by birds and leaves caught in their descent, coupled with a haunting soundtrack. It is as if the perspective is that of post-mortem, of the dead, of all of those

[16] Thomas Elsaesser, 'The Mind-Game Film', in Warren Buckland (ed.), *Puzzle Films: Complex Storytelling in Contemporary Cinema* (Hoboken, NJ: Wiley-Blackwell, 2009), 13–41. Drew Grant, the reviewer of *Salon.com*, did not particularly like *Melancholia*, yet she accurately identified its generic make-up as a mind-game film. Titling her review 'What happens when *Rachel Getting Married* meets *Donnie Darko*?', she ended a sarcastic summary of the plot's supposed inanities and improbabilities with the backhanded compliment that 'it could be *Festen* [Thomas Vinterberg] meets *Southland Tales* [Richard Kelly], which is a film I would very much like to see', Drew Grant, 'Lars von Trier's "Melancholia": an apocalyptic wedding', *Salon.com*, 8 April 2011, http://www.salon.com/2011/04/08/melancholia_trailer_von_trier/ (accessed 10 January 2017).

[17] For more on productive pathologies, see Elsaesser, 'The Mind-Game Film', 24–30.

> who will be subsequently living to die until the slow motion shots in the opening match to complete the circle. Who then, survives to narrate the story, none . . . but cinema alone![18]

Not only does this rhetorical question 'who survives – the cinema alone' suggest the special status of cinema as outliving or outlasting in some sense mankind itself, as if to intimate that the purpose of the world might be to end up as a film, but it also implies the reverse – that everything recorded on film has its existence fatally re- and devalued, and can be handed over to destruction.[19] More specifically when understood as thought experiments, many of von Trier's films rely on situations that at first sight seem improbable or arbitrary, but are set up in order to examine the consequences of taking extreme positions, without deviation, compromise or hesitation. Insofar as these are versions of 'what if' scenarios, they are both in line with (and a response to) a typical feature of contemporary social life, namely the tendency towards testing: running tests and simulations to determine possible outcomes on every conceivable topic, be it in matters of health or finance, policy calculations or insurance risks, weaponry or consumer products.[20] What is special and unique about von Trier is that he takes moral dilemmas and intractable personal relations, such as gender a-symmetry or couple relations, but also concepts such as 'liberty', the 'social contract', 'justice, faith, trust' or key social roles such as 'motherhood', and puts them to the test, by running them through his lab procedures in order to observe the outcome.

It is this apparent coldness of *Melancholia* that divided critics, eliciting often ambiguous or even self-contradictory appraisals.[21] The *Guardian*'s

---

[18] Priyaa Ghosh, 'Melodrama of Melancholia', *Edit Room*, 4 January 2012, http://blogs.widescreenjournal.org/?p=2275 (accessed 10 January 2017).

[19] This is a powerful thought, often hinted at when documentaries invariably collude with the destruction of that which they claim to discover and record, but whose small change, as it were, is our habit of looking at the world's sights and wonders merely though a viewfinder, snapping them on our cell phones and moving on, no longer giving the object itself more than a passing glance.

[20] See Avital Ronnell, *The Test Drive: A Philosophical and Cultural Analysis of the Motivation for and Ubiquity of Testing* (Chicago: University of Illinois Press, 2007).

[21] *Melancholia*, it will be recalled, was a media event before it had even been properly released. It provoked the single most noted scandal of the Cannes 2011 Film Festival, when the director, asked about his reaction to discovering that his biological father wasn't Jewish, as he had been led to believe, but of German extraction, claimed to now know what it feels like to be a Nazi. As the video with the unfortunate remark went viral on the web, and the press went into a feeding-frenzy, the Cannes board of directors declared the Danish director, a former Palme d'Or winner and festival favourite for his *enfant terrible* image as much as his taboo-breaking films, 'persona non grata, with effect immediately'. This apparently despite the fact that the organizers had asked the director for an explanation, and he had posted his apology: 'If I have hurt someone this morning by the words I said at the press conference, I sincerely apologize. I am not anti-Semitic or racially prejudiced in any way, nor am I a Nazi.' But his contrition was clearly not sufficient for the board, and von Trier – though not his film – was banned from Cannes. See my comment on the further significance of the incident in Chapter 12.

Peter Bradshaw found the film 'entirely ridiculous, often quite boring, with a script showing worrying signs of being cobbled together', but ended his review with an apparent non-sequitur: 'for all its silliness and self-consciousness, [*Melancholia*] is the happiest experience I've had with von Trier for some time'.[22] Writing for the *Observer*, Philip French concluded that 'the movie is heavy, though without weight or gravitas – a solipsistic, narcissistic, inhuman affair', but discovers pertinent Shakespearean echoes:

> *Melancholia*, like von Trier's oeuvre as a whole, is, to quote the most famous, most melancholy of Danes, 'sicklied o'er with the pale cast of thought.' Indeed like Hamlet, von Trier is a depressed, attention-seeking malcontent, forever insulting and playing malevolent games with those around him and inventing dramas such as Hamlet's 'The Mousetrap', designed to disturb and expose the audience and leave it in a state of disarray.[23]

Looked at more dispassionately, French's comparison is quite apt: 'The Mousetrap' in *Hamlet* as a *mise en abîme* of the main plot might well serve as theatrical precedent for both mind-game films and thought experiments, since von Trier routinely plays cat and mouse with his audience's moral and emotional responses, while Hamlet does indeed set up a 'what if' scenario in order to observe the outcome, thereby testing something that cannot be proven directly: 'the (bad) conscience of a king'. To think of *Melancholia* as staging a play-within-a-play has the further advantage of highlighting the way part one and part two both mirror and inverse each other, set off as they are by different cinematic styles as well as distinct ethical-metaphysical perspectives.

As will be recalled, the film has two acts and a prologue: the prologue consists of a series of tableau shots in extreme slow motion, which prefigures several of the key scenes in the film to come, and end with the collision between Earth and Melancholia. Noteworthy is the fact that this section opens with Justine looking straight ahead – at us, but also past us and through us. As Christiane Striewski remarked, 'The overture with which *Melancholia* sets in, does literally what the cinema does best: it makes us see.'[24] To which I would add, it makes us see that there is nothing (more) to

[22] Peter Bradshaw, 'Lars von Trier, *Melancholia*', *Guardian*, 29 September 2011, http://www.theguardian.com/film/2011/sep/29/melancholia-film-review (accessed 10 January 2017).

[23] Philip French, 'Lars von Trier's would-be apocalyptic take on the end of the world is a narcissistic and humourless exercise', *Observer*, 2 October 2011, http://www.theguardian.com/film/2011/oct/02/melancholia-lars-von-trier-review (accessed 10 January 2017).

[24] Christiane Striewski, 'Nichts, das ist kein schlechter Slogan', *Perlentaucher*, 3 November 2011, http://www.perlentaucher.de/essay/nichts-das-ist-kein-schlechter-slogan.html (accessed 14 June 2015).

see. The missing reverse shot folds Justine's diegetic outer field of vision into an inner world of lunar beauty and destructive force, at the same time as it alerts the audience, anxious to deflect this direct gaze, that they will be implicated in the film in ways that are indeed 'designed to disturb and expose'.[25]

The first part, called 'Justine', is taken up mostly with her disastrous wedding reception at Claire's husband's palatial country house, filmed in typical *Dogme* style, hand-held camera and fly-on-the wall realism, its unravelling of family bonds and social decorum presented as a pastiche of Thomas Vinterberg's paradigmatic *Festen*. The second part, entitled 'Claire', starts with Justine coming to stay with Claire, her husband John and their son Leo. At first unable to carry on a normal life, Justine eventually gets better over time, thanks to Claire's ministrations. John, an amateur astronomer, explains that Melancholia, the massive blue telluric planet that had before been hidden behind the sun, has become visible in the sky, and is approaching Earth. Excited by the prospect of a rare cosmic spectacle, he and Leo prepare for the 'fly-by' expected by scientists, confident that Earth and Melancholia will pass by each other without colliding.

Claire, on the other hand, is becoming ever more fearful, believing the end of the world to be imminent. After a search on the internet, she reads about the slingshot effect, and using her son's makeshift wire-contraption, realizes that Melancholia has not passed Earth, but is circling back and will collide with Earth after all. John, also now aware that he was wrong, commits suicide by taking a pill overdose. Justine, on the other hand, seems to grow more composed and faces the impending doom with stoic equanimity and even quiet satisfaction. As Claire becomes increasingly agitated, Justine grows uncannily calm, preparing for the coming event by building a teepee with Leo, where the three huddle and hold hands as the collision occurs and they are enveloped by a huge fireball. Given that the central parts of the film are named after the two sisters, it is significant that one key structural feature and psychological enigma of the film is the reversal of the power relation between the sisters, the shift from Claire as the dominant to Justine as the more resilient. The play-within-the-play, or *mise en abîme* structure, thus takes two principal forms: one concerns the status of the prologue as a frame tale, 'nesting' the subsequent narrative in an uncertain temporal and causal relation to this prologue, but confirming Justine as the 'author' of what we are given (not) to see, and – following on from this – the way von Trier eventually flips our fascination with these oneiric images when we realize the extent to which for much of the second part we are seduced into sharing Justine's chillingly beautiful version of life, all but voided of meaning.

[25] Striewski, 'Nichts, das ist kein schlechter Slogan'.

Critical contexts, hermeneutic moves and frames of reference

In what follows I want to reconcile such 'end of . . .' cinematic melancholy with the proposed status of contemporary films as thought experiments; first of all, by issuing a disclaimer: the relation of film to philosophy has to be specified and needs to acknowledge its limits. As Tom McClelland concluded, 'Though film cannot itself perform full philosophical exercises, it can make an active contribution to such exercises by presenting narratives to its audience that serve the role of thought-experiments. In this way film can actively prompt us to reach the general and precise propositions characteristic of philosophy, despite its inability to express such propositions itself.'[26] In other words, films as thought experiments, if they cannot formulate philosophical propositions proper, can prompt us to 'reach general and precise propositions', which is to say, can enable several – equally valid, equally consistent – interpretative moves and hermeneutic strategies. The 'voiding of meaning' of the melancholy cast of mind would thus be something like a tabula rasa moment, creating a precondition for thinking differently, for thinking in several dimensions at once: a characteristic of the thought experiment as well as of the mind game.

The second objective is to argue that to think of *Melancholia* as a thought experiment does not preclude other hermeneutic approaches, but invites them as 'what-if' hypotheses. Similar to the frame tales, *mise en abîme* constructions or mind-game narratives from *The Cabinet of Dr Caligari* (1920) to *Inception* (2010), the point to make is that *Melancholia*'s status as a thought experiment is strengthened by the film's ability to solicit a number of interpretations within precise conceptual frameworks.[27] Some of these will be discussed below, privileging those that focus on melancholy as a psychological condition, but not excluding others. At the same time, each hermeneutic move can be a 'mousetrap' of sorts that catches the spectator at his or her own projective game, insofar as such interpretations 'make sense', while also reversing or even seeming to contradict each other. At a meta level, this raises the question of what constraints could either limit the validity of such readings or help discover the common denominator that unites them under a compelling core concern. It will be addressed in the final

---

[26] McClelland, loc. cit., http://cjpmi.ifl.pt/2-mcclelland (accessed 14 June 2015).

[27] 'Lars von Trier's *Melancholia* is the kind of film critics love: enigmatic, stunning, beautiful, self-conscious, and rich in philosophical, historical, and cinematic references. *Melancholia makes us write*. As if to say, "No, no – the Earth has not been destroyed. I know you, *Melancholia*; I interpret you; I own you."' Bettina Mathes, 'Waiting to Happen', *Division Review* 7 (Spring 2013): 44. Prefaced with a quote from Melanie Klein, the review that follows this passage uses a Kleinian conceptual framework; www.bettinamathes.net/resources/D-R-Melancholia-printed.pdf (accessed 14 June 2015).

section, where a cluster of interrelated paradoxes are shown to address a problem that may only have hypothetical solutions.

A further point is relevant: because Lars von Trier uses us, the audience, for his own purposes (whatever these may be, from film to film),[28] the temptation is to use his films for our own critical agendas. This can produce a sense of welcome mastery (we have the director on the hook, however much he might wriggle) or its opposite: a nagging frustration, because sensing the limits of our own powers as readers, we come to suspect that our interpretative games are either internally self-validating, making of the films mere illustrative material, or are already accommodated and thus targeted by von Trier himself, in order to better engage or rile us. Put in the terms of the games the characters play in his film *The Idiots* (1999), if von Trier tries to 'spass' us, that is, provoke us into revealing our hidden assumptions and facing our own prejudices, is it for a Socratic purpose of self-reflexivity and humility, or just a prankster's inability to be serious about anything? Lars von Trier has always been a master at this, trying to put us into cognitive double binds, making us worry whether he is a misogynist or a feminist, a shameless self-promoter or a Danish ironist in the mold of Kierkegaard, wrestling with metaphysical angst or merely out to provoke, whether he is the *Dogme* iconoclast when it comes to breaking cinematic conventions, or at heart an old-fashioned genre director, perfectly at home with melodrama and horror, film noir and musical comedy, television series formats as well as out-and-out avant-garde experiments.

However, beyond the mousetraps of (illusory) mastery and (self-)doubt thus sprung, the hermeneutic moves and implicit philosophical propositions can also liberate the mind by generating hypotheticals. With respect to *Melancholia*, the combination of undecidability (regarding mood and texture) and reversibility (in the power relations between sisters, husbands and wives) can be especially productive, allowing for a number of 'what-if' scenarios, once one gets past the critics' perplexed or outraged responses. As I sketch several such interpretations – 'auteurist', psychoanalytic, feminist – the idea will be to show how these can support the philosophical propositions of a thought experiment in general, and how they connect with von Trier's mind games in particular.

Male and female depression – with Lacan, Žižek and Stanley Cavell

The most prevalent critical context for European auteur cinema, especially when premiered at prestigious film festivals (such as Cannes) in the presence

[28] According to Philip French, 'to disorient and disturb'. Peter Bradshaw is more blunt; he calls von Trier 'a wind-up merchant' ('Windup merchant Lars von Trier is back with a film about the end of the world – but it's not to be taken entirely seriously'). See references above (notes 21 and 22).

of the director, is still a biographical or autobiographical interpretation, and von Trier's public persona, as well as his pronouncements, do little to discourage such readings. Thus we learn that the idea for the film appears to have originated during a therapy session when von Trier, being treated for his bouts of depression, was told by a therapist that depressive people tend to act more calmly than others under pressure, because they already expect the worst to happen. Von Trier then developed the story not primarily as a cosmic disaster film, and without any ambition to portray astrophysics realistically, but as a way to examine the human psyche during calamities, whether man-made or natural. Once settled on an 'end of the world' scenario, von Trier decided early on that it would be clear from the outset that the planet would collide with Earth, so that audiences would not be distracted by the suspense of not knowing.[29]

The concept of the two sisters as main characters developed via an exchange of letters between von Trier and the Spanish actress Penélope Cruz. Cruz wrote that she would like to work with Trier, and spoke enthusiastically about the play *The Maids* by Jean Genet. As von Trier subsequently tried to write a role for the actress, the two maids from the play evolved into the sisters Justine and Claire in *Melancholia*. In other words, Cruz was initially expected to play the lead, but dropped out when the filming schedule of another project was changed. Von Trier then offered the role to Kirsten Dunst, who had been suggested by the American filmmaker Paul Thomas Anderson (the director of *Magnolia* (1999) – another 'end of the world' film in the art-house mode) during a discussion about the film between him and von Trier.

This could be called the biographical-auteurist reading, where the vicissitudes of casting expose a different dynamics between the sisters, which refers us first of all to Jean Genet, but via the notorious *fait divers* that inspired Genet – the Papin sisters who murdered their employers, a mother and daughter – associates Jacques Lacan's first published essay, 'Motifs du crime paranoïaque – Le crime des sœurs Papin' (Motives of Paranoiac Crime – The Crime of the Papin Sisters).[30] Given that the incident also preoccupied Jean-Paul Sartre and Simone de Beauvoir, the fact that behind Claire and Justine stands an entire erotico-philosophical-psychoanalytic tradition, with deep resonances across the arts and the humanities, considerably raises the stakes for us as interpreters, potentially taking the film right out of the autobiographical realm. At the same time, in view of von Trier's fondness for trilogies or series, the intertext of *Melancholia* might have been von Trier's own previous film,

---

[29] See various interviews, for instance http://www.dfi.dk/Service/English/News-and-publications/FILM-Magazine/Artikler-fra-tidsskriftet-FILM/72/The-Only-Redeeming-Factor-is-the-World-Ending.aspx, and Cannes Press Kit, downloadable at http://www.festival-cannes.com/assets/Image/Direct/042199.pdf (both accessed 14 June 2015).

[30] Lacan's essay was published in the surrealist journal *Minotaure* 3/4 (1933–4).

Antichrist, in which Claire, aka Charlotte Gainsbourg, played the terminally depressive, destructive-self-destructive She (to be followed by Gainsbourg's Joe in *Nymphomaniac*). Choosing Penélope Cruz, on the other hand, would have been a nod in the direction of Pedro Almodóvar's *Volver* (2006), where she plays Raimonda, a woman willing to hide in a deep-freeze the husband her daughter had just killed with a knife, now retroactively resonating with parallels to Genet's *The Maids*, but with a twist: the switch of victims as perpetrators or perpetrators as victims.

A further auteurist, but more trans-individual reading would note that rather than with Terrence Malick's *Tree of Life* (2011), shown in Cannes the same year and frequently compared with *Melancholia* by critics and academic commentators, the more pertinent analogies would be between Lars von Trier and David Lynch, since both directors have specialized in making films about female depression: in von Trier's case, this applies to *Breaking the Waves*, *Dancer in the Dark*, *Dogville*, *Manderley*, *Antichrist*, *Melancholia* and *Nymphomaniac*, while among David Lynch's films one could name *Blue Velvet*, *Twin Peaks*, *Mulholland Drive* and *Inland Empire*. Even without citing Roberto Rossellini's films with Ingrid Bergman (*Voyage in Italy*, *Stromboli*, *Europe 51*), Ingmar Bergman's *Persona* or *The Passion of Anna*, Antonioni's *Red Desert* or *La Notte*, Tarkowski's *Nostalghia*, or Kieslowski's *Three Colors: Blue* and *La Double Vie de Véronique*, it is remarkable how central the depressive female has been for European cinema. In fact, in recent years, Juliette Binoche has made this role her forte, not only in *Blue* and *Code Inconnu*: she takes it to perfection in Abbas Kiarostami's *Copie Conforme*. If melancholia is a state of being that is uncommunicative to the outside, the fact of showing female protagonists as its afflicted bearers would act as an amplifier, given our culture's identification of women with empathy and multiple affective channels attaching them to the world and to others. *Melancholia* accentuates the rift between inner self and outer reality, even signalling the kind of post-traumatic condition that Hal Foster typified as 'it hurts so much, I can't feel a thing'.[31] Lynch and von Trier would then be directors who establish a gap between body and the senses, via female depression and melancholia, staging in their heroines acts of protest or refusal. This in turn could be interpreted politically or psychoanalytically: a (Freudian) unwillingness to abandon the lost object, or a (post-patriarchal) refusal to accede to the symbolic order – of marriage, the law of the father, societal norms – but also to any imaginary sensory plenitude. What seems like masochism can be a different form of externalization, which works via 'perverse' identifications: for instance, with the aggressor, in order to regain agency, if one concedes that female depression turns on problems of agency and identification – a point to which I shall return. In a Lacanian reading this would indicate the depressive's closer relation to the

[31] Hal Foster, 'Obscene, Abject, Traumatic', *October* 78 (Autumn 1996): 106–24.

Real, heroically depriving herself of the support of either the imaginary (desire, fantasy) or the symbolic (law, rules) as external constraints.

Such a conjunction of melancholia and women protagonists invites several paths of analysis: for instance, one from a (female) feminist perspective, in particular the re-readings of Freud by Julia Kristeva and Judith Butler, and one from a male (feminist?) perspective, such as Freud re-read by Slavoj Žižek, but also by Stanley Cavell, notably in Cavell's *Contesting Tears: The Hollywood Melodrama of the Unknown Woman*.[32] Both Žižek (referring himself to Lacan) and Cavell (exploring the ramifications of philosophical scepticism) have highlighted the mutual deadlock of the genders. In Lacan, we find the notorious formula 'woman doesn't exist', or 'woman is a function of man', implying that 'she' depends on 'him' to tell her who she is, but if he does not know what 'she' wants, there is a deadlock, a stalemate. Seeking to elucidate these enigmatic statements, Žižek has devoted several studies to the issue of female depression, in particular by analysing the films of David Lynch, by focusing on the reversibility of cause and effect, and on retroactive causality as being grounded in the asymmetry of gender relations.[33]

---

[32] Stanley Cavell, *Contesting Tears: The Hollywood Melodrama of the Unknown Woman* (Chicago: University of Chicago Press, 1997).

[33] '[T]he elementary matrix of the relationship between cause and effect is offered by the sexual relationship. In the last analysis, the irreducible gap that separates an effect from its cause amounts to the fact that "not all of feminine enjoyment is an effect of the masculine cause." ... At the center of *Blue Velvet* (and of all of Lynch's opus), there is the enigma of woman's depression. That the fatal Dorothy (Isabella Rossellini) is depressed goes without saying, since the reasons for it seem obvious: her child and husband were kidnapped by cruel Frank (Denis Hopper). The causal link seems thus clear and unambiguous. Frank is the cause of all troubles, he broke into the happy family and provoked the trauma; Dorothy's masochistic enjoyment is a simple after-effect of this initial shock – the victim is so bewildered and thrown off by the sadistic violence she is subjected to, that she "identifies with the aggressor" and sets out to imitate his game. However, a detailed analysis of the most famous scene from *Blue Velvet* – the sadomasochistic sexual play between Dorothy and Frank, observed by Jeffrey (Kyle MacLachlan) while he is hiding in the closet – requires us to reverse the entire perspective [for there is] a third possible reading, centered on Dorothy ... [My point is] the following: what if – bearing in mind that, with woman, the linear causal link is suspended, and even reversed – *depression is the original fact?* What if depression comes first, and all subsequent activity – Frank's terrorizing of Dorothy – far from being its cause, is rather a desperate "therapeutic" attempt to prevent her from sliding into the abyss of absolute depression, a kind of "electroshock" therapy which endeavors to attract her attention? ... In this sense, Lynch can be said to be a true anti-Weininger. In Otto Weininger's *Sex and Character*, the paradigm of modern anti-feminism, woman proposes herself to man, endeavoring to attract and fascinate his gaze and thus drag him down from spiritual heights into the lowliness of sexual debauchery ... [For] Lynch, the "original fact" is woman's depression, her sliding into the abyss of self-annihilation and absolute lethargy, whereas man, on the contrary, proposes himself to woman as the object of her gaze. Man "bombards" her with shocks in order to arouse her attention and thereby shake her out of her numbness in short, in order to re-include or reinstate her in the "proper" order of causality.' Slavoj Žižek, 'David Lynch, or, Feminine Depression', in *The Metastases of Enjoyment: Six Essays on Women and Causality* (London: Verso, 1994), 119–20.

In Cavell, the deadlock takes the form of 'gendering' post-Kantian scepticism. Scepticism, the philosophical issue whose apparent resolution attracted Cavell to Wittgenstein and ordinary language philosophy, turns out to be a problem – as well as the displacement of a problem – constitutive of the male. Cavell traces it back to the break-up of the feudal order, tied to legitimacy and inheritance, and grounded in the doubts expressed most poignantly in Shakespearean tragedy, such as in *Othello* or *King Lear*, but articulated most nakedly in *The Winter's Tale*, which turn on the question of whether men can ever really know that their children are theirs.[34] With this formulation, Cavell seeks to rephrase issues of recognition, the search for the lost object and its miscognition, which he sees enacted in the Hollywood melodramas of the unknown woman.

Melodrama valorizes several different temporalities: from the empty time of waiting, to the 'too late' of missed encounters as well as the temporality of 'if only' (i.e., remorse and regret): all conditions of repetition and return, but marked crucially by gaps that open up between an event and its return in the constitution of the subject. Both trauma and melodrama know and speak about this repetition, but from the vantage point of a barrier, a limit. This limit – the blockage to exchange, or to 'conversation' in Cavell's terms – is what Cavell calls 'female subjectivity', 'the woman's insistence on unknownness' – her willingness to sustain the irrecoverable loss, that is, melancholy, for the sake of this unknownness, in the double bind of gendered subjectivity. The first part of von Trier's *Melancholia* very much plays like such a family melodrama, where Justine's increasing isolation and alienation from her husband-to-be is explicitly coded around the question of 'What does the woman want?', in the form of a gift from her husband that she both wants and does not want, leaving her in a paralysing blockage of affect and agency, withdrawing into an unknownness to which the groom/husband can only respond with the violence of physical force.[35]

Julia Kristeva's *Black Sun of Melancholia*

The paradoxes of such mutually generated deadlocks between failed communicative exchange and successful refusal-withdrawal ('unknownness')

---

[34] Luckily for Shakespeare – and also Cavell – DNA paternity tests had not yet been invented.

[35] '[Lacan's] "not-all" designates inconsistency and not incompleteness: in the reaction of a woman, there is always something unforeseen. A woman never reacts as expected – all of a sudden, she does not react to something that, up to that time, infallibly aroused her, yet she is aroused by something that a man does in passing, inadvertently. Woman is not fully submitted to the causal link. With her, this linear order of causality breaks down or, to quote Nicholas Cage when, in Lynch's *Wild at Heart*, he is surprised by an unexpected reaction of Laura Dern's: "The way your mind works is God's own private mystery."' Žižek, 'David Lynch, or, Feminine Depression', 119.

requires further probing. Complementing the male take on (female) depression in Cavell's *Contested Tears*, one must turn to Julia Kristeva, the theorist par excellence who has devoted much of her critical work to the enigmas of female melancholia, notably in her two books *Powers of Horror: An Essay on Abjection* (1982) and *Black Sun: Depression and Melancholia* (1990). From among Kristeva's many subtle and intricate arguments, the features of her theory particularly relevant to a reading of von Trier's *Melancholia* would seem to be her return to Freud's paper on 'Mourning and Melancholia'. There, Freud makes his famous distinction between two ways of dealing with loss, grief and absence. He sees mourning as the 'normal' way to deal with loss, the necessarily painful abandonment from what has been lost, a way of withdrawing libidinal investment from the lost object/person over time, eventually achieving closure. In the case of 'melancholia', it is not clear what has been lost because the identification/investment has involved unconscious components, such as over-identification or ambivalent self-identification. The unconscious components entail a loss of self-regard and a sense that it is the ego which is emptied, not the external world. Melancholia leaves the wound open in order to keep the lost object alive. Following Freud in this, Kristeva posits a difference between male and female melancholia, and in *Black Sun* and *Powers of Horror* (female) melancholia is diagnosed as a heightened (or unresolvable) ambivalence in the attachment to the imago of the mother, the originary 'lost object' for both sexes.

In light of the Oedipal trajectory insisted on by Freud for gendered/sexed identity-formation, this process can be much more traumatic for the woman, because she not only has to transfer libido to another object, but to the (barred) object of another sex, the father, and the acceptance of castration under the sign of the phallus. Kristeva, in this respect quite an orthodox Freudian, sees female melancholia as the consequence of an abusive mother, or a mother who abandoned her female child, thereby making the transfer that leads to the formation of a stable ego immeasurably more difficult, since the sense of self is fatally tied up with the maternal image, experienced as threatening and (self-)destructive. Developing these thoughts further in *Black Sun*, depression is characterized by a denial of this normal childhood prehistory, by what Kristeva calls 'the denial of negation'. This negation – the usual infantile acceptance of the loss of oneness with the mother – is unconsciously refused by the depressive, who clings to (and dreads) the fantasy of union with the mother.[36]

It is an apt diagnosis of at least one of the mother–daughter relationships on display in *Melancholia*, that of Justine and her mother. In what seems like a textbook case, von Trier demonstrates the 'thought experiment' of the

[36] A Hollywood film, which even in its title alludes to this Kristevan constellation, is Darren Aronofsky's *Black Swan* (2010), a melodrama-horror story about a mother–daughter relationship that feels like a pastiche/homage of Julia Kristeva.

abusive mother fully enacted by Charlotte Rampling as a bitter maternal ogre, who uses the wedding reception to publicly humiliate her husband and heap scorn on her daughters and sons-in-law. Although called 'Justine', this first part shows us the energized, efficient, bustling world of Claire, in which Justine is progressively lost, ill at ease and out of place, to the point of paralysis, erratic behaviour and catatonia. The second part, while nominally devoted to 'Claire', concentrates on the now saturnine world of Justine, where Claire plays nurse to her sister, ministering to her needs, as if to make up for the nurturing mother that their own mother neglected or refused to be. Yet such help comes too late, is fraught with ambivalence or cannot compensate for what the mother did not give, and progressively it is Claire who loses her bearings to the point of panic and hysteria, further focusing the film's turning-points on the vicissitudes of motherhood, as Claire obsesses about her son Leo.

The maternal in *Melancholia*

If we follow a Kristevan reading, and put at the centre of the first part this truly abusive phallic mother, it is the proximity of the mother, and thus the return of the traumatic love object, that throws Justine off balance. In fact, Justine becomes acutely depressive only after her mother interrupts her father's giving-away speech, which shows her castrating power in full force. Justine taking a bath by absenting herself from the reception could then be seen as a way of trying to heal, reimmersing herself in the amniotic fluid, and returning to the womb of the lost mother, as it were. But we also see the price on the mother: both mother and daughter break off the reception to 'take a bath', that is, regress, reimmerse themselves into womb-like warmth and fusion, as if they wish they had never been born/separated. In this context, which points to a generational repetition, it is important that the father, played by John Hurt, is both a harmless philanderer and a useless father, indicative of the lack of paternal authority that may have set off the abusive chain reaction in the first place.

Justine will eventually emerge from this stupor by learning to embrace the destructive element of this mother-image, which is to say, by identifying with the planet, which can now be deciphered as the externalization and materialization of the maternal imago, the planet being the explicitly named metaphor of her melancholy with its inexorably destructive force. As John, the husband, throws Gaby, the mother, out of his house, so the planet 'returns', as if to make the parallel/transfer/substitution even more explicit and literal. In the logic of this family constellation, and gendered melancholia, the planet is not only the externalization/objectification of this destructive maternal force. Its collision with Earth is also ambiguously visualized, because reminiscent of a pregnant belly into which the smaller one wants to re-enter. What is destruction and annihilation for one sister is absorption and reunification for the other.

Indeed, even Claire oscillates between a friendly and a hostile view of the planet, with homely and uncanny feelings towards it. The primitive wire-sling measuring device of the planet's relative distance and proximity may be a way of 'managing' the uncanny, making it toy-like ('the moon is a sixpence'). But the images we see also remind one of a kind of monstrous pregnancy, and recall the maternal body as 'abject'[37]

In other words, once the 'benefits' of melancholy are factored in, which according to Freud are a particularly 'realistic' assessment of others as well as of one's own shortcomings, freed of illusions, past all hope, denial and self-deception, then the inexorable destructiveness of the planet can be seen as a form of (desperate, terminal) self-empowerment (on the part of Justine), different from (but perhaps nonetheless related to) the self-empowerment that Kristeva and others see in the aesthetic productivity of melancholia. It is certainly a plausible reading of the changing power relations between Justine and Claire, whose own attempts to aestheticize the impending apocalypse Justine mercilessly (dis-)qualifies as 'a piece of shit'. The more the planet and annihilation approach, the stronger, more resolute and pragmatic Justine seems to become. If viewed as the maternal body, the planet causes Claire, the successfully adjusted heterosexually socialized mother (i.e. successfully repressing the destructive side of the mother image) to feel stifled, oppressed and break down in tears, while it liberates Justine from her repressed ambivalences towards the same mother image.

As a further consequence, the Kristeva reading of female melancholia allows one to make sense of the two principal male figures. Claire's husband John, an authoritarian choleric macho version of male identity – a possible projection of the melancholic's object choice in the image of the phallic mother – collapses into nothingness, that is, commits suicide, under the pressure of the planet asserting its destructive inevitability. By contrast Michael, Justine's groom and husband to be, is a typical softie, the 'new man', all solicitude and concern, who will be rejected – along with his gift – by a Justine overcome with nameless grief. He subsequently tries to impersonate a domineering masculinity by attempting to 'take' her, thereby definitively ejecting himself from Justine's psychic economy (i.e., unconscious identifications with the phallus of the mother). In this respect, both bride and groom 'inherit' the constellation of the bride's parents, with Michael the replica of Justine's father, and Justine's escape and rape of the young man on

---

[37] A fuller version of Kristeva's positions on abjection can be found in Chapter 5, but the specific reference here is to Julia Kristeva, *Powers of Horror: An Essay on Abjection*, trans. Leon S. Roudiez (New York: Columbia University Press, 1982), 2–3. See also Anne-Marie Smith, 'The Abject, the Maternal and Melancholy', in Anne-Marie Smith, *Julia Kristeva Speaking the Unspeakable* (London: Pluto Press, 1998), 3–48.

the golf course the absurd impersonation and travesty of her mother's unfulfilled marriage.

As a practising psychoanalyst and therapist, Kristeva accepts for her patients the need for an eventual subordination and reinsertion into the symbolic order, while as a thinker and literary theorist, she valorizes the aesthetic potential that melancholia gives the woman, endowing her with that special sense of beauty and empowerment which comes from spinning the delicate web of language around the melancholy core-void of being, as well as dispassionate lucidity. In *Black Sun*, Kristeva insists on the paradox that the work of art born out of melancholy is less an act of auto-therapy than a perpetually nurtured hurt: '[W]e are confronted with an enigmatic paradox that will not cease questioning us: if loss, bereavement, and absence trigger the work of the imagination and nourish it permanently as much as they threaten and spoil it, it is also noteworthy that the work of art as fetish emerges when the activating sorrow has been repudiated.'[38]

The anatomy of melancholy and the autonomy of art

Given that both the narrative trajectory and the peculiar inversions of the sisters' power relations closely follow Kristeva's analysis of the mother–daughter dyad and even enact her paradoxical turns (leaving it open whether the parts of the film thus named are in fact devoted to Justine and to Claire, or whether each is merely seen from the other's point of view), one might rest one's case and close the interpretation by reaffirming a broadly Freudian reading. One can justify the psychoanalytic reading on the further grounds that it serves as a special *mise en abîme*, by pointing to the fact that the haunting beauty of *Melancholia*'s images – identified as the film progresses, with the perfectly clear, lunar and untouchable vision that will become Justine's – makes her the stand-in for the melancholic-as-artist and thus an alter-ego for the director, not only claiming his *auteurist* mastery, but reclaiming retroactively that disconcertingly direct look into the camera of a now no longer dreamily sleepwalking but on the contrary, piercingly 'clair'voyant Justine.

Yet this might be a premature conclusion, another hermeneutic mousetrap, and this for several reasons. For instance, Kristeva's account of Freud's 'Mourning and Melancholia' has not gone unchallenged. While she may have been aware of the dilemma of her conflicting roles as therapist and theorist, acknowledging the circularity of returning women to a patriarchal symbolic order that contributes to the production of female melancholia in

[38] Julia Kristeva, *Black Sun: Depression and Melancholia* (New York: Columbia University Press, 1992), 9.

the first place, Kristeva laid herself nonetheless open to a more fundamental critique: that her reading is heterosexist. And it is on these grounds that Judith Butler, in *The Psychic Life of Power*, mounts a deconstruction of Freud and Kristeva, insofar as both ultimately consider 'mourning' the path of psychic health and normativity. In terms of Butler's gender discourse and the valorization of same sex identity, on the other hand, it is 'melancholia' that is the more 'authentic' way of commemorating loss and being true to one's same-sex originary love object/identity, while mourning is the heterosexist way of dealing with loss, by repressing the memory of this part of one's identity. For Butler, prioritizing mourning over melancholia reflects a hegemonic normative model of object-loss and how to deal with it.[39]

Again, how can we be sure that von Trier has not allowed for this twist, too? Flaubert's claim that his female characters are alter egos[40] grants some leeway when trying to fix his films' (if not the director's) sexual orientation, even leaving aside the admission in an interview about 'his desire to be a homosexual'.[41] As pointed out, one of the great strengths of von Trier's cinema in general is the reversibility of (ideological) positions, with structured ambiguities, also with respect to gender, often poised on the cusp of their own dialectical about-face. This is no less true of *Melancholia*, so that the interpretative moves should remain proportionate to the director's own tactical moves. The hypothetical proposition would then be that the Freudian readings, Lacanian re-readings and Butlerian counter-readings should be seen to complement rather than compete with Cavell's notion of female depression as acts of resistance across the gender divide, in an open (or recursive) series of interpretations, which do not contradict but instead interpret each other. While Cavell thematizes male scepticism regarding the woman's sexual fidelity, as amenable to either comic (screwball comedy) or tragic (melodrama) generic emplotments, the addition of

---

[39] Judith Butler's most explicit critique of Julia Kristeva is in 'The Body Politics of Julia Kristeva', *Hypatia* 3, no. 3, French Feminist Philosophy (Winter 1989): 104–18. The more general argument is elaborated in Judith Butler, *The Psychic Life of Power* (Stanford, CA: Stanford University Press, 1997), 132–50.

[40] 'Trier has been open about the fact that Justine is an autobiographical character, springing from his own experience with depression. When he interviewed Charlotte Gainsbourg, Andrew O'Hehir suggested that Trier is "extracting the feminine aspects of himself and projecting them onto the screen." Gainsbourg agreed: "he is giving the parts to women, but there's a lot of himself in there." Trier himself claims that these women are not female at all, but his alter egos.' Emma Robinson, 'Lars von Trier – Misogynist?', *Cinema Scandinavia* 1 (April 2014): 13, https://www.academia.edu/6848264/Cinema_Scandinavia_Issue_1 (accessed 14 June 2015).

[41] '[V]on Trier and his cast have promoted [*Melancholia*] with vim and energy in the weeks leading up to release. . . . In his last UK interview, given to BBC Radio 3's Night Waves, the director discussed making a calendar of Björk's menstrual cycle during the shooting of *Dancer in the Dark*, his desire to be homosexual and a career spent "running around with a camera between the tits of very young women".' Cited in Catherine Shoard, 'Lars von Trier Makes Vow of Silence After Cannes Furore', *Guardian,* 5 October 2011, http://www.theguardian.com/film/2011/oct/05/lars-von-trier-cannes (accessed 10 January 2017).

the Kristeva–Butler debate reinterprets both genres as arising from the affect of female melancholia. Such an *interpretation of an interpretation* intriguingly complicates not only *Melancholia* but the social symbolic of these cinematic genres, by allowing for a normatively heterosexual version and a polemically same sex version of (female) subject formation.

A further reversal of perspective that diagnoses melancholia as a crisis not of identity or subject formation but of agency (and its blockages) within the broader context of the West's current malaise over its democracy is put forward by philosopher and art historian Boris Groys, who speaks of the 'paradox of urgency': a combination of 'intimations of mortality, of radical finitude and lack of time', which he sees as symptomatic for our epochal moment, where the enormity of the challenges confronting mankind goes hand in hand with an ominous inability to act, thus producing the kind of 'end of the world' syndrome that *Melancholia* both performs and dissects:

> A good example of this performance of urgency can be seen in Lars von Trier's film *Melancholia*. Two sisters see their approaching death in [the] form of the planet Melancholia as it draws closer to the earth, about to annihilate it. Planet Melancholia looks on them, and they read their death in the planet's neutral, objectifying gaze . . . Here we find a typical modern, secular case of extreme urgency – inescapable, yet at the same time purely contingent. The slow approach of Melancholia is a call for action. But what kind of action? One sister tries to escape this image – to save herself and her child. It is a reference to the typical Hollywood apocalyptic movie in which an attempt to escape a world catastrophe always succeeds. But the other sister welcomes the death – and becomes seduced by this image of death to the point of orgasm. Rather than spend the rest of her life warding off death, she performs a welcoming ritual – one that activates and excites her within life. Here we find a good model of two opposing ways to react to the feeling of urgency and lack of time.[42]

Thought experiments and mathematical game theory

'Urgency and the lack of time' arising from a crisis of agency is as good a description as any for the reason why the thought experiment imposes itself

[42] Boris Groys adds, 'this feeling of urgency and lack of time prevents us from making long-term projects; from basing our actions on long-term planning; from having great personal and historical expectations concerning the results of our actions'. Boris Groys, 'Under the Gaze of Theory', *e-flux* 35 (2012), http://www.e-flux.com/journal/35/68389/under-the-gaze-of-theory/ (accessed 10 January 2017).

as a strategic cinematic form for a filmmaker like von Trier, who treats the uneven struggle between the sisters as a balancing act on the cusps of several kinds of impossibilities or deadlocks, which so far have been mainly analysed across the different but also complementary psychoanalytic frames of reference. By shifting the emphasis on agency as a 'paradox of urgency', *Melancholia* emerges as a thought experiment within the broader objectives of von Trier's work, since all his films turn on three distinct hypothetical propositions that actually complement each other, to reveal the common core I mentioned earlier. The propositions are the paradox of 'creative constraints', the paradox of 'identifying with the aggressor' and the paradox of 'the prisoner's dilemma'. All three are versions of each other, depending – in true thought experiment fashion – on the perspective from which a situation is conceived or judged, and all have the same goal or pose the same question: *how to gain control and retain agency under complex, contradictory or in other ways extreme and adverse conditions*. The first of these paradoxes was already in evidence in the formulation and dissemination of the *Dogme* manifesto, also known as the 'vow' of chastity, where the salient gesture is that of the 'vow', a seemingly old-fashioned term, but useful since it emphasizes the self-assent or self-imposition of the rules which make up the manifesto. True to von Trier strategies of reversibility and structured ambivalence, critics were unable to decide whether the *Dogme* rules were meant to be observed and adhered to, or were only written down in order to be flouted; whether they were a pastiche of the rebellious gesture of the Nouvelle Vague in 1959, or a serious, albeit coded, attempt to lay down some ground rules for the cinema as it entered the digital age. Questions of realism and ontology, of the function of the moving image in a media-saturated world, and the status of filmed objects that no longer function as representations, but as realities and energies in their own right: all these aspects are touched on in the manifesto, but in a curiously indirect and oblique form, as if in disguise, performing a kind of masquerade.[43]

At issue was also the question of rules as such, or rather, the uses and functions of creative constraints, that is, of self-imposed rules. The idea of creative constraints in this specific sense of representing a solution to a problem, goes back to Jon Elster who, in *Ulysses Unbound*, defines creative constraints as ways in which, in a certain situation, one tries to anticipate the outcome by taking deliberately self-limiting initiatives.[44] Besides 'vows', von Trier will call these constraints 'obstructions', as in the film *The Five*

---

[43] A collection of essays, some of them trying to unravel the enigma, is Mette Hjørt and Scott MacKenzie (eds), *Purity and Provocation: Dogma '95* (London: BFI Publishing, 2003).

[44] Jon Elster, 'Creativity and Constraints in the Arts', in Jon Elster, *Ulysses Unbound: Studies in Rationality, Precommitment, and Constraints* (Cambridge: Cambridge University Press, 2000), 175–268. For a fuller discussion of 'creative constraints' also in relation to Lars von Trier, see Chapter 12.

Obstructions, which he imposed on his friend and mentor Jürgen Leth; more recently he explicitly referred to them as 'mind-games' notably in his commentary on his television film *The Boss of it All*.[45] According to Elster, two kinds of situations make creative constraints necessary or productive. You impose rules (constraints) on yourself, either because the environment does not give them to you, or you do not (yet) fully understand the situation or phenomenon you are confronted with. The main benefit in each case is to combat powerlessness under conditions where you are objectively not in charge. By having chosen the constraints yourself, you have a chance to regain agency and thus you are once more in control.

Quite clearly, the dilemmas of agency through self-submission apply to *Melancholia* in several senses, reflected as they also are in Žižek's and Cavell's female depression scenarios, in Kristeva's paradox of melancholy and in Groys' paradox of urgency. The second paradox – of identifying with the aggressor – is also much in evidence in *Melancholia* if we think of the rogue planet as the malevolent agent into whose force field Justine is increasingly drawn. It confirms once again that Justine is at the narrative core and creative centre of the film, while nonetheless giving Claire's desperate need for control the function of the necessary foil, in fact, making her the potential double of Justine, rather than her opposite or opponent.

Identifying with the aggressor – also known as the Stockholm syndrome – often manifests itself in intimate personal relations: it determines the power relations between a couple, and as such it is depicted in several of von Trier's films, notably *Antichrist* and *Breaking the Waves*, with Beth's sexual submission representing both a gift of love and an atonement for imagined transgression. In other of his films, identifying with the aggressor can shift the balance of a-symmetrical power relations within a community, as is the case in *Dogville* and *Manderlay*, or it can push seemingly tragic and ineluctable dilemmas to their (violent) resolution, as in *Europa* and *Dancer in the Dark*. An exceptionally explicit (and complicated) examination of the Stockholm syndrome is *Nymphomaniac*, which takes us to the next paradox.

The third paradox, the 'prisoner's dilemma', may turn out to be nothing other than a more formal version of such self-imposed, seemingly perverse or counter-intuitive strategies of maintaining control and having access to agency. It also illustrates more directly than the other two paradoxes the idea of 'cinema as thought experiment', since the prisoner's dilemma is a staple of mathematical game theory, itself the domain of thought experiments *par excellence*. In *Playing the Waves*, Jan Simons has applied game theory to Lars von Trier's films, demonstrating in detail how each one enacts a

[45] Mark Brown, 'Lookey here: Lars von Trier is at it again', *Guardian*, 8 December 2006, http://film.guardian.co.uk/News_Story/Guardian/0,,1967275,00.html?82%3A+Film+news (accessed 10 January 2017).

variation on the 'prisoner's dilemma'.[46] Simons also points out that game theory has found application in many diverse fields, such as the Cold War between the US and the Soviet Union, trade union disputes with employers, chess, poker and other multi-player competitive games, so that von Trier's interest in how communities only survive if they find a modus vivendi between antagonisms and cooperation, around self-interest and altruism, joins a wide spectrum of practical and philosophical uses of mathematical game theory:

> The basic question of the prisoner's dilemma is how to make sure I can trust the other to collaborate with me. This paradoxical formula, which is eventually an unanswerable question, is the bare bone of all of von Trier's films, and it has been developed to its extreme in *Antichrist* where the underlying uncertainty and distrust unavoidably leads up to mutual defection and destruction . . . In as far as von Trier's films keep elaborating on the basic structure of the (infinite) prisoner's dilemma, it looks as if his films will have predictable outcomes indeed: punish or perish, revenge or defeat, survival or death . . . von Trier has always succeeded in surprising his audience with completely new visual styles, cinematographic approaches, and apparently new settings and themes, to the extent that the very consistent continuity of structure and narratives in his films has hardly been noticed at all.[47]

Insofar as von Trier's 'prisoner's dilemma' scenarios are about cooperation and trusting the other, they also echo the issues of scepticism, other minds and the antagonistic relation between male violence and female unknownness already discussed in connection with Cavell and Žižek, as well as probing the conditions for communal survival, which brings us back to the fate of Western democracy and its crisis of both legitimacy and agency. These strategies for regaining agency and autonomy, under precarious, but urgent conditions of cooperation, not only describe the narrative momentum of *Melancholia*. Its successor film, *Nymphomaniac*, is an even more outstanding example of a film built on the same principles and paradoxes. *Creative constraints* are at work in the competition of how many men Joe and her friend can have sex with on a single train journey, and the Little Flock's vow

[46] For a description of 'the prisoner's dilemma', see Avinash Dixit and Barry Nalebuff, 'Prisoners' Dilemma', in *The Concise Encyclopedia of Economics*, 2008, http://www.econlib.org/library/Enc/PrisonersDilemma.html (accessed 10 January 2017).

[47] Jan Simons, 'Lars von Trier's Antichrist: Natures, Couples, Rules, Games', *Seachange: Art, Communication, Technologies* (Spring 2010) ('The Face-To-Face'): 128–9, http://www.seachangejournal.ca/PDF/2010_Face%20to%20Face/Simons_ANTICHRIST.pdf (accessed 10 January 2017). For a fuller examination of the prisoner's dilemma, see Jan Simons, *Playing the Waves: Lars von Trier's Game Cinema* (Amsterdam: Amsterdam University Press, 2007).

to have sex but no boyfriends also counts as a creative constraint. Constraints are once more foregrounded in the way Joe's narrative is triggered by the objects (and evolves around the cues) she takes from Seligman's room. *Identifying with the aggressor* in order to gain agency seems the guiding principle underlying the sadomasochistic episode with K, which frees Joe from the onerous role as a mother as well as helps her achieve orgasm, after a seemingly endless spell of 'feeling nothing'. The *prisoner's dilemma* – the third version of self-selected constraints or perverse identifications as a way of gaining freedom – typifies the framing situation of the film, namely the night that Joe and Seligman spend together: not only is Seligman's room a kind of cell; both are, in more than a merely metaphoric sense, 'prisoners' whose hope of escaping their private hell is to find a modus of cooperation, which acknowledges their differences and asymmetries, and still results in a win–win strategy. It nearly works – Joe hopes to find friendship in Seligman's company, Seligman hopes to lose his virginity – but things go horribly wrong when each misconstrues the other's message.

Cinema/melancholy

To sum up, starting with the hypothesis that there may be a connection between end of the world scenarios and end of the cinema arguments, my initial purpose was to show that both revolved around an idea of 'limits of representation': in the case of cinema, clearing the ground, as it were, for digital film which may look and behave like the films we know, but in some crucial respects constitute the groundless ground of another cinema, and with it, of another understanding of what is (the meaning of) the world. Or, in the terms of *Melancholia*, digital cinema may have 'absorbed' into itself that indexical Earth-bound cinema we built our theories on, put our hopes in and made our cinephile home – a prospect both wished for and dreaded. Loss and melancholy are deeply ingrained in our view of cinema, cinephilia being the very name for the fetish of the irretrievable moment and fidelity to its immanent loss, almost in the spirit of Judith Butler's fidelity to the primary love object.[48]

What then does it take to 'accept' digital cinema as the only sustainable future of cinema? The answer is an aesthetics of melancholy in the fullest sense, which includes both a sense of irreparable loss (as well as the grieving that goes with it) and an acknowledgement of the luminous (if lunar and cold) beauty that beckons with the swooning, Wagnerian strains of the

[48] Thomas Elsaesser, 'Cinephilia, or The Uses of Disenchantment', in Marijke De Valck, and Malte Hagener (eds), *Cinephilia: Movies, Love and Memory* (Amsterdam: Amsterdam University Press, 2005), 27–44.

Tristan overture, inviting us to yield and to submit to the longing for oblivion.

The counter-music that resists and balances this desire towards self-abandon is also founded in melancholy, as the philosopher's persistence to think beyond the limits of the possible, to imagine the unrepresentable and to pose problems that require the self-imposed rules and rigours of the thought experiment. In cinema, the thought experiment invites participation from the spectator, perhaps not in the interactive sense of augmented reality but in the form of 'augmented hermeneutics', forestalling efforts at fixing meaning, while enabling encounters with a film that allows for the exploratory play of 'what if' possibilities.

Such an 'anatomy of melancholia' would then be the ground for a new 'ontology of the cinema', whether in the sense of Cavell (for whom ontology entails redefining the felicity conditions of 'trust', 'belief' and 'faith' in the world) or in the sense of von Trier: cinema as a cold and voided world of saturnine beings and objects, producing images so beautiful and ravishing as to make reality superfluous. It would give an unintended diagnostic value to Philip French's description of *Melancholia* as 'solipsistic, narcissistic, inhuman', because he would have been characterizing (digital) cinema itself, rather than von Trier, either the man or his film. It would also put in a different perspective Werner Herzog's sentence with which I began: 'If I knew that tomorrow a meteorite would destroy our planet, I would start shooting a new film today.' For there to watch it, if we follow the logic of post-cinema, would be 'the cinema alone', signalling a move from the dystopic 'end of world' *Weltschmerz* to a possible – possible only in its persistence and fidelity to cinema – new beginning, one without requiring either rescue or redemption, free of that surfeit of meaning that is the cause of so much pain.

11

Anatomy Lesson of A Vanished Country

Christian Petzold's *Barbara*

How aware – and wary – are European directors of the kind of self-exoticism that is often the temptation of an 'auteur cinema' showcased at film festivals? On the one hand, auteurs need to assert their artistic autonomy and unique voice and vision, while on the other hand they are invariably pressed into the service of 'representing' their country, especially where they are this country's critical or dissenting voices.[1] If today it is directors from Iran, Israel and Turkey who face the dilemma of having to be 'representative' by their very unrepresentativeness, films from Central and Eastern Europe have to meet other expectations: they will be judged by how they address the communist past, while struggling to redefine their post-communist 'national identity' without becoming nationalists or trading on religious or tribal identities. One option for a director to keep his or her own voice is to make 'trilogies' – Lars von Trier, Michael Haneke – using the same actress to define a tone and a worldview. Another strategy is to create a 'school' as a unifying label. This was the case with the Danish *Dogme* movement in the mid-1990s, and more recently was tried with the Berlin School, a term launched in Paris as the 'nouvelle vague allemande', rebranded Berliner Schule in Germany and the US, conveniently forgetting (or cleverly over-writing) that there had already been a Berlin School in the 1970s. The present chapter focuses on a director in whose work several of these lines converge.

---

[1] For a fuller discussion of the contemporary auteur's dilemmas and counter-moves, see Chapter 12.

Abject bodies, abject nation

Throughout this study I have been considering a feature that has struck me as potentially threading a tenuous ribbon through different directors, schools, countries and styles. It seems symptomatic of an effort to imagine a European community from the ground up, as it were, asking what kind of social contract, what kind of singularity and what kind of community can we imagine as emerging? In an earlier chapter I outlined what I consider an important constellation of figures and tropes that has emerged, taken up by directors who try to come to terms with what I have called post-heroic narratives of identity, nationhood and community. These tropes seem to centre on the figure of the abject body, as both outcast and sacred, as both no-longer-alive and not-yet-dead, who by marking the margins of the community is nonetheless an essential part of the community.

Also in the preceding chapters we saw how such abject bodies in European cinema take different forms, come in different genders and are part of different narratives. Abject bodies challenge not only grand narratives of progress or unlimited growth; they also do not fit into the Europe of technocrats favoured by politicians, or the fusion of multitudes, as celebrated in sport and popular culture. In other words, the states of abjection in this context are not (only) the result of hospitality not extended to migrants, to the undocumented or to refugees, nor does it name those at the margins exposed to economic precariousness. Abjection can be a momentary state, a sudden realization of exclusion and groundlessness, but it also addresses the tendency of 'native' Europeans to consider themselves as victims, and mainly as victims of European history. In which case the abject bodies are both the extension and the verso of a victimhood that seems tied to the historical catastrophes still haunting Europe, even as these traumas paradoxically constitute the continent's cultural identity and moral authority. Abjection can also amount to an act of defiance, against a Europe that risks losing this moral authority, by reneging on its republican values and giving in to the pressures put on democracy by global capitalism and the dictates of 'the markets'.

In this situation, the figure of the abject fulfils a need: to place oneself outside the existing symbolic order; but it also exerts a fascination: the abject refuses the position of the victim, but asserts a stance of radical equality, which endows the abject with a certain power. It is the power of absolute negativity, resistance and refusal, embodied in the much-quoted figure of Herman Melville's Bartleby the Scrivener, who 'prefers not to'. As demonstrated in Chapter 4, this stance is embraced by several of the philosophers discussed, some of whom see Bartleby's motto asserted also in those protest movements that put no positive demands, famously the Occupy Wall Street movement, and other manifestations of the public sphere, where bodies merely insist on making their presence manifest: they refuse to go away, but they also refuse to be co-opted into any pre-existing agenda or ideology.

Authorial identity

The above is something like the outer horizon and frame of reference for an extended reading of Christian Petzold's *Barbara* (2012), a film that can be discussed under several headings: that of the distinctive themes and style of the recognized auteur, that of an actress-led trilogy (along with *Yella* (2007) and *Jerichow* (2008)), and as belonging to the Berlin School, of which Petzold is the reluctant figurehead.[2] I want to add another heading, and approach *Barbara* across a particular kind of reflexivity and self-reference, which I have called throughout this study 'film as thought experiment', across the trope of the abject body, but extended to also connote a larger entity, namely the body politic of an entire country, in this case that of the former German Democratic Republic (GDR) and its complicated relation to West- (and its afterlife within a united) Germany.

Were I to make an argument about *Barbara* reflecting Petzold's authorial identity, or defining and refining the aesthetics of the Berlin School, it would probably go something like this – here taken from the Toronto Film Festival catalogue, where *Barbara* had its North American premiere:

> Christian Petzold has established himself as the most internationally recognized representative of the so-called 'Berlin School,' the unofficial new wave of filmmakers who have reinvigorated German cinema with films marked by a precise, observational style that manages to be simultaneously enigmatic and radically lucid. Like many of his colleagues, Petzold is adept at infusing his attentive psychological and sociological portraits with genre elements, and his new film – a suspenseful chamber piece set in 1980s East Germany, which he co-wrote with . . . Harun Farocki – is no exception . . . Petzold uses his meticulously calibrated pacing and almost unnervingly crisp visual style to create a foreboding atmosphere of ever growing paranoia and claustrophobia. Working for the fifth time with his *Yella* and *Jerichow* star Hoss – whose measured, icy restraint is the perfect actorly analogue for Petzold's expertly muted style – he creates a brilliantly incisive study of what becomes of human nature when totalitarian states weave suspicion into the fabric of everyday life.[3]

---

[2] Like many of the films discussed in this study, *Barbara*, too, has given rise to extensive scholarly coverage. See references in the footnotes.

[3] Dimitri Eipides, 'Barbara', *Toronto International Film Festival 2012*, http://www.bytowne.ca/movie/barbara (accessed 4 June 2017).

This neatly combines a number of potentially incompatible attributes and condenses them into 'the Petzold paradox', while drawing an intriguing, if questionable, analogy between Petzold's minimalist style as a director and his leading actress's emotionally restrained, introvert and 'sullen' (the Stasi-officer's word) performance. These epithets have become clichés – so much so that German critics speak of 'das System Petzold', once more demonstrated to perfection in *Barbara*: 'keine Geste, kein Wort, keine Kamerabewegung ist zu viel, jede Szene ist ein eigener, kleiner Spannungsbogen für sich'.[4]

A thought experiment

Given that my ostensible purpose is to make a space for *Barbara* as part of European cinema, in the sense of films that use an inherent reflexivity in order to examine the status and current fate of the political goals and ethical values embodied in the Enlightenment, I am also contesting the notion – subscribed to by almost all commentators – that *Barbara* is a particularly realistic depiction of life under a totalitarian regime, or as Dimitri Eipides puts it, 'a brilliantly incisive study of what becomes of human nature when totalitarian states weave suspicion into the fabric of everyday life'.[5] I would argue, not very controversially, that *Barbara* is an extremely stylized film, but that the stylization is neither to heighten realism nor to block identification, but the stylization typical of what throughout I have dubbed 'film, as thought experiment'.[6]

By treating *Barbara* as a thought experiment, I mean to highlight a number of features, notably the rather schematic plot and minimalist *mise en scène*, taking the almost didactic form of a Brechtian *Lehrstück*, while also deploying the structuring devices of mirroring, doubling and repetition that characterize both fairy tales and classical Hollywood narratives.

But *Barbara* could also be regarded as a thought experiment, in the sense that it tries to recreate, as precisely as possible, the conditions of how the GDR might have looked and felt 'from the inside', at a point in time when

[4] 'No gesture, no word, no movement of the camera is superfluous. Each scene has its own dramatic arc.' Hans-Georg Rodek, 'Die Angst der Nina Hoss, sich anzuvertrauen', *Berliner Morgenpost*, 11 February 2012, http://www.morgenpost.de/kultur/berlinale/article1903370/Die-Angst-der-Nina-Hoss-sich-anzuvertrauen.html (accessed 4 June 2017).

[5] Eipides, 'Barbara'.

[6] To recapitulate the definition of the thought experiment given previously. What is a thought experiment? A thought experiment is generally understood to mean setting up an imaginary situation in order to help understand the way things really are or were, in circumstances where one does not have direct access to the phenomenon in question. Thought experiments display a patterned way of thinking, they operate under a number of self-imposed, but explicit constraints, and they are designed to explain, predict or control events, often employing subjunctive reasoning, such as 'What happens if. . .?', or 'What might have happened, if . . .?'

its rigidity, stasis and paralysis were evident to all concerned, but when there was no specific indication of whether or how this experiment in socialism might transform, adapt or terminate itself.

Thirdly, *Barbara* as a thought experiment wants to draw attention to the structuring role that the internal references to paintings and to literary works exert on the narrative arc and on the overall conception of the film, giving *Barbara* a kind of self-allegorizing and self-referential dimension, which acts as a counterweight to its purported psychological depth and outwardly so meticulously researched phenomenal realism. Most prominent, for my purposes, is Rembrandt's *The Anatomy Lesson of Dr. Nicolaes Tulp*, along with its literary and art historical interpretations.

Finally, *Barbara* as a thought experiment implies that the film poses for itself a particular problem, which the experimental set-up (or in German, *die Versuchs-Anordnung*) is meant to elucidate and elaborate. This problem may be summarized as, what to do with the double legacy of the GDR, consisting of the (almost wholly negative) image that the West has of it, and the (more ambiguously coloured) memories its own citizens have retained of it?

Concerning the life and afterlife of the GDR, the standard view is that the films which since 1990 have been made in or about the former GDR tend to come in two flavours: those tinted by mildly self-critical but also self-congratulatory nostalgia for the good old days of communal crèches, controlled rents and pickled cucumbers (the famous *Ostalgie*); and those that show a police state of arbitrary arrests, everyday fear, corrupt elites and petty chicanery, little short of the totalitarian regime that preceded it. For most of us, *Good Bye, Lenin!* (2003) stands for the first, and *The Lives of Others* (2006) for the second category. This is no doubt a gross over-simplification, but my assumption is that Petzold distances *Barbara* from the respective template used by these – it should not be forgotten – internationally immensely popular films, both of which were made by West German directors.

Petzold is credited with a personal reason for avoiding this either/or 'mental straight-jacket'.[7] His parents fled the GDR before he was born, but they retained fond memories, which frequent visits by the young Christian only confirmed and made more precious. But Petzold also had political reasons, insofar as his West Berlin training as a filmmaker took place in a milieu that was Marxist and pro-socialist, never quite relinquishing the belief in the possibility of a more just and equitable society, despite the

[7] 'Thus it all starts out as the classic tale of East versus West, freedom versus oppression, that forever wants to limit us to remaking the same old ideological choice between Stalinism and market capitalism. However, as the film goes on, Barbara develops two new relationships that bit by bit open up this mental straightjacket.' Daniel Lindvall, 'Barbara: Beyond East vs West', *Film International*, 6 September 2012, http://filmint.nu/?p=5881 (accessed 5 June 2017).

manifest failure of the state that claimed to realize these ideals. More generally, Petzold's particular challenge – the one that might be said to make a thought experiment necessary – was to prevent the viewer from inhabiting too quickly or too securely a twofold superior position of knowledge: firstly, that from hindsight (i.e. the knowledge that this oppressive and stultifying regime eventually imploded, almost from one day to the next, bankrupting not only lives and livelihoods, but sending into free fall the meaning of collective memories), and secondly, that from the superior position of a Wessi (i.e. the West German, or for that matter, the US spectator), tempted to feel self-righteous about living in a democracy, where such abuses do not happen, while quick to sort the Ossis into perpetrators, collaborators, informers and victims. In the words of Petzold:

> You see the past as present, but our present from today, our knowledge that we know that in 1989, everything would break down . . . People feel that something is happening. They feel something's dying and something will be broken and how can you live in a society that starts to vanish? Because in this society, it's not an abstraction. When the state is vanishing, your identity is vanishing, your history is vanishing, your memories are vanishing and how you can stop this entropy?[8]

'Seeing the past as present' accounts for a good deal of the pleasure of a historical film, but it is also one of its pitfalls, precisely because of this superior position of knowledge. So how to unsettle such pre-emptive certainty? One of the main resources, I think, is a subtle use of motifs that belong more to the horror film than to historical reconstruction or even to the thriller, never mind to a love story. I'm not even thinking of some obvious hints, such as the spooky tour of the cellar that the landlady or block supervisor forces upon Barbara in the early hours of the morning.[9] More

[8] Christian Petzold, in 'Christian Petzold on the Skillful Seduction of "Barbara"', interview with Stephen Saito, *Moveablefest*, 20 December 2012, http://www.moveablefest.com/moveable_fest/2012/12/christian-petzold-barbara-interview.html (accessed 5 June 2017).

[9] 'You hear the dog and you think, "okay this is maybe a horror film, the basement is dungeon, this whole thing is like a fairy tale, the old lady is taking her to a place that she didn't want to go to, she's going to show her something, later we'll go back there and find there's dead bodies there," or something. Which is also the case with the Stasi in the film, and so on. The movie keeps giving these hints of an outer world that Barbara is looking at, that she's reacting to, and yet it's all framed as a mystery that's never resolved, that might not be a mystery at all. Just like a horror film without an explanation as to the truth beneath or any kind of resolution.' David Phelps, in Daniel Kasman and David Phelps, 'Spatial Suspense: A conversation with Christian Petzold'; Christian Petzold, 'Spatial Suspense: A Conversation with Christian Petzold', interview with Daniel Kasman and David Phelps, *Mubi*, 16 October 2012, https://mubi.com/notebook/posts/spatial-suspense-a-conversation-with-christian-petzold (accessed 5 June 2017).

pervasive and effective is the soundscape carefully designed for the film, dispensing with any kind of extra-diegetic music or score.[10] Instead, the director relies on the amplified sounds of everyday objects, such as a rusty doorbell or the wind catching treetops, interspersed with eerie bird-calls and the distant barking of dogs, startling the heroine into turning around or cocking her head.[11] Apparently, it was Fassbinder's *The Merchant of Four Seasons* – the 1970s looking back at the 1950s – that inspired Petzold to let the extra space between people, their slightly delayed reaction to each other, and the amplified aural cues, signal a temporal distance that makes the past uncannily present to our senses, while removing from our minds the certitude of our knowing it, by letting the shadow of dreaded anticipation ever so slightly cloud the lush autumnal landscape and the well-lit interiors.[12]

In addition to the film having to create a temporal lag, and a narrative tense that distances the events and situations, at the same time as it brings them close, Petzold needed to balance that as viewers we not only sense the pervasive surveillance of a ubiquitous state, but also recognize our potential complicity with this surveillance, insofar as our own historical curiosity and cinematic voyeurism are scrutinizing Barbara, just as she is being scrutinized by others.

> I always had to ask myself and the cameraman: This is a movie where all people are under surveillance, but *our* camera can't share the position

---

[10] The wind in the trees – that quintessential Berlin School visual motif – can also be given a double meaning: 'The roaring wind that typically comprises the entire soundtrack for these shots is strangely comforting: it is the sound of microphones being drowned out, of surveillance deafeningly interrupted. That brief respite ends whenever Barbara makes her way back into town after nightfall, the eerie silence of idle neighborhoods and the encasing amber of streetlights trapping her once more.' Jake Cole, review of *Barbara*, *Spectrum Culture*, 20 December 2012, http://spectrumculture.com/film/barbara/ (accessed 5 June 2017).

[11] 'Then they started remembering the acoustics. They didn't have traffic [because] there [weren't] so many cars and they didn't have so many planes. But when you hear a plane or a car or even a bird, it's very loud. So I decided to throw out all the music score. The smell also opens the remembrance always. You smell something and you say, oh this reminds me of grandma and pancakes or something . . . [laughs] So for two days it's like a collective voyage into history.' Petzold, 'Christian Petzold on the Skillful Seduction of "Barbara"'.

[12] 'In East Germany, in 1980, no one is to be trusted, and Petzold creates that sense of oppression with meticulous sound design (never has a doorbell sounded so frightening), and yawning gaps in between conversations, gaps filled with sound: wind, echoing footsteps in a hallway, trees rustling, the crunch of gravel under bicycle wheels. There is no score. The only music comes from the radio, once, and when Barbara plays her newly-tuned piano alone in her apartment. Barbara's landlady stares at her with cold expressionless eyes, a piano tuner shows up unexpectedly, freaking Barbara out (he must be there to inform on her), and every interpersonal interaction is charged with suspicion.' Sheila O'Malley, *Barbara*, 6 March 2013, http://rogerebert.suntimes.com/apps/pbcs.dll/article?AID=/20130306/REVIEWS/130309996/1023 (accessed 5 June 2017).

> with the State. Therefore, our position of storytelling must be between the people, the angle of *their* eyes. Because we have to see the tension of the social life, the tension based on the surveillance – we don't want to choose the Stasi's position.[13]

And yet, in *Barbara* the marked preference for long- and medium-shots implies another's gaze, while investing a special power in the intermittent close-ups, for even these are often framed and held as if to imply she is being watched.

If these and other remarks by the director – notably about how he rehearsed the actors by making sure they felt the weight and shape of the objects from the period, as well as by playing the sounds that would eventually accompany or trigger their actions – suggest that Petzold is aiming at a certain controlled and stylized naturalism, the film itself also mounts a counter-argument, contained in the different strategies that to my mind make *Barbara* a thought experiment, one that involves testing a hypothesis under controlled but schematized conditions.

There is first of all, the schematic plot. Petzold quite generally uses stripped-down dramatic situations, condensed human relationships and laconic interactions, whose basic dramatic structure is set out from the start, then undergoes variations and permutations within this given constellation, but rarely opens up into new terrain or totally unforeseen consequences. This is true of *Die Innere Sicherheit* (2000), *Gespenster* (2005), *Yella* (2007) and *Jerichow* (2008), and it holds for *Barbara*: we have two doctors, one male, the other female, in an outwardly antagonistic but, at several levels, also mutually interdependent situation. Each has a young adult as patient, who becomes a kind of mirror or double of the main characters' predicament, more clearly in the case of Barbara, for whom Stella, the runaway teenager from a work camp, becomes an alter ego, both in the sense of a younger self and of an alternative self. But André's patient Marco, the boy who tried to commit suicide, and whom he is not sure he has diagnosed correctly, is a reminder of his earlier failure with two premature babies, who, because of an error for which he had to take responsibility, became permanently blind. Each doctor has been penalized by the authorities, assigned to a post or outpost well below their professional capabilities or qualifications. Other schematic elements in the plot are the repetitions: two train journeys, two house visits from the Stasi officer plus strip searches by a female officer, two bike-rides to the wooden cross by the sea, two trysts with her Western lover, the second one – in the Inter-Hotel – doubling her date with that of her lover's driver, whose equally blonde girlfriend visits Barbara in her room

[13] Petzold, 'Spatial Suspense: A conversation with Christian Petzold'.

while the men are away, to exchange views on engagement rings, thus giving Barbara another, more ironic double as a kept woman, for whom 'freedom' is cheap champagne, luxury lingerie and jewellery out of a mail-order catalogue.

The exchange with her lover at the Inter-Hotel also puts in sharp focus what emerges as one of the major binaries of the film: the gender roles and equality between men and women, across a mutual commitment and respect for work.[14] It is through their dedication as doctors that André and Barbara adjust, test and recalibrate their personal relationship, letting us glimpse some of the work ethos and camaraderie of the old GDR – admittedly in the relatively privileged setting of a hospital rather than a factory. In an interview, Petzold tries to bridge the gap:

> In the movies of the German Democratic Republic, they start at a factory in the morning. We start our movies when they come out of the factory, when the shift is over, and for me, the hospital is a possibility to have a factory at the heart of the movie, work as something that is more important than seduction between man and woman. Barbara opens her mind to André not because he has fantastic eyes. It's because he has skills and he knows how to work and the only people she can respect are people that can work.[15]

This respect and self-respect through work is put in sharp relief when held against the West German lover's promise that once she joins him in the West, she'd never have to work again: a not altogether subtle hint at an entirely different set of societal values and gender norms.[16] Work and love, work as love, and work versus love are the terms put in circulation. They are allowed

[14] 'Barbara shrinks at her boyfriend's suggestion that, once she's settled in the West, she'll be affluent enough that she won't have to work. In this small town deep in East Germany, work is her respite from her loneliness and the airless restraint of her surroundings, but it is also where she finds purpose and fulfillment. Work is also something that she shares with André, and as they treat patients together, she begins to let her guard down. When André offers his own story of why he ended up in the provinces, and then tells Barbara that she owes the state her services, she chafes momentarily at his moralizing but she doesn't disagree.' Anna Altman, 'Go East', *New Yorker*, 11 January 2013, http://www.newyorker.com/online/blogs/culture/2013/01/east-germany-in-barbara.html (accessed 5 June 2017).

[15] Petzold, 'Christian Petzold on the Skillful Seduction of "Barbara"'.

[16] 'In this situation work becomes the bridge between them. Only on this subject is straight communication possible. Their attraction is therefore built initially on mutual professional respect and the honest care they both express for their patients. But on this foundation the film suggests the possibility of an egalitarian and comradely ideal relationship, a possibility that puts Barbara's relationship with Jörg in a new light. It is Barbara and Jörg that most strikingly fail to communicate.' Lindvall, 'Barbara: Beyond East vs West'.

to permutate, in order to set us up for Barbara's surprise decision at the end, which thus has a retroactive logic, prepared for all along. The work–love binary is among the didactic elements that shape the film like a parable, giving it something approaching a moral, to the effect that the final denouement confirms for us – spectators of today – the importance, in the pursuit of happiness, of a fulfilling job, at a time when even in developed countries, employment is getting scarce, and for most people, takes forms that are scarcely meaningful or satisfying, even when adequately remunerated.

But *Barbara* also has the functional simplicity of a fairy tale, with ancillary characters remaining one-dimensional, unencumbered by psychology or humanizing nuance. Even Stella, the young runaway, just does one thing: run away. The Stasi officer, too, doesn't seem to do anything other than park his car outside her door, and he isn't any less odious for having a wife dying of cancer, so that Barbara can ask André, 'Do you often do this?' – and he asks, 'You mean, assisting patients to die by giving them morphine?' – to which she replies, 'No, helping ass-holes.' A nice metaphor for this aspect of the film – the use of clearly defined subsidiary characters – is also the bowl of vegetables that a grateful neighbour gives the doctor: tomatoes, onions, courgettes and aubergines, so no wonder that all André can offer Barbara is to cook her ratatouille. The director, too, shows us his ingredients, and then puts them all to good use.

Another feature of Petzold's major films is that they tend to be remakes: often of well-known or lesser-known Hollywood films, such as *Die Innere Sicherheit*, a remake of Sidney Lumet's 1988 film, *Running on Empty*, or *Jericho*, a more obvious remake of *The Postman Always Rings Twice* (1981). As Barton Byg pointed out to me, *Barbara* is the remake of the 1977 GDR film *Die Flucht* (*The Flight*), by Roland Gräf, probably better known in the GDR than in West Germany, even though its main lead as the doctor, Armin Müller-Stahl, successfully left the GDR immediately after, to become an international star. Add to this the fact that Nina Hoss evoked for many critics one of the 'icy blondes' of Hitchcock, a director Petzold has expressed immense admiration for, and *Barbara* emerges as all calculation and premeditation, drawing us in and putting us at a distance.[17] However, *Barbara*, understood as a remake not of *Marnie* but of *The Flight*, could also

[17] 'Now she's this long, gorgeous, glamorous blonde in a sleepy town of brunettes, an alien, really. The movie is set in 1980, and her expulsion is overseen by the Stasi, the oppressive East German secret police. Officers drop by to inspect both Barbara's modest apartment and eventually Barbara herself.' Wesley Morris, 'Barbara is one film to watch', *Boston.com*, 20 December 2012, http://www.boston.com/ae/movies/2012/12/20/movie-review-barbara-one-film-watch/UxzYhn0kJGHcckvJbVJ0bO/story.html (accessed 5 June 2017).

lead us back into GDR history,[18] insofar as some of the plot holes and character inconsistencies that Western critics detected in Gräf's *The Flight* – made about the then extremely touchy subject of *Republikflucht* (and brain drain) at the height of renewed tensions between West and East Germany – were inevitable for the film in order to be approved and pass the censor. Remade by Petzold thirty-eight years later, the story could be presented from a more even-handed perspective, so that hesitation whether to stay in the East or abscond to the West when given the chance no longer seems an ideological fudge, made to appease the authorities. At one point, in reply to Barbara, when somewhat scornfully, she cites the official mantra – that the GDR had schooled and trained them, so they owed the socialist collective some solidarity, as return on this investment – André says, '*Eigentlich nicht falsch*' – 'Not so wrong, after all, is it?' But since by then they are both under no illusion as to how the regime has abused (or enforced) such solidarity, their tentative willingness to live by it reflects a post-GDR awareness, or as one commentator puts it, 'In their own personal way, Barbara and André liberate the good idea from its historical cage.'[19]

Assuming that *Barbara* is a film about the GDR as much in sorrow as in anger, another way that Petzold recasts the 'GDR past' in terms more commensurate to the outsider's view and the future perfect of historical retrospection is in his treatment of surveillance. The film depicts the pervasive presence of the state not through any clunky GDR technology of spying and eavesdropping, of metal filing cabinets and faulty typewriters, as does *The*

[18] Christian Petzold has pointed out that the film is based on literary models, rather than on Gräf's film: 'There are two books that served as an inspiration for me this time: Hermann Broch's novella *Barbara*, which is set in 1928 and tells the story of a female doctor who takes a job in a rural hospital in order to hide her communist activities from the police, and Werner Bräunig's novel *Rummelplatz*. In Bräunig's book a doctor's son is consumed by physical work for the first time in a uranium mine. He defines himself through this work, which is interesting because work as a theme had almost completely disappeared from the literature and cinema in the West. Another aspect that appealed to me was that the book tells how women replaced the workers who had been wooed by the West, which somewhat gave those women a new purpose and self-understanding, and I wanted to tell a story about this.' Pamela Jahn, 'Barbara: Interview with Christian Petzold', 28 September 2012, http://www.electricsheepmagazine.co.uk/features/2012/09/28/barbara-interview-with-christian-petzold/ (accessed 5 June 2017); Christian Petzold, 'Barbara: Interview with Christian Petzold', interview with Pamela Jahn, *Electric Sheep*, 28 September 2012.

[19] 'Paradoxically, the choices that Barbara eventually ends up making – after a dramatic chain of events, that I will not detail here – could be described in terms superficially compatible with those of the ideal citizen of the GDR: an egalitarian, comradely relationship and "solidarity with the workers and peasants that have paid for her education", quoting a piece of propaganda-speak that occurs in one of Barbara and André's conversations. At that point, however, it is clear that André is as aware as Barbara is of the discrepancy between reality and propaganda. But, as he points out, "it is not *really* such a bad idea". In their own personal way, Barbara and André liberate the good idea from its historical cage.' Lindvall, 'Barbara: Beyond East vs West'.

Lives of Others, but translates it into the interpersonal dynamics of trust, doubt and distrust, of individual human beings obliged to depend on each other, both on the job and in daily life, while not knowing the grounds on which such mutual dependence can be sustained. From the start, Barbara appears as the outsider, at once reviled and envied, having to decide whether to ingratiate herself in order to integrate, or keep her integrity and independence at the price of remaining alienated, and alienating others, through her standoffishness or gruff rebuffs. As one reviewer aptly sums up her predicament,

> . . . living in a police state, you are as suspect to the state as others are to you, and you to them. This comes out nicely, if a bit too neatly, too schematically, in *Barbara*, where ostensibly conventions of the thriller and of the romance overlap: 'Am I attracted to him?' becomes, or *is*, 'Do I trust him?' 'Will I sleep with him?' becomes 'Is this man a Stasi agent?' One could hardly imagine a more exhausting existence – which certainly explains Petzold's usual steely restraint and impeccable, heightened precision: a *mise en scène* held in check as everyone in it must, too, hold themselves in reserve to forestall a tell that could mean their lives.[20]

Another reviewer focuses on the male doctor: 'André Reiser's pleasantries can be read equally as genuine romantic interest and/or ingratiating attempts to lower her guard and get her to reveal a juicy tidbit for the secret police.'[21] This balancing act is also noted by Jonathan Romney: 'The film is built on the delicate play of trust and doubt. When Barbara arrives in town, her defences raised, people see her as a haughty Berliner; she's warned not to be too "separate" (in a nation then defined by separation).'[22]

In order to demonstrate this precise *mise en scène* in action, and also to follow how Petzold establishes his theme of trust, repeats it and varies it, consider a scene near the opening, which also illustrates an earlier point, namely how each scene establishes a complete narrative arc. Barbara attends a consultation, where André tends to a boy with an injured leg. She observes the doctor, but also the junior doctors and nurses in the room – her new colleagues. When it is over they all go for lunch to the canteen. Here, several versions of trust/doubt and integrity/integrate/ingratiate are successively put on display. First, the doctor engages the sick boy in banter over football, to gain his trust and distract his attention from the pain to come with the removal of the bandage. The boy, however, makes eye contact with the

---

[20] Kasman, 'Spatial Suspense: A conversation with Christian Petzold'.

[21] Jake Cole, *Barbara*.

[22] Jonathan Romney, review of *Barbara*, *Independent*, 30 December 2012, http://www.independent.co.uk/arts-entertainment/films/reviews/barbara-christian-petzold-105-mins-12a-8190724.html (accessed 5 June 2017).

junior doctor, who – in empathetic anticipation of the pain – screws up his face and looks away, which in turn is read, mirror-fashion, by the boy, who now screams with pain and has to be held down by the nurses. Over lunch, the doctor reprimands the junior, who defends himself by arguing that the boy knew the doctor was trying to distract him, that is, that he knew he was being deceived. At this point, Barbara enters the picture with her food tray, but instead of sitting down on the chair ostensibly kept empty for her, she walks past the group and joins a nurse in the corner of the room, whereupon female doctor number one at the table leans forward and says, 'Berliners!', before reclining, while female doctor number two leans forward and mumbles, 'Such a stuck-up . . .' A choreography of 'as-if's', of 'I know that you know that I know', of gazes that meet but do not intersect, sketches for us, in the most banal of settings, but also in the most economical terms, a culture of doublespeak and distrust, of empathy reprimanded and of encounters rife with suspicion and misunderstandings.

Barbara: rebel among the resigned or abject among abjects?

Yet what ultimately attracted me to the film, and justifies, I think, me calling it a thought experiment, is its self-allegorizing, inwardly-directed momentum, embodied in the scene where André signals to Barbara that he is sympathetic to her attempt to leave the GDR, albeit for different reasons: 'I'd like to go to The Hague', he says, and after a pause, 'to see the Rembrandt', pointing to a reproduction of Rembrandt's *Anatomy Lesson* on his laboratory wall, to which she sarcastically replies, 'Submit an application' (i.e. make the move that got her into trouble). André then offers a passionately personal interpretation of the painting, which – in response to her hesitation and dubious look – he half takes back and relativizes. This scene – as indeed the painting – is open to many different readings, several of which seem to me pertinent, including some that imply a self-scrutiny of the film's own premise and procedure, which finally helps address the question of how to depict a country, a national or state entity, with a distinct history and identity, that has ceased to exist, but which – by this very fact of having ceased to exist – exerts a certain power and emanates a negative energy. What draws the attention of André in the picture is not, as one might expect, any identification with the medical profession or with the renowned Dr Tulp, but with the dead man, the corpse. This is what he says:

> 'Did you notice something – in the picture?' – She looks and does indeed spot some errors: they should have started the autopsy by cutting open the abdomen, so no poisonous gases develop, and the hand that's

> sectioned is the wrong one and much too big. 'I don't think Rembrandt made a mistake', André says, 'do you see the anatomical atlas in the corner?' They all stare at it – he, he, and he – and the hand looks exactly like the one in the atlas. Rembrandt paints something into the picture, which we cannot actually see. Thanks to this apparent mistake, we do not see with the eyes of the doctors: we see him, Aris Kindt, the victim. We are with him, and not with those up there.

Chapter 5 examined how, in any theoretical elaboration of the notion of the abject body, notably when following Julia Kristeva, the corpse especially exemplifies this concept, since it literalizes or stages the breakdown of several key boundaries that assure identity and subjectivity. What we are confronted with when we see a human corpse is not only our own inevitable death made palpably real; its radical objectness also makes us doubt the very possibility of being a subject.[23]

To recapitulate briefly the main articulations of abjection we have been considering, there is a psychology of abjection: for Kristeva the abject intervenes in and breaks open the opposition between subject and object, between the living and inanimate: the abject can have too much life – in the form of the death drive – and too little life – in the case of the corpse still uncannily bearing all the features of the living body. Between victimhood and agency, the abject appears as an intermediary but also mediating category, inhabiting the liminal spaces, where a terminal state of nothingness has as its verso something more indeterminate and transitional, and the rejects of reason retain or regain the disturbing potency of taboos.

There is an ethics of abjection: the abject is beyond victimhood, because it can embody an inhuman 'power' – the power of the one so far outside the symbolic, who has nothing to lose, and therefore experiences a certain freedom that probes the limits of such freedom *and* the law.

And there is a politics of abjection. It is sometimes said that the Israelis and Palestinians are each other's abjects, in the sense that the Palestinians, in their state of destitution, also remind Israelis of their own past, the precariousness of their former stateless existence, their fragility, as well as their duties of love thy neighbour, and the endlessly deferred, endlessly complicated, feelings of guilt, and the disavowal of such guilt, mingled with the originary trauma of the Zionist pioneers, who were in search of 'a land without people for the people without land'.

Evidently, I am not suggesting that the relationship between the GDR and the Federal Republic is anything like the Palestinian–Israeli one, even if one were to grant that the notion of the 'abject' is a helpful term in

---

[23] As Kristeva famously puts it, 'The corpse, seen without God and outside of science, is the utmost of abjection. It is death infecting life.' Julia Kristeva, *Powers of Horror: An Essay on Abjection*, trans. Leon S. Roudiez (New York: Columbia University Press, 1982), 4.

understanding the Middle Eastern dilemma (a big 'if'). Nor am I offering a one-to-one relation between Kristeva's abject body and Barbara's position within the community in which she finds herself as outsider and pariah. But if I am right in claiming that the trope of abjection is one that, in different circumstances, but across almost all of Europe, seems to preoccupy filmmakers today, then the constellation I am here sketching is highly pertinent, also in relation to Petzold's *Barbara*.

For once alerted to the significance given to the corpse in Rembrandt's picture, we find it elsewhere in the film as well: Marco the suicidal boy, for instance, is framed in his bed all rigid and stiff, in much the same position as the hanged man in *The Anatomy Lesson*, strengthening the empathetic identity of Marco as André's alter ego. But the most telling reference to a corpse occurs when Barbara reads to Stella from *The Adventures of Huckleberry Finn*, for the passage she chooses is the one in Chapter 7, where Finn fakes his own murder:

> I says to myself, they'll follow the track of that sackful of rocks to the shore and then drag the river for me. And they'll follow that meal track to the lake and go browsing down the creek that leads out of it to find the robbers that killed me and took the things. They won't ever hunt the river for anything but my corpse [dead carcass]. They'll soon get tired of that, and won't bother no more about me.

This passage allows for at least two readings: it tells of a happy escape, thanks to a successful camouflage of a living body as a corpse, which applies to Stella's rigid body as much as to Barbara's emotional stiffness (she later identifies herself with Marco the comatose boy who needs to be operated upon because he has lost access to his feelings). But the Huck Finn corpse also suggests another interpretation that aligns it more directly with Barbara, and with André's comments on the centrality of the corpse in Rembrandt's painting: a comment now interpretable as another way of letting her know obliquely that he understands her situation and sympathizes with it. Barbara, more than André, has reason to consider herself the (living) corpse that the Stasi officers and informers study and dissect, following the bureaucratic rules, with little regard of her actual person.

At the same time, it is significant that André refers to the dead man as 'victim', because the political and ethical interest of the notion of the abject is that he/she is precisely not a victim, as the abject retains an uncanny agency and power, even as a corpse, indeed especially as a corpse. Furthermore, the abject is beyond the binary of inclusion and exclusion, since s/he rearticulates the power relations that ensue after an act of exclusion, where the abject has an 'intimate' relationship to the other – a proximity, a familiarity, an affective bond, be it of hatred, disgust, shame, or guilt. By implying Barbara to be a victim, André offers a gesture of sympathy that Barbara has to reject, because for her it would be an admission of defeat. To quote once more Kristeva:

> There looms, within abjection, one of those violent, dark revolts of being, directed against a threat that seems to emanate from an exorbitant outside or inside, ejected beyond the scope of the possible, the tolerable, the thinkable. It lies there, quite close, but it cannot be assimilated. It beseeches, worries, and fascinates desire, which, nevertheless, does not let itself be seduced. Apprehensive, desire turns aside; sickened, it rejects. A certainty protects it from the shameful – a certainty of which it is proud to hold on to it.[24]

Anatomy lesson

To return to Rembrandt's *Anatomy Lesson*, the interpretation offered of the painting is in fact not André's own nor that of Petzold or his co-screenwriter Harun Farocki. Rather, it is lifted from another German author's rumination on the Rembrandt painting, W. G. Sebald's *The Rings of Saturn*. This is what Sebald has to say:

> The spectacle, presented before a paying public drawn from the upper classes, was no doubt a demonstration of the undaunted investigative zeal in the new sciences; but it also represented (though this surely would have been refuted) the archaic ritual of dismembering a corpse, of harrowing the flesh of the delinquent even beyond death, a procedure then still part of the ordained punishment. That the anatomy lesson in Amsterdam was about more than a thorough knowledge of the inner organs of the human body is suggested by Rembrandt's representation of the ceremonial nature of the dissection – the surgeons are in their finest attire, and Dr Tulp is wearing a hat on his head – as well as by the fact that afterwards there was a formal, and in a sense symbolic, banquet. If we stand today before the large canvas of Rembrandt's *The Anatomy Lesson* in the Mauritshuis we are standing precisely where those who were present at the dissection in the Waaggebouw stood, and we believe that we see what they saw then: in the foreground, the greenish, prone body of Aris Kindt, his neck broken and his chest risen terribly in rigor mortis. And yet it is debatable whether anyone ever really saw that body, since the art of anatomy, then in its infancy, was nor least a way of making the reprobate body invisible. It is somehow odd that Dr Tulp's colleagues

[24] Kristeva, *Powers of Horror*, 1.

> are not looking at Kindt's body, that their gaze is directed just past it to focus on the open anatomical atlas in which the appalling physical facts are reduced to a diagram, a schematic plan of the human being, such as envisaged by the enthusiastic amateur anatomist René Descartes, who was also, so it is said, present that January morning in the Waaggebouw. In his philosophical investigations, which form one of the principal chapters of the history of subjection, Descartes teaches that one should disregard the flesh, which is beyond our comprehension, and attend to the machine within, to what can fully be understood, be made wholly useful for work, and, in the event of any fault, either repaired or discarded. Though the body is open to contemplation, it is, in a sense, excluded, and in [much] the same way the much-admired verisimilitude of Rembrandt's picture proves on closer examination to be more apparent than real. Contrary to normal practice, the anatomist shown here has not begun his dissection by opening the abdomen and removing the intestines, which are most prone to putrefaction, but has started (and this too may imply a punitive dimension to the act) by dissecting the offending hand. Now, this hand is most peculiar. It is not only grotesquely out of proportion compared with the hand closer to us, but it is also anatomically the wrong way round: the exposed tendons, which ought to be those of the left palm, given the position of the thumb, are in fact those of the back of the right hand. In other words, what we are faced with is a transposition taken from the anatomical atlas, evidently without further reflection, that turns this otherwise true-to-life painting (if one may so express it) into a crass misrepresentation at the exact centre point of its meaning, where the incisions are made. It seems inconceivable that we are faced here with an unfortunate blunder. Rather, I believe that there was deliberate intent behind this flaw in the composition. That unshapely hand signifies the violence that has been done to Aris Kindt. It is with him, the victim, and not the Guild that gave Rembrandt his commission, that the painter identifies. His gaze alone is free of Cartesian rigidity. He alone sees that greenish annihilated body, and he alone sees the shadow in the half-open mouth and over the dead man's eyes.[25]

In other words, both Sebald's narrator and André identify with the corpse, or rather, they intimate that Rembrandt identifies with the corpse more than with his learned patron, but his sympathies with common humanity can only manifest themselves in a mistake, a parapraxis, that is, a *lapsus* or *slip* which in retrospect seems charged with significance.

Petzold gives a slightly different, though complementary, reason for its significance. While Sebald sees in the picture a struggle between an abstract

[25] W. G. Sebald, *The Rings of Saturn* (New York: New Directions, 1998), 12–13.

enlightenment logic (Descartes) and the forces embodied in mortality that resist it, Petzold extracts from the *Anatomy Lesson* a deliberately anachronistic allegory, insofar as the picture depicts for him, in the figures of the learned doctors, the functionaries or *nomenclatura* of the GDR, staring at their Marxist-Leninist Texts, while the patient – whether true communism or the people of the GDR – are dead or dying under their inattentive eyes. What unites these two readings is, of course, a distrust or disenchantment with the Enlightenment as such, inclining them towards a Nietzschean, Freudian or post-ideological verdict, which is ready to infer or project upon the corpse in Rembrandt's painting a will to resistance, even in death, especially in death, a negative energy of refusal, thwarting the powers that have taken his life and that now are in the process of taking possession of his body, too.

Sebald's ingeniously idiosyncratic reading, however, is itself indebted to at least two precursors – the Viennese Alois Riegl (1902) and the Dutchman William Heckscher (1958), the two foremost art historical commentators on the painting – who in 1902 and 1958 respectively had already unpeeled several layers of meaning. Heckscher in particular had added extensive historical contexts, one of which is relevant to the case in hand, namely the complex negotiations between the Catholic Church, the state and the Medical Guilds around the cutting up of human bodies, given that every human being is a divine creation, whose wilful destruction is technically a sin. By allowing a criminal body to be dissected, that is, an abject to be reclaimed for science, a certain transubstantiation had to take place also at the spiritual plane. By releasing hanged criminals for autopsy, evil deeds are redeemed and turned into serving a greater good, thus helping to expiate both the crime and the severe manner of its punishment. It gives the corpse in Rembrandt's picture the ambiguous status of the *homo sacer*, in his abjection closer to the divine and the sacred than were he still alive.

Alois Riegl, on the other hand, had studied the geometry of gazes, as well as the intensity of each character's look, that together create an extraordinary and entirely novel atmosphere of attentiveness, especially when compared to earlier Dutch group portraits:

> The listeners subordinate themselves to Dr Tulp through their attention, but each in a different way. There is a common psychological attention among them, although this expresses itself physically in an independent, individual form in every case. It is most animated, because most externalized, among the three surgeons placed at the head of the corpse: one leans forward in order to see better, and his neighbour in order to hear better-so that his face almost takes on an expression of suffering (pathos=internal movement) – and the third figure probably does so for both purposes . . . The same applies to the doctor at the left below, whose gently inclined head is turned slightly outward [if only to avoid the *profil perdu* pose inimical to portraiture]. His downcast gaze and the deep

> wrinkles around the eyes prove that he, too, does not make coquettish glances at some beholder but painstakingly follows the words of the professor . . . That leaves the seventh doctor, who, in a no less rigidly vertical pose, rises high above all the others and constitutes the single exception: he turns en face with his full gaze toward the beholder and points with his right index finger to the demonstration scene. Whereas the remaining seven figures appear connected in an internal unity – insofar as six surgeons subordinate themselves through attention to the speaking professor – the eighth figure establishes an external unity with the beholder, whom he subordinates through his pointed finger and thereby connects with the lecture scene. The picture accordingly contains a double unity through subordination: first, between Tulp and the seven surgeons, all of whom subordinate themselves to him as the lecturer and, second, between the crowning surgeon and the beholder, the latter subordinated to the former and indirectly through him to Tulp in turn.[26]

Riegl, in other words, unlocks the extraordinarily vivid movements that separate the individuals and joins them as a group, in what Michael Fried would later call 'absorption',[27] although Riegl sees a special value in the 'theatricality' of the upright surgeon whose Matthias Grünewald index finger links the protagonists of the painted scene to the spectators in front of the picture. What Sebald has added is the painter's own moral point of view, and through him, our own perspective as spectators. Translated into Petzold's – and *Barbara*'s – terms, every character has an entry point: the learned surgeons looking at the book, Dr Tulp, looking out at the paying audience assembled in his anatomical theatre, the look of Rembrandt, directing our gaze to the corpse. All are doubled by the look of André, of Barbara, of Petzold the director, and our looks as the film's spectators, having to make sense of these points of view, while at the same time wondering how we are meant to read any of this in relation to the stalled romance of our two protagonists. In other words, although none of the gazes meet and join, all of them are active, and all of them belong to the experience of seeing this picture.

Therefore, we have to assume that behind Petzold's reference to communism, there is another kind of reference, now more a self-reference to himself as artist rather than an analogy associating the corpse with Barbara or 'the people' at once dissected and disregarded by 'the system'. Sebald's Rembrandt has a problem: how to please his patron, Dr Tulp and his fellow surgeons, who commissioned the painting, and how to do justice to the

[26] Alois Riegl, 'The Dutch Group Portrait', trans. Benjamin Binstock, *October* 74 (Fall 1995): 5–7.

[27] See Michael Fried, *Absorption and Theatricality: Painting and Beholder in the Age of Diderot* (Chicago: University of Chicago Press, 1988); Cole, *Barbara*.

humanity of the poor wretch Aris Kindt, hanged for trying to steal a cloak. Extending Sebald's reading, Petzold uses *The Anatomy Lesson* as an allegory of himself as an artist and self-divided German, confronted with the problem of doing justice to the now defunct GDR at a point in time when it was still alive, and in terms that neither betray its people nor minimizes their complicity with a criminal regime. But Petzold also makes the painting serve as a guide to the formal construction of this particular film, into which are inscribed at least two, if not three, distinct, even antagonistic, but perhaps after all mutually interdependent moral and political vantage points. There is that of the black congress of authority figures, who dominate the picture, which is to say, whose tense attentiveness acknowledges the ubiquity of control and surveillance in the GDR, but whose demeanour also speaks of seriousness of purpose and of higher intent, since as surgeons (of a sick system – fascism, capitalism), they consider themselves the benefactors of mankind. Then there is the second perspective: that of the corpse, whose greenish-grey-white body pallor is ominously glowing in a kind of luminous hue, and whose prostate body elicits a mixture of curiosity, empathy and queasy discomfort. While the gazes of the surgeons do not meet the spectator's, the closed eyes of the corpse solicit and attract our eyes, giving the picture its push–pull, attraction–repulsion, leaning forward–stepping back dynamic – all of which can be viewed as applying equally to Petzold's film, insofar as it answers to the problem of representing the vanished GDR in a manner that allows for multiple perspectives to interact, without obliging them to converge – the multi-focal parallax view embodied in Rembrandt's work becomes the master trope for Petzold's own film aesthetic and political ideal. Finally, the fact that the anatomy of the arm is copied from the book, and is, as it were, at once exterior and integral to the body, also hints at an allegorical aptness: it acknowledges the schematism of the plot, but also its functionality, while hinting at Petzold's dependence on other sources – whether we see *Barbara* as a remake of another film, an adaptation from literature, or as indebted to Hitchcock and Hollywood genre films: references that are as obliquely central and at the margins of *Barbara* as the book of Vaselius's anatomical drawings is to Rembrandt's *Anatomy Lesson*.

Consequently, the work of the spectator lies less in identifying the relevance of the *Anatomy Lesson* in all its details, and more in making the enigma of its geometry of gazes resonate, in the sense of recognizing each perspective within its own space – a space made narratively present through the space between the characters, as well as in the shots held slightly longer than the plot requires, and it is present in the time lags and pauses between the characters' respective responses to each other, which makes the film too slow for some American viewers and thus so 'European', quite apart from the fact that the open ending confirms that other complaint about European films, namely that they do not solve problems but merely probe dilemmas. *Barbara*'s open end is thus an additional irritation.

What, finally, is gained by suggesting that Barbara might qualify not just as an alien (which is, after all, the meaning of the name Barbara) but as an abject? As abject, I have tried to argue, *Barbara* helps redefine what it means to refuse, and not just in a situation where overt resistance or rebellion is swiftly punished, as is so clearly demonstrated in the case of Stella, the young runaway. Escaping to the West, by the grace of Jörg, might give Barbara one kind of freedom, but would by the same token deprive her of agency or even nullify the personal meaning of this freedom. Staying, on the other hand, would mean resigning herself to being the victim, and thus to surrendering control over her life. In this situation, the abject marks a position both below and beyond victimhood, as well as staking out a different freedom, the freedom to choose, even if she appears to choose the very instance that oppresses her. Barbara's choice becomes an ethical act, precisely due to the fact that she decides to stay, that is, by seemingly giving in to the system, she is resisting the system, not only because she exercises choice: exactly what the regime is intent on depriving her of. Rather, she acts ethically also because her choice challenges the regime, by not giving in to the system's own cynicism and taking literally the values it only pretends to defend; to return to an earlier quote, she 'liberates a good idea from its historical cage'. Perhaps she thereby even breaks open the very opposition East versus West, GDR versus FRG, communism versus capitalism – and in doing so, confirms that the film that carries her name is indeed a 'thought experiment', namely how to think ourselves beyond these oppositions, as well as beyond cynical resignation, which assumes and accepts that our present system is the untranscendable horizon of how humans can organize their lives and collectively shape their societies. In short, *Barbara* is not a film about wanting the GDR back, nor about surveillance poisoning lives, but the thought experiment as anatomy lesson, performed on the body of a country that in its vanishing has turned abject, but whose abjectness might still contain moments of refusal and models of agency that deserve to be remembered for the future. That, too, is perhaps part of the Petzold paradox and maybe even the lesson of the Petzold system.

12

Control, Creative Constraints and Self-Contradiction

The Global Auteur

The author: impossible and indispensable

There are many reasons why the concept of the auteur, as it applies to the film director, should not be carried over into the twenty-first century. First of all, because it has always been a contested notion, serving sometimes highly polemical and partisan agendas under unique historical circumstances (e.g. first in post-war Europe, then in 1970s Hollywood). Secondly, while it was strategically useful when helping film- and cinema-studies gain a foothold in academia by modelling itself on literary studies and art history, this objective had been (over-)achieved by the mid-1980s, by which time the historical conditions of the original auteur theory (i.e. validating Hollywood's popular art by employing high culture criteria) also no longer applied. Throughout the 1980s and into the 1990s, film, media and cultural studies programmes were eagerly inaugurated everywhere in higher education in order to come to the rescue of humanities departments and to provide training for the ever-expanding 'creative' media industries.

Cultural studies in particular had little need of the individual author, having shifted attention from creation and production to reception and spectatorship: works of art as well as of popular culture (which meant art cinema and the mainstream) were assumed to be social texts carrying ideologically encoded messages, and thus had larger systems, for example capitalism or patriarchy, as their 'authors'. Such deconstructions (and 'deaths') of the author were theoretically supported by no less authoritative authors than Roland Barthes and Michel Foucault, who in turn provided models of analysis that supported close readings of specific texts without resorting to self-expression, intentionality or individual moral and legal accountability.[1]

No doubt, there are even more pertinent philosophical reasons, why authorship is such a vexing problem for a popular and collaborative art such as the cinema, and why it should be dropped from the list of important topics, quite apart from the industrial and capitalist context in which filmmaking has invariably taken place.[2] None of these critiques are new nor have they been laid to rest,[3] yet precisely because even art cinema has become thoroughly pervaded by market considerations, the author debate deserves another look. Given that the film director as author, and the author as auteur, have survived even the most well founded set of counter-arguments, one can only conclude that being philosophically problematic and conceptually vague merely reinforces the author's indispensability, both as a reality and as a concept. In fact, more than ever, (film) authorship is taken for granted, filling an evident gap by fulfilling its 'author-function' (Foucault), which at its most basic rests on the assumption that the work (the film) in question possesses a degree of coherence and purposiveness, which convention and the need for meaning likes to attribute to a nameable instance and an origin – the author.[4] This author-function was initially more important to film critics and scholars than for the directors themselves (many Hollywood veteran directors were baffled and amused, before they became flattered and intrigued, by the French *politique des auteurs*). Responding to such a disconnect between person and function, authorship was redefined as implicit and inferred rather than expressive and embodied. The author, famously, became an 'effect of the text', a 'necessary fiction', a projection and over-identification by the enthusiastic cinephile, requiring one to carefully (and ontologically) separate John Ford from 'John Ford' – the latter the sum of the narrative structures and stylistic effects that the critic was able to assemble around a body of work 'signed' by a given director. Yet in subsequent decades, as the director as auteur increasingly became a fixture of the popular media's general personality cult, the author

[1] Roland Barthes, *S/Z: An Essay*, trans. Richard Miller (New York: Hill & Wang, 1970); Michel Foucault, 'Ceci n'est pas une pipe', *October* 1 (Spring 1976); 6–21.

[2] There is no shortage of essays problematizing the notion of the author or auteur. Among the best-known collections are John Caughie (ed.), *Theories of Authorship* (London and New York: Routledge, 1981); Virginia Wright Wexman (ed.), *Film and Authorship* (Piscataway, NJ: Rutgers University Press, 2003); David A Gerstner and Janet Staiger (eds), *Authorship and Film* (New York: Routledge, 2003); and Barry Keith Grant (ed.), *Auteurs and Authorship: A Film Reader* (Malden, MA: Wiley-Blackwell, 2008).

[3] For a philosophical discussion of the cases for and against film authorship, see Aaron Meskin, 'Authorship', in Paisley Livingston and Carl Plantinga (EDS), *The Routledge Companion to Philosophy and Film* (New York: Routledge, 2008), 12–27.

[4] For Meskin, most of the authorship debates revolve around 'evaluation, interpretation, and stylistic attribution'. Meskin, 'Authorship', 18–19.

began doing duty not only as the (imaginary or real) anchor for presumed, perceived or projected coherence, but was actively deployed as a brand name and marketing tool, for the commercial film industry as well as in the realm of independent and art cinema.

Questions of access and control

Adding the word 'global' to 'author' reflects this shift of register which raises the stakes, and acknowledges that 'global' applies to both Hollywood's global reach and coverage and to world cinema and transnational cinema – terms that have all but replaced the labels 'art cinema' and 'independent cinema' (where the author as both function and person survived the longest without being either contested critically or seen as tainted by commercialism). Globalizing auteurism is therefore the inevitable consequence of art cinema now being part of the market and of the urgent need to resituate the old debates in an enlarged context. Concerning the latter, however, I follow the lead of those writers who have narrowed the question of authorship in cinema down to the issue of control:

> V. F. Perkins claims . . . that the 'director's authority is a matter not of total creation but of sufficient control' (184). Bordwell and Thompson suggest that 'usually it is through the director's control of the shooting and assembly phases that the film's form and style crystallize' (Bordwell and Thompson 1993: 16) . . . [Paisley] Livingston, who has argued that some studio films are singly authored, points to the 'high degree of control' and 'huge measure of authority' that some directors have (Livingston 1997: 144).[5]

Control, of course, can be exercised in many different ways: organizational, financial, political, artistic and intellectual, and many of these types of control are indeed involved in the making, marketing, distributing and 'owning' of a film. Not all of these forms of control need to fall to the same physical individual, or indeed any individual, given the abstract nature of some of the controlling forces and functions at work. I have elsewhere argued that contemporary Hollywood should be understood within such an extended, 'reflexive' authorial dynamic of providing 'access for all' at the same time as 'keeping control'. Which is to say, Hollywood sets out to make films that are formally and intellectually accessible to as wide as possible a range of audiences, diverse in language, race, religion, region and nationality, all the while trying to control not only legal ownership and property rights

[5] Meskin, 'Authorship', 22.

and the platforms of distribution and exhibition, but also steering the scope of interpretations and forms of (fan-) appropriation thanks to a combination of (textual) structured ambiguity and (paratextual) feedback loops.[6] By way of example, I examined the authorial persona of the director James Cameron and the narrative structure of his most successful film, *Avatar* (2009), arguing that both instantiate a convergence of these basically antagonistic forces of 'access' and 'control' under the intensified conditions of a global market and an increasingly polarized political world (dis)order.[7]

One consequence to draw from this situation is that the author in the global context is both a *construct* and a *person*(ality). Being a locus of agency (control) as well as a focal point of projection (access), s/he is positioned at the intersection of a theoretical impossibility and a practical indispensability. A figure of contradiction as well as a construct, the global author exists within antagonistic forces, whose effects need not work against each other, but can be harnessed so as to re-energize rather than block the different levels of circulation in play. It aligns authorship with other aspects of globalization, where multiple variables are simultaneously interacting with each other, where traditional categories of linear cause-and-effect chains have opened up to recursive network effects and where our idea of autonomy, that is, single source, rational agency, is complicated by models of distributed agency, contingency and mutual interdependence. These 'rhizomatic' tendencies are reinforced by electronic communication and the internet, whose architecture is the very site of simultaneous, multi-directional, reciprocal, recursive and looped interactions.

Similarly 'distributed', antagonistic and yet interdependent forces are typical of today's cinema as a whole, thriving as it does between ostensibly incompatible identities of big screen spectacle, digital video disk and download file, with viewers effortlessly switching between online viewing and visits to the local multiplex, and with the culture at large treating 'the cinema' as part of the urban fabric and 'the cinematic' as part of our collective memory and imaginary. In these contexts and definitions, the author does not seem to be crucial to the system, being only one of the pieces of information and markers of recognition by which audiences identify a film as worthy of their attention.

As laid out in Chapter 1, most significant and symptomatic in the present context is the author's place in that other network which competes with and complements global Hollywood: the film festival network. Its nodes are no longer merely in Europe (Cannes, Venice, Berlin, Rotterdam) but extend to North America (Toronto, New York, Sundance, Telluride), Africa (Ouagadougou), Latin America (Buenos Aires, Sao Paulo) and Asia (Busan,

[6] Thomas Elsaesser, *The Persistence of Hollywood* (New York: Routledge, 2013), 319–40.

[7] Thomas Elsaesser 'James Cameron's *Avatar*: access for all', *New Review of Film and Television Studies* 9, no. 3 (2011): 247–64.

Hong Kong, Shanghai, Mumbai). As has been evident for some time, it is at these festivals that the auteur is the only universally recognized currency, yet this currency is stamped and certified at only very few of the world's many festivals, with Cannes (and France) still the decisive place for authenticating internationally recognized auteurs.

The idea that auteur*s* are constructs of the festivals merely underscores and makes more historically specific the point made earlier about the problematic status of cinematic authorship, insofar as the discursive construct auteur is now doubled by an institutional construct under the control of the film festival system. In another sense, however, calling respected directors of great films 'constructs' is both counter-intuitive and demeaning, yet it can also become subversively productive, if it opens up a number of otherwise unrecognized contradictions, which filmmakers themselves have identified as challenges and (sometimes welcome) opportunities – having to do with autonomy and forms of agency that turn the question of control inside out. This is what I intend to illustrate by introducing two distinct but complementary notions – that of creative constraint and of performative self-contradiction, which together outline potentially productive counter-strategies from *within* the system, rather than continuing to pursue (increasingly ineffective) oppositional stances from without.

On the face of it, the extraordinary dependency of most of the world's non-Hollywood filmmakers on festivals for validation, recognition and cultural capital makes a mockery of the term 'independence'. Yet it is a reminder that the festivals' increase in power does not sit easily on them either, since it contradicts the very purpose of the festivals, namely to celebrate film as art and to acknowledge the filmmaker as artist and auteur – all notions supposedly synonymous with autonomy. In other words, a dynamic of reciprocal dependencies is implicit in this relationship between auteur and festival, chief among these being that the festival, in order to fulfil its mission, has to encourage and even constrain the filmmaker to behave as if s/he was indeed a free agent and an autonomous artist, dedicated solely to expressing a uniquely personal vision, and thus to disavow the very pressures the festival has to impose. One such pressure, for instance, comes from the increasingly conflicted force field of schedules and dates, hierarchies, competition and selection mechanisms into which the festival network places both the filmmakers and the festivals. With festivals being both portals and gatekeepers, both windows of attention and platforms for dissemination, a filmmaker has to plan and produce his or her film to fit the timetable of the respective festival, that is, effectively making his/her film to measure, to order and to schedule. In the case of established auteurs, the dilemma is aggravated by having to weigh loyalty against opportunity, when accepting a festival invitation: 'What if I commit to Berlin in February and a month later, I hear that Cannes wants to show my film in May?' Festivals are in competition with each other over exclusive premieres, forcing filmmakers into yet another form of dependence.

Double occupancy, self-exoticism and 'serving two masters'

Yet these examples may only scratch the surface of the kinds of controls and contradictory demands the global author is exposed to: festivals pride themselves on their internationalism, of transcending the boundaries of national cinema by providing an open forum for the world's films and filmmakers. But this openness can be a trap: it is an open invitation to self-conscious ethnicity and retribalization, it quickly shows its affinity or even collusion with cultural tourism, with fusion-food-world-music-ethnic-cuisine third-worldism in the capitals of the first world, and more generally, with a post-colonial and subaltern sign-economy, covering over and effacing the new economy of downsizing, outsourcing and the relentless search for cheap labour on the part of multinational companies. Because cinema (as part of the creative industries) is not exempt from these pressures, but cannot avow them openly, there is a tendency of films within the festival circuit – whether from Asia, Africa or Europe – to respond and to comply, by gestures that amount to a kind of 'self-exoticizing' or 'auto-orientalism': that is, a tendency to present to the world (of the festivals) a picture of the self, a narrative of one's nation or community that reproduces or anticipates what one believes the other expects to see. It is the old trap of the colonial ethnographer, of the eager multiculturalist who welcomes the stranger and is open to otherness, but preferably on one's own terms and within one's own comfort zone.

In Chapter 4 and especially Chapter 5 I detailed the reasons why, in order to highlight these asymmetrical but reciprocal dependencies, I once proposed the term 'double occupancy'. It was meant to draw attention, first of all, to some of the fallacies implicit in identity politics: 'rather than diversity or multiculturalism, [double occupancy wants to] signal our discursive as well as geopolitical territories as always already occupied. It can convey right away a concrete [history of occupation, colonialism and globalization] as well as the need to reflect the reality of competing claims in the identity-wars, while also keeping alive the political and philosophical associations that the term may carry.' Secondly, the term was meant to allude to and include contemporary theories of the subject: 'in Lacanian psychoanalysis it is language that speaks us, rather than the other way around; for Foucault, religion and social institutions inscribe themselves as discursive regimes and micro-politics on our bodies and senses. [Double occupancy] also calls to mind Jacques Derrida's practice of putting certain words "under erasure", in order to indicate the provisional nature of a text's authority, and the capacity of textual space to let us see both itself and its opposite.'[8]

In the present study, I revised and radicalized this notion of double occupancy. First, I substituted for it the concept of 'abjection', whose different connotations nonetheless cover crucial aspects of the earlier formulation, notably the negative reciprocity. Second, in order to refocus the political aspects, as they apply specifically to global auteurs, I now argue that their double occupancy is better characterized as the state of constitutively *serving at least two masters*. These masters can be a government exerting censorship, versus the master embodied by the international film festival whose director expects dissidence and resistance from the filmmaker (think China, think Iran); one master can be public service television which in Europe acts as the major producer and exhibitor, versus the other master, the big screen as endorsement of the director as auteur (an accolade not available on television). Yet the split can also be on the side of audience address: trying to satisfy a domestic critical establishment, while hoping to seduce an international audience that expects exoticism either in the form of gritty realism or picturesque squalor (international successes such as *City of God* (2002) and *Slumdog Millionaire* (2008) provide the relevant examples). For instance, Matteo Garrone's *Gomorrah* (2008) and Paolo Sorrentino's *La Grande Bellezza* (2013) may not at first glance have much in common, but both carefully balance biting criticism of contemporary Italy with a seductive allure of 'crime and violence' in the former and 'glamour and decadence' in the latter. Each film is also very conscious of its national cinematic lineage (neo-realism, spaghetti Western and Pasolini in one case, Fellini and Antonioni in the other). It is a heritage that the films performatively enact, which is one reason why European cinema in the age of globalization should be called 'post-nationalist', in the sense of 'performing nationalism'.

Also servants of two masters – another meaning of the term 'double occupancy' – are auteurs such as Krzysztof Kieslowski and Michael Haneke, Abbas Kiarostami and Hou Hsiao-Hsien, when they make films outside their home country, while still 'representing' it, by associating its national stereotypes. This double occupancy can also be proven negatively, when directors throw in their lot with one master only, as in the case of Kim ki-Duk or Cristian Mungiu, who have more or less given up on their domestic Korean or Romanian audiences and now make films mainly for the Cannes and Venice festivals, after having been ignored or vilified in their own country.

---

[8] Thomas Elsaesser, 'Real Location, Fantasy Space, Performative Place: Double Occupancy and Mutual Interference in European Cinema', in Temenuga Trifonova (ed.), *European Film Theory* (New York and London: Routledge, 2009), 50, 52.

In the same vein, the Russian director Alexander Sokurov would be another telling case of a film auteur 'serving two masters'. Targeted by film censorship during the Soviet period (all the while producing films that were almost systematically shelved), he became heralded as one of the major figures representing his national cinema, as it was being showcased abroad, at the time of *perestroika* in the mid-1980s. But with film funds dwindling during the late Soviet period and throughout the 1990s, Sokurov had to utilize Western European subsidy infrastructures and production funds in order to continue to make films, while still identified with (sometimes clichéd) Russianness, even in cases where his films dealt with non-Russian topics and even when shot in foreign languages, such as German or Japanese. Benefiting from finance obtained through both local and foreign (mostly German, but also French) production companies, the director famously reached out to Vladimir Putin himself when trying to find additional money for his *Faust* (2011), or, more confidentially, obtained funding from the Wolff-Metternich estate for his latest film, *Francofonia* (2015), which, lo and behold, portrays Count Wolff-Metternich in a rather positive light. A sign of his own awareness of his dependency on a variety of non-commercial, 'art cinema' funds and investors is Sokurov's consistent habitus of rebellious insubordination in interviews, 'performing' the radical free spirit and independent auteur, both on and off film sets. It seems to have served him well on the festival circuit:

> [A]fter being lionized (or 'leopardized') at Locarno in the late 1980s, he was later 'upgraded' to Cannes award-winner (with *Moloch* (1999)) and the prestigious off-festival screening, both in 35mm and digital, of *Russian Ark* (2002). He later sternly criticized the festival for its commercialism, including in major interviews and in his book *V Tsentre Okeana* (2012), and has since found a new home at the Venice film festival (where he took the Golden Lion, to everyone's astonishment, for *Faust*).[9]

A third, possibly more profitable and productive servitude can be noted when filmmakers turn gallery artists, which has been the case with directors Harun Farocki, Wim Wenders, Ulrike Ottinger and Chantal Akermann from an earlier generation, and more recently applies to Isaac Julien and John Akomfrah, but also to Apichatpong Weerasethakul from Thailand, and Abbas Kiarostami from Iran. The reverse is also becoming more common, when established contemporary artists undertake major film productions, as in the case of Julian Schnabel (*Before Night Falls* (2000), *The Diving Bell and the Butterfly* (2007)), Steve McQueen (*Hunger* (2008), *Shame* (2011),

[9] I owe much of this information and the quotation to a personal communication from Jeremi Szaniawski.

Twelve Years a Slave (2013)) and Sam Taylor-Wood as Sam Taylor-Johnson (*Nowhere Boy* (2009), *50 Shades of Grey* (2015)).

Such transitions from the gallery to Hollywood are still relatively rare.[10] Most film directors continue to lend their talents to the festival circuit as their lifeline for cultural capital and recognition. In this respect, European auteurs are not exempt from being part of the globalization of creative labour more generally, which positions them in proximity to the creative precariate of the art world, unless they are able to craft and maintain a suitable self-image that can support the festival brand. Cannes is very jealous of 'its' directors, and so are Venice, Berlin, Rotterdam and Toronto. One way to account for the paradoxes of such 'enabling dependency' or 'master–slave dialectic' that binds the auteur to the festival and vice versa is to invoke – besides the second-order performed nationalism just mentioned – also a sort of second-order performed auteurism, where films are not the self-expression of a uniquely gifted individual or the expression of the moral conscience of a nation(al cinema), but rather the products of 'specialists' working within conditions of possibility – the festival circuit – that are also limiting conditions and structural constraints.

The much invoked but still under-defined 'typical festival film' may be a case in point.[11] If I am right in suggesting that certain non-Hollywood films are made with festivals rather than audiences in mind, then this would go some way to explain why, not only European but also Asian directors (e.g. Wong Kar-wai or Hou Hsiao-Hsien) tend at some point to make films in and for France, using iconic French actors. Juliette Binoche is typical in this respect, having provided Frenchness and festival credibility – as well as memorable instances of female melancholy and depression, discussed in Chapter 10 – to directors as diverse as Krzysztof Kieslowski, Michael Haneke, Abbas Kiarostami, Anthony Minghella, Hou and David Cronenberg. While these auteurs are transnational filmmakers who have sometimes been co-opted as additional creative labour into the ranks of French film art, European directors such as the Dardenne Brothers, Mike Leigh, Ken Loach and Wim Wenders have become Cannes favourites (or even 'mascots'), also helping to confirm France's strategic role as a regional power with global reach in matters cinema, banking on Paris and the French language as a luxury brand. A counter-tendency should also be noted. In the past, French filmmakers were careful not to dilute this Frenchness into a transnationalism over which they might lose control, yet France is now also producing films, stars and a number of directors that successfully establish themselves as internationals, with Binoche playing a Swiss-German with perfect English in

[10] See Melis Behlil, *Hollywood is Everywhere: Global Directors in the Blockbuster Era* (Amsterdam: Amsterdam University Press, 2016).

[11] See Cindy H. Wong, *Film Festivals: Culture, People, and Power on the Global Screen* (New Brunswick, NJ: Rutgers University Press, 2011), 145–8.

The Clouds of Sils Maria (2015), Marion Cotillard playing Edith Piaf for the global market in *La Vie en rose* (2007) and directors such as Jean Pierre Jeunet (*Amélie* (2001)), Michel Hazanavicius (*The Artist* (2011)) and above all Luc Besson (*La Femme Nikita* (1990), *The Professional* (1994), *The Fifth Element* (1997), *Lucy* (2014)) 'exporting' Frenchness into Anglophone films, not always to the liking of their critics back home.[12]

Creative constraints

The moves by filmmakers in the face of the pressures of globalized authorship, which I identified above as auto-exoticism, becoming a festival talent for hire or outsourcing oneself to Hollywood, are by and large 'adaptive' strategies. They implicitly accept the conditions of the market in cultural capital, in reputation and recognition, and they acknowledge the asymmetrical power relations that auteurs find themselves in vis-à-vis the global film business, film festivals, their international audiences and national governments or funding bodies. Yet there are other ways of confronting the 'antagonistic mutualities', already discussed in Chapter 3, when what keeps the system going are often arrangements that on the surface are antagonistic, but hide mutual benefits, or conversely, situations that appear mutually beneficial but hide hidden conflicts. Such strategies – for which I borrow the term 'creative constraints' – are neither adaptive nor do they necessarily require the kind of outright challenge, sabotage or refusal that Jean-Luc Godard has made his forte.[13]

Control from an external source, whether individual or institutional, is usually experienced as a constraint – constraint on one's freedom: of expression, of action, of movement. If we follow Lawrence Lessig, four sorts of constraints both 'regulate behaviour in the real world' and are the levers for bringing about change: the law, the market, social norms and what he calls 'architecture' – the technological infrastructure which has increasingly replaced 'nature' as the regulating and constraining force in

[12] Luc Besson has fared especially badly in this respect, with critics deriding his international success: 'Besson thinks he can buy himself the title of auteur, but all he attains is a parvenu's vulgarity.' Cited in Jamie Wolf, 'Le Cinéma du Blockbuster', *New York Times*, 20 May 2007, http://www.nytimes.com/2007/05/20/movies/20wolf.html (accessed 31 July 2015).

[13] Jean-Luc Godard's battles with Cannes date back to 1968, when along with other filmmakers of the *nouvelle vague* he forced the festival to shut down. In 2014, when his thirty-ninth film, *Adieu au Langage*, won the Jury Prize at the festival, he refused to attend the press conference, sending a video letter instead. Elyse Schein and Paula Bernstein, 'Jean-Luc Godard Explains Why He Skipped Cannes Press Conference', *IndieWire*, 21 May 2014, http://www.indiewire.com/2014/05/watch-jean-luc-godard-explains-why-he-skipped-cannes-press-conference-26396/ (accessed 10 January 2016).

human lives.[14] Much the same constraints operate in an activity like filmmaking, except that the schema takes no account of the areas of freedom and autonomy we call 'art'. In one sense, it would be the appeal to the autonomy of art that acts as the counter-force, but as already pointed out, it is the very notion of the unfettered freedom of the imagination and the claim of being in control which defines the auteur and sustains the authorial myth *within* the system rather than being an effective defence *against* the system by resisting its constraints or destabilizing its mechanisms. Whichever way one looks at it, effective counter-strategies or subversion have to come from within rather than without, and they do so in the form of *additional constraints*: these, however, must be *freely chosen* rather than submitted to under protest, or adopted by way of compromise. Such a freely chosen constraint is what I mean by *creative constraint*. As explained in Chapter 1, it was the sociologist Jon Elster who has made the term popular and even applied it to the cinema. Yet it names a practice with a longer history, usually in the context of addressing a contradiction, without pretending to resolve it. In the context of the present study, the purpose and benefit of imposing on oneself such a constraint is in order to master a situation by first making it worse: to aggravate it, turn it against oneself, and to internalize it, as a way of regaining some form of agency and control.

The auteur as Ulysses

In *Ulysses Unbound: Studies in Rationality, Pre-commitment and Constraints*, where he develops the idea of creativity and constraint most fully, Elster initially distinguished between *essential* and *incidental* constraints. Essential constraints are chosen for the sake of expected benefits, while incidental constraints may turn out to have benefits but are not chosen for the sake of these benefits: 'When the constraints are imposed from the outside, [the artist] may or may not benefit. If he does, we are dealing with incidental constraint . . . Sometimes, an incidental constraint may turn into an essential one, if the artist chooses to abide by the constraint even when it is no longer mandatory.'[15] In the chapter on the arts, entitled 'less is more', Elster also introduces the idea of local maximization, by which he means that such constraints can be a trade-off between the fullness of possibilities (e.g. daydreaming) and the parsimony of means (e.g. conceptual art), but that they can also have economic benefits, insofar as constraints create

[14] Lawrence Lessig, 'The Laws of Cyberspace', Draft 3, presented at the Taiwan Conference, Taipei, March1998, 2–3, http://cyber.law.harvard.edu/works/lessig/laws_cyberspace.pdf (accessed 10 January 2017).

[15] Jon Elster, *Ulysses Unbound: Studies in Rationality, Pre-commitment, and Constraints* (Cambridge: Cambridge University Press, 2000), 176.

scarcity, which in turn maximizes value.[16] An example of external constraints leading to local maximization, discussed by Elster, would be the Hays Code, often said to have been a boon for sexual innuendo in classical Hollywood movies, for example in films like *Casablanca* (1942).[17] More generally, the code was a training ground for the kind of structured ambiguity mentioned earlier, but Elster's argument regarding the Hays Code also engages with the well-known but not uncontroversial notion that (political) censorship is beneficial to literature and the arts because it forces writers to become more oblique, more allusive and indirect in their means of expression, and therefore more subtle and profound.

The part of Elster's theory relevant to the present argument is his claim that artists 'self-bind' themselves (hence the reference to Ulysses in the title of his book, tying himself to the mast in order to resists the Sirens' song) not only by accepting *imposed* (hard) constraints, and learning how to turn them into *chosen* (soft) constraints (Elster cites the Lubitsch touch, which works by innuendo and inference). Artists also self-bind themselves by a third type, the invented constraint, the most often cited example being Georges Perec's novel *La Disparition*, written without the vowel 'e', which thereby disappears.[18] Artists may invent constraints in the face of unlimited time and means ('For a movie director, an unlimited budget may be disastrous. For a TV producer, having too much time may undermine creativity'),[19] which is to say, faced with a situation where there is not sufficient pressure present in their primary environment (i.e. when there is too much 'freedom' and when 'everything goes').

But a filmmaker may also invent constraints when a new technology comes along that allows for so many options that the very notion of a mistake disappears, because it can always be put right afterwards, or as

---

[16] Elster defines maximization as follows: 'The process of artistic creation is guided by the aim of maximizing aesthetic value under constraints,' and adds in as footnote: '(1) The idea of a maximum implies that in a good work of art, "nothing can be added and nothing subtracted" without loss of aesthetic value. The idea of a good work of art as embodying both fullness and parsimony seems naturally captured by the idea of a maximum. (2) By arguing that artists aim at producing a local maximum rather than "the" best work they can make, I believe I can make sense of several properties of works of art and their creation, (a) Many artists experiment with small variations before they decide on the final version, (b) The notion of a "minor masterpiece" has a natural interpretation in this framework, (c) The notion of a "flawed masterpiece" also receives a natural interpretation.' Elster, *Ulysses Unbound*, 200.

[17] See Richard Maltby, 'A Brief Romantic Interlude: Dick and Jane Go to 3½ seconds of the Classical Hollywood Cinema', in David Bordwell and Noël Carroll (eds), *Post-Theory: Reconstructing Film Studies* (Madison: University of Wisconsin Press, 1996), 434–59, and Slavoj Žižek's commentary, 'Shostakovich in Casablanca', *Lacanian Ink*, 2007, www.lacan.com/zizcasablanca.htm (accessed 10 January 2017).

[18] Elster, *Ulysses Unbound*, 196.

[19] Elster, *Ulysses Unbound*, 210–11.

Elster puts it 'the artist deliberately increases the cost of making mistakes, in the hope that fewer mistakes will ensue'[20] – in other words, when the problem of expression through form (as opposed to self-expression) has not been redefined clearly enough.

To translate the condition of not sufficient pressure present in the environment into the terms of 'independent' filmmaking, one could argue as follows: the fact that European filmmakers receive much, if not all, the funding for their films from non-commercial sources, and mostly via the taxpayer, effectively deprives them (or liberates them) of the constraint of the box office. How to compensate for this in the environment of the festival? As indicated, even national representativeness that once acted as both incentive and constraint for directors like Bergman or Fellini, Bresson or Chabrol, Antonioni or Bertolucci, began to wane in the 1990s, making some form of self-binding artistically, but perhaps also politically, necessary, in order to mark the shift from national cinema to global. Fassbinder, beginning in the 1980s, deliberately chose 'commercial' producers (a major constraint for an auteur) because they gave him access to international distribution, but also because they allowed an escape from the bureaucratic constraints of the governmental film funding system. Given that at the time the national audiences preferred American films by more than 3 to 1 over films made by their own directors, one can see why a filmmaker might want to raise the bar for him or herself, in order to be in touch with some kind of generic (i.e. external) constraint coming from the popular medium or the melodramatic story material: Fassbinder's *The Marriage of Maria Braun* (1979) or *Lili Marleen* (1981) may have owed their existence partly to the director not sensing sufficient constraints present in the art cinema of his day.

The second reason cited by Elster as to why creative constraints are necessary – when a new technology turns artistic skill into automated effect and an abundance of stylistic options oblige the filmmaker to redefine what is the relation between expression and form – would take us to the situation with which I started: the fact that art cinema is now part of the market, under conditions of globalization; that digital tools and platforms have made self-expression the very opposite of autonomy; and that the binaries once dividing Hollywood from the rest have been replaced by asymmetrical and heteronomous forces. Detailing these forces – variously described as 'double occupancy', 'antagonistic mutuality', 'servants of two masters', 'states of abjection' – and identifying their effects within each of the films chosen as case studies has been the main aim of this study. The result has been to map not a level playing field for European cinema, but an uneven and conflicted one, with porous boundaries between Hollywood and independent cinema, between independent cinema and festival films, and

[20] Elster, *Ulysses Unbound*, 196

between festival films and artists' cinema. Yet what also emerge are the tactical advantages and strategic possibilities that arise from European cinema finding itself in the weaker position.

Modifying Elster's terminology in order to make it applicable to the state of cinema authorship, I draw a distinction between *external constraints* and *creative constraints*, with the external constraints the ones named by Lessig as enabling humans to engage with their lived environment and to effect change, and creative constraints the ones that renegotiate a different kind of autonomy and freedom. To these distinctions one should add the further difference between the *classic auteur (of Hollywood cinema)* and the *romantic auteur*, the latter more relevant to the *European auteur*, but also to be found on the margins of the studio system and championed by the French *nouvelle vague* as *auteurs maudits*. These apparent outsiders or misfits (Orson Welles, a notorious 'enemy of promise', Nicholas Ray or Sam Fuller) were regarded as rebels against the system – if necessary at the cost of failure – and their authorship would indeed have been celebrated by defining it as that of the creative exception, giving expression to his vision, his beliefs or inner demons through the medium that he has chosen, or that has chosen him.

By contrast, an example of the classic auteur would be the already mentioned John Ford, who famously introduced himself by saying 'My name is John Ford, I make Westerns.' His identity and self-image was that of a craftsperson and professional, not as an artist with a personal vision; the same goes for Alfred Hitchcock (at least before he was interviewed by François Truffaut and turned into a 'great artist' and 'master of pure cinema'). A classic auteur welcomes the external constraints of genre (the Western or the thriller), can cope with the pressures of the studio system (interference by the producer; the stipulations of the Hays Code) and accept the verdict of the box office ('you're only as good as your last film's gross'). It may seem as if the classical auteur merely accommodates himself to the system, but in the examples given (and one would want to add directors like Howard Hawks or Clint Eastwood), the external constraints become inner resources, leading to the kind of *mise en scène*, of staging, dialogue or generating suspense that made these directors into auteurs in the first place. As with metre and rhyme in poetry or the formal constraints of the sonnet or the sonata, 'genre' in classical Hollywood could become an incentive for invention.

European auteurs from the 1960s to the 1980s faced a different set of constraints: they were often regarded as representative of their particular 'national cinema' and even their nation: think of Bergman as the archetypal gloomy Swede, or the New German Cinema, whose directors – especially Hans Jürgen Syberberg, Werner Herzog or Wim Wenders – had to be romantics, rebels, dissenters or outsiders: for example they had to be both cliché Germans and critics of Germany. Rainer Werner Fassbinder, for instance, became the representative anti-representative of Germany in the 1980s, by making himself the epitome of the 'ugly' German: no one in Germany recognized themselves in him, nor did he want to be a representative of anyone, and yet these very contradictions were the condition of a director's international representativeness in post-war West Germany until 'unification'. Berating their government for not facing up to the country's horrible past, Fassbinder and his fellow New German Cinema directors were seen, mainly abroad, as representatives of a 'better' Germany. However, *the more critical they were, the more credible they became as representatives* – an irony that did not escape the West German government and its cultural institutions, which subsidized and sponsored such dissidence because they realized the benefits for the country's international image.[21] It confirms the well-known dilemma of dissenting art, insofar as it can be co-opted or recuperated by the system – a mechanism also observable in an auteur's relation to the film festival system, which needs his/her dissidence and values transgression as proof of its own integrity and authenticity.

Creative constraints and the author-function: beyond self-expression and genre

Now that filmmaking has become as popular, inexpensive and the results as easy to diffuse as is the case with digital tools, equipment and platforms, self-expression can no longer count as a reliable touchstone of a work's meaning and value. When YouTube is the very name of self-expression-as-self-exhibition ('broadcast yourself') and the 'selfie' of the sovereign Me rules social media, the author-function must also change. Rather than a guarantor of authenticity, or the last autonomous subject in an alienated and reified world, the contemporary filmmaker is an auteur only to the extent that s/he accepts the inherent anachronism of the label, as and when conferred by international film festivals. Thanks to Cannes and other A-festivals, European auteurs – like their Asian counterparts – are part of a star system of world cinema, assuming they possess the requisite attention value in the marketplace of reputations. Under conditions of overproduction and lacking agreed standards of value, the auteur as quality brand secures a

[21] Artists in West Germany had to be sages, the conscience of the nation, the upholders of values, but also the rebels against conventions, the avant-garde artists and international icons. Many were perceived as the nation's moral compass as well as modern masters: Joseph Beuys, Anselm Kiefer, Gerhard Richter; or they were public intellectuals: Heinrich Böll, Günter Grass, Christa Wolf, Heiner Müller. Today, as even these artists' and writers' subsequent reputations prove, things have become more complicated, and nowhere more so than for filmmakers.

stable horizon of expectation, with the director's image functioning like a 'genre', a notion often consolidated via 'trilogies', as in the case of Bergman (the Faith trilogy), Antonioni (the Alienation trilogy), Polanski (the Apartment trilogy), Fassbinder (the BRD trilogy) and Michael Haneke's so-called 'Glaciation trilogy'.

For a long time, roughly from Rossellini in the late 1940s to Jean-Luc Godard in the early 1980s, the European director could still assume the mantle of the modernist artist, responsible only to his work and answerable only to his own inclinations. Shielded from the full force of the market either by patronage (i.e. commercial producers like Pierre Braunberger or Carlo Ponti, who liked the prestige that came with investing in art cinema) or taxpayers' subsidy, their autonomy was a given, and indeed it was what made the auteurs valuable for the complex cultural politics of the country or nation ('cultural nationalism') whose critical conscience they were called upon to embody. No such protection or mission for the next generation: Michael Haneke, Lars von Trier, Aki Kaurismäki; or indeed for their American counterparts: David Lynch, Quentin Tarantino, Steven Soderbergh, Richard Linklater, Wes Anderson. They are obliged either to craft a self-image – the rebel, the cinephile, the eccentric, the slacker, the whimsical geek – and manage this image like a commercial brand, or they have to invent for themselves forms of resistance or paranoia, when the system no longer generates the friction conducive to creativity that a hostile society or an offended public used to provide.

Since the 1990s, one of the key figures of European auteur cinema in the global context has been Lars von Trier, one of the inspirations for this book, who has already featured in several previous chapters, including Chapter 10, devoted in part to his film *Melancholia* (2011). A credible representative of his country (he put Denmark back on the map as not only a filmmaking country, but as an internationally important and intriguing one), he is also wholly non-representative for a national cinema, insofar as his films are mostly in English and only rarely set in Denmark. His early ones camouflaged themselves as German films: *Element of Crime* (1984), *Epidemic* (1987) and *Europa* (1991), while the later ones were either Scottish (*Breaking the Waves* (1996)) or more often, American (*Dancer in the Dark* (2000), *Dogville* (2003), *Manderlay* (2005) and *Antichrist* (2009)). He, too, established his personal genre identity via trilogies (first the 'Europa' trilogy, then the 'Golden Heart' trilogy), but these designations were invoked by Trier ironically because the practice had become a cliché. Following Fassbinder, Trier courted negative epithets such as 'enfant terrible', 'controlling' and 'chaotic', but he, too, deployed them knowingly and strategically. Energizing the Nordic filmmaking infrastructure, he built up state-of-the-art studio capacity in Sweden's 'Trollhättan' with structural funds from the European Union for distressed manufacturing regions. He also, for a period, provided the international independent filmmaking community with a legitimating discourse, the *Dogme* manifesto. To this day it is not clear whether 'Dogme' is a pastiche of a manifesto or was to be taken at face value. What is certain, however, is that the *Dogme* members' 'vow of chastity' is an outstanding example of a set of creative constraints, put in place in order to stimulate talent and competition.[22] Unlike Bergman, who cast a long shadow on Swedish cinema, for much of the time stifling new talent, von Trier encapsulates the transition from the idea of the auteur-artist to that of the auteur as entrepreneur, as brand name, as well as facilitator and enabler.

Trier was also one of the first to practise an explicit poetics of creative constraints, giving them the name of 'obstructions' or 'mind-games' – the latter a term that has been mentioned throughout this study, and highlighted especially in connection with the 'thought experiment' in Chapter 3. So far, Trier has defined and redefined these obstructions several times: 1) the *Dogme* rules (as applied in *The Idiots* (1998)); 2) the *Five Obstructions* (2003, signed by Jørgen Leth, his former mentor), is effectively von Trier's meta-film about his own creative method); 3) directing by remote control a television feature called *D-Day*, about the last day of the previous millennium (2000); 4) using a computerized camera and so-called 'Lookeys' in *The Boss of it All* (2006); and 5) making a close adaptation of *The Hammer of Witches*, the *Malleus Malificarum* – an anti-women tract of the Inquisition – that is, about Christianity at its most fundamentalist and paranoid, in *Antichrist*.[23] Elsewhere I have tried to demonstrate how Trier's poetics of creative constraints fits into a broader overall strategy of re-establishing rules by first breaking them, and to show how the principle of arbitrary rules as creative constraints is fully on display also in *Nyphomaniac* (2013).[24] They are present in the competition about how many men Joe and her friend can have sex with on a single train journey, and the Little Flock's vow to have sex but no boyfriends also counts as a creative constraint. Constraints are once more foregrounded in the way Joe's narrative is triggered by the objects (and evolves from the cues) she notices in Seligman's room. Taken together these instances of breaking social norms by setting up arbitrary rules are so prominent in *Nymphomaniac* as to qualify it as a meta-film, where von Trier explores his own formal and narrative preoccupations, at least as much as exorcizing his personal demons or 'therapizing' his traumas. Besides von Trier's self-imposed obstructions, one could cite Wes Anderson's

---

[22] For a discussion of constraints in reference to the *Dogme* movement and manifesto (citing Jon Elster), see Mette Hjørt, 'Dogme 95', in Paisley Livingstone and Carl Plantinga (eds), *The Routledge Companion to Philosophy and Film* (London: Routledge, 2009), 487.

[23] See Bodil M. Thomsen, 'Antichrist – Chaos Reigns: the event of violence and the haptic image in Lars von Trier's film', *Journal of Aesthetics and Culture* 1 (2009): n.p.

[24] See Chapter 10 in this study.

highly stylized hyper-symmetrical visual compositions as similarly motivated creative constraints.

Performative self-contradiction

This returns me to the other move, already discussed in Chapter 1, by which some European auteurs try to counter the system *from within* rather than accommodating themselves to their servitude of double occupancy. Instead of accepting it covertly and with ironic knowingness, or denouncing the golden cage of contemporary auteurism by refusing to inhabit it, this alternative strategy – for which I introduced the philosophical concept of 'performative self-contradiction' – aims at carving out a kind of negative autonomy specifically under the capitalist conditions prevailing in the creative industries. Besides Fassbinder, who was my first prototype of performative self-contradiction, I have identified a similar tactic in the film work and self-presentation of Michael Haneke, one of the most militant – and seemingly unreconstructed – defenders of the film auteur as autonomous artist. As outlined at the end of Chapter 1, there is a link between Europe's dilemma of national self-interest in relation to shared transnational sovereignty, and the European auteur's autonomy in relation to the various kinds of antagonistic mutuality. In both cases, adopting either creative constraints or practising performative self-contradiction may be the only way forward.

Here I want to focus on performative self-contradiction by showing that, far from being a logical error (to be avoided in rational argument), it can become a risky but efficient tactic when trying to stand one's ground in situations where one's mutual entanglement with an adversary allows the latter to absorb and recuperate all forms of protest and critique. Just like the move towards self-imposed rules or creative constraints becomes necessary when the problem has not been defined clearly enough, so performative self-contradiction is part of the same set of counter-intuitive, dynamic but also potentially destructive strategies, all designed to regain or retain agency and control under complex, contradictory or in other ways adverse conditions. It adds a further, more aggressive or provocative layer, by exacerbating the hidden contradictions and exposing the ideological blind spots of the outwardly so mutually beneficial symbiosis between film directors and film festivals, by enacting that even as one dissents and resists, one is part of a market (of promotion and self-promotion) and its written and unwritten rules.

What is a performative self-contradiction? Briefly put, one enacts a performative self-contradiction when one makes a claim that contradicts the validity of the means that are used to make it, that is, which contradicts your performance of the claim. One of the best-known examples goes back to the logical or semantic paradoxes of the Greek philosopher Epimenides, who famously claimed that 'all Cretans are liars', while being himself a Cretan. In other words, in a performative self-contradiction, there is a conflict between one's presuppositions and one's conclusions. One affirms something, knowing that there are no grounds that could validate it, but doing so tries to put the addressee or adversary in a cognitive double bind, thus retroactively creating a space for oneself (where there is none) by putting oneself as the enunciator under erasure, that is, negatively securing an enunciative presence. It is thus a strategy that tries to control forces you cannot control, of finding a way out of moral or metaphysical deadlocks, without merely 'destabilizing' the categories or binary options, but aggravating their inherent contradictions.

As it happens, von Trier is one of those directors most acutely aware of this dilemma. A master of the performative self-contradiction, he had adopted it as his preferred counter-strategy, seen in action most provocatively in his public appearances at film festivals. A poster ahead of his appearance at the Berlin Film Festival in February 2014 to promote *Nymphomaniac* showed him with duct tape plastered over his mouth, signalling the fact that he had been 'silenced' by the Cannes festival, and was now 'vowing silence' after the disastrous press conference for *Melancholia* in May 2011. Yet the very gesture is so eloquent that it contradicts the assertion that he has been silenced. The same goes for his 'persona non grata-special selection' t-shirt display at the photocall also in Berlin.[25] There, von Trier was wearing his rejection and ejection from Cannes as a badge of honour, turning himself into a spectacle of abjection: we can now see how this state of abjection, as the key concept running through virtually all the chapters – once acknowledged as a force from outside that is best resisted by being positively assumed – can become an auteur's way to assert autonomy as an artist within the untranscendable horizon of commodification and the discourse of advertising and branding. Using the Cannes logo (a festival proud of being only about art) as the enunciator (and 'brand') of the utterance adorning his chest, von Trier entangles Cannes in a simple self-contradiction (Cannes makes 'art' its commercial 'brand'), which allows him to carve out for himself a performatively self-contradictory space between 'persona non

[25] 'For the world premiere of the director's cut of *Nymphomaniac, Vol. 1* von Trier maintained his vow to refrain from all public statements, and did not attend the press conference. But he had a message, nevertheless. At the photo call preceding the *Nymphomaniac* panel, the helmer sported a t-shirt emblazoned with the Cannes Film Festival logo followed by the words "Persona Non Grata, Official Selection." The sartorial choice was a nod to 2011 when von Trier was dubbed a *persona non grata* by Cannes for Nazi-flavored comments he made at a press conference for *Melancholia*.' Nancy Tartaglione, *Deadline Hollywood*, 9 February2014, http://deadline.com/2014/02/berlin-lars-von-trier-sports-persona-non-grata-t-shirt-shia-labeouf-abruptly-exits-nymphomaniac-press-conference-680154/) (accessed 10 January 2017).

grata' and 'special selection', and to show himself at his most independent when being taken hostage (or 'hosted') by the very institution to which he owes his reputation and fame.

Michael Haneke

In Michael Haneke, the creative constraints are finely balanced with enabling conditions. These include his decision, as a German by birth, to be an 'Austrian' director, some of whose major films have a distinctly 'French' identity. They also comprise a carefully calibrated relation to European cinema's father figures – an Oedipal 'anxiety of influence' matched by 'elective paternity' – even more complexly figured than that of Fassbinder (Douglas Sirk), Wenders (Nicholas Ray) and Herzog (F. W. Murnau). Restricting myself to only the French films, one finds Ingmar Bergman in *Le Temps du Loup/Time of the Wolf*, and – by choosing actresses like Isabelle Huppert, Juliette Binoche and Annie Girardot – Claude Chabrol, Francois Truffaut and André Téchiné. More generally, Haneke inscribes himself in a particular French tradition of 'bourgeois' cinema (with a cruel twist in the tail), a tradition which includes other illustrious foreign directors working in France, such as Luis Buñuel, Roman Polanski and Krzysztof Kieslowski. In *The White Ribbon*, apparently 'returning' to Germany, the 'freely chosen paternal constraint' (besides the photographer August Sander and the novelist Theodor Fontane) is once more Ingmar Bergman, who looms large. Not many critics seem to have noticed that in *The White Ribbon* the doctor's vicious verbal assault on his housekeeper and mistress is taken from Bergman's *Winter Light*, where Gunnar Björnstrand as the pastor who has lost his faith tongue-lashes his last and most loyal parishioner, the bespectacled Ingrid Thulin, because he cannot bear her love for him.

In another register of self-binding or creative constraints, Haneke is one of those European directors who are in a productively ambivalent dialogue with the different versions of Christianity, often choosing to adopt the faith that is adversarial or in tension with that of their upbringing: Bresson, Rohmer and Rivette are French cinema's most Jansenist Catholics, just as Kieslowski is Catholic Poland's most Protestant director. Tom Tykwer, the German Protestant, explores in *Run Lola run* and *Der Krieger und die Kaiserin* 'grace' as if he was a Catholic. And as with Lars von Trier, born Jewish, but who makes a Presbyterian film with *Breaking the Waves*, and a Catholic film with *Dogville* (the female protagonist is called 'Grace'), so the Catholic Michael Haneke examines in *The White Ribbon* the most severe version of Northern Protestantism, after having given us more Jansenist moral anguish, guilt without absolution or redemption in his French films, notably in *La Pianiste/The Pianist*, *Code Inconnu/Code Unknown* and *Caché*.

With Haneke, however, creative constraints take on quite another level of severity: they become what I have been calling 'performative self-contradictions'.[26] It reflects both the gravity of the situation European filmmakers finds themselves in, one marked by all manner of contradictions, and yet offering all kinds of freedom. I return to Jon Elster's definition of 'arbitrary' self-constraints, namely when there isn't sufficient constraint present in either their environment or if the problem at hand is not yet defined clearly enough. In support of the first condition ('not sufficient constraint present in the environment', one could argue that because European filmmakers receive much, if not all, the funding for their films from non-commercial sources, and mostly via the taxpayer), it deprives them *as it liberates them* of the constraint of the box-office. Added to this is the fact that national representativeness (and the constraints that come with it) has always been more of a side effect of the film festival circuit rather than an indigenous expression of the nation and is nowadays mainly reserved for filmmakers coming from the emerging nations of Asia, the Far East or Africa. Finally, this problem of representativeness is compounded by the peculiar a-symmetry which makes 'the cinema' in Europe a highly-valued *cultural* asset ('heritage', 'patrimoine', our 'living memory'), but a negligible *economic* factor ('a cottage industry'), which not only creates contradictions at the heart of the Brussels bureaucracy over the status of cinema, but may well demand some kind of boundary or resistance coming from the medium, the material or the maker.

This is the situation that Haneke finds himself in: when you look at the credits of *The White Ribbon*, for instance, you will find no fewer than five different production companies from four different countries (X-Filme Creative Pool, Hamburg; Wega Film, Vienna; Les Films du Losange, Paris; Lucky Red, London; and Canal +, Paris). In addition, Haneke was financially supported by the Medienboard Berlin-Brandenburg, the Mitteldeutsche Medienförderung, Leipzig, the German Federal Film Board, the Mini-Traité Franco-Canadien, the Deutsche Filmförderfonds (DFFF), the Austrian Film Institute, the Vienna Film Financing Fund and the French Ministère de la Culture et de la Communication and Eurimages (the Media Directive of the European Union). It is a further argument why films that advertise themselves as 'national' – 'eine *deutsche* Kindergeschichte' [a German children's story], in Gothic script, no less – do so invariably in a gesture that is both performatively national and post-national.

Performing the nation rather than representing it, Haneke responds, in *Das Weisse Band*, to two other crises, and in each case by creative constraints

[26] For an earlier discussion of this concept in relation to Haneke's work, see Thomas Elsaesser, 'Performative Self-Contradictions: Michael Haneke's Mindgames', in Roy Grundmann (ed.), *A Companion to Michael Haneke* (Chichester: Wiley-Blackwell, 2010), 53–74.

that reveal themselves as acts of liberation. One set of constraints answers to the crisis that European cinema is no longer 'cinema', other than in constant and constantly self-defeating differentiation from television. Haneke has gone all out in his denunciations of television, both in his films and in interviews, but given that most of his films were produced and financed by television, one must regard this stance as a performative self-contradiction, rather than merely seeing it as yet another case of an artist biting the hand that feeds him: the performativity helps to underline – and bring to the fore – the structural contradictions inherent in European filmmaking which wants 'cinema' but can only afford 'television'.

The second crisis acknowledges that this cinema's primary source of aesthetic value is realism, but that such realism is in jeopardy, at least as traditionally understood, once cinema has become a digital medium. In the debate over the so-called 'death' of cinema, the loss of photographic indexicality brought about by the digital image means that there can be no essential contact between physical reality and the image, one of the defining features of 'cinema'. But there can also be no friction and resistance emanating from the real, and thus no more encounter, no more disclosure of being, as envisaged by the aesthetics of realism in the spirit of André Bazin. In other words, the dilemma is either consent to the death of cinema and cease making films, or accept digital cinema as something other than a contradiction in terms, and cease claiming realism as your aesthetics: a difficult decision for European filmmaking, which – it will be recalled – has always defined itself against Hollywood on the basis of its greater realism. Whether one thinks of Italian neo-realism, the French *nouvelle vague*'s semi-documentary *cinéma vérité*, or Ingmar Bergman's clinically probing psychological realism, our notions of non-Hollywood filmmaking are generally tied to some version of a realist aesthetics. Here, too, Haneke has tackled the issue of digital realism head-on. *The White Ribbon* was shot digitally and in colour, before remastering it in post-production to a point where it appears as the most pristine of silver emulsion black and white. An underhand fake, or a gesture of performative self-contradiction? Haneke's self-constraint, in Elster's terms, would thus have flipped over from abitrariness to necessity: the consequence not of the environment offering insufficient constraints, but of the problem at hand (in this case, 'digital realism') not yet being defined clearly enough.

The White Ribbon, finally, is also an important contribution at the story level to the political and philosophical narrative I began with: the reassessment of the legacy of the Enlightenment across a different kind of anti-anti-foundationalism and new universalism. The film might show a parochial, self-enclosed world, imminently threatened with internal implosion – as well as external destruction – by the chaos and upheavals of the Great War, but Haneke has also set it up as a laboratory situation, where many of the postures and forces that have shaped Europe over the past 200 years are once more pitted against each other. As a parable about the origins of Western values, re-examining the Enlightenment heritage, *The White Ribbon* once more unfolds the classic 'bourgeois' triad of pastor, doctor and schoolteacher, across whose stances a good deal of nineteenth-century fiction tried to 'work through' and resolve the tensions between Church authority, lay-secularism and modern science and technology. Rather than about the origins of fascism, *The White Ribbon* is more pertinently about the origins of the nation state and national identity, through the conflictual interplay of schoolteacher, state Church, feudal master and medical doctor – each standing for aspects of both the costs and the benefits of progress and modernity winning out over tradition and authority.

Into this classical schema, Haneke introduces a significant 'revision' and a twist, in that it is the representative of science and progress, the doctor, who seems to have lost 'faith', rather than the pastor, while the schoolteacher – along with his bride to be – is and remains the outsider (gentle and compassionate; but when it matters, passive and reactive). It is as if the old (literary, Enlightenment) oppositions pastor versus doctor, religion versus science, socialism (equality, democracy) versus authoritarianism (obedience in exchange for feudal benevolence) are now revealed as two sides of the same coin, in that neither can claim legitimacy or provide the moral grounds for exercising authority and sovereignty. We see the sins of the fathers, visited upon the children, which visit them on (each) other(s) in their turn, in a circuit where 'crime' and 'punishment' are not reciprocal, even though there may be eventual 'justice' – though not by the institutions here present. *The White Ribbon* as thought experiment of a new authoritarianism?

From 'servant of two masters' to 'performative self-contradiction': the philosophical turn

This last conundrum returns me to the philosophical context in which performative self-contradiction can function as a further stage and possible response to the global auteur's state of double or triple servitude, as discussed above. Performative self-contradiction came to prominence in the late 1980s, when Jürgen Habermas levelled a thoroughgoing critique against, among others, Jacques Derrida, feeling compelled to defend the 'unfinished project of modernity' that began with the Enlightenment, against post-Nietzschean, Heidegger-inspired anti-humanism and deconstruction. In his *The Philosophical Discourse of Modernity* (1987), Habermas tries to prove that postmodern philosophers – he has in mind especially Derrida, Foucault and Bataille – are taking apart Enlightenment reason and post-Kantian philosophy of the subject, while unwittingly relying on the philosophical concepts they are critiquing. He even includes Adorno:

> Adorno's 'negative dialectics' and Derrida's 'deconstruction' can be seen as different answers to the same problem. The totalizing self-critique of reason gets caught in a performative contradiction since subject-centered reason can only be convicted of being authoritarian when having recourse its own tools. The tools of thought, which . . . are imbued with the 'metaphysics of presence,' (Derrida) are nevertheless the only available means for uncovering their insufficiency.[27]

In other words, according to Habermas, Derrida remains trapped within the theoretical framework against which he is writing, so that his performative self-contradiction consists in sawing off the branch on which he is himself sitting. Clearly, for Habermas, this is a serious shortcoming, one that he would expect a philosopher to avoid.

Yet, as many commentators have pointed out, Habermas may be misunderstanding the very project of deconstruction, which is not to critique or dismantle reason from a position outside, but to offer an immanent critique, a form of argument that acknowledges this trap, this necessary self-binding of philosophy. To go a step further, what from the point of view of logic or analytical philosophy might seem a grievous error, may turn out, from a rhetorical or political perspective, to offer another way of reading, another way of looking and thus a space of freedom, of movement that loosens the shackles even if it does not remove them. As Seyla Benhabib puts it:

> It is not difficult to show that any theory which denies . . . the possibility of distinguishing between [truth] and sheer manipulative rhetoric would be involved in a 'performative self-contradiction.' This may not be terribly difficult, but it does not settle the issue either. For, from Nietzsche's aphorisms, to Heidegger's poetics, to Adorno's stylistic configurations, and to Derrida's deconstructions, we have examples of thinkers who accept this performative self-contradiction, and who self-consciously draw the consequences from it by seeking a new way of writing and communicating.[28]

This, then would be the stake: if, for the many reasons I have indicated, the global auteur is only an auteur as long as s/he is inside and part of the system, then the self-binding creative constraints, exacerbated to the point of performative self-contradiction, become, unavoidably, the only possible

---

[27] Jürgen Habermas, *The Philosophical Discourse of Modernity*, trans. Frederick Lawrence (Cambridge: Polity Press, 1987), 185 (translation modified).

[28] Seyla Benhabib, 'Epistemologies of Postmodernism: A Rejoinder to J.F. Lyotard', in Victor E. Taylor and Charles E. Winquist (eds), *Postmodernism: Disciplinary Texts* (New York: Routledge, 1998), 488.

enunciative position, and thus the only form of authenticity and autonomy. While the hidden antagonisms, the unforeseeable contingencies and the asymmetrical power dynamics that make creative constraints necessary seem to speak of the auteur's dependency and weakness both vis-à-vis the market (of reputation and revenue) and vis-à-vis the auteur's chief benefactor (the film festival circuit), in actual fact, any acts of performative self-contradiction would signal a more properly 'philosophical' turn or gesture. It would begin to grant filmmakers as auteurs the place and value that film-philosophy has long tried to bestow on their films, namely of putting forward philosophical positions in their own right. We seem to have come full circle: the anachronism or obsolescence of the auteur as a representative of art against commerce and commodification, with which I started, now turns out – under conditions of globalization and the film festival circuit – to be the very precondition for a paradoxical kind of autonomy and agency that has the potential of helping to reinvent the cinema: not as an art form, nor as a life form, but as a form of philosophy. The *politique des auteurs* has never seemed more urgent, and never seemed more timely: as both autonomous agent and abject, as performer of a living self-contradiction, the auteur may be the *last action hero* in a post-heroic Europe.

BIBLIOGRAPHY

Agamben, Giorgio, *Homo Sacer: Sovereign Power and Bare Life*, trans. Daniel Heller-Roazen, Stanford, CA: Stanford University Press, 1999.

Agamben, Giorgio, 'Notes on Gesture', in *Means Without End: Notes on Politics*, trans. Vincenzo Binetti and Cesare Casarino, Minneapolis: University of Minnesota Press, 2000, 49–62.

Agamben, Giorgio, *State of Exception*, trans. Kevin Attell, Chicago: University of Chicago Press, 2005.

Agamben, Giorgio, 'Introductory Note on the Concept of Democracy', in Alain Badiou and Slavoj Žižek (eds), *Democracy in What State?*, trans. William McCuaig, New York: Columbia University Press, 2012, 1–5.

Altman, Anna, 'Go East', *New Yorker*, 11 January 2013, http://www.newyorker.com/online/blogs/culture/2013/01/east-germany-in-barbara.html (accessed 5 June 2017).

Anderson, Benedict, *Imagined Communities: On The Origins of Nationalism*, London: Verso, 1983.

Anderson, Perry, 'Depicting Europe', *London Review of Books* 29, no. 18 (September 2007): 13–21, http://www.lrb.co.uk/v29/n18/perry-anderson/depicting-europe (accessed 4 September 2017).

Andrew, Dudley, 'Fatih Akin's Moral Geometry', in Seung-hoon Jeong and Jeremi Szaniawski (eds), *The Global Auteur: The Politics of Authorship in 21st Century Cinema*, New York: Wallflower, 2015, 179–98.

Appiah, Kwame Anthony, *Cosmopolitanism: Ethics in a World of Strangers*, New York: W.W. Norton, 2006.

Arendt, Hannah, 'The Decline of the Nation-State and the End of the Rights of Man', in *The Origins of Totalitarism*, London and New York: Harcourt, 1951.

Aristotle, *The Complete Works of Aristotle Vol. II*, ed. Jonathan Barnes, Princeton, NJ: Princeton University Press, 1984.

Atran, Scott, 'Religion in America', *Huffington Post*, US edition, 25 May 2011, http://www.huffingtonpost.com/scott-atran/religion-in-america-why-m_b_126225.html > (accessed 9 January 2017).

Aumont, Jacques, 'Que reste-t-il du cinéma?', *Trafic* 79 (September 2011): 95–107.

Aumont, Jacques, *Que reste-t-il du cinéma?*, Paris: Vrin, 2013.

Badiou, Alain, *Deleuze – The Clamour of Being*, Minneapolis: University of Minnesota Press, 1999.

Badiou, Alain, *Ethics: An Essay on the Understanding of Evil*, trans. Peter Hallward, London: Verso, 2001.

Badiou, Alain, 'The Democratic Emblem', in Giorgio Agamben et al., *Democracy in What State?*, trans. William McCuaig, New York: Columbia University Press, 2012, 6–15.

Baecker, Dirk 'Zukunftsfähigkeit: 22 Thesen zur nächsten Gesellschaft', *The Catjects Project* (blog), 2 July 2013, https://catjects.wordpress.com/2013/07/02/zukunftsfahigkeit–22-thesen-zur-nachsten-gesellschaft (accessed 9 January 2017).

Bal, Mieke, 'Exhibition as Film', in Robin Ostow (ed.), *(Re)Visualizing National History: Museums and National Identities in the New Millennium*, Toronto: University of Toronto Press, 2008, 15–43.

Balibar, Étienne, *We the People of Europe? Reflections on Transnational Citizenship*, trans. James Swenton, Princeton, NJ: Princeton University Press, 2004.

Balibar, Étienne, 'On Universalism: In Debate with Alain Badiou', *European Institue for Progressive Cultural Policies*, 2007, http://eipcp.net/transversal/0607/balibar/en > (accessed 5 September 2017).

Balibar, Étienne and Immanuel Wallerstein, *Race, Nation, Class: Ambiguous Identities*, trans. Chris Turner, London: Verso, 1991.

Balke, Friedrich, 'Tristes Tropiques: Systems Theory and the Literary Scene', *Soziale Systeme* 8 (2002): 27–37.

Barber, Benjamin and Sondra Myers, *The Interdependence Handbook: Looking Back, Living the Present, Choosing the Future*, New York: International Debate Education Association, 2004.

Barthes, Roland, *S/Z An Essay*, trans. Richard Miller, New York: Hill & Wang, 1970.

Bartsch, Anne, 'Vivid Abstractions: On the Role of Emotion Metaphors in Film Viewers' Search for Deeper Insight and Meaning', *Midwest Studies in Philosophy* 34 (2010): 240–60.

Bataille, Georges, 'Informe', *Documents* 7 (December 1929): 382.

Baudry, Jean-Louis, 'The Apparatus: Metapsychological Approaches to the Impression of Reality in Cinema', *Camera Obscura* 1 (1976): 104–26.

Bauman, Zygmund, *Modernity and the Holocaust*, Cambridge: Polity, 1989.

Bauman, Zygmund, *Europe: An Unfinished Adventure*, Cambridge: Polity, 2004.

Bauman, Zygmund, *Wasted Lives: Modernity and its Outcasts*, Cambridge: Polity, 2004.

Bazin, André, 'The Ontology of the Photographic Image', trans. Hugh Gray, *Film Quarterly* 13, no. 4 (Summer 1960): 4–9.

Beck, Ulrich, 'Time to Get Angry, Europe', Lecture, Guggenheim Museum, Bilbao, 1 December 2011, http://globernance.org/ulrich-beck-time-to-get-angry-europe/ (accessed 9 January 2017).

Beck, Ulrich and Edgar Grande, *Cosmopolitan Europe*, Cambridge: Polity, 2007.

Behlil, Melis, *Hollywood is Everywhere: Global Directors in the Blockbuster Era*, Amsterdam: Amsterdam University Press, 2016.

Beller, Jonathan, 'Cinema, Capital of the 20th Century', *Postmodern Culture* 3, no. 3 (1994), http://pmc.iath.virginia.edu/text-only/issue.594/beller.594 (accessed 12 January 2017).

Bellour, Raymond, *La Querelle des dispositifs: Cinéma – installations, expositions*, Paris: P.O.L., 2012.

Benhabib, Seyla, 'Epistemologies of Postmodernism: A Rejoinder to Jean-François Lyotard', in Victor E. Taylor and Charles E. Winquist (eds), *Postmodernism: Disciplinary Texts*, New York: Routledge, 1998, 479–500.

Benjamin, Walter, *Ursprung des deutschen Trauerspiels*, Frankfurt: Suhrkamp Verlag, 1963.

Benjamin, Walter, 'Paris, Capital of the Nineteenth Century', in Rolf Tiedman (ed.), *The Arcades Project*, trans. Howard Eiland and Kevin McLaughlin, Cambridge, MA: Harvard University Press, (1939) 1999.

Bensaïd, Daniel, 'Permanent Scandal', in Alain Badiou and Slavoj Žižek (eds), *Democracy in What State?*, trans. William McCuaig, New York: Columbia University Press, 2012, 16–43.

Berghahn, Volker R., 'The debate on "Americanization" among economic and cultural historians', *Cold War History* 10, no. 1 (February 2010): 107–30.

Bergson, Henri, *Creative Evolution*, trans. Arthur Mitchell, New York: Cosimo, 2005.

Berlant, Lauren, 'Nearly Utopian, Nearly Normal: Post-Fordist Affect in *La Promesse* and *Rosetta*', *Public Culture* 19, no. 2 (2007): 273–301.

Bernstein, J. M., 'Movies as the Great Democratic Artform of the Modern World', in Jean-Philippe Deranty and Alison Ross (eds), *Jacques Rancière and the Contemporary Scene*, London and New York: Continuum (2012), 15–42.

Beugnet, Martine, 'The Wounded Screen', in Tanya Horeck and Tina Kendall (eds), *The New Extremism in Cinema: From France to Europe*, Edinburgh: Edinburgh University Press, 2011, 29–42.

Beugnet, Martine and Jane Sillars, 'Beau travail: time, space and myths of identity', *Studies in French Cinema* 1, no. 3 (2001): 166–73.

Blanchot, Maurice, *The Unavowable Community*, trans. Pierre Joris, New York: Station Hill Press, 1988.

Böhme, Hartmut, *Albrecht Dürer, Melencolia I: im Labyrinth der Deutung*, Frankfurt: Fischer, 1989.

Bois, Yves-Alain and Rosalind Krauss, *Formless: A User's Guide*, New York: Zone Books, 1997.

Bowser, Eileen, *History of the American Cinema: The Transformation of Cinema, 1907–1915*, Berkeley: University of California Press, 1990.

Bradshaw, Peter, review of *Beau Travail*, dir. by Claire Denis, *Guardian*, 14 July 2000, https://www.theguardian.com/film/2000/jul/14/1 (accessed 21 August 2017).

Bradshaw, Peter, review of *Melancholia*, dir. by Lars von Trier, *Guardian*, 29 September 2011, http://www.theguardian.com/film/2011/sep/29/melancholia-film-review (accessed 10 January 2017).

Branigan, Edward and Warren Buckland (eds), *The Routledge Encyclopaedia of Film Theory*, New York: Routledge, 2014.

Brassier, Ray, *Nihil Unbound*, London: Palgrave Macmillan, 2007.

Breger, Claudia, 'Configuring Affect: Complex World-Making in Fatih Akin's *Auf der anderen Seite*', *Cinema Journal* 54, no. 1 (Fall 2014): 65–87.

Breton, Andre, 'Limits Not Frontiers of Surrealism', in *What Is Surrealism? – Selected Writings*, New York: Pathfinder, 1978, 199–211.

Brinckmann, Christine Noll, 'Die Arbeit der Kamera', in Isabella Reicher and Michael Omasta (eds), *Claire Denis: Trouble Every Day*, Vienna: Filmmuseum-Synema, 2005, 18–33.

Brown, Mark, 'Lookey here: Lars von Trier is at it again', *Guardian*, 8 December 2006, https://www.theguardian.com/world/2006/dec/08/filmnews.film (accessed 10 January 2017).

Brown, Wendy, 'We Are All Democrats Now', in Alain Badiou and Slavoj Žižek (eds), *Democracy in What State?*, trans. William McCuaig, New York: Columbia University Press, 2012, 44–57.

Buckland, Warren, 'Between Science Fact and Science Fiction: Spielberg's Digital Dinosaurs, Possible Worlds, and the New Aesthetic Realism', *Screen* 40, no. 2 (Summer 1999): 177–92.

Burgin, Victor, 'Geometry and Abjection', *Public* 1 (Winter 1988): 12–30. Reprinted in John Fletcher and Andrew Benjamin (eds), *Abjection, Melancholia, and Love: The Work of Julia Kristeva* (London: Routledge, 1990), 104–23.

Butler, Judith, 'The Body Politics of Julia Kristeva', *Hypatia* 3, no. 3, French Feminist Philosophy (Winter 1989): 104–18.

Butler, Judith, *The Psychic Life of Power*, Stanford, CA: Stanford University Press, 1997.

Butler, Judith, *Frames of War: When Is Life Grievable?*, London: Verso, 2010.

Carroll, Noël, 'Movies, the Moral Emotions, and Sympathy', *Midwest Studies in Philosophy* 34 (2010): 1–19.

Carroll, Noël and Jinhee Choi (eds), *Philosophy of Film and Motion Pictures: An Anthology*, Malden, MA, and London: Blackwell, 2005.

Castells, Manuel, 'European Cities, the Informational Society and the Global Economy', *New Left Review* 1, no. 204 (March–April 1994): 18–32.

Castells, Manuel, *End of Millennium*, The Information Age: Economy, Society and Culture Vol. 3, Oxford: Blackwell, 1996.

Castells, Manuel, 'The Construction of European Identity', in Maria João Rodrigues (ed.), *The New Knowledge Economy in Europe*, Cheltenham: Edward Elgar, 2002, 232–41.

Caughie, John (ed.), *Theories of Authorship*, London and New York: Routledge, 1981.

Cavell, Stanley, *The World Viewed: Reflections on the Ontology of Film*, Cambridge, MA: Harvard University Press, 1971.

Cavell, Stanley, *The Claim of Reason: Wittgenstein, Skepticism, Morality, and Tragedy*, Oxford: Oxford University Press, 1979.

Cavell, Stanley, *Contesting Tears: The Hollywood Melodrama of the Unknown Woman*, Chicago: University of Chicago Press, 1997.

Caygill, Howard, *Levinas and the Political*, New York: Routledge, 2002.

Chanter, Tina, *The Picture of Abjection: Film, Fetish, and the Nature of Difference*, Bloomington: Indiana University Press, 2007.

Clark, Andy and David J. Chalmers, 'The Extended Mind', *Analysis* 58 (1998): 7–19.

Clover, Carol, *Men, Women and Chainsaws*, Princeton, NJ: Princeton University Press, 1992.

Cole, Jake, review of *Barbara*, dir. by Christian Petzold, *Spectrum Culture*, 20 December 2012, http://spectrumculture.com/2012/12/20/barbara/ (accessed 5 June 2017).

Collett-White, Mike. 'Lars von Trier film "Antichrist" Shocks Cannes', *Reuters*, 17 May 2009, http://www.reuters.com/article/us-cannes-antichrist-idUSTRE54G2JF20090517 (accessed 27 November 2017).

Conley, Tom, 'Cinema and its Discontents: Jacques Rancière and Film Theory', *SubStance* 34, no. 3 (2005): 96–106.

Connolly, Kate, 'Pegida: what does the German far-right movement actually stand for?', *Guardian*, 6 January 2015, https://www.theguardian.com/world/shortcuts/2015/jan/06/pegida-what-does-german-far-right-movement-actually-stand-for (accessed 18 December 2016).

Cooper, Robert, *The Breaking of Nations: Order and Chaos in the Twenty-First Century*, New York: Atlantic Books, 2003.

Cooper, Sarah, 'Je sais bien, mais quand même . . .: Fetishism, Envy, and the Queer Pleasures of Beau travail', *Studies in French Cinema* 1, no. 3 (2001): 174–82.

Cooper, Sarah, *Selfless Cinema? Ethics and French Documentary*, Oxford: Legenda, 2006.

Cooper, Sarah, 'Moral Ethics: Reading Levinas with the Dardenne Brothers', *Film-Philosophy* 11, no. 2 (2007).

Cooper, Sarah (ed.), 'The Occluded Relation: Levinas and Cinema', Special issue, *Film-Philosophy* 11, no. 2 (2007).

Corrigan, Timothy and Patricia White, *The Film Experience*, 5th edn, New York: Macmillan Learning, 2017.

Coveney, Michael, *The World According to Mike Leigh*, New York: Harper Collins, 1996.

Creed, Barbara, *The Monstrous-Feminine: Film, Feminism, Psychoanalysis*, London and New York: Routledge 1993.

Critchley, Simon, 'Five Problems in Levinas's View of Politics and a Sketch of a Solution to Them', *Political Theory* 32, no. 2 (April 2004): 172–85.

Critchley, Simon, *Infinitely Demanding*, London: Verso, 2007.

Dardenne, Luc, *Au dos de nos images, 1991–2005*, Paris: Editions du Seuil, 2008.

De Gruyter, Caroline, 'Wat is er mis met Europa, en wat doen we er an?', *NRC Handelsblad*, 13 February 2016, http://www.nrc.nl/nieuws/2016/02/13/wat-is-er-mis-is-met-europa-en-wat-doen-we-er-an-1587839-a850793 (accessed 4 September 2017).

De Vries, Hent and Lawrence Eugene Sullivan, *Political Theologies: Public Religions in a Post-secular World*, New York: Fordham University Press, 2006.

Dean, Tim, review of *Masculinity, Psychoanalysis, Straight Queer Theory: Essays on Abjection in Literature, Mass Culture, and Film*, by Calvin Thomas, *MFS Modern Fiction Studies* 55, no. 4 (Winter 2009): 871–4.

Deleuze, Gilles, *Cinema 1: The Movement-Image*, trans. Hugh Tomlinson, Minneapolis: University of Minnesota Press, 1986.

Deleuze, Gilles, *Cinema 2: The Time-Image*, trans. Hugh Tomlinson, Minneapolis: University of Minnesota Press, 1989.

Deleuze, Gilles, *Negotiations 1970–1990*, New York: Columbia University Press, 1997.

Denis, Claire, 'Film-makers on film: Claire Denis', interview by Sheila Johnston, *Daily Telegraph*, 16 August 2003.

Deranty, Jean-Philippe and Alison Ross (eds,) *Jacques Rancière and the Contemporary Scene*, London: Continuum, 2012.

Derrida, Jacques, *Adieu à Emmanuel Levinas*, Paris: Galilee, 1997.

Derrida, Jacques, 'Hospitality, Justice, and Responsibility: A Dialogue with Jacques Derrida', in Richard Kearney and Mark Dooley (eds), *Questioning Ethics: Contemporary Debates in Philosophy*, New York: Routledge, 2002.

Derrida, Jacques, 'Violence and Metaphysics', in Claire Elise Katz and Lara Trout (eds), *Emmanuel Levinas*, London: Routledge, 2005, 1–88.

Derrida, Jacques and Anne Dufourmantelle, *Of Hospitality*, trans. Rachel Bowlby, Stanford, CA: Stanford University Press, 2000.

Dixit, Avinash and Barry Nalebuff, 'Prisoners' Dilemma', *The Concise Encyclopedia of Economics*, 2008, http://www.econlib.org/library/Enc/PrisonersDilemma.html (accessed 10 January 2017).

Doane, Mary Ann, *The Desire to Desire*, Bloomington: Indiana University Press, 1987.

Donnelly, Jack, 'Cultural Relativism and Human Rights', *Human Rights Quarterly* 6, no. 4 (1984): 400–19.

Dosse, Francois, *Gilles Deleuze and Félix Guattari: Intersecting Lives*, New York: Columbia University Press, 2011.

Douchet, Jean, Lecture press handout, *Le Cinéma: Vers son deuxième siècle*, conference held at the Odéon, Paris, 20 March 1995.

Douglas, Mary, *Purity and Danger: An Analysis of Concepts of Pollution and Taboo*, London: Routledge and Kegan Paul, 1966.

Ebert, Roger, review of *Bad Lieutenant*, dir. by Abel Ferrara, *Chicago-Sun Times*, 22 January 1993, https://www.rogerebert.com/reviews/bad-lieutenant-1993 (accessed 12 November 2017).

Eipides, Dimitri, 'Barbara', *Toronto International Film Festival, 2012*, http://www.bytowne.ca/movie/barbara (accessed 4 June 2017).

Elsaesser, Thomas, 'Cinephilia, or The Uses of Disenchantment', in Marijke De Valck and Malte Hagener (eds), *Cinephilia: Movies, Love and Memory*, Amsterdam: Amsterdam University Press, 2005, 27–44.

Elsaesser, Thomas, *European Cinema: Face to Face with Hollywood*, Amsterdam: Amsterdam University Press, 2005.

Elsaesser, Thomas, 'The Mind-Game Film', in Warren Buckland (ed.), *Puzzle Films: Complex Storytelling in Contemporary Cinema*, Hoboken, NJ: Wiley-Blackwell, 2009, 13–41.

Elsaesser, Thomas, 'Real Location, Fantasy Space, Performative Place: Double Occupancy and Mutual Interference in European Cinema', in Temenuga Trifonova (ed.), *European Film Theory*, New York and London: Routledge, 2009, 47–61.

Elsaesser, Thomas, 'Performative Self-Contradictions: Michael Haneke's Mindgames', in Roy Grundmann (ed.), *A Companion to Michael Haneke*, Chichester: Wiley-Blackwell, 2010, 53–74.

Elsaesser, Thomas, 'James Cameron's *Avatar*: access for all', *New Review of Film and Television Studies* 9, no. 3 (2011): 247–64.

Elsaesser, Thomas, *The Persistance of Hollywood*, New York: Routledge, 2013.

Elsaesser, Thomas, *Film History as Media Archaeology*, Amsterdam: Amsterdam University Press, 2016.

Elsaesser, Thomas, 'Media Archaeology as Symptom', *New Review of Film and Television Studies* 14, no. 2 (2016): 181–215.

Elsaesser, Thomas, 'Contingency, Causality, Complexity: Distributed Agency in the Mind-game Film', *New Review of Film and Television Studies* 16, no. 1 (2018): 1–39.

Elsaesser, Thomas and Malte Hagener, *Film Theory: An Introduction Through the Senses*, 2nd edn, London and New York: Routledge 2015.

Elster, Jon, 'Creativity and Constraints in the Arts', in *Ulysses Unbound: Studies in Rationality, Precommitment, and Constraints*, Cambridge: Cambridge University Press, 2000, 175–268.

Epstein, Jean, 'Bonjour Cinéma [1921]', [or 'The Senses I (b)'], in Richard Abel (ed.), *French Film Theory and Criticism: A History/Anthropology, 1907–1939*, trans. Tom Milne, Volume 1: 1907–1929, Princeton, NJ: Princeton University Press, 1988, 241–6.

Esposito, Dawn, 'Mafia Women and Abject Spectatorship', *Melus* 28, no. 3 (Autumn 2003): 91–109.

Esposito, Roberto, 'An Interview with Roberto Esposito', interviewed by Diego Ferrante and Marco Piasentier, *The Philosophical Salon*, http://thephilosophicalsalon.com/from-outside-a-philosophy-for-europe-an-interview-with-roberto-esposito-part-one/ (accessed 27 December 2016).

Esposito, Roberto, *From Outside: A Philosophy for Europe*, London: Polity Press, 2017.

Everett, Wendy (ed.), *European Identity in Cinema*, Bristol: Intellect Books, 2005.

Everett, Wendy and Axel Goodbody (eds), *Revisiting Space: Space and Place in European Cinema*, Brussels: Peter Lang, 2005.

Ezra, Elizabeth (ed.), *European Cinema*, Oxford: Oxford University Press, 2004.

Ezra, Elizabeth and Terry Rowden (eds), *Transnational Cinema: The Film Reader*, London and New York: Routledge, 2006.

Falzen, Chris, 'Philosophy Through Film', *Internet Encyclopedia of Philosophy*', http://www.iep.utm.edu/phi-film/ (accessed 9 December 2016).

Fontana, Josep, *The Distorted Past: A Reinterpretation of Europe*, Cambridge, MA: Blackwell, 1995.

Foster, Hal, 'Obscene, Abject, Traumatic', *October* 78 (Autumn 1996): 106–24.

Foster, Hal, 'Precarious', *Artforum*, December 2009, https://www.artforum.com/inprint/issue=200910&id=24264 (accessed 9 January 2017).

Foster, Hal, Benjamin Buchloh, Rosalind Krauss, Yves-Alain Bois, Denis Hollier and Helen Molesworth, 'The Politics of the Signifier II: A Conversation on the *Informe* and the Abject', roundtable discussion, *October* 67 (Winter 1994).

Foucault, Michel, 'Ceci n'est pas une pipe', *October* 1 (Spring 1976): 6–21.

Foucault, Michel, *Archaeology of Knowledge*, trans. A. M. Sheridan Smith, London and New York: Routledge, (1969) 1989.

Foucault, Michel, *The Order of Things: An Archaeology of the Human Sciences*, New York and London: Routledge, (1966) 1989.

Fowler, Catherine (ed.), *European Cinema Reader*, London: Routledge, 2002.

Frampton, Daniel, *Filmosophy*, London: Wallflower, 2006.

Franke, Anselm, 'A Critique of Animation', *e-flux* 59 (November 2014), http://www.e-flux.com/journal/59/61098/a-critique-of-animation/ (accessed 12 December 2016).

Freeland, Cynthia A. and Thomas E. Wartenberg (eds), *Philosophy and Film*, London and New York: Routledge, 1995.

French, Philip, review of *Melancholia*, dir. by Lars von Trier, *Observer*, 2 October 2011, http://www.theguardian.com/film/2011/oct/02/melancholia-lars-von-trier-review (accessed 10 January 2017).

Freud, Sigmund, 'Mourning and Melancholia', *The Standard Edition of the Complete Psychological Works of Sigmund Freud* 14, (1917) 1976, 239–60.

Freud, Sigmund, *Civilization and its Discontents*, London: Penguin, 2002.

Fried, Michael, *Absorption and Theatricality: Painting and Beholder in the Age of Diderot*, Chicago: University of Chicago Press, 1988.

Galt, Rosalind, *The New European Cinema: Redrawing the Map*, New York: Columbia University Press, 2006.

Gassert, Philipp. 'The Spectre of Americanization: Western Europe in the American Century', in Dan Stone (ed.), *The Oxford Handbook of Postwar European History*, Oxford: Oxford University Press, 2012, 182–200.

Gaudreault, André and Philippe Marion, *The End of Cinema? A Medium Crisis in the Digital Age*, New York: Columbia University Press, 2015.

Geller, Jeffrey, review of *Profanations*, by Giogio Agamben, *Notre Dame Philosophical Reviews*, 2008, http://ndpr.nd.edu/news/23591/?id=13409 (accessed 26 October 2017).

Gerstner, David A. and Janet Staiger (eds), *Authorship and Film*, New York: Routledge, 2003.

Ghosh, Priyaa, 'Melodrama of Melancholia', *Edit Room*, 4 January 2012, http://blogs.widescreenjournal.org/?p=2275 (accessed 10 January 2017).

Gibson, John (ed.), *The Philosophy of Poetry*, Oxford: Oxford University Press, 2015.

Grant, Barry Keith (ed.), *Auteurs and Authorship: A Film Reader*, Malden, MA: Wiley-Blackwell, 2008.

Grant, Drew, 'Lars von Trier's "Melancholia": An Apocalyptic Wedding', *Salon.com*, 8 April 2011, http://www.salon.com/2011/04/08/melancholia_trailer_von_trier/ (accessed 10 January 2017).

Greif, Mark, 'Apocalypse Deferred', review of *State of Exception*, by Giorgio Agamben, *N+1* 2 (2005), https://nplusonemag.com/issue-2/reviews/apocalypse-deferred/ (accessed 26 November 2017).

Groys, Boris, 'Under the Gaze of Theory', *e-flux* 35 (2012), http://www.e-flux.com/journal/35/68389/under-the-gaze-of-theory/ (accessed 10 January 2017).

Habermas, Jürgen, *The Philosophical Discourse of Modernity*, trans. Frederick Lawrence, Cambridge: Polity Press, 1987.

Haidt, Jonathan, 'What Makes People Vote Republican?', *Edge.org*, 9 October 2008, https://www.edge.org/conversation/jonathan_haidt-what-makes-people-vote-republican (accessed 4 September 2017).

Haidt, Jonathan, *The Righteous Mind: Why Good People Are Divided By Politics and Religion*, London: Allen Lane, 2012.

Hake, Sabine and Barbara Mennel, *Turkish German Cinema in the New Millennium: Sites, Sounds, and Screens*, Oxford: Berghahn Books, 2012.

Hallward, Peter, *Think Again: Alain Badiou and the Future of Philosophy*, London: Continuum, 2004.

Hansen, Miriam Bratu, 'The Mass Production of the Senses: Classical Cinema as Vernacular Modernism', *Modernism/Modernity* 6, no. 2 (April 1999): 59–77.

Hansen, Miriam, *Cinema and Experience: Siegfried Kracauer, Walter Benjamin, and Theodor W. Adorno*, Berkeley: University of California Press, 2011.

Hanssen, Beatrice, 'Portrait of Melancholy (Benjamin, Warburg, Panofsky)', *MLN* 114, no. 5, Comparative Literature Issue (December 1999): 991–1013.

Hardt, Michael and Antonio Negri, *Empire*, Cambridge, MA: Harvard University Press, 2000.

Harrod, Mary, Mariana Liz and Alissa Timoshkina (eds), *The Europeanness of European Cinema*, London: I.B. Tauris, 2015.
Haug, Mathew C., review of 'Can Philosophical Thought Experiments be Screened?', by David Davies, in Melanie Frappier, Letitia Meynell and James Robert Brown (eds), *Thought Experiments in Science, Philosophy, and the Arts*, *Analysis* 74, no. 1 (2014): 169.
Hayek, Friedrich, *The Road to Serfdom*, London: Routledge, 1944.
Herzog, Werner, 'Werner Herzog: Trust in My Wild Fantasies', interview with Sven Schumann and Johannes Bonke, *The Talks*, 30 January 2013, http://the-talks.com/interview/werner-herzog/ (accessed 10 January 2017).
Hess, Sabine, 'Gerade "Leistungsträger" treten nach unten', interview with Gitta Düperthal, *jungeWelt*, 7 September 2013, https://www.jungewelt.de/loginFailed.php?ref=/2013/09-07/062.php (accessed 4 September 2017).
Higbee, Will, *Post-beur Cinema: North African Emigré and Maghrebi-French Cinema*, Edinburgh: Edinburgh University Press, 2013.
Hjørt, Mette, *Small Nation, Global Cinema: The New Danish Cinema*, Minneapolis: University of Minnesota Press, 2005.
Hjørt, Mette, 'Dogme 95', in Paisley Livingston and Carl Plantinga (eds), *The Routledge Companion to Philosophy and Film*, London: Routledge, 2009, 483–93.
Hjørt, Mette and Scott MacKenzie (eds), *Purity and Provocation: Dogma '95*, London: BFI Publishing, 2003.
Hoberman, J, 'Work in Progress', review of *Beau Travail*, dir. by Claire Denis, *Village Voice*, 28 March 2000, http://www.villagevoice.com/film/work-in-progress-639509 (accessed 21 August 2017).
Hodge, Robert and Gunther Kress, *Language as Ideology*, London: Routledge, 1993.
Honneth, Axel, *The Struggle for Recognition: The Moral Grammar of Social Conflicts*, Cambridge, MA: MIT Press, 1995.
Jameson, Frederic, *Postmodernism, or, the Cultural Logic of Late Capitalism*, Durham, NC: Duke University Press, 1991.
Jameson, Frederic, *A Singular Modernity: Essay on the Ontology of the Present*, London: Verso, 2002.
Jay, Martin, *Cultural Semantics: Keywords of Our Time*, Amherst: University of Massachusetts Press, 1998.
Jouhandeau, Marcel, *De l'abjection*, Paris: Gallimard, 1939.
Kant, Immanuel, 'Idea for a Universal History With a Cosmopolitan Aim' (1784), in James Schmidt and Amélie Oksenberg Rorty (eds), *Kant's Idea for a Universal History with a Cosmopolitan Aim*, Cambridge: Cambridge University Press, 2009.
Kaufman, Linda, 'David Cronenberg's Surreal Abjection', in *Bad Girls and Sick Boys: Fantasies in Contemporary Art and Culture*, Berkeley: University of California Press, 1998, 115–45.
Kierkegaard, Søren, *Works of Love*, trans. Howard V. Hong and Edna H. Hong, Princeton, NJ: Princeton University Press, 1995.
Kittler, Friedrich, *Gramophone, Film, Typewriter*, Stanford, CA: Stanford University Press, 1999.
Klein, Naomi, *Shock Doctrine: The Rise of Disaster Capitalism*, Toronto: Random House, 2007.

Konstantarkos, Myrto (ed.), *Spaces in European Cinema*, Exeter: Intellect Books, 2000.

Kretzschmar, Laurent, 'Is Cinema Renewing Itself?', *Film-Philosophy* 6, no. 15 (July 2002), http://www.film-philosophy.com/index.php/f-p/article/view/679 (accessed 14 December 2017).

Kristeva, Julia, *Powers of Horror: An Essay on Abjection*, trans. Leon S. Roudiez, New York: Columbia University Press, 1982.

Kristeva, Julia, *Black Sun: Depression and Melancholia*, New York: Columbia University Press, 1992.

Labanyi, Jo, Luisa Passerini and Karen Diel (eds), *Europe and Love in Cinema*, Bristol: Intellect Books, 2012.

Lacan, Jacques, 'Motifs du crime paranoïaques – Le crime des sœurs Papin', *Minotaure* 3/4 (1933–4).

Lakoff, George and Mark Johnson, *Metaphors We Live By*, Chicago: University of Chicago Press, 1980.

Lessig, Lawrence, 'The Laws of Cyberspace', Draft 3, presented at the Taiwan Conference, Taipei, March 1998, https://cyber.harvard.edu/works/lessig/laws_cyberspace.pdf (accessed 10 January 2017).

Latour, Bruno, *We Have Never Been Modern*, trans. Catherine Porter, Cambridge, MA: Harvard University Press, 1993.

Latour, Bruno, 'Why Has Critique Run Out of Steam? From Matters of Fact to Matters of Concern', *Critical Inquiry* 30 (Winter 2004): 225–48.

Lefort, Claude, *Essais sur le politique*, Paris: Seuil, 1986.

Lemert, Charles (ed.), *Social Theory: The Multicultural, Global, and Classic Readings*, 6th edn, Boulder, CO: Westview Press, 2017.

Lévi-Strauss, Claude, *Structural Anthropology*, trans. Claire Jacobson and Brooke Grundfest Schoepf, New York: Basic Books, 1963.

Lévi-Strauss, Claude, *Tristes Tropiques*, New York: Penguin, 1992.

Levinas, Emmanuel, *Totality and Infinity: An Essay on Exteriority*, trans. Alphonso Lingis, Pittsburgh: Duquesne University Press, 1969.

Levinas, Emmanuel, *Otherwise than Being or Beyond Essence*, trans. Alphonso Lingis, Dordrecht and Boston: Kluwer Academic Publishers, 1978.

Lewis, Jon (ed.), *The End of Cinema As We Know It*, New York: NYU Press, 2001.

Lewis, Simon L. and Mark A. Maslin, 'Defining the Anthropocene', *Nature* 519 (12 March 2015): 171–80.

Lilla, Mark, 'The End of Identity Liberalism', *New York Times*, 18 November 2016, https://www.nytimes.com/2016/11/20/opinion/sunday/the-end-of-identity-liberalism.html (accessed 15 December 2016).

Lindvall Daniel, 'Barbara: Beyond East vs West', *Film International*, 6 September 2012, http://filmint.nu/?p=5881 (accessed 5 June 2017).

Livingston, Paisley, 'Theses on Cinema as Philosophy', *Journal of Aesthetics and Art Criticism* 64, no. 1 (2006): 11–18.

Livingston, Paisley and Carl Plantinga (eds), *The Routledge Companion to Philosophy and Film*, London: Routledge, 2009.

López, Cristina Álvarez and Adrian Martin, 'Béla Tarr's Repulsion', *FilmScalpel.com*, http://www.filmscalpel.com/bela-tarrs-repulsion/ (accessed 12 December 2016).

Luhmann, Niklas, 'Beyond Barbarism', *Soziale Systeme* 14, no. 1 (2008): 38–46.

Mai, Joseph, *Jean-Paul and Luc Dardenne*, Urbana: University of Illinois Press, 2010.

Maltby, Richard, 'A Brief Romantic Interlude: Dick and Jane Go to 3½ Seconds of the Classical Hollywood Cinema', in David Bordwell and Noël Carroll (eds), *Post-Theory: Reconstructing Film Studies*, Madison: University of Wisconsin Press, 1996, 434–59.

Manovich, Lev, 'To lie and to act: Potemkin's villages, cinema and telepresence. Notes around Checkpoint '95 project', *Ars Electronica*, 1995 catalogue, Linz, Austria, http://manovich.net/index.php/projects/to-lie-and-to-act-potemkin-s-villages-cinema-and-telepresence (accessed 14 December 2016).

Manovich, Lev, *The Language of New Media*, Cambridge, MA: MIT Press, 2001.

Maratti, Paola, *Cinema and Philosophy*, Baltimore, MD: Johns Hopkins University Press, 2003.

Marchart, Oliver, *Post-Foundational Political Thought: Political Difference in Nancy, Lefort, Badiou and Laclau*, Edinburgh: Edinburgh University Press, 2007.

Martin, Adrian, 'Fleeing the Unconscious', *Filmkrant*, http://www.filmkrant.nl/world_wide_angle/244 (accessed 7 December 2016).

Massumi, Brian, 'The Autonomy of Affect', *Cultural Critique* 31 (Autumn 1995): 83–109.

Mathes, Bettina, 'Waiting to Happen', *Division Review* 7 (Spring 2013): 44, www.bettinamathes.net/resources/D-R-Melancholia-printed.pdf (accessed 14 June 2015).

May, Todd, *The Political Thought and Jacques Rancière*, Edinburgh: Edinburgh University Press, 2008.

McClelland, Thomas, 'Philosophy of Film and Film as Philosophy', *Cinema: Journal of Philosophy and the Moving Image* 2 (2011): 11–35.

Merleau-Ponty, Maurice, 'Le cinéma et la nouvelle psychologie', *Les Temps Modernes* 26 (November 1947): 930–43

Meskin, Aaron, 'Authorship', in Paisley Livingston and Carl Plantinga (eds), *The Routledge Companion to Philosophy and Film*, New York: Routledge, 2008, 12–27.

Metz, Christian, 'Cinéma: langue ou language?', *Communications* 4, no. 1 (1964): 52–90.

McGill, Hannah, 'Blood and Sand', review of *Beau Travail*, dir. by Claire Denis, *Sight & Sound*, May 2012, http://old.bfi.org.uk/sightandsound/feature/49855 (accessed 21 August 2017).

Moretti, Franco, *Distant Reading*, London: Verso, 2013.

Morin, Edgar, *The Cinema, or the Imaginary Man*. Minneapolis: University of Minnesota Press, 2015.

Morris, Wesley, '*Barbara* is one film to watch', *Boston.com*, 20 December 2012, http://www.boston.com/ae/movies/2012/12/20/movie-review-barbara-one-film-watch/UxzYhn0kJGHcckvJbVJ0bO/story.html (accessed 5 June 2017).

Mulhall, Stephen, *On Film*, 2nd edn, London and New York: Routledge, 2008.

Mullarkey, John, 'Film as Philosophy: A Mission Impossible?', in Temenuga Trifonova (ed.), *European Film Theory*, New York and London: Routledge, 2009, 65–79.

Mullarkey, John, *Refractions of Reality: Philosophy and the Moving Image*, London and New York: Palgrave MacMillan, 2009.

Müller, Werner, 'The Failure of the Intellectuals', *Eurozine*, 11 April 2012, http://www.eurozine.com/the-failure-of-european-intellectuals/ (accessed 24 October 2017).

Mulvey, Laura, 'Pandora's Box', in *Fetishism and Curiosity*, London: BFI, 1996, 53–64.

Musser, Charles, *The Emergence of Cinema: The American Screen to 1907*, Berkley: University of California Press, 1990.

Nancy, Jean-Luc, *The Inoperative Community*, ed. Peter Connor, Minneapolis: University of Minnesota Press, 1991.

Nancy, Jean-Luc, *Being Singular Plural*, trans. Robert D. Richardson and Anne E. O'Byrne, Stanford, CA: Stanford University Press, 2000.

Nancy, Jean-Luc, 'L'areligion', *Vacarme* 14 (January 2001), http://www.vacarme.org/article81.html (accessed 21 August 2017).

Nancy, Jean-Luc, *L'Evidence du film: Abbas Kiarostami/The Evidence of Film*, bilingual edn, French–English, Brussels: Yves Gevaert, 2001.

Nancy, Jean-Luc, 'Love and Community: A Roundtable Discussion with Nancy', Roundtable Discussion, European Graduate School, August 2001.

Nancy, Jean-Luc, *La Création du monde ou la mondialisation*, Paris: Galilée, 2002.

Nancy, Jean-Luc, 'A-religion', *Journal of European Studies* 34, no. 1/2 (2004): 14–18.

Nancy, Jean-Luc, *Dis-Enclosure: The Deconstruction of Christianity*, trans. Gabriel Malenfant, Michael B. Smith and Bettina Bergo, New York: Fordham University Press, 2008.

Neilson, Heather L. E., 'The Reluctant Voyeur: The Spectator and the "Abject" in Gillean Mears' Fineflour', *Sydney Studies in English* 21 (1995–6): 103–16.

Nelson, Eric S., 'Who Is the Other to Me? Levinas, Asymmetrical Ethics and Socio-Political Equality', *Mono Kurgusuz Labirent* 8–9 (2010): 454–66.

Nesbit, Thomas, 'Otto Mühl and the Aesthetics of Seduction', paper for the Institut für die Wissenschaft des Menschen, Vienna, 2005, http://www.iwm.at/publications/5-junior-visiting-fellows-conferences/vol-xviii/thomas-nesbit/ (accessed 26 November 2017).

O'Malley Sheila, review of *Barbara*, dir. by Christian Petzold, *Rogerebert.com*, 6 March 2013, http://rogerebert.suntimes.com/apps/pbcs.dll/article?AID=/20130306/REVIEWS/130309996/1023 (accessed 5 June 2017).

Pagden, Anthony, review of *The Distorted Past: A Reinterpretation of Europe*, by Josep Fontana, *American Historical Review* 102, no. 5 (1 December 1997): 1469–70.

Panofsky, Erwin and Fritz Saxl, *Dürers' Melencolia I. Eine Quellen- und typengeschichtliche Untersuchung*, Leipzig and Berlin: Studien der Bibliothek Warburg, 1923.

Paul, Ian Alan, 'Desiring-Machines in American Cinema', *Senses of Cinema* 56 (2010), http://sensesofcinema.com/2010/feature-articles/desiring-machines-in-american-cinema-what-inception-tells-us-about-our-experience-of-reality-and-film/ (accessed 10 December 2017).

Paulus, Tom, 'A Lover's Discourse: Cinephilia, or, The Color of Cary Grant's Socks', *CINEA*, 25 October 2012, https://cinea.be/a-lovers-discourse-cinephilia-or-the-color-cary-grants-socks/ (accessed 12 December 2017).

Pearson, James, 'Interpreting Disturbed Minds: Donald Davidson and The White Ribbon', *Film-Philosophy* 16, no. 1 (2012): 1–15.

Petzold, Christian, '*Barbara*: Interview with Christian Petzold', interview with Pamela Jahn, *Electric Sheep*, 28 September 2012, http://www.electricsheepmagazine.co.uk/features/2012/09/28/barbara-interview-with-christian-petzold/ (accessed 5 June 2017).

Petzold, Christian, 'Spatial Suspense: A Conversation with Christian Petzold', interview with Daniel Kasman and David Phelps, *Mubi*, 16 October 2012, https://mubi.com/notebook/posts/spatial-suspense-a-conversation-with-christian-petzold (accessed 5 June 2017).

Petzold, Christian, 'Christian Petzold on the Skillful Seduction of "Barbara"', interview with Stephen Saito, *Moveablefest*, 20 December 2012, http://moveablefest.com/moveable_fest/2012/12/christian-petzold-barbara-interview.html (accessed 5 June 2017).

Pfaller, Robert, *Interpassivität*, Vienna: Springer, 2000.

Pheasant-Kelly, Frances, *Abject Spaces in American Cinema*, London: I.B. Tauris, 2013.

Pippin, Robert, 'Psychology Degree Zero? The Representation of Action in the Films of the Dardenne Brothers', *Critical Inquiry* 41, no. 4 (2015): 757–85.

Pisters, Patricia, *The Matrix of Visual Culture: Working with Deleuze in Film Theory*, Stanford, CA: Stanford University Press, 2003.

Pisters, Patricia, *The Neuro-Image: A Deleuzian Film-Philososphy of Digital Screen Culture*, Stanford, CA: Stanford University Press, 2012.

Plato, *Five Dialogues: Euthyphro, Apology, Crito, Meno, Phaedo*, trans. G. M. A. Grube, Indianapolis, IN: Hackett Publishing, 2002.

Pluckrose, Helen, 'How French "intellectuals" ruined the West', *aeromagazine*, 27 March 2017, https://areomagazine.com/2017/03/27/how-french-intellectuals-ruined-the-west-postmodernism-and-its-impact-explained/ (accessed 24 October 2017).

Poore, Jonathan, 'Bartleby's Occupation: "Passive Resistance" Then and Now', *Nonsite.org*, 1 May 2013, http://nonsite.org/article/bartlebys-occupation-passive-resistance-then-and-now (accessed 5 September 2017).

Qlipoth, 'Easier to imagine the end of the world . . .', 11 November 2009, http://qlipoth.blogspot.co.uk/2009/11/easier-to-imagine-end-of-world.html (accessed 10 January 2017).

Rabinowitz, Dan, 'The Right to Refuse: Abject Theory and the Return of Palestinian Refugees', *Critical Inquiry* 36, no. 3 (Spring 2010): 494–516.

Radden, Jennifer, *The Nature of Melancholy: From Aristotle to Kristeva*, Oxford: Oxford University Press, 2002.

Rancière, Jacques, *The Ignorant Schoolmaster: Five Lessons in Intellectual Emancipation*, trans. Kristin Ross, Stanford, CA: Stanford University Press, 1991.

Rancière, Jacques, 'Ten Theses on Politics', *Theory & Event* 5, no. 3 (2001), http://muse.jhu.edu/article/32639 (accessed 4 September 2017).

Rancière, Jacques, 'The Aesthetic Revolution and its Outcomes', *New Left Review* 14 (2002): 133–51.

Rancière, Jacques, *The Politics of Aesthetics*, trans. Gabriel Rockhill, London: Continuum, 2003.

Rancière, Jacques, *Malaise dans l'esthétique*, Paris: Galilée, 2004.

Rancière, Jacques, 'The Ethical Turn of Aesthetics and Politics', *Critical Horizons: A Journal of Philosophy and Social Theory* 7, no. 1 (2006): 1–20.

Rancière, Jacques, *Film Fables*, trans. Emiliano Battista, Oxford: Berg, 2006.
Rancière, Jacques, 'The Politics of Aesthetics', *Mute*, 14 September 2006, http://www.metamute.org/editorial/articles/politics-aesthetics (accessed 21 October 2017).
Rancière, Jacques, *Hatred of Democracy*, trans. Steve Corcoran, London: Verso, 2009.
Reader, Keith, *The Abject Object: Avatars of the Phallus in Contemporary French Theory, Literature and Film*, Amsterdam: Rodopi, 2006.
Richter, Hannah, 'Beyond the "Other" as Constitutive Outside: The Politics of Immunity in Roberto Esposito and Niklas Luhmann', *European Journal of Political Theory* (July 2016), http://ept.sagepub.com/content/early/2016/07/14/1474885116658391.abstract (accessed 18 December 2016).
Riegl, Alois, 'Excerpts from "The Dutch Group Portrait"', trans. Benjamin Binstock, *October* 74 (Fall 1995): 3–35.
Rilke, R. M., 'Die erste Duineser Elegie', *Insel-Verlag*, 1923.
Robert, John, 'Dogme 95', *New Left Review* 1, no. 238 (November–December 1999): 138–44.
Robinson, Emma, 'Lars von Trier – Misogynist?', *Cinema Scandinavia* 1 (April 2014): 9–13, https://www.academia.edu/6848264/Cinema_Scandinavia_Issue_1 (accessed 14 June 2017).
Rodek, Hans-Georg, 'Die Angst der Nina Hoss, sich anzuvertrauen', *Berliner Morgenpost*, 11 February 2012, http://www.morgenpost.de/kultur/berlinale/article1903370/Die-Angst-der-Nina-Hoss-sich-anzuvertrauen (accessed 4 June 2017).
Rodowick, David, 'An Elegy for Theory', *October* 122 (Fall 2007): 91–109.
Romney, Jonathan, review of *Barbara*, dir. by Christian Petzold, *Independent*, 30 December 2012, http://www.independent.co.uk/arts-entertainment/films/reviews/barbara-christian-petzold-105-mins-12a-8190724.html (accessed 5 June 2017).
Ronnell, Avital, *The Test Drive: A Philosophical and Cultural Analysis of the Motivation for and Ubiquity of Testing*, Chicago: University of Illinois Press, 2007.
Rorty, Richard, *Achieving Our Country: Leftist Thought in Twentieth-Century America*, Cambridge, MA: Harvard University Press, 1998.
Rose, Steve, 'Werner Herzog on death, danger and the end of the world', *Guardian*, 14 April 2012, http://www.theguardian.com/film/2012/apr/14/werner-herzog-into-the-abyss (accessed 12 January 2017).
Rosen, Michael, *Dignity: Its History and Meaning*, Cambridge, MA: Harvard University Press, 2012.
Rosenbaum, Jonathan, 'Unsatisfied Men', review of *Beau Travail*, dir. by Claire Denis, *Chicago Reader*, 25 May 2000, http://www.chicagoreader.com/chicago/unsatisfied-men/Content?oid=902343 (accessed 21 August 2017).
Rothberg, Michael, review of *Ethics: An Essay on the Understanding of Evil*, by Alain Badiou, *Criticism* 43, no. 4 (2001): 478–84.
Roxborough, Scott, 'Michael Haneke on "Happy End" and the Art of Making Audiences Uncomfortable', *Hollywood Reporter*, 30 November 2017, https://www.hollywoodreporter.com/news/oscars-michael-haneke-happy-end-art-making-audiences-uncomfortable–1062407 (accessed 1 December 2017).

Rushton, Richard, 'Empathetic Projection in the Films of the Dardenne Brothers', *Screen* 55, no. 3 (Autumn 2014): 303–16.

Ryan, Michael and Douglas Kellner, *Camera Politica: The Politics and Ideology of Contemporary Hollywood Film*, Bloomington: University of Indiana Press, 1988.

Sawhney, Cary Rajinder, 'Asian-British cinema – from the margin to the mainstream', *Screenonline*, http://www.screenonline.org.uk/film/id/475617/ (accessed 31 December 2017).

Schein, Elyse and Paula Bernstein, 'Jean-Luc Godard Explains Why He Skipped Cannes Press Conference', *IndieWire*, 21 May 2014, http://www.indiewire.com/2014/05/watch-jean-luc-godard-explains-why-he-skipped-cannes-press-conference–26396/ (accessed 10 January 2016).

Scruton, Roger, 'Poetry & Truth', in John Gibson (ed.), *The Philosophy of Poetry*, Oxford: Oxford University Press, 2015, 149–61.

Sebald, W. G., *The Rings of Saturn*, New York: New Directions, 1998.

Seitz, Matt Zoller, 'The Death/Decay of Cinema @15', *Rogerebert.com*, 31 July 2014, http://www.rogerebert.com/mzs/death-of-filmdecay-of-cinema-at–15-a-conversation-with-godfrey-cheshire (accessed 10 January 2017).

Shapiro, Michael, *The Politics of Representation*, Madison: University of Wisconsin Press, 1988.

Shaw, Daniel, *Film and Philosophy: Taking Movies Seriously*, London and New York: Wallflower, 2008.

Shoard, Catherine, 'Lars von Trier Makes Vow of Silence After Cannes Furore', *Guardian*, 5 October 2011, http://www.theguardian.com/film/2011/oct/05/lars-von-trier-cannes (accessed 10 January 2017).

Silvey, Vivien and Roger Hillman, 'Akin's *Auf der anderen Seite (The Edge of Heaven)* and the widening periphery', *German as a foreign language* 3 (2010): 98–116, http://www.gfl-journal.de/3-2010/SilveyHillman.pdf (accessed 9 January 2017).

Simons, Jan, *Playing the Waves: Lars von Trier's Game Cinema*, Amsterdam: Amsterdam University Press, 2007.

Simons, Jan, 'Lars von Trier's Antichrist: Natures, Couples, Rules, Games', *Seachange: Art, Communication, Technologies*, The Face-To-Face (Spring 2010): 120–34, http://www.seachangejournal.ca/PDF/2010_Face%20to%20Face/Simons_ANTICHRIST.pdf (accessed 10 January 2017).

Sinnerbrink, Robert, *New Philosophies of Film: Thinking Images*, London and New York: Continuum, 2011.

Sloterdijk, Peter, *Critique of Cynical Reason*, trans. Michael Eldred, Minneapolis: University of Minnesota Press, 1987.

Sloterdijk, Peter, *Rage and Time: A Psychopolitical Investigation*, trans. Mario Wenning, New York: Columbia University Press, 2010.

Smith, Anne-Marie, 'The Abject, the Maternal and Melancholy', in *Julia Kristeva Speaking the Unspeakable*, London: Pluto Press, 1998, 3–48.

Smith, Murray, 'Film Art, Argument and Ambiguity', in Murray Smith and Thomas E. Wartenberg (eds), *Thinking Through Cinema: Film As Philosophy*, Hoboken, NJ: Wiley-Blackwell, 2006, 33–42.

Smith, Murray and Thomas E. Wartenberg (eds), *Thinking Through Cinema: Film as Philosophy*, Hoboken, NJ: Wiley-Blackwell, 2006.

Smith, Tim J., 'Watching You Watch Movies: Using Eye Tracking to Inform Cognitive Film Theory', in Arthur P. Shimamura (ed.), *Psychocinematics*, Oxford: Oxford University Press, 2013, 165–91.

Smuts, Aaron, 'In Defense of a Bold Thesis', *Journal of Aesthetics and Art Criticism* 67, no. 4 (Fall 2009): 409–20.

Sokal, Alan and Jean Bricmont, *Fashionable Nonsense: Postmodern Intellectuals' Abuse of Science*, New York: Picador, 1998.

Sonderegger, Ruth, review of *Jacques Rancière and the Contemporary Scene*, ed. Jean-Philippe Deranty and Alison Ross, *Constellations* 20, no. 2 (2013): 365–7.

Sonderegger, Ruth, 'Do We Need Others to Emancipate Ourselves? Remarks on Jacques Rancière', *Krisis – Journal for Contemporary Philosophy* 1 (2014): 54–67.

Sontag, Susan, *Under the Sign of Saturn*, New York: Picador, 1972.

Stephan, Alexander (ed.), *The Americanization of Europe: Culture, Diplomacy, and Anti-Americanism after 1945*, New York: Berghahn Books, 2007.

Streiter, Anja, 'The Community According to Jean-Luc Nancy and Claire Denis', *Film-Philosophy* 12, no. 1 (2008): 49–62, http://www.film-philosophy.com/2008v12n1/streiter.pdf (accessed 9 January 2017).

Striewski, Christiane, 'Nichts, das ist kein schlechter Slogan', *Perlentaucher*, 3 November 2011, http://www.perlentaucher.de/essay/nichts-das-ist-kein-schlechter-slogan.html (accessed 14 December 2017).

Sullivan, Gordon M., 'Fascinated Victims: Aspects of Abjection in the Films of David Cronenberg', MA thesis, North Carolina State University, Raleigh, 2007.

Tanke, Joseph J., 'What is the Aesthetic Regime?', *Parrhesia* 12 (2011): 71–81.

Tarr, Carrie, *Reframing Difference: Beur and Banlieue Filmmaking in France*, Manchester: Manchester University Press, 2005.

Tartaglione, Nancy, 'Belin: Lars von Trier Sports "Persona Non Grata" T-Shirt; Shia LeBeouf Abruptly Exits "Nymphomaniac" Press Conference', *Deadline.com*, 9 February 2014, http://deadline.com/2014/02/berlin-lars-von-trier-sports-persona-non-grata-t-shirt-shia-labeouf-abruptly-exits-nymphomaniac-press-conference–680154/ (accessed 10 January 2017).

Taubin, Amy, 'Body Language', *Village Voice*, 28 March 2000, http://www.villagevoice.com/film/body-language-6395085 (accessed 9 January 2017).

Taubin, Amy, 'Under the Skin', *Film Comment* 36, no. 3 (May/June 2000): 22–8.

Thomas, Calvin, *Masculinity, Psychoanalysis, Straight Queer Theory: Essays on Abjection in Literature, Mass Culture, and Film*, New York: Palgrave, 2008.

Thomsen, Bodil M., 'Antichrist – Chaos Reigns: the event of violence and the haptic image in Lars von Trier's film', *Journal of Aesthetics and Culture* 1 (2009): n.p.

Treuting, Jennifer, 'Eye Tracking and the Cinema: A Study of Film Theory and Visual Perception', *SMPTE Motion Imaging Journal* 115, no. 1 (January 2006): 31–40.

Trotter, David, *Cinema and Modernism*, Oxford: Blackwell, 2007.

Tyler, Imogen, *Revolting Subjects: Social Abjection and Resistance in Neoliberal Britain*, London: Zed Books, 2013.

Usai, Paolo Cherchi, *The Death of Cinema*, London: BFI Publishing, 2000.

Von Trier, Lars, 'The Only Redeeming Factor is the World Ending', interview with Per Juul Carlsen, *Danish Film Institute*, 4 May 2011, http://www.dfi.dk/Service/English/News-and-publications/FILM-Magazine/Artikler-fra-tidsskriftet-FILM/72/The-Only-Redeeming-Factor-is-the-World-Ending.aspx (accessed 10 January 2017).

Voster, Amy Jane, 'Film, Fear and the Female: An Empirical Study on the Female Horror Fan', *Off-Screen* 18, no. 6–7 (2014), http://offscreen.com/view/film-fear-and-the-female (accessed 27 November 2017).

Walsh, David, 'The Dardennes Brothers', World Socialist Website, 29 September 2008, https://www.wsws.org/en/articles/2008/09/tff5-s29.html (accessed 12 December 2017).

Walzer, Michael, 'Two Kinds of Universalism', Lecture, *Nation and Universe: The Tanner Lectures on Human Values*, Brasenose College, Oxford University, 1 and 8 May 1989, http://tannerlectures.utah.edu/_documents/a-to-z/w/walzer90.pdf (accessed 9 January 2017).

Wartenberg, Thomas, *Thinking on Screen: Film as Philosophy*, London: Routledge, 2007.

Webster, John, 'A Map to Freud's *Civilization and its Discontents*, Especially with Respect to Spenser's *Faerie Queene*', http://faculty.washington.edu/cicero/Freud.htm (accessed 5 September 2017).

Wexman, Virginia Wright (ed.), *Film and Authorship*, Piscataway, NJ: Rutgers University Press, 2003.

Wills, David, 'Dorsal Chances: An Interview with David Wills', interviewed by Peter Kilroy and Marcel Swiboda, *Parallax* 13, no. 4 (2007): 4–15.

Wilson, Laura, *Spectatorship, Embodiment and Physicality in the Contemporary Mutilation Film*, Amsterdam: Springer, 2015.

Wolf, Jamie, 'Le Cinéma du Blockbuster', *New York Times*, 20 May 2007, http://www.nytimes.com/2007/05/20/movies/20wolf.html (accessed 31 July 2015).

Wong, Cindy H., *Film Festivals: Culture, People, and Power on the Global Screen*, New Brunswick, NJ: Rutgers, 2011.

Wood, Mary P., *Contemporary European Cinema*, London: Bloomsbury, 2007.

Žižek, Slavoj, *Enjoy Your Symptom! Jacques Lacan in Hollywood and Out*, New York: Routledge, 1992.

Žižek, Slavoj, *The Metastases of Enjoyment: Six Essays on Women and Causality*, London: Verso, 1994.

Žižek, Slavoj, 'Multiculturalism, Or the Cultural Logic of Multinational Capitalism', *New Left Review* 1, no. 225 (1997): 28–51.

Žižek, Slavoj, *The Ticklish Subject: The Absent Centre of Political Ontology*, London: Verso, 1999.

Žižek, Slavoj, *The Fright of Real Tears: Krzysztof Kieslowski between Theory and Post-Theory*, Cambridge, MA: MIT Press, 2001.

Žižek, Slavoj, 'Neighbors and Other Monsters', in Kevin Reinhard, Eric Santner and Slavoj Žižek, *The Neighbor: Three Inquiries in Political Theology*, Chicago and London: University of Chicago Press, 2006, 134–90.

Žižek, Slavoj, *The Parallax View*, Cambridge, MA: MIT Press, 2006.

Žižek, Slavoj, 'Smashing the Neighbor's Face: On Emmanuel Levinas's Judaism', *Lacan.com*, 2006, http://www.lacan.com/zizsmash.htm (accessed 9 January 2017).

Žižek, Slavoj, 'Resistance is Surrender', *London Review of Books* 29, no. 22 (15 November 2007): 7.
Žižek, Slavoj, 'Shostakovich in Casablanca', *Lacanian Ink*, 2007, http://www.lacan.com/zizcasablanca.htm (accessed 10 January 2017).
Žižek, Slavoj, 'Liberal multiculturalism masks an old barbarism with a human face', *Guardian*, 3 October 2010, https://www.theguardian.com/commentisfree/2010/oct/03/immigration-policy-roma-rightwing-europe (accessed 4 September 2017).
Žižek, Slavoj, interview in Levi Bryant, Nick Srnicek and Graham Harman (eds), *The Speculative Turn: Continental Materialism and Realism*, Victoria: re.press, 2011.
Žižek, Slavoj, *Living in the End Times*, London: Verso, 2011.
Zourabichvili, Francois, *Deleuze: A Philosophy of the Event: Together with the Vocabulary of Deleuze*, Edinburgh: Edinburgh University Press, 2012.

FILMOGRAPHY

4 luni, 3 saptamani si 2 zile/4 Months, 3 Weeks and 2 Days, dir. by Mungiu, Cristian (2007)
12 Years a Slave, dir. by Steve McQueen (2013)
24 Hour Party People, dir. by Michael Winterbottom (2002)
50 Shades of Grey, dir. by Sam Taylor-Johnson (2015)
A Ma Soeur/Fat Girl, dir. by Catherine Breillat (2001)
A Scanner Darkly, dir. by Richard Linklater (2006)
Abigail's Party, dir. by Chris Yates (2006)
Abraham's Gold, dir. by Jörg Graser (1990)
Abre los ojos/Open Your Eyes, dir. by Alejandro Amenábar (1997)
Aguirre Wrath of God, dir. by Werner Herzog (1972)
Aimée & Jaguar, dir. by Max Färberböck (1999)
Ali: Fear Eats the Soul, dir. by Rainer Werner Fassbinder (1974)
Amélie, dir. by Jean-Pierre Jeunet (2001)
American Sniper, dir. by Clint Eastwood (2014)
Amour, dir. by Michael Haneke (2012)
Annie Hall, dir. by Woody Allen (1977)
Antichrist, dir. by Lars von Trier (2009)
Argo, dir. by Ben Affleck (2012)
Armageddon, dir. by Michael Bay (1998),
Au Revoir les Enfants, dir. by Louis Malle (1987)
Auf der anderen Seite/The Edge of Heaven, dir. by Fatih Akin (2007)
Bad Lieutenant, dir. by Abel Ferrara (1992)
Barbara, dir. by Christian Petzold (2012)
Beau Geste, dir. by William A. Wellman (1939)
Beau Travail, dir. by Claire Denis (1999)
Before Night Falls, dir. by Julian Schnabel (2000)
Benny's Video, dir. by Michael Haneke (1992)
Berlin Alexanderplatz, dir. by Rainer Werner Fassbinder (TV series 1980)
Bitter Tears of Petra von Kant, dir. by Rainer Werner Fassbinder (1972)
Black Swan, dir. by Darren Aronofsky (2010)
Blue Velvet, dir. by David Lynch (1986)
Brazil, dir. by Terry Gilliam (1985)
Breaking the Waves, dir. by Lars von Trier (1996)
Bride and Prejudice, dir. by Gurinder Chadha (2004)
Bridge of Spies, dir. by Steven Spielberg (2015)
Caché, dir. by Michael Haneke (2005)
Casablanca, dir. by Michael Curtiz (1942)

Chocolat, dir. by Claire Denis (1988)
Cidade de Deus/City of God, dir. by Fernando Meirelles (2002)
Cinema Paradiso, dir. by Giuseppe Tornatore (1988)
Citizen Four, dir. by Laura Poitras (2014)
Cloud Nine, dir. by Andreas Dresen (2008)
Code Inconnu/Code Unknown, dir. by Michael Haneke (2000)
Container, dir. by Lukas Modysson's (2006)
Copie Conforme/Certified Copy, dir. by Abbas Kiarostami (2010)
Dancer in the Dark, dir. by Lars von Trier (2000)
Das Leben der Anderen/The Lives of Others, dir. by Florian Henckel von Donnersmarck (2006)
D-Dag, dir. by Lars von Trier and Søren Kragh-Jacobsen and Kristian Levring and Thomas Vinterberg (2000)
Der Krieger und die Kaiserin/The Princess and the Warrior, dir. by Tom Twyker (2000)
Diary of a Country Priest, dir. by Robert Bresson (1951)
Die Flucht (The Flight), dir. by Roland Gräf (1977)
Die Innere Sicherheit/The State I Am In, dir. by Christian Petzold (2000)
Die Schöpfer der Einkaufswelten/The Creators of Shopping Worlds, dir. by Harun Farocki (2001)
Dirty Pretty Things, dir. by Stephen Frears (2002)
Dogville, dir. by Lars von Trier (2003)
Downfall, dir. by Oliver Hirschbiegel (2004)
Dr Strangelove or: How I Learned to Stop Worrying and Love the Bomb, dir. by Stanley Kubrick (1964)
Element of Crime, dir. by Lars von Trier (1984)
Enter the Void, dir. by Gaspar Noé (2009)
Epidemic, dir. by Lars von Trier (1987)
Eternal Sunshine of the Spotless Mind, dir. by Michel Gondry (2004)
Europa, dir. by Lars von Trier (1991)
Europe 51, dir. by Roberto Rossellini (1952)
Faust, dir. by Aleksandr Sokurov (2011)
Faustrecht der Freiheit/Fox and His Friends, dir. by Rainer Werner Fassbinder (1975)
Festen, dir. by Thomas Vinterberg (1998)
Force Majeure, dir. by Ruben Östlund (2014)
Forrest Gump, dir. by Robert Zemeckis (1994)
Francofonia, dir. by Aleksandr Sokurov (2015)
Funny Games, dir. by Michael Haneke (1997)
Funny Games, dir. by Michael Haneke (2007)
Gaslight, dir. by George Cukor (1944)
Gegen die Wand/Head On, dir. by Fatih Akin (2004)
Gespenster/Ghosts, dir. by Christian Petzold (2005)
Ghost Dance, dir. by Ken McMullen (1983)
Gomorra/Gomorrah, dir. by Matteo Garrone (2008)
Good Bye Lenin!, dir. by Wolfgang Becker (2003)
Good Kill, dir. by Andrew Niccol (2014)
Grizzly Man, dir. by Werner Herzog (2005)

Happy End, dir. by Michael Haneke (2017)
Happy-Go-Lucky, dir. by Mike Leigh (2008)
Holy Motors, dir. by Leos Carax (2012)
Hunger, dir. by Steve McQueen (2008)
I, Daniel Blake, dir. by Ken Loach (2016)
Idioterne/The Idiots, dir. by Lars von Trier (1998)
Images of the World, dir. by Harun Farocki (1989)
In einem Jahr mit 13 Monden/In a Year of Thirteen Moons, dir. by Rainer Werner Fassbinder (1978)
In this World, dir. by Michael Winterbottom (2002)
In Vanda's Room, dir. by Pedro Costa (2000)
Inception, dir. by Christopher Nolan (2010)
Independence Day, dir. by Roland Emmerich (1996)
Inland Empire, dir. by David Lynch (2006)
Interstellar, dir. by Christopher Nolan (2014)
Ivan The Terrible (I/II), dir. by Sergei Eisenstein (1945/1958)
Jeanne Dielman, dir. by Chantal Akerman (1975)
Jerichow, dir. by Christian Petzold (2008)
Kauas pilvet karkaavat/Drifting Clouds, dir. by Aki Kaurismäki (1996)
Kebab Connection, dir. by Anno Saul (2004)
Kurz und schmerzlos/Short Sharp Shock, dir. by Fatih Akin (1998)
L'Enfant, dir. by Jean-Pierre Dardenne and Luc Dardenne (2005)
L'humanité, dir. by Bruno Dumont (2000)
La Bandera, dir. by Julien Duvivier (1935)
La Chinoise, dir. by Jean-Luc Godard (1968)
La Double Vie de Véronique, dir. by Krzysztof Kieslowski (1991)
La Femme Nikita, dir. by Luc Besson (1990)
La Finestra di Fronte/Facing Windows, dir. by Ferzan Ozpetek (2003)
La Graine et le mulet, dir. by Abdellatif Kechiche (2007)
La Grande Bellezza/The Great Beauty, dir. by Paolo Sorrentino (2013)
La Haine, dir. by Mathieu Kassovitz (1995)
La Jeteé, dir. by Chris Marker (1962)
La Nostra Vita, dir. by Daniele Luchetti (2010)
La Notte, dir. by Michelangelo Antonioni (1961)
La Promesse, dir. by Jean-Pierre Dardenne and Luc Dardenne (1996)
La Vie en rose, dir. by Olivier Dahan (2007)
La Vita e bella, dir. by Roberto Benigni (1997)
Lacombe Lucien, dir. by Louis Malle (1974)
Last Resort, dir. by Pawel Pawlikowski (2000)
Le Dernier Métro, dir. by François Truffaut (1980)
Le Fils/The Son, dir. by Jean-Pierre Dardenne and Luc Dardenne (2002)
Le Havre, dir. by Aki Kaurismäki (2011)
Le Petit Soldat, dir. by Jean-Luc Godard (1963)
Le Silence de Lorna/Lorna's Silence, dir. by Jean-Pierre Dardenne and Luc Dardenne (2008)
Leningrad Cowboys Go America, dir. by Aki Kaurismäki (1989)
Léon: The Professional, dir. by Luc Besson (1994)
Les Anges du péché/Angels of Sin, dir. Robert Bresson (1943)

Life and Nothing More, dir. by Abbas Kiarostami (1991)
Lili Marleen, dir. by Rainer Werner Fassbinder (1981)
Lilja 4-ever/Lilya 4 Ever, dir. by Lukas Moodysson (2002)
Lincoln, dir. by Steven Spielberg (2012)
Lola, dir. by Rainer Werner Fassbinder (1981)
Lola rennt/Run Lola Run, dir. by Tom Tykwer (1998)
Lorenzo's Oil, dir. by George Miller (1992)
Los Olvidados/The Forgotten Ones, dir. by Luis Buñuel (1950)
Lost Highway, dir. by David Lynch (1997)
Lucy, dir. by Luc Besson (2014)
M. Klein, dir. by Joseph Losey (1976)
Magnolia, dir. by Paul Thomas Anderson (1999)
Manderley, dir. by Lars von Trier (2005)
Männer/Men, dir. by Doris Dörrie (1985)
Margin Call, dir. by J.C. Chandor (2011)
Melancholia, dir. by Lars von Trier (2011)
Memento, dir. by Christopher Nolan (1999)
Mies vailla menneisyyttä/The Man without a Past, dir. by Aki Kaurismäki (2002)
Minority Report, dir. by Steven Spielberg (2002)
Miracolo a Milano/Miracle of Milan, dir. by Vittorio de Sica (1951)
Moloch, dir. by Aleksandr Sokurov (1999)
Monsoon Wedding, dir. by Mira Nair (2001)
Morocco, dir. by Josef von Sternberg (1930)
Mulholland Drive, dir. by David Lynch (2001)
Muriel, dir. by Alain Resnais (1963)
My Big Fat Greek Wedding, dir. by Joel Zwick (2002)
Naked, dir. by Mike Leigh (1993)
Nibelungen, dir. by Fritz Lang (1924)
Nostalghia/Nostalgia, dir. by Andrej Tarkowski (1983)
Nowhere Boy, dir. by Sam Taylor-Johnson (2009)
Nymphomaniac, dir. by Lars von Trier (2013)
Oslo 31 August, dir. by Joachim Trier (2011)
Persona, dir. by Ingmar Bergman (1966)
Phoenix, dir. by Christian Petzold (2014)
Pickpocket, dir. by Robert Bresson (1959)
Prometheus, dir. by Ridley Scott (2012)
Psycho, dir. by Alfred Hitchcock (1960)
Rebecca, dir. by Alfred Hitchcock (1940)
Red Desert, dir. by Michelangelo Antonioni (1964)
Rosenstrasse, dir. by Margarethe von Trotta (2003)
Rosetta, dir. by Jean-Pierre Dardenne and Luc Dardenne (1999)
Running on Empty, dir. by Sidney Lumet (1988)
Russian Ark, dir. by Aleksandr Sokurov (2002)
Sans toit ni loi/Without Roof or Law, dir. by Agnès Varda (1985)
Secret Beyond the Door, dir. by Fritz Lang (1947)
Seul contre tous/I Stand Alone, dir. by Gaspar Noe (1998)
Shame, dir. by Ingmar Bergman (1968)
Shame, dir. by Steve McQueen (2011)

Shoah, dir. by Claude Lanzmann (1985)
Slumdog Millionaire, dir. by Danny Boyle (2008)
Snowdon, dir. by Oliver Stone (2016)
Son of Saul, dir. by Nemes László (2015)
Songs from the Second Floor, dir. by Roy Andersson (2000)
Soul Kitchen, dir. by Fatih Akin (2009)
Stromboli, dir. by Roberto Rossellini (1950)
Stroszek, dir. by Werner Herzog (1977)
Syriana, dir. by Stephen Gaghan (2005)
The Act of Killing, dir. by Joshua Oppenheimer (2012)
The Artist, dir. by Michel Hazanavicius (2011)
The Big Short, dir. by Adam McKay (2015)
The Boss of it All, dir. by Lars von Trier (2006)
The Cabinet of Dr Caligari, dir. by Robert Wiene (1920)
The Clouds of Sils Maria, dir. by Olivier Assayas (2015)
The Cut, dir. by Fatih Akin (2014)
The Day After Tomorrow, dir. by Roland Emmerich (2004)
The Death of Mr. Lăzărescu, dir. by Cristi Puiu (2005)
The Diving Bell and the Butterfly, dir. by Julian Schnabel (2007)
The Fifth Element, dir. by Luc Besson (1997)
The Five Obstructions, dir. by Jørgen Leth and Lars von Trier (2003)
The Hunt, dir. by Thomas Vinterberg (2012)
The Man Who Shot Liberty Valance, dir. by John Ford (1962)
The Marriage of Maria Braun, dir. by Rainer Werner Fassbinder (1979)
The Matrix, dir. by Lana Wachowski and Lilly Wachowski (1999)
The Merchant of Four Seasons, dir. by Rainer Werner Fassbinder (1972)
The Passion of Anna, dir. by Ingmar Bergman (1969)
The Piano Teacher, dir. by Michael Haneke (2001)
The Postman Always Rings Twice, dir. by Bob Rafelson (1981)
The Reader, dir. by Stephen Daldry (2008)
The Sacrifice, dir. by Andrej Tarkowski (1986)
The Sixth Sense, dir. by M. Night Shyamalan (1999)
The Skin I Live in, dir. by Pedro Almodóvar (2011)
The Son's Room, dir. by Nanni Moretti (2001)
The Third Man, dir. by Carol Reed (1949)
The Turin Horse, dir. by Béla Tarr (2012)
The White Ribbon, dir. by Michael Haneke (2009)
The Wolf of Wall Street, dir. by Martin Scorsese (2013)
Three Colours Trilogy (Blue, White, Red), dir. by Krzysztof Kieslowski (1993–4)
Time of the Wolf, dir. by Michael Haneke (2003)
To See If I Am Smiling, dir. by Tamar Yarom (2007)
Toni Erdmann, dir. by. Maren Ade (2016)
Trainspotting, dir. by Danny Boyle (1996)
Tree of Life, dir. by Terrence Malick (2011)
Twelve Monkeys, dir. by Terry Gilliam (1995)
Twelve Years a Slave, dir. by Steve McQueen (2013)
Twin Peaks, dir. by David Lynch (TV series 1990–1)
Two Days, One Night, dir. by Jean-Pierre Dardenne and Luc Dardenne (2014)

Vagabond, dir. by Agnès Varda (1985).
Vanilla Sky, dir. by Cameron Crowe (2001)
Veronika Voss, dir. by Rainer Werner Fassbinder (1982)
Viaggio in Italia/Voyage in Italy, dir. by Roberto Rossellini (1954)
Vivre sa Vie, dir. by Jean Luc Godard (1962)
Volver, dir. by Pedro Almodóvar (2006)
Waltz with Bashir, dir. by Ari Folman (2008)
War of the Worlds, dir. by Steven Spielberg (2005)
We Need to Talk About Kevin, dir. by Lynn Ramsay (2011)
Winter Light, dir. by Ingmar Bergman (1963)
Winter Sleepers/Winterschläfer, dir. by Tom Tykwer (1997)
Yella, dir. by Christian Petzold (2007)
Young Adam, dir. by David Mackenzie (2003)
Youth, dir. by Paolo Sorrentino (2015)
Zero Dark Thirty, dir. by Kathryn Bigelow (2012)

INDEX